AVIATION AND TOURISM

Aviation and Tourism
Implications for Leisure Travel

ANNE GRAHAM
University of Westminster, United Kingdom

ANDREAS PAPATHEODOROU
University of the Aegean, Greece

PETER FORSYTH
Monash University, Australia

ASHGATE

Reprinted 2010
First published in paperback 2010

Published by
Ashgate Publishing Limited
Wey Court East
Union Road
Farnham
Surrey, GU9 7PT
England

Ashgate Publishing Company
Suite 420
101 Cherry Street
Burlington, VT 05401-4405
USA

www.ashgate.com

British Library Cataloguing in Publication Data
Aviation and tourism : implications for leisure travel
1. Tourism 2. Tourism - Government policy 3. Aeronautics
and state 4. Aeronautics, Commercial - Passenger traffic
I. Graham, Anne II. Papatheodorou, Andreas, 1974-
III. Forsyth, P. (Peter)
338.4'791

ISBN: 978-0-7546-7187-9 (hbk)
ISBN: 978-1-4094-0232-9 (pbk)
ISBN: 978-0-7546-9248-5 (ebk)

Library of Congress Cataloging-in-Publication Data
Aviation and tourism : implications for leisure travel / edited by Anne Graham, Andreas Papatheodorou, and Peter Forsyth.
      p. cm.
Includes bibliographical references and index.
ISBN 978-0-7546-7187-9
1. Tourism. 2. Tourism--Government policy. 3. Aeronautics and state. I. Graham, Anne. II. Papatheodorou, Andreas, 1974- III. Forsyth, P. (Peter)

G155.A1A84 2008
338.4'791--dc22

2008007605

Printed and bound in Great Britain by
TJ International Ltd, Padstow, Cornwall.

Contents

PART I
LEISURE TRAVEL DEMAND

PART II
REGULATION AND GOVERNMENT POLICY

PART III
AIRLINE ISSUES

PART IV
IMPLICATIONS FOR AIRPORTS

PART V
ECONOMIC AND ENVIRONMENTAL IMPACTS

PART VI
DESTINATION CASE STUDIES

PART VII
CONCLUSIONS

List of Acronyms

A	Airbus
AACO	Arab Air Carriers Organization
AAI	Airport Authority of India
ACARE	Advisory Council for Aeronautics Research in Europe
ACI	Airports Council International
ACSA	Airports Company South Africa
ADP	Aéroports de Paris
ADR	Aeroporti di Roma
AEA	Association of European Airlines
AFCAC	African Civil Aviation Commission
ANAC	National Civil Aviation Agency (Brazil)
APD	Air Passenger Duty (UK)
APU	Auxiliary Power Units
AQS	Air Quality Standards
ARIMA	Autoregressive Integrated Moving Average
ASK/M	Available Seat Kilometres/Miles
ASEAN	Association of South East Asian Nations
ASPA	Association of South Pacific Airlines
ATAG	Air Transport Action Group
ATC	Air Traffic Control
ATI	Air Transport Intelligence
ATOL	Air Travel Organisers' Licensing (UK)
ATR	Avions de Transport Régional
B	Boeing
BA	British Airways
BAE	BAE Systems plc
(B)ASA/BATA	(Bilateral) Air Services Agreements/Bilateral Air Transport Agreements
BCBP	Bar Coded Boarding Pass
BSCA	Brussels South Charleroi Airport
CAA	Civil Aviation Authority (UK)
CAAC	Civil Aviation Administration of China
CAAS	Civil Aviation Authority of Singapore
CASK/M	Operating Cost per Available Seat Kilometre/Mile
CEO	Chief Executive Officer
CGE	Computable General Equilibrium
CNTA	China National Tourism Administration

CPI	Consumer Price Index
CRJ	Canadair Regional Jet (Bombardier)
CRS	Computer Reservation System
CRT	Centre for Regional and Tourism Research (Denmark)
CUSS	Common Use Self Service
CWC	Carriers Within Carriers
DAC	Department of Civil Aviation (Brazil)
DfT	Department for Transport (UK)
DoT	Department of Transport (USA)
DRDNI	Department for Regional Development Northern Ireland
DVT	Deep Vein Thrombosis
EAS	Essential Air Service
EASA	European Aviation Safety Agency
EC	European Commission
ECA	Economic Commission for Africa
ECAA	European Common Aviation Area
ECAC	European Civil Aviation Conference
EEA	European Economic Area
EEC	European Economic Community
ELFAA	European Low Fares Airlines Association
ERJ	Embraer Regional Jet
ETS	Emissions Trading Scheme
EU	European Union
EUDGE	European Union Directorate General for the Environment
FAST	Fully Automated Seamless Travel
FFP	Frequent Flyer Programme
FSC	Full Service Carrier
GCC	Gulf Cooperation Council
GDP	Gross Domestic Product
GDS	Global Distribution System
GE	General Electric
GFF	Global Futures and Foresight
GNP	Gross National Product
GPS	Global Positioning System
GST	General Sales Tax
HIAL	Highlands and Islands Airports Limited
HSBC	Hong Kong and Shanghai Banking Corporation
IACA	International Air Carrier Association
IACS	Immigration Automated Clearance System
IATF	International Airline Training Fund (IATA)
IBM	International Business Machines
ICAO	International Civil Aviation Organisation
IMF	International Monetary Fund
IOSA	IATA Operational Safety Audit
IPCC	Intergovernmental Panel on Climate Change
IPS	International Passenger Survey (UK)
IT/ICT	Information/Information and Communication Technologies
KADCO	Kilimanjaro Airport Development Company (Tanzania)

KLM	Koninklijke Luchtvaart Maatschappij (Royal Dutch Airlines)
LCC	Low Cost Carrier
MIA	Malta International Airport
MIISPA	Managed Integrated Independent South Pacific Airlines
MMS	Multimedia Message Service
MTA	Malta Tourism Authority
NCAA	Nigerian Civil Aviation Authority
NIMBY	Not-In-My-Back-Yard
OAG	Official Airline Guide
OECD	Organisation for Economic Co-operation and Development
OEF	Oxford Economic Forecasting
OFT	Office of Fair Trading (UK)
ONDA	Office National des Aéroports (Morocco)
OPEC	Organization of the Petroleum Exporting Countries
PATA	Pacific Asia Travel Association
PM	Particulate Matter
PNR	Passenger Name Records
PPP	Private – Public Partnership
PSO	Public Service Obligation
RASK/M	Passenger Revenue per Available Seat Kilometre/ Mile
RFID	Radio Frequency ID
RJ	Regional Jet (associated with BAE)
RTIC	Registered Traveller Inter-operability Consortium
RPK/M	Revenue Passenger-Kilometres/Miles
RTP	Registered Travellers Programmes
RUCUR	Relative Unit Cost – Unit Revenue
SAA	South African Airlines
SARS	Severe Acute Respiratory Syndrome
SAS	Scandinavian Airline Systems
SDR	Special Drawing Rights
SE	South-East
SMS	Short Message Service
SP1	Standard Provision 1
SPTO	South Pacific Tourism Organization
SRA	Strategic Research Agenda (European Union)
ST-EP	Sustainable Tourism - Eliminate Poverty (Africa)
STSM	Structural Time-Series Model
TAAI	Travel Agents Association of India
TDP	Tourism Development Plan (Mauritius)
TINA	The INtelligent Airport (Heathrow, UK)
T&T	Travel and Tourism
TSA	Transport Security Administration (USA)
UAE	United Arab Emirates
UK	United Kingdom
UN	United Nations
UNESCO	United Nations Educational, Scientific and Cultural Organization
UNWTO	United Nations World Tourism Organization
USA (or US)	Unites States of America

VARIG	Viação Aérea RIo Grandense (Brazil)
VASP	Viação Aérea São Paulo (Brazil)
VAT	Value Added Tax
VFR	Visiting Friends and Relatives
VOC	Volatile Organic Compounds
VWP	Visa Waiver Program (USA)
WCED	World Commission on Environment and Development
WTO	World Tourism Organization (former name of UNWTO)
WTTC	World Travel and Tourism Council

List of Figures

List of Maps

List of Tables

List of Editors

Anne Graham is a Senior Lecturer in Air Transport and Tourism at the University of Westminster in London, UK. She has a First Class Honours BSc degree in Mathematics from the University of Newcastle, a MSc in Tourism from the University of Surrey and a PhD in Air Transport and Tourism Management from the University of Westminster. Before joining the University, Anne worked in air transport consultancy. Anne has been involved in the teaching, research and consultancy of air transport and tourism for over 20 years and has developed two key research interests. First, is the analysis and forecasting of tourism and aviation demand and the relationship between the tourism and aviation industries. Her other research interest is airport management, economics and regulation. Her latest publication in this area will be the third edition of her key book entitled '*Managing Airports: An International Perspective*' (published by Elsevier/Butterworth-Heinemann). She has written many conference papers and articles about these two research areas and is on the Editorial Board of the Journal of Airport Management. She is a member of the Tourism Society and the Chartered Institute of Logistics and Transport, UK.

E-mail: grahama@wmin.ac.uk

Andreas Papatheodorou is an Assistant Professor in Industrial Economics with emphasis on Tourism at the School of Business Administration, University of the Aegean, Greece. He is also an Honorary Research Fellow at the Nottingham University Business School and a Visiting Senior Fellow at the University of Surrey, UK. Andreas holds a MPhil in Economics from the University of Oxford and a DPhil in Geography from the same university. He started his academic career as a Lecturer in Tourism at the University of Surrey. Dr Papatheodorou is actively engaged in tourism research, focusing on issues related to competition, pricing and corporate strategy in air transport and travel distribution. Most of his work is related to the Mediterranean Region and has been published in international academic journals. He has also edited two books, i.e. '*Corporate Rivalry and Market Power: Competition Issues in the Tourism Industry*' (published by IB Tauris in 2006) and '*Managing Tourism Destinations*' (published by Edward Elgar in 2006). Andreas has also offered his services as an Advisor to the Greek Government on tourism policymaking, education and development and conducts air transport and tourism executive courses organised in Africa and the Middle East on behalf of IATF and AACO. He is a Fellow of the Tourism Society, UK and sits on the Executive Board of the Hellenic Aviation Society. He is also a Partner at the Air Consulting Group and presided over the Executive Committee of the 2008 Air Transport Research Society Conference held in Athens, Greece.

E-mail: academia@trioptron.org and a.papatheodorou@aegean.gr
Website: www.trioptron.org

Peter Forsyth has been Professor of Economics at Monash University since 1997, and prior to this he was at the University of New England, Australian National University and the University of New South Wales. He studied at the University of Sydney and gained a DPhil in Economics from the University of Oxford. Most of his research has been on applied microeconomics, with particular reference to the economics of air transport, tourism economics and the economics of regulation. He has done extensive research on air transport, including on international aviation regulation and Australian domestic air transport. He has published several papers on airport regulation, and is the joint Editor of a book on the subject (*The Economic Regulation of Airports: Recent developments in Australasia, North America and Europe*, Ashgate, 2004). Recently he published, with Larry Dwyer, a jointly edited volume, (*International Handbook on the Economics of Tourism*, Edward Elgar, 2006). In 2003 he was awarded an Australian Research Council Discovery Grant for research on Airport Privatisation and Regulation. He has also done substantial research on tourism economics and policy. This has covered measurement of the benefits of tourism, assessment of international price competitiveness of tourism industries, foreign investment in tourism and taxation of tourism. Recent work has involved using Computable General Equilibrium models to assess the economic impacts of tourism, including events, and to analyse tourism and aviation policy issues. Current research includes climate change policies and their impact on aviation, and developing models to assess the implications of climate change policies for the tourism industry. This work has been supported by the Australian Sustainable Tourism Cooperative Research Centre.

Email: peter.forsyth@buseco.monash.edu.au

List of Contributors

Khaula Alkaabi is a doctoral candidate in the Department of Geography at the University of North Carolina at Greensboro, USA. Her research interests include the geography of air transportation and its impact on regional economies, and urban sprawl. She has published a co-authored article in the *Journal of Air Transport Management* and presented a paper at the Annual Meeting of the Association of American Geographers in Denver, CO in 2005. Upon graduation, Khaula will take a position as an Assistant Professor in the Department of Geography at the United Arab Emirates University at Al-Ain City.

Email: alkaabik@hotmail.com

Pavlos Arvanitis is a Partner at the Air Consulting Group. He has worked in the airline industry and has been a lecturer at Bedford College UK, teaching transport and tourism. He conducted research at Cranfield University, UK. He holds a BA in Tourism Business Administration and completed his thesis in Sustainable Tourism Development, at Hogeschool Delft, Netherlands as an Erasmus Student Exchange Programme Scholar. He obtained an MSc in Tourism Management and Planning from Bournemouth University, UK. His thesis discussed air transport deregulation in Greece. He is currently pursuing studies at a doctoral level at the University of the Aegean, Greece.

Email: p.arvanitis@airconsulting.aero
Website: www.airconsulting.aero

Sean Barrett is a Senior Lecturer at the Department of Economics and a Fellow of Trinity College, Dublin, Ireland. He is a graduate of University College, Dublin, and McMaster University, Canada. He is a Government of Ireland nominee to the National Economic and Social Council of Ireland and a member of the international Editorial Board of the *Journal of Air Transport Management*. He has participated in international research on airline and airport competition under the auspices of the European Science Foundation, the European Union, the OECD/ECMT and CESifo. He is a Board Member of the Alfred Beit Foundation and the Kenmare Economic Policy Conference and academic adviser to the FBD Trust.

Email: sbarrett@tcd.ie

Nuno Brilha heads the Strategic Partnerships and Special Projects Division at ANA, the Portuguese airport authority, managing seven international airports. He has been involved with non-aviation businesses for the last six years, after returning from London where he concluded his Business Studies BA (Hons) degree at University of Westminster. Currently he holds a Post-Graduate degree in Air Transport, Airports and Intermodality from ISTC and a Master's degree in Tourism Management from the University of Aveiro and several executive courses at Westminster, Cranfield and INSEAD. His key research interests comprise management, air transport and tourism industries.

Email: mailnmb@yahoo.com

Ben Daley is a Research Associate at the Centre for Air Transport and the Environment (CATE) at Manchester Metropolitan University. He has a background in geography and environmental history. He has worked on a range of projects concerned with aviation environmental impacts, including studies of operational improvements at airports, revised air traffic management technologies and procedures, and climate change mitigation. He also has a research interest in the relationship between aviation and economic development, especially the ways in which air transport can be used effectively to promote sustainable development.

Email: b.daley@mmu.ac.uk

Keith G. Debbage is a Professor of Urban Development in the Department of Geography at UNC-Greensboro and the 2008 GlaxoSmithKline Faculty Fellow with the Institute of Emerging Issues at North Carolina State University, USA. His specific research interests include airline route networks and how they shape regional economies, and the economic geography of the tourist industry. Dr. Debbage is the author of over 50 publications in book chapters, contracted reports and various academic journals including the *Journal of Air Transport Management*, the *Journal of Transport Geography*, and *Transportation Quarterly*.

Email: kgdebbag@uncg.edu
Website: www.uncg.edu/~kgdebbag

Dimitrios Dimitriou has expertise in transportation engineering and air traffic demand modelling. He has produced specialist work in the subject of routes with high seasonal fluctuations, using stochastic forecasting methods. He has worked particularly on air transport demand forecasting for the Greek tourist islands. He has been involved in strategic planning in relation to a range of topics: upgraded transport systems in Athens, road safety, surface transport to Chios port, and the Athens Metro operational plan during the 2004 Olympic Games. He is a member of numerous expert committees and professional organisations.

Email: d.dimitriou@cranfield.ac.uk

Rafael Echevarne is an economist with a PhD in Airport Economics from Cranfield University. He is an independent airport advisor and academic and was a Director of International Airport Development at Copenhagen Airports, Technical Director at Ferrovial Airports and Marketing and Commercial Director at Spain's first private airport. He also held positions in companies in Australia, New Zealand and the UK, working on airport privatisation and the provision of consultancy services in the fields of airports and air traffic control.

Email: echevarne@gmail.com

Respicio Espirito Santo Jr is Adjunct Professor at the Federal University of Rio de Janeiro in Brazil. His main fields of consulting, advisory and academic research are: public policies in air transport and tourism; political/economic regulation of air transport and tourism; strategic planning for airlines and airports; and scenario planning. He is President of the Brazilian Institute of Strategic Studies and Public Policies in Air Transport. He is a member of a number of industry organisations including the Executive/Networking Committee of the Air Transport Research Society (ATRS) and the International Aviation Law Institute.

Email: respicio@institutocepta.org

Brian Graham is Professor of Human Geography at the University of Ulster, UK. He is a Chartered Geographer of the Royal Geographical Society and was formerly Chair of its Transport Geography Research Group. Brian Graham is a member of the Editorial Boards of *Journal of Transport Geography* and *Transport Reviews* and has published widely on many aspects of air transport. His present research interests focus on the interconnections between air transport, economic development and the environment. He is the author of *Geography and Air Transport* (1995), has acted as an advisor on aviation matters to government departments in Northern Ireland and is a Director of Air Route Development (NI) Ltd.

Email: bj.graham@ulster.ac.uk

Nigel Halpern is Associate Professor in Transport and Tourism at Molde University College, Norway. He was previously Principal Lecturer in Aviation at London Metropolitan University, UK. Nigel joined academia from industry where he worked for the UK Civil Aviation Authority and Department for Transport, Local Government and the Regions. He has also worked in the tourism and hospitality industry in the UK, France, Spain and Italy. Nigel has an MSc in Tourism Management and a PhD in Air Transport Management. He currently teaches and conducts research and consultancy in transport and tourism, focusing on airports and the development of tourism in remoter regions.

Email: nigel.halpern@himolde.no.

Kostas Iatrou is a partner of Air Consulting Group and holds a PhD in Air Transport Management from Cranfield University, UK. He is co-author of the book *Airline Choices for the Future: From Alliances to Mergers*. He has conducted seminars on alliances under the auspices of IATF of IATA and at Cranfield University. Kostas has presented his work and research on alliances, including the impact of alliances on airlines and alliance branding, at the ICAO Liberalisation Symposium, IATA Commercial Strategy Symposium and at several Air Transport Research Society (ATRS) World Conferences. His articles have featured in numerous air transport publications such as *Airline Business*, the *Journal of Air Transport Management*, the *Journal of Air Transportation*, the *Annals of Air and Space Law* of McGill University and *Aerlines*. Finally, he is Editor and Publisher of AirTransportNews. aero.

Email: k.iatrou@airconsulting.aero
Website: www.airconsulting.aero

Zheng Lei is a Senior Lecturer in Tourism at Anglia Ruskin University, UK. He has a PhD in Management from the University of Surrey, UK. Zheng's research interests include air transport and tourism management, regional economic development and research methodology.

Email: z.lei@anglia.ac.uk

Gang Li is a Lecturer in Economics in the Faculty of Management and Law at the University of Surrey, UK. He received his PhD in Tourism Economics from the same institution. His major research interests are econometric modelling of international travel and tourism demand and assessment of the accuracy of different forecasting methods within the tourism context.

Email: g.li@surrey.ac.uk

Jukka Niskala is Airport Manager at the expanding Pajala-Ylläs Airport (PJA/ESUP) in the very north of Sweden. He has a wide and varied background in aviation including an accident free 14,000 hour bush pilot career in East Africa. Tourism and aviation have gone hand in hand since the development and pioneering of new routes in Africa to the present creation and running of an entirely new airport and destination in the Arctic. Additional current assignments include flight duty at regional carriers and relevant flight instruction and examination.

Email: airport@pajala.se

John F. O'Connell completed an MSc in Air Transport Management from Cranfield University (UK) and an MBA (Aviation) from Embry-Riddle Aeronautical University (USA), later returning to Cranfield to complete a PhD. He is also a certified IATA instructor and holds a pilot's licence. John currently works as an Airline Lecturer at the Department of Air Transport, Cranfield University. Previously, he worked for the Boeing Commercial Aircraft Company in Europe and Seattle as a marketing analyst for over six years. He then lectured at Embry-Riddle Aeronautical University extended campus in the San Francisco Bay Area for a further five years. He is also an aviation instructor travelling to the world's airlines on behalf of IATA, IATF and AACO where he provides airlines with seminars on strategy, management, marketing, cost reduction, distribution and no-frills operations.

Email: john_f_o_connell@hotmail.com

Neelu Seetaram is a Lecturer in the Department of Economics and Statistics at the University of Mauritius. She holds a B.Sc (Hons) in Economics from the University of Mauritius and an M.Sc. in Economics and Econometrics from Nottingham University (UK). She has been awarded the Sustainable Tourism (Qantas) Scholarship and is currently pursuing doctoral research at Monash University (Australia). Her research interests are mainly tourism and transport economics.

Email: Neelu.Seetaram@buseco.monash.edu.au

Stephen Shaw is the Managing Director of SSA Ltd, a consultancy which specialises in providing courses in marketing, economics and business strategy to firms in the aviation industry. He is also a part-time member of the faculty of City University, London, UK, where he lectures on the university's M.Sc in Air Transport Management. The sixth edition of his book *Airline Marketing and Management* has recently been published by Ashgate Books.

Email: ssassoc@dsl.pipex.com

Marianna Sigala is a Lecturer at the University of the Aegean, Greece and previously, she had been lecturing at the Universities of Strathclyde and Westminster in the UK. Her interests include service operations management, Information and Communication Technologies (ICT) in tourism and hospitality, and e-learning. She has professional experience from the Greek hospitality industry, while she has also contributed to several international research and consultancy projects. She has published three books, and numerous research papers at academic journals and international conferences. She had served as President of Euro-CHRIE (2004 – 2005) and she currently serves at the Board of Directors of IFITT and HeAIS.

Email: m.sigala@aegean.gr
Website: www.ba.aegean.gr/m.sigala

Semisi Taumoepeau is the Head of the Hospitality and Tourism Management Programme, AIS St Helens, New Zealand. He is also the Associate Director of the New Zealand Tourism Research Institute. Previous positions include directorship of Tourism for the Government of Tonga (1979-2002) and CEO of the Tonga National Airline (1999-2001). Semisi holds a BSc from Auckland University (New Zealand), a MSc degree from the University of Surrey (UK) and a DBA from the University of the Sunshine Coast, Australia. His research interests include economic sustainability of Pacific airlines, tourism planning and development as well as linkages between tourism and education.

Email: semisit@ais.ac.nz and semisi.taumoepeau@gmail.com
Website: www.ais.ac.nz

Callum Thomas is Professor of Sustainable Aviation in the Centre for Air Transport and the Environment (CATE) at Manchester Metropolitan University. He worked for over fifteen years at Manchester Airport where he established the Bird Control Department, Environment Department and Community Relations Unit. He has worked on various international and national projects investigating the management of aircraft noise, community affairs and bird control at airports. His main focus is on the sustainable development of aviation – especially in relation to environmental capacity constraints at airports. He is a member of several UK Government, EU and industry working parties and committees.

Email: c.s.thomas@mmu.ac.uk

Elena Tsitsiragou has studied law, history, political science and translation. She lives and works in Athens.

Email: elenat@otenet.gr

Anastasia Vasiliadou is an Attorney at Law and member of Thessaloniki Bar Association in Greece since 2000. She has previously worked as a *stagiaire* in the Centre of International and European Economic Law. She received her degree in Law from Democritus University of Thrace (Greece) and holds a Masters Degree in Tourism Business Management from the Hellenic Open University with a specialisation in the aviation field. Her MSc thesis addressed the issue of passenger protection in a liberal aviation market. Anastasia's main research interests include sustainable tourism development, environmental and land use implications of tourism, consumer protection, aviation law. She speaks Greek, English, Spanish and Italian.

E-mail: vasiliadou.a@dsthe.gr

George Williams is a Reader in Airline Economics at the Department of Air Transport, Cranfield University, UK. He has extensive international lecturing experience and has written two books and over 50 papers and research reports all exploring the impact of deregulation on the airline industry. He has led major studies into airline service provision in Ireland, the Netherlands, Norway, Portugal, Spain, Sweden and the UK on behalf of the European Commission, Government departments, regulatory authorities, airlines and airport authorities. He heads the Centre for Air Transport in Remoter Regions, which organises a biennial international Forum devoted to issues concerning air transport provision in Remoter Regions, the next of which will take place in Bergen in May 2009.

Email: g.williams@cranfield.ac.uk
Website: www.cranfield.ac.uk/soe/departments/airtransport

John Zammit is a Senior Executive Assistant to Chairman & CEO at Air Malta plc. He joined the airline in 1977 after graduating in economics at the University of Malta. John's airline experience comprises fleet planning, aircraft leasing, aircraft maintenance cost monitoring, market research and statistics, route economics, traffic forecasting and budgeting, schedules planning. He has also implemented Balanced Scorecard for the airline. He is a regular participant at the Aircraft Finance & Commercial Aviation Forum in Geneva, speaking mostly on fleet planning and LCCs issues. In 2003 John became an MBA graduate with distinction from the Danube University, Krems, Vienna, Austria.

E-mail: john.f.zammit@airmalta.com

Petros Zenelis works at the Bank of Cyprus in Athens, Greece. He obtained an MSc in International Banking and Financial Services from the University of Reading, U.K. His Thesis was about price discrimination in the airline market. He previously graduated from the University of Athens, Greece, with a BSc in Economics. From August 1999 to January 2000, he attended the University of Linköping, Sweden, to study at the Department of Business Administration as an Erasmus Student Exchange Programme Scholar. Petros is currently pursuing his doctorate at the University of the Aegean, Greece. His research interests include low-cost air carriers and tourism development.

Email: p.zenelis@chios.aegean.gr

Preface

It may not be immediately obvious why three academics from different parts of the world (namely United Kingdom, Greece and Australia) would want to join forces in editing this book. The answer is very simple. We have all specialised in tourism and aviation teaching and training, research and consulting for many years and remain fascinated by developments in these dynamic industries. Nonetheless, we continue to be surprised at the failure of academia, governments, industry and other stakeholders to fully recognise and appreciate the close and complex relationships which exist between aviation and tourism, particularly when leisure travel is concerned. It is this common view that has united and motivated us to invite 26 distinguished experts in different specialist areas to contribute to this book. Hopefully, this publication will help in some way to expand and develop the knowledge and understanding of the important links between these two industries.

Anne Graham
Andreas Papatheodorou
Peter Forsyth

London, May 2008

Acknowledgements

We would like to thank Kyriaki Boulasidou and Konstantinos Polychroniadis for their invaluable contribution to the production of the manuscript, Elliott Kefalas for providing the striking photos for the cover, and Eleftherios Tsouris for preparing the maps in the destination case studies

Thanks are also due to Guy Loft and others at Ashgate for all their helpful advice and assistance.

Finally, we must express our gratitude to our families and friends for their continuing love, support and understanding.

1

Introduction

Anne Graham
Andreas Papatheodorou
Peter Forsyth

Transport is a fundamental component of tourism, providing the vital link between the tourist generating areas and destinations. Hence there are very close links between the transport and tourism industries where a two-way relationship exists. On the one hand good accessibility, which is determined by the transport services provided, is essential for the development of any tourist destination. Conversely for the transport industry, there can be substantial benefits from tourism because of the additional demand which this type of travel can produce.

Aviation is an increasingly important mode of transport for tourism markets. Whilst geography has meant that, in modern times, air travel has always been the dominant mode for long distance travel and much international tourism, moves towards deregulation, and in particular the emergence of the low cost carrier sector, have also increased aviation's significance for short and medium haul tourism trips. Thus, developments in aviation are having very major implications for many leisure and business tourism markets. However , the characteristics and needs of leisure travellers are generally so very different from business travellers that this necessitates a separate consideration of these markets if a detailed understanding of the relationship with aviation is to be gained.

In spite of the obvious closeness between the aviation and the leisure tourism industries, there are very few specialist texts on this subject. Most tourism focused books consider aviation as just one component of the tourism industry which needs to be discussed, whereas aviation specialist texts rarely concentrate on just leisure travel. In addition there is very little literature that gives a detailed appreciation of the complexities and potential conflicts associated with the development of coherent and effective aviation and tourism policies. Therefore it is the aim of this book to fill this important gap which exists with a comprehensive, in-depth study of the relationship between aviation and leisure travel.

This book is particularly timely because of recent developments in both the aviation and tourism world. The demand for leisure travel continues to grow in most world regions but is changing as tourists become more experienced, adventurous and demanding travellers. At the same time the general climate of deregulation is producing very significant structural developments within the airline industry. The nature of network, charter and low cost carriers, and the way that they each serve the leisure market is changing, as is the distribution channels that are used. In addition, airports are becoming much more proactive and experienced in trying to attract leisure demand and in providing a level of service which is appealing to leisure travellers.

The present edited volume deals exclusively with issues related to the synergies and conflicts in the relationship between aviation and leisure travel. The key underlying theme which is emphasised throughout the book is that it is essential for all to recognise the two-way linkages which exist between the aviation and tourism industries and to ensure that these are fully understood during any decision making process. The authors of each chapter are each highly recognised authorities on the specific subject area that they are considering. Moreover, the exact mix of the authors has been carefully chosen so as to create a balanced representation from both industry and academia and also from different world regions. The end result is that a wide range of different topics related to the aviation-tourism interface have been examined from a mixture of different viewpoints.

The book is divided into seven parts. Each part covers a different and important aspect of the aviation and tourism relationship and provides a useful insight into some of the key challenges which both industries face. Part I explores the nature of demand whilst Part II looks at government policy. Parts III and IV then focus on supply issues, related to both airlines and airports. The focus of this first half of the book, therefore, is geared towards demand, supply and governmental trends that will shape the future of the aviation and tourism industries and the interface between them. Part V then considers broader industry impacts, from economic, social and environmental viewpoints. This is followed by Part VI which offers a selection of case studies from different regions of the world which explores the complementary nature of the air transport and tourism products in these areas and investigates some of the key themes discussed in the previous chapters. Part VII provides the conclusions.

In detail, Part I contains three chapters and looks in depth at the nature of leisure travel demand and assesses the implications of serving this demand for the aviation industry. This is important as clearly the aviation and tourism industries must understand their demand and recognise changing trends in order to fulfil their customers' needs. Gang Li begins by discussing the nature of leisure travel demand in Chapter 2 principally from an economic perspective. He identifies key influencing factors of leisure travel demand and relates this to the concept of demand elasticities. This is developed into a discussion of forecasting methodologies which can be used to forecast leisure travel demand. This is followed by Chapter 3 written by Anne Graham which explores recent trends and characteristics of leisure demand with specific reference to travel by air. Global and regional patterns of demand are explored and distinctions made between mature and emerging markets. This leads onto a consideration of the changing demographic characteristics of leisure tourists and evolving travel preferences. Steven Shaw then builds on these two last two chapters in his Chapter 4 by examining the implications of the specific nature of leisure travel demand for airline marketing and by applying various marketing techniques, such as a PESTE analysis, to explore the current marketing practices within the airline industry for this market segment.

Part II, which also contains three chapters, focuses on regulation and government policy related to both industries and assesses the consequences of this for the development of tourism. The aviation and tourism sectors have mutual interests in supporting government policy which encourages the well being of both industries. Andreas Papatheodorou in Chapter 5 identifies the role of the prevailing institutional economics regimes in the aviation industry and examines how the traditionally highly regulated environment has been gradually liberalised. He studies the rationale and operating principles of aviation regulation as well as the advantages but also the potential dangers arising from market liberalisation. Anastasia Vasiliadou then looks in more specific detail at the current aviation legislation which is specifically relevant to leisure travel in her Chapter 6. Areas covered include safety, security, the Single European Sky and data protection. Reference is also made to the legislation related to denied boarding, cancellation and delays. This leads onto Chapter 7 by Peter Forsyth which explores aviation policy and associated tourism benefits. It begins by reviewing aviation policy and its impact on tourism flows. This is followed by a discussion which identifies tourism benefits and highlights key issues related to their measurement. Then these two sections are brought together by assessing aviation-tourism trade-offs with the aid of a number of examples from around the world.

Part III, is the first of two parts which consider supply issues, with the focus in this part being on airlines. Much of the emphasis is on the changing role of different types of airlines which serve the leisure market. These changes have been primarily driven by demand trends (as discussed in Part I) and developments towards a more liberal environment (as discussed in Part II). In particular, George Williams in Chapter 8 considers charter operations. He investigates the main airlines and markets within Europe and the relationship between the charter airlines and the tour operators. This leads onto a discussion of the factors influencing charter operating and economic performance and the consequences for the future. Then, Chapter 9 written by Sean Barrett describes the emergence of the low cost carrier sector. He examines the cost savings, product features, and benefits of low cost airlines. He also explores the low cost sector's role within the European aviation leisure market, in relation to growth patterns and competition, and further elaborates on the impacts on charter airlines. The next Chapter 10 by John Zammit builds on the discussion in these two chapters (and Part II) in presenting a case study of how Air Malta has changed from a national airline to an EU leisure based carrier since Malta's accession to the European Union. Moreover, he explains how Malta's evolution is intricately intertwined with the development of Malta's tourism and travel industry. The final Chapter in this part by Keith Debbage and Khaula Alkaabi has an equally as important but somewhat different orientation in that it examines how the airline industry has utilised market power and scale economies to shape consumer demand and accessibility levels in both major leisure destinations and also in small and emerging destinations. It investigates the use of vertical integration and vertical alliances within the aviation and tourism industries and concludes with a case study of the rapid growth of Dubai and its clear links to the emerging market power of Emirates Airlines.

The common topic for Part IV is airports and Nuno Brilha in Chapter 13 begins by identifying the various types of customers at airports and assesses their different requirements. He then explores how an airport can maintain a safe and secure environment without deterring tourists, how the right airport image and non-aeronautical facilities can contribute to the leisure experience and how airports can best cope with the peaks and troughs of leisure demand. The focus of Chapter 14 which follows by Rafael Echevarne is on the emergence of airport marketing which is set within the context of deregulation, low cost carriers and competition. The needs of low costs carriers in terms of financial incentives and airport design are discussed. Nigel Halpern and Jukka Niskala in the next Chapter 15 revisit the marketing theme and develop it further by considering the practices used by airports in Europe's northern periphery to exploit the potential for tourism and to compete in destination markets. A case study from a remote region in Sweden is used to illustrate some of the key points made. Finally, the last Chapter 16 of this part by Marianna Sigala focuses on airport ICT applications that are changing the way travellers are processed and are experiencing air travel. To begin, the key ICT applications are described along with their operational and customer benefits. This leads onto an assessment of their impacts on leisure travellers' air travel experiences. Numerous examples of international ICT initiatives and pilot programmes are also provided.

There are two chapters in Part V which together explore the broader impacts of aviation and tourism development. The focus of this part is very important as undoubtedly developing more sustainable tourism and travel products is one of the greatest challenges which face the aviation and tourism sectors. In Chapter 17, Brian Graham's emphasis is on discussing the relationships between aviation, tourism and economic development. He begins by explaining why these relationships are complex and often contradictory. The chapter then concentrates on the overlapping networks and interconnections between heritage and cultural tourism; accessibility, mobility and air services; and the cultural economy, air services and sustainability. The sustainability theme is further developed in Chapter 18 written by Ben Daley, Dimitris Dimitriou and Callum Thomas. This looks at the environmental impacts of both tourism and aviation and examines the pressures for greater sustainability, which in part have been caused by increased consumer awareness. The main implications for tourism and air travel for leisure demand are discussed and various measures to mitigate aviation environmental impacts are explored.

Part VI has a regional perspective and examines key issues and trends in aviation and tourism focusing on specific areas of the world. This concentrates on regions in less developed countries where aviation is playing a very significant role in the development of tourism. Each chapter considers the historical developments of the two industries in the chosen region and identifies current trends. Major policy issues are then examined which lead to a consideration of the way forward for aviation and tourism in each of the chosen regions. There are seven destination case study chapters. These are Chapter 19: Brazil (Respicio Espirito Santo Jr), Chapter 20: India (John O'Connell), Chapter 21: China (Zheng Lei), Chapter 22: The Middle East (John O'Connell), Chapter 23: Africa (Pavlos Arvantis and Petros Zenelis), Chapter 24: Mauritius (Neelu Seetaram) and Chapter 25: South Pacific (Semisi Taumoepeau).

Finally, the last Part VII contains Chapter 26 where the editors present the conclusions. This reflects upon the main themes identified in the book, explores the implications of these, and discusses unresolved issues and further directions for the future. In particular, the chapter refers to a number of themes such as the changing nature of the aviation industry, the relationship between aviation policy and leisure tourism, the tyranny of economies of density, the emergence of airports as tourism stakeholders, the importance of constraints in aviation and tourism growth and the significance of innovation and its impacts. It then elaborates on unresolved issues such as future developments of airline business models, the importance of climate change and its implications, the need to resolve the trade-off between development and environmental protection and the role of the emerging superpowers (namely India and China) in shaping the future of aviation and tourism. Having all the above in mind, the chapter closes with a positive note on the contribution of this book into this fascinating area of research!

PART I

Leisure Travel Demand

2

The Nature of Leisure Travel Demand

Gang Li

INTRODUCTION

The first section of this book considers leisure travel demand. A knowledge and understanding of such demand is crucial if the links between the aviation and tourism industries are to be fully appreciated. This initial chapter considers the nature of demand and the factors affecting it; whilst the next chapter explores demand trends and characteristics. The remaining chapter in this section then examines the implications of this specific nature of leisure travel demand for airline marketing.

This chapter aims to provide an overview of the nature of the leisure travel demand, principally from the economic perspective. It starts with defining what leisure travel demand means in economics, followed by discussions of key influencing factors of the demand for leisure travel and air transport with a particular focus on various economic determinants. Subsequently, the concept of demand elasticities is illustrated in the context of leisure travel and air transport, with particular attention paid to air fare elasticities. Finally, some methods of forecasting leisure travel demand are illustrated using empirical examples.

In general, a travel product involves a complex consumptive experience that results from a process where tourists use multiple travel services, including accommodation, food service, transportation, travel agencies and tour operators, recreation and entertainment, and other travel trade services, during the course of their visit (Gunn 1988). Leisure is associated with the discretionary time, i.e., 'the time remaining after working, commuting, sleeping and doing necessary household and personal chores which can be used in a chosen way' (Tribe 1995: 3). Thus leisure travel can be understood as a tourist's travel experience at his or her discretionary time (instead of working time). From an economic perspective, the definition of demand refers to 'effective' demand, that is, buyers must possess the wherewithal to buy as well as the willingness (Uysal 1998). Leisure travel demand can be defined as the quantity of leisure travel products (such as air transport) that a tourist is willing and able to purchase. The following discussions of the nature of leisure travel demand are based on this economic definition.

FACTORS AFFECTING LEISURE TRAVEL DEMAND

A variety of factors influence the demand for leisure travel and tourism. This section focuses on the economic determinants such as income and various price factors, with non-economic factors being briefly summarized in the end.

Trade-off Between Paid Work and Unpaid Leisure

The demand for leisure travel from the economic perspective is derived from the classical consumer theory, which assumes that consumers always take rational decisions, face constraints of limited income and time, and their decisions are made on the basis of maximizing their overall utility (or satisfaction).

Leisure time represents a key element of the choice set faced by a consumer. Maximization of his or her utility involves a trade-off between paid work (i.e. labour supply) and unpaid time for leisure activities (i.e., consumption, such as air travel) (Tribe 1995). Considering the limited time (24 hours a day) people have, to increase the time for leisure means to give up some time for paid work. From this view, leisure has a cost, which is the earnings foregone by giving up the paid work in order to pursue certain leisure activities. It is called the 'opportunity cost' of leisure time. The changes in wages affect people's decisions on combination between paid work and unpaid leisure. For example, an increase in the wage rates suggests that more income can be earned to afford more leisure and travel consumption (i.e., income effect); but on the other hand, it means leisure time becomes more expensive and people may tend to consume less leisure but work more (i.e., substitution effect).

The net effect depends on the individual's preference and other issues such as his or her current income level, working conditions, and government taxation and spending policies. At a lower level of wage rates, people are likely to choose to work more in order to increase their income until their wage rates go up to a certain level. When wage rates continue to increase, people tend to give up some work and pursue more leisure. If the wage rates keep going up, the opportunity cost of leisure time is too high and people begin to favour more work. Thus the relationship between the labour supply and wage rates can be illustrated by an 'S' shaped curve.

Price of a Leisure Travel Product

As with the demand for any other 'normal' product, the demand for leisure travel and air transport follows 'the law of demand', i.e., 'other things remaining the same, the higher the price of a good, the smaller is the quantity demanded' (Parkin *et al.* 1997: 71). Given a decrease in price of a leisure travel product such as air transport, with other factors being held constant, the quantity demanded of this product will increase. In the past three to four decades, there have been substantial decreases in the prices of package holidays across the whole Mediterranean region, which, coupled with other factors, have led to a constantly increasing number of international tourists to this region.

Income

With other factors remaining constant, given the same price level, increased income will lead to a growth of demand for leisure travel. Figure 2.1 shows the growth of real disposable income of UK households and the growth of their overseas leisure travel demand measured by the number of visits abroad. It can be clearly seen that following the gradual increase in income over time, British people's international leisure travel demand has grown more proportionally, especially over the past decade.

Prices of Substitutes and Complements

In addition to the changes of income of tourists and the price of the leisure travel product concerned (e.g., a holiday in Spain), the changes of alternative leisure travel products (such as a holiday in Italy) may affect the leisure travel demand concerned (i.e., the holiday in Spain). For British tourists, Spain and Italy can be regarded as competing destinations for a package holiday. Therefore, if a package holiday in Italy is cheaper than a similar alternative in Spain, given other factors remaining unchanged, British tourists will probably choose the package in Italy. In other words, demand for leisure travel to Spain will decrease if the price of its substitute product (i.e., a package in Italy) decreases.

If transportation is regarded as a product, two alternative transport means, by air and by rail, can be regarded as substitutes. For instance, people who want to travel from London to Paris can choose to go either by air or by Eurostar. Therefore, an increase in the air fare will encourage more people to travel by Eurostar and less by air.

The demand for leisure travel can also be influenced by the price of a complementary product, which is consumed together with the product concerned. For example if a British tourist is planning his or her holiday in Spain and decides to book flights and accommodation separately (instead of an all-inclusive package), then an increase in the air fare is likely to result in a decrease in his or her demand for hotel accommodation in Spain, given his or her limited budget for this holiday.

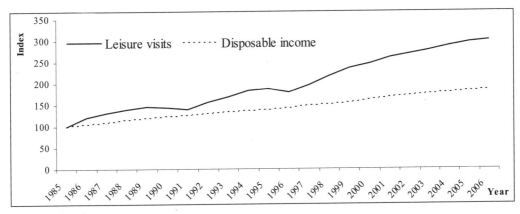

FIGURE 2.1   Indices of leisure visits abroad by UK residents and household disposable income (1985=100)

Source: Office for National Statistics (UK).

Exchange Rates

The price becomes more complicated as far as the demand for international travel is concerned, because tourists need to consider the relative exchange rate between tourism generating and receiving countries if different currencies are used. For example, the continuous weakening of the US dollar against the UK sterling since 2002 has made the UK an increasingly expensive destination for American tourists. Therefore, an unfavourable variation of the exchange rate tends to reduce the American tourists' demand for travel to the UK. Tourists may cut their spending in this destination or choose a relatively cheaper destination for their holidays (i.e., substitution effect). On the other hand, the favourable exchange rate creates a further incentive for UK tourists to travel to the USA and other dollar-based countries such as the Caribbean.

Effective Prices of Tourism and Real Exchange Rates

It can be seen from the above discussion that both fluctuations of exchange rates and price evolution (i.e. inflation) in a potential destination relative to that in the origin country affect the demand for leisure travel. The combination of these two effects leads to two important notions: 'the effective price of tourism' (Durbarry and Sinclair 2003) and 'the real exchange rate' (Vanhove 2005). The effective price of tourism means the price level in a destination relative to that in the origin country, adjusted by the exchange rate between the two countries. The general price level is normally represented by the consumer price index (CPI). Real exchange rates measure the joint effects of price evolution and exchange rates in a different way. The real exchange rate refers to the market rate of exchange between the origin country's currency and the destination's currency, adjusted by an index of relative inflation rates between the two countries.

Using the UK as an origin country of leisure travel, and the USA as a destination, Figure 2.2 shows that the general price levels (CPIs) in the origin and destination countries, the exchange rates between the two countries' currencies and the effective price of tourism in the destination relative to that in the origin country, all fluctuate to a different extent. This is particularly evident in the most recent years (2001–2006). For a rational decision making, the effective prices of tourism or real exchange rates should be considered, as they reflect the joint effect of all of the above price factors. However, the effect of changes in exchange rates on international travel is not similar to the effect of differential rates of inflation. The consequences of a change in an exchange rate can be immediately perceived by potential travellers, while people may not be well informed about recent price developments in foreign countries (Artus 1970). Thus in light of the complex effects of various price factors, the rate of exchange is regarded by many potential travellers to be a prime indicator of expected prices in their travel decision making process (Gray 1966).

Travel Costs

Travel costs refer to the costs of round-trip travel between the origin and destination countries or regions. Transportation, as one of the most necessary elements of a travel product, accounts for a considerable proportion of the total travel expenses, especially for long-haul travel. Hence, travel costs may be an important determinant of leisure travel

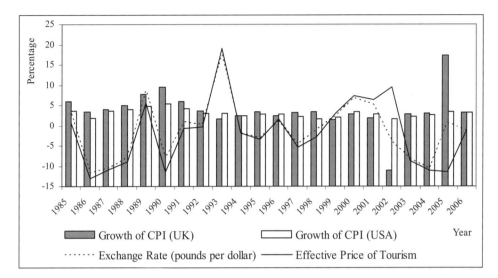

FIGURE 2.2   Growth rates of UK and US CPIs, exchange rates between Sterling and Dollar, and effective price of tourism

Source: International Monetary Fund (IMF).

demand. Oil prices are often regarded as a key indicator of travel costs, especially for air travel. An increase in oil prices, for instance, leads to higher air travel costs and therefore makes leisure travel dearer. Arguably, the continuous decreases of air fares over time have contributed, to a great extent, to the constant growth of world-wide travel over the past half an century. More recently, the booming of no-frills (or low-cost) carriers in Europe has stimulated phenomenal growth of air travel domestically and within Europe. According to the Civil Aviation Authority (CAA) (2006a), the demand for air travel with low-cost carriers from the UK to EU countries experienced a remarkable growth of 35 per cent annually on average between 2000 and 2005. It contributed significantly to the overall demand for air travel.

Non-economic Factors

In addition to the above key economic determinants of the demand for leisure travel, a number of non-economic factors have been identified in the literature (see, for example, Middleton and Clark 2001; Vanhove 2005). Firstly, demographic factors, in terms of both the size and the structure of a source market's population, influence the demand for leisure travel. Secondly, governments may use their regulatory powers to exert interventions with respect to tourism, which will further affect the demand for tourism and travel products. Thirdly, the development of the information and communication technologies (ICT) and the spread of mobile technologies and navigation systems (GPS), all have strong impacts on people's travel decision-making and their choice of destinations and travel distribution channels. Lastly, social and cultural events, along with natural and man-made disasters, can all affect people's travel decisions, at least in the short term. These factors are considered in greater detail by A. Graham in Chapter 3 and Shaw in Chapter 4.

DEMAND ELASTICITIES AND THEIR IMPORTANCE

As the previous discussions have shown, income and prices are regarded as the key economic determinants for demand of a product or service such as leisure travel. Information regarding the extent to which changes in demand result from each of these variables is also important for both tourism suppliers and policy-makers (Sinclair and Stabler 1997). The responsiveness of demand for a product to changes in income, own-price and prices of related products is measured by income elasticity of demand, own-price elasticity of demand and cross-price elasticity of demand, respectively.

Income Elasticity of Demand

The income elasticity of demand is measured by the proportional change which occurs in the quantity demanded (Q) relative to the proportional change which has taken place in income (Y). It can be defined as follows:

$$E_y = \frac{\text{Percentage change in quantity demanded}}{\text{Percentage change in income}} = \frac{\%\Delta Q / \bar{Q}}{\%\Delta Y / \bar{Y}}$$

where $\bar{Q}$ and $\bar{Y}$ are average quantity demanded and average income, respectively, between the two points on a demand curve.

Most goods and services have positive income elasticities. The effect of income on tourism demand is subject to the type of tourism. General vacation or holiday demand is more income-elastic than visiting friends and relatives (VFR) demand, and secondary vacations are the most income-elastic. However, demand for business travel and convention tourism is relatively income-inelastic (Bull 1995). A number of tourism economics studies have provided empirical evidence for this (see Li *et al.* 2005 for a summary).

The study of Crouch (1995) supports the assumption that demand elasticities for international tourism vary regionally, as far as both source markets and destinations are concerned. Hence, knowledge of the income elasticity is important for tourism planners and policymakers in different origins and destinations. A low income elasticity of demand implies that the demand for leisure travel to a particular destination is relatively insensitive to the economic situation in the origin country. However, if the calculated income elasticity exceeds unity, then a rise in income in the origin country will be accompanied by a more than proportionate rise in the demand for travel to the destination. Destinations should pay particular attention to forecasting the future levels of economic activities in those tourism generating countries associated with high income elasticities.

Own-price Elasticity of Demand

Own-price elasticity of demand is a measure of the proportional change in the quantity demanded (Q), relative to the proportional change in the own price of the product (P). It is measured through the formula:

$$E_p = \frac{\text{Percentage change in quantity demanded}}{\text{Percentage change in price}} = \frac{\%\Delta Q / \bar{Q}}{\%\Delta P / \bar{P}}$$

Own-price elasticity is usually negative, which indicates that there is an inverse relationship between a travel and tourism product's price and the demand for it.

In general, the greater the degree of competition (or substitutability) amongst products, the higher the price elasticity of demand is likely to be, as price-conscious tourist search for cheaper alternatives (Bull 1995). Thus, the magnitude of the estimated own-price elasticity of demand can provide useful information for travel and tourism service providers. For example, if the absolute value of own-price elasticity is over unity ($|E_p|>1$) the demand for travel and tourism is price elastic. It means that an increase in the price will result in a more than proportionate decrease in the quantity demanded. As a result, the total sales revenue will fall. If the absolute value of own-price elasticity equals unity ($|E_p|=1$) the increase in the price will result in the proportionate decrease in the quantity demanded so the total revenue will remain constant. If the absolute value of own-price elasticity is less than unity ($|E_p|<1$) the demand for travel and tourism is price inelastic. It means an increase in tourism price will result in a less than proportionate decrease in the quantity demanded, and the total revenue will rise. Therefore, to identify the magnitude of own-price elasticity can help tourism suppliers in a destination to adopt appropriate pricing strategies.

Cross-price Elasticity of Demand

Another important concept in demand analysis is the cross-price elasticity of demand between different products. It can be expressed as follows:

$$E_{cp} = \frac{\%\text{ change in quantity demanded for product A}}{\%\text{ change in price of product B}} = \frac{\%\Delta Q_A / \overline{Q}_A}{\%\Delta P_B / \overline{P}_B}$$

If E_{cp} is positive it means product A and B are substitutes, while the two products are viewed as complementary if E_{cp} is negative.

Cross-price elasticity of tourism demand has important policy implications for the destination concerned. A significant substitution effect indicates strong competition and the implication would be that planners and decision-makers in the destination under consideration should keep a close eye on the prices in its competing destinations in order to ensure that the relative price level does not increase significantly. At the same time appropriate strategies should be adopted based on the specific attributes that the destination possesses to target on differentiated markets segments. In other words, that is to make full use of their competitive advantages. When complementary effects are in place, the destinations involved may consider launching joint marketing programmes to maximise their overall profits (Li et al. 2005).

AIR FARE ELASTICITY

The above discussion of various elasticities of demand is based on the aggregate level of travel and tourism products, which include all elements of a travel experience. Considering the great contribution of air transport to the world's travel and tourism development, it is of increasing interest to investigate price (i.e., fare) elasticity of demand for air travel.

Moreover, 'the importance of air fares has undoubtedly increased in recent years from the viewpoint of individual airlines because of greater transparency and more substitution possibilities' (Njegovan 2006: 33). Therefore, a good understanding of air fare elasticity is of great importance for air transport operators to project effective pricing strategies in such a competitive aviation market. Moreover, it provides useful policy implications for the relevant regulatory bodies.

The principle of demand price elasticity is readily applicable to air fare elasticity analysis. This mainly focuses on own-price elasticity, with cross-price elasticity being largely ignored. This is probably due to the difficulty in collecting air fare data from competitors. As far as the own-price (air fare) elasticity analysis of demand for air travel is concerned, the demand is normally measured by the number of air passengers or passenger-kilometres (or miles), and the price refers to the air fare or air fare per kilometre (or mile) related to a particular route or carrier.

A number of factors may affect the value of air fare elasticity, including the degree of competition in the air travel market, the number of competing operators (i.e., substitutes) available, the proportion of income spent on air tickets, the transparency of alternative fares, and the duration of the time period under study. A more competitive market, a larger number of competitors offering the same or similar air travel services, a higher proportion of income on air tickets, and more transparent fare information easy for people to compare competitors' fares, are all related to a higher air fare elasticity. In addition, people often take time to adjust their consumption patterns to price changes. Therefore, air travel demand generally becomes more and more fare-elastic over time.

Gillen *et al.* (2003) provided empirical evidence in their comprehensive overview of air fare elasticity analysis based on 254 demand elasticity estimates from 21 past studies. It is found that long-haul air travel is generally less fare-elastic than its short-haul counterpart, international travel is less fare-elastic than domestic travel, and business travel is much less fare-elastic than leisure travel. Moreover, international business travel is the least sensitive to fare changes, while the domestic leisure travel has the highest fare elasticity. It is also found that the demand for air travel has become increasingly sensitive to fare changes over time. The reason for higher fare elasticity of demand for short-haul air travel in comparison to the demand for its long-haul counterpart is that, for a short distance travel, other substitute transport modes (e.g., by car or train) are more likely to be available. The increasingly competitive aviation market, challenges from the low-cost carriers, and more and more transparent fare information available on internet, all explain why people become increasingly sensitive to air fare changes over time. To recognise the differences of air fare elasticity between business and leisure travellers is useful for an airline's effective yield management by taking the appropriate price discrimination strategy with respect to different fare classes.

FORECASTING LEISURE TRAVEL DEMAND

Based on data availability, travel and tourism forecasting techniques generally fall into two major categories: quantitative and qualitative forecasting. Quantitative forecasting methods can be further divided into causal and non-causal approaches, depending on whether there is any influencing factor of travel demand being included in the forecasting model.

Qualitative Techniques

Qualitative methods, also called 'judgmental methods' or 'subjective forecasting', rely on the experience and the judgment of experts in the field under study. This approach is particularly appropriate where past data are insufficient or inappropriate for statistical analysis, or where changes of a previously inexperienced dimension make numerical analysis of past data inappropriate (Uysal and Crompton 1985). Qualitative methods are useful for short-term forecasting, as the relationships between variables are likely to remain constant over this short time period. The disadvantages are that errors can arise due to the lack of expertise or the bias of chosen judges, the human tendency to confuse desires for the future with forecasts of it and judges' predisposition to be anchored in the present and underestimate future changes. Qualitative forecasting techniques such as the Delphi method, scenario writing, jury of executive opinion, and consumer intentions survey have all been used in the context of tourism demand (for example see Frechtling 2001).

Quantitative Forecasting Methods

There are two major approaches to quantitative forecasting: causal (principally econometric) and non-causal (mainly time-series) methods. They are based on different philosophical premises and serve different purposes. Causal methods assume a cause and effect relationship between the inputs to the system and the outputs (Makridakis *et al.* 1983). The system refers to the object that is being forecasted. So, causal forecasting intends to identify the causal relationship by observing the features of the output. The identified relationship will be used to predict the future states of the system. On the contrary, non-causal forecasting methods treat the system as a 'black box' and the prediction of the future output only depends on the pattern of the input data and randomness. Hence, comparably speaking, causal forecasting methods can provide useful information for both policy evaluation in the public sector and strategy formulation in various tourism businesses; whilst non-causal models, as they only require historical observations of a variable, are less costly in terms of data collection and model estimation.

Evidently, travel and tourism demand forecasting techniques have been advanced dramatically over the past four to five decades, as both non-causal and causal approaches are concerned (for example see Li *et al.* 2005; Song and Witt 2000; Frechtling 2001). Two simple examples are provided here for the purpose of illustrating the concepts and usefulness of non-causal and causal forecasting in the travel and tourism context.

Non-causal forecasting of seasonal variations: Additive model Leisure travel features significant seasonal variations due to different climates, school holidays and other reasons. Figure 2.3 shows clear evidence that, for British leisure travellers, the second and third quarters of each year are the peak season to travel abroad for holidays by air, and the first and fourth quarters are the off-peak season. It is therefore necessary to predict both the long-term trend of travel demand and seasonal variations in each quarter of a year.

To forecast seasonal travel demand, it is useful to separate the values of the demand series (X_t) into long-term trend (T_t) plus seasonal component (S_t), i.e., $X_t = T_t + S_t$, and then forecast them individually. Such a model is called an additive model (Thomas 1997). In order to isolate the trend, the method of moving averages can be used to smooth out the values of a series. Where the number of the values is even (as the case shown in Table 2.1), centred moving averages should be considered. First of all, 4-point moving averages are calculated, but these values are placed in the centre of the range of values used (Column (b) in Table 2.1). For example, the first 4-point moving average value 8.16 corresponds to the midway between the second and the third values of the actual demand, i.e., 8.59 and 11.84, respectively. Then the 2-point moving averages (i.e., centred moving averages) need to be calculated based on the values of the 4-point moving averages, in order to make the average values correspond to the actual demand figures. For instance, the centred moving average 8.18 corresponds to the demand in 2003 Q3 (11.84). The smoothed out values in Column (c) captures the trend of the travel demand series concerned. If the number of the total values is odd, only 3-point or 5-point average calculation is needed, instead of the calculations of both 4-point averages and then 2-point averages.

According to the formula of the additive model, $S_t = X_t - T_t$, seasonal variations can be obtained by subtracting the trend from the original series (see Column (d) in Table 2.1). The average of the seasonal variations corresponding to each quarter can be further calculated. For example: the average seasonal variation in Quarter 1 is (-2.49-2.48-2.56)/3=-2.51. Similarly, the average seasonal variations of Quarters 2, 3 and 4 are (0.46+0.44+0.84)/3=0.58, (3.66+3.72+3.90)/3=3.76, and (-1.75-1.65-1.89)/3=-1.77, respectively. These estimates of the seasonal variations can be combined with the trend estimates to obtain forecasts for future travel demand.

In Figure 2.3 the straight line shows the trend, which is drawn as the line of 'best fit' through the moving average values. The estimated trend in 2007 can be obtained by extending the line. Alternatively, a regression method could be used to obtain the precise values on the trend line (the mathematical illustration is omitted here). The trend estimates for the 4 quarters in 2007 are: 9.68, 9.80, 9.91 and 10.02, respectively. Combining

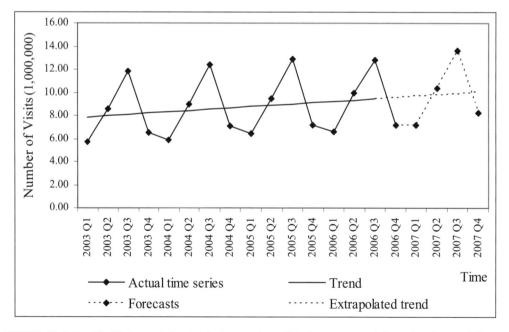

FIGURE 2.3   **British residents' international leisure travel by air: Actual data, trend and forecast**

Source: Overseas Travel and Tourism (MQ6), Office for National Statistics (UK).

TABLE 2.1 British residents' international leisure travel by air: Isolating the trend and seasonal variations

Time	Actual Demand (a)	4-point Moving Averages (b)	Centred Moving Averages (c)	Deviations (d) (d)=(a)-(c)
2003 Q1	5.72			
2003 Q2	8.59	8.16		
2003 Q3	11.84	8.20	8.18	3.66
2003 Q4	6.49	8.29	8.24	-1.75
2004 Q1	5.86	8.42	8.35	-2.49
2004 Q2	8.96	8.58	8.50	0.46
2004 Q3	12.37	8.72	8.65	3.72
2004 Q4	7.13	8.84	8.78	-1.65
2005 Q1	6.43	8.98	8.91	-2.48
2005 Q2	9.43	9.00	8.99	0.44
2005 Q3	12.92	9.05	9.02	3.90
2005 Q4	7.22	9.18	9.11	-1.89
2006 Q1	6.61	9.15	9.17	-2.56
2006 Q2	9.98	9.14	9.15	0.84
2006 Q3	12.78			
2006 Q4	7.20			

Source: Overseas Travel and Tourism (MQ6), Office for National Statistics (UK).

the trend estimates and the average seasonal variations, British residents' international leisure travel demand by air in 2007 can be predicted as follows and illustrated in Figure 2.3:

2007 Q1: 9.68-2.51=7.17	2007 Q2: 9.80+0.58=10.38
2007 Q3: 9.91+3.76=13.67	2007 Q4: 10.02-1.77= 8.25

The additive model should be used when the seasonal elements are relatively constant over time as with the above case (see Figure 2.3). It seems most travel and tourism series follow this pattern. However, if the seasonal elements change in proportion to the trend values over time, a multiplicative model should be used and it can be expressed as: $X_t = T_t \times S_t$ (Thomas 1997). Once sufficient historical data are available more advanced non-causal time-series forecasting methods can be employed, such as exponential smoothing, autoregressive integrated moving average (ARIMA) model, and structural time-series model (STSM). The applications of these methods to travel and tourism forecasting can be seen in the studies, for example, of Kulendran and Witt (2003) and Witt S.F. and Witt C.A. (1991).

Causal or econometric forecasting   Causal forecasting methods are principally regression based models. As far as international travel and tourism demand is concerned, the demand can be expressed as a function of various influencing factors (i.e., explanatory variables) and a disturbance term as follows:

$$Q_{ij} = f(Y_j, P_i, P_s, T_{ij}, Ds, \varepsilon)$$

where Q_{ij} is the aggregate demand for travel and tourism in destination i by tourists from country j; Y_j is the level of the income of tourists in origin country j; T_{ij} is the travel cost from origin country j to destination i; P_i is the price of travel and tourism products in destination i; P_s is the aggregate price level of travel and tourism products in substitute destinations s; Ds represent dummy variables which capture the effects of one-off events (such as the September 11 terrorist attack) on the demand for travel and tourism; ε is the disturbance term that captures the effects of all other factors which may influence the travel and tourism demand. It should be noted that travel costs (measured by the average air fare as far as air travel is concerned) are often ignored in empirical studies of international aggregate travel and tourism demand due to the complex fare structure and difficulties in constructing the average fare at the aggregate level.

With regard to the functional form, the above relationship between the demand and its influencing factors is normally specified as a linear or log-linear function. For example, the log-linear function can be written as:

$$\ln Q_{ij} = a_0 + a_1 \ln Y_j + a_2 \ln P_i + a_3 P_s + a_4 T_{ij} + a_5 D_1 + a_6 D_2 + ... + \varepsilon \tag{2.1}$$

In a log-linear function, the coefficients of explanatory variables, a_1, a_2, a_3 and a_4, can be interpreted as demand elasticities. Therefore, the log-linear functional form is the most popular in empirical studies, although, strictly speaking, the choice of the functional form should be subject to statistical testing. Equation (2.1) is a simplified representation of an econometric model without any dynamic features of a demand system. A variety of dynamic specifications can be selected and the optimal one is determined based on a number of diagnostic tests of the estimation results (the details can be seen in Song and Witt 2000). The best-fit model can be used for demand elasticity analysis and to generate forecasts of future demand. To predict the demand variable, all explanatory variables need to be forecasted first by using non-causal forecasting methods. The sum of the productions of the forecasted explanatory variables and their estimated coefficients leads to the forecast of travel and tourism demand.

For example, Song *et al.* (2003) used various econometric models including most of the key explanatory variables in Equation (2.1) to predict the international tourism demand in Thailand by 7 key source markets. Using the historical data up to 2000, most econometric models used in this study predicted that the average annual growth rate of travel demand from the USA is about 4–5 per cent between 2001 and 2010 (see Figure 2.4). The actual demand between 2001 and 2006 also showed an average growth rate of 4.7 per cent per annum. Apart from the unpredictable effect of SARS on travel and tourism in most Asian countries including Thailand, these econometric models accurately predicted the average growth of the demand for the destination.

Econometric forecasting of future demand and its growth is of great importance for the destination country and its tourist service providers. For example, Song *et al.* (2003) also predicted that South Korea will be the fastest growing key source market for Thai

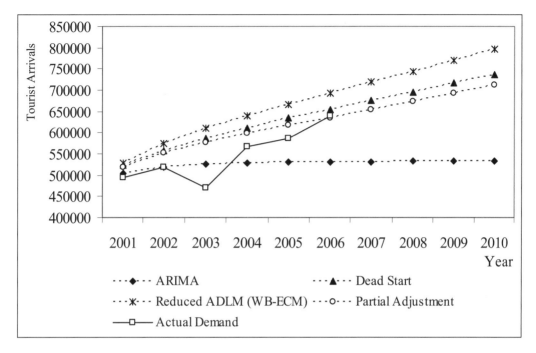

FIGURE 2.4   Actual numbers and forecasts of tourist arrivals from USA to Thailand

Sources: Song *et al* (2003) (for the forecasts) and Tourism Authority of Thailand (for actual demand figures).

tourism in this decade (i.e. 2001–2010), and this has been confirmed by the statistics in the past six years. The implication for the destination is to increase its budget for marketing and to launch effective promotion campaigns in the source market. In addition, as the econometric models showed that substitute prices had a significant effect on Korean tourists' demand, the Thai tourism industry should closely monitor its competitors' offers and react promptly.

The above discussion of econometric forecasting of travel and tourism demand is based on the aggregate demand at the international level. Considering the predominant role that air transport plays in leisure travel and tourism activities, it is useful to forecast the demand for air transport. In addition to the importance for airlines' route planning and capacity management, the forecasts of air travel demand can provide useful policy implications to the government agencies with respect to air transport regulation and regional economic development. In an air transport demand model, the demand is normally measured by the number of air passengers or passenger miles, and the key explanatory variables include the income of passengers, air fare of the route or carrier being concerned, air fares of competing carriers or travel costs by other transport modes and travel time (see, for example, Abrahams 1983; Agarwal and Talley 1985). The principle of econometric forecasting of air travel is the same as that discussed above.

CONCLUSION

This chapter has provided an insight into the nature of leisure travel and tourism demand from the economic perspective. Travellers' income, the price of a travel and tourism product, prices of substitute and complementary travel products and travel costs are the key economic determinants of leisure travel demand. As far as international travel is concerned, the real exchange rates or effective tourism prices are important influencing factors, although the nominal exchange rates are often used by potential travellers as a direct indicator of price changes of an international travel.

Demand analysis, associated with income, own-price and cross-price elasticities, has useful managerial implications for travel service providers in a destination. In particular, the air fare elasticity analysis provides air transport operators with important information for their effective pricing strategies and yield management. To sustain competitive advantages and explore potential markets, accurate forecasting of future travel demand is necessary. Both qualitative and quantitative forecasting approaches and both non-causal and causal quantitative methods can be used where appropriate. Since each method has its strengths and limitations, it would be favourable to employ multiple approaches and combine their forecast results.

3

Trends and Characteristics of Leisure Travel Demand

Anne Graham

INTRODUCTION

To complement the previous chapter which focused on looking at the economic factors which influence leisure demand, it is the aim of this chapter to identify recent trends and characteristics of leisure demand with specific reference to travel by air. It begins by considering global patterns of demand and the factors affecting these patterns. It then goes on to assess developments which have been occurring as regards origin countries for leisure tourists and makes the distinction between mature and emerging markets. This leads onto a discussion of the changing demographic characteristics of leisure tourists and evolving travel preferences.

Before examining current demand characteristics, it is necessary to highlight some major shortcomings with the data used in this chapter. In spite of the closeness between the aviation and tourism industries, there are significant differences between the two in their approach to measuring demand. This can make it difficult for the two industries to interpret each other's data without additional guidance or co-operation (International Air Transport Association/United Nations World Tourism Organisation 2002). Within the aviation industry the most usual measurements are passengers or passenger-kilometres but it is often not possible to identify purpose, or true origin and destination of travel. Tourism demand is usually measured by looking at tourist numbers or tourist-nights, although it is not always feasible to get this split by purpose of visit, or mode of transport. Another commonly used measure is tourism expenditure but often this only includes expenditure at the destination and excludes spending on transport. All this means that it is frequently not possible to quantify trends related specifically to leisure air travel demand as the aviation and tourism data is not always produced at this required level of disaggregation. In such cases, a more subjective assessment has had to be made here as to the relevance of broader tourism and aviation trends to the specific leisure air travel market.

TRENDS IN GLOBAL PATTERNS OF LEISURE TRAVEL DEMAND

Travel by air for leisure purposes is an important part of the growing global demand for tourism. According to the United Nations World Tourism Organisation (UNWTO), 846 million international tourist arrivals were recorded in 2006 which represents an average annual growth rate of around four per cent since 1995. Around half of these arrivals were for leisure, recreation and holiday purposes. A further quarter of these were for visiting friends and relative (VFR), religion and 'other' purposes. Hence arguably well over half of all arrivals are for leisure purposes if VFR is considered as an additional leisure purpose which is often the case. Moreover the air share of arrivals is increasing, accounting for 46 per cent of all the arrivals in 2006 compared to 38 per cent in 1995 (United Nations World Tourism Organisation, 2007a). These figures do not include domestic arrivals, which overall are of a greater magnitude than international arrivals, but are generally less dependent on air transport because of the smaller distances involved. In the aviation industry, there were 2,128 million total passengers carried in 2006, which similarly represented an average annual growth rate of just over four per cent since 1995. Around a third of these (762 million) were on international services (International Civil Aviation Organisation, 2007).

There are clearly a multitude of factors which have been driving this growth in aviation and tourism. Economic causes, particularly increasing real income and declining real price, have played a key role and are discussed in detail in Chapter 2. Numerous other political, social, technological and environmental factors have also had major influences (see Chapter 4). Of particular significance in recent years has been the impact of 'shock' or crisis/disaster events. These are associated with terrorist attacks, war or internal conflict, climatic incidents, crime waves or health concerns. Such events have always been present but now appear to be occurring more often and with greater severity and hence seem to be creating a more volatile or uncertain operating environment for both the aviation and tourism industries. They tend to have negative impacts on the traveller's perceptions of the safety and security of their transport mode and destination, as well as on their overall motivation to travel, and hence influence travel patterns, particularly in the short-term.

Since 2000 the most significant 'global' shocks have been 9/11 in 2001 and the outbreak of SARS (combined with the Iraq War) in 2003. The former had the greatest impact in North America and the latter in Asia (Figure 3.1). However there is some evidence to suggest that generally leisure traffic was not affected as much as business traffic – indeed this can be observed by examining the growth in passenger numbers at London Heathrow (mainly a business airport) and London Stansted (mainly a low cost leisure airport), and also by comparing the premium (more business) and non-premium or 'normal' (more leisure) traffic of British Airways (Figures 3.2 and 3.3).

When the events are more limited and only 'one-off,' recovery time varies according to local circumstances but generally demand appears to bounce back relatively quickly. This can be observed with the case of the terrorism attacks in November 1997 at the Luxor Temple in Egypt and in October 2002 in a popular nightclub in Kuta on the Indonesian island of Bali. Various measures of aviation and tourism demand showed a very significant decline in the year following the attacks but in the next year there were clearly signs of recovery (Table 3.1).

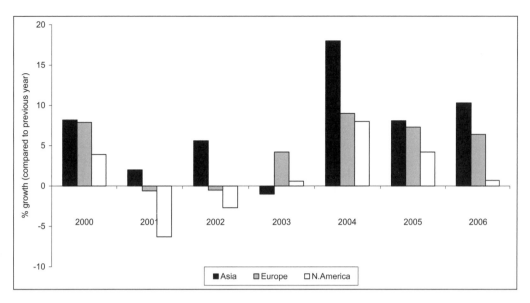

FIGURE 3.1   Passenger growth by main region 2000–2006
Source: ACI.

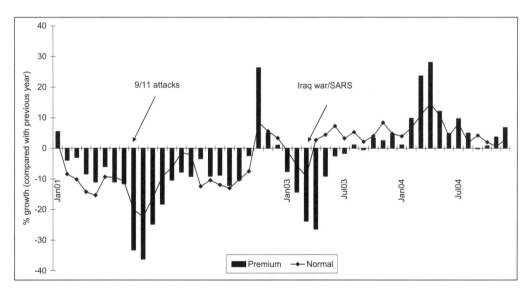

FIGURE 3.2   Monthly passenger-km growth on BA services 2001–2004
Source: BA.

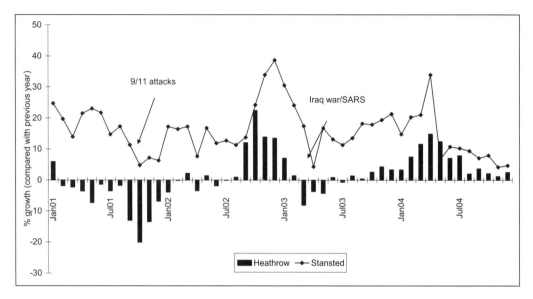

**FIGURE 3.3   Monthly passenger growth at London Heathrow and Stansted
airports 2001–2004**

Source: CAA.

**TABLE 3.1   Impact of terrorism attacks on air transport and tourism in
Egypt and Indonesia**

Percentage Growth (compared to previous year)					
Egypt (a)	**1995**	**1996**	**1997**	**1998**	**1999**
International air visitors	28.7	24.2	6.5	-17.0	55.3
UK-Egypt air passengers	31.3	25.6	13.4	-37.5	35.5
Egyptair: RPKs	27.1	-3.8	14.6	-11.5	12.8
International spending (c)	93.9	19.4	16.3	-31.2	52.2
Indonesia (b)	2000	2001	2002	2003	2004
International air visitors	12.7	0.2	-0.8	-20.7	28.1
UK-Bali air passengers	54.0	-12.8	-33.7	-85.2	n/a
Garuda: RPKs	11.2	-8.4	0.8	-11.5	7.7
International spending (c)	22.1	-5.9	-2.3	-23.6	18.9

Notes:
(a) Luxor bombings November 1997
(b) Bali bombings October 2002
(c) Does not include spending on international fares

Sources: UNWTO, Airline Business.

MATURE AND EMERGING MARKETS

The global patterns of demand hide the significantly different growth rates in outbound tourism which have been experienced in different world regions. This has resulted in changes to the global distribution of outbound tourism with the dominant markets of Europe and America reducing their market share from 81 to 75 per cent since 1995. There is a similar trend for air traffic with the Europe/American share declining from 70 to 66 (although the relative shares of the two regions are different from the tourism statistics because of the inclusion of domestic traffic, exclusion of charter traffic and the different proportion of leisure trips taken by air in the two regions).

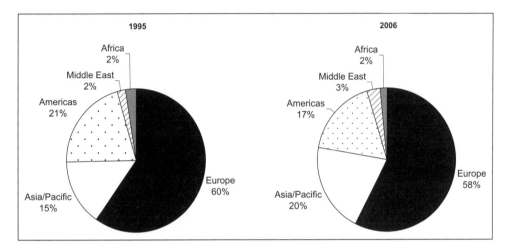

FIGURE 3.4   Outbound tourism by region 1995 and 2006

Source: UNWTO.

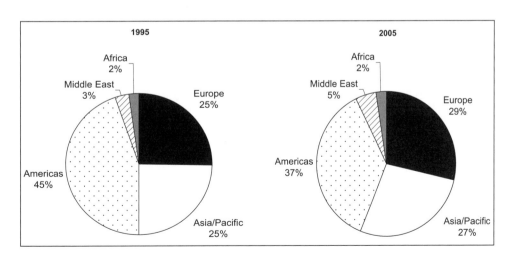

FIGURE 3.5   Airline traffic by region of registration (scheduled passenger-kms) 1995 and 2006

Source: ICAO.

Much of the growth in the other regions, particularly in Asia-Pacific, is related to changing economic factors which are raising living standards and this, when combined with a more liberal air transport environment, is giving many an opportunity to travel for the first time. For example Boeing (2006) comments on how the proportion of middle class in China is expected to rise from 13 per cent in 2010 to around 40 per cent in 2020 which will produce 100 million outbound tourists by this year. Likewise in India and in other Asian/Pacific countries such as Indonesia, Thailand and Malaysia, rapidly developing economies and the emergence of substantial numbers of middle-class travellers will substantially boost outbound tourism numbers. Various aviation forecasts predict that this trend will continue into the future with North America and Europe being the slowest growth regions, and Asia-Pacific having the highest or second highest growth (Table 3.2). Notable examples of lesser developed countries in other regions which are also likely to generate substantial numbers of 'new' tourists are Mexico and Brazil (Tretheway and Mak 2006).

Differences in travel patterns or propensities can also be investigated by looking at arrivals generated per 100 population per year. Globally this measure equalled unity at around 1950, rose to nearly 12 in 2002 and is expected to reach 21 by 2020 (Kester 2005). Europeans currently have the highest values with at the extreme the Netherlands, UK, Sweden and Switzerland recording values of over 100. This means that these countries generate more than one trip per capita per year (VisitBritain 2006). By 2020 the Asian propensity to travel is expected to be at a level comparable to Europe in 1980 (Figure 3.6).

In more mature markets, growth is likely to be largely as the result of more frequent trips rather than from new travellers. Within Europe, for example in 2004, there were eight EU member states where at least two trips per year per tourist lasting 4 nights or more were made and indeed the EU average was 2.1 trips. The highest values were recorded for France (2.7), Germany (2.3) and the UK (2.2) whereas at the other extreme Greece, Ireland, Estonia and Slovakia only had measures of 1.1 (Bovagnet 2006). This indicates that there could be significant scope for growth in countries within the EU with the smaller values. On the other hand it may be that for countries with higher propensities, maturity could

TABLE 3.2   Long-term air transport forecasts 2006–2025

% Average Annual Growth	Boeing	Airbus	Rolls-Royce	ACI
Asia-Pacific	6.2	6.2	6.6	5.8
North America	4.1	4.0	3.6	2.7
Europe	4.3	4.6	4.1	3.6
Latin America	6.2	5.8	5.0	4.5
Middle East	5.5	6.4	5.3	4.6
Africa	5.7	5.3	(a)	5.8
Total	**4.9**	**4.8**	**4.8**	**4.0**

Notes:
Units are revenue passenger kilometres/miles for Boeing/Airbus/Rolls-Royce and passengers for ACI.
(a) included in Middle East

Sources: Boeing, Airbus, Rolls-Royce, ACI.

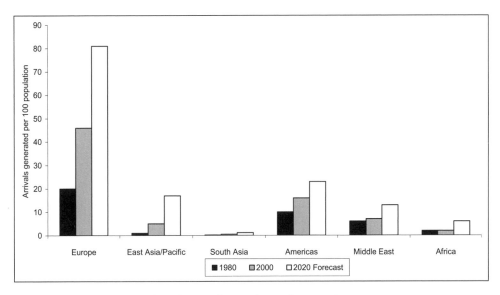

FIGURE 3.6   Participation in outbound tourism 1980–2020
Source: UN WTO.

be setting in because of the lack of income and/or leisure time for further travel, or a lack of motivation to take additional trips. Hence high growth here of the overall demand for travel may be more difficult to achieve in the future.

However, when looking specifically at air travel it is important to remember that this is just one of a number of different travel markets. Growth in leisure air travel may be caused by two factors, firstly market extension (growth in the total leisure market) and secondly market penetration (growth caused by a shift in demand from another transport mode whilst the total demand remains relatively constant). If the total demand remains relatively constant as it could when travel propensities are high, the opportunity for growth in air travel is likely to be limited to the degree of future substitution between different markets which can take place. As an example, it has been suggested by the Civil Aviation Authority (2005a) that the UK outbound leisure air market appears relatively immature but it has been argued by A. Graham (2006) that whilst this does appear to be the case, the overall leisure travel market (all modes and all destinations) seems to be much nearer to full maturity and consequently future air travel growth may have to come primarily from increased market penetration.

CHANGING DEMOGRAPHIC AND SOCIAL CHARACTERISTICS

In addition to the economic factors which are having major influences on the regional distribution of outbound tourism globally, there are a number of inter-related changing demographic and social characteristics which are having an impact on leisure travel demand. A key development is the growth of the so-called 'grey' or over 55s market. In recent years leisure travel by this market segment has grown considerably in many developed countries, not only as people in this group have the time to travel, but also because they are wealthier, healthier and more experienced travellers than before. For example in the UK the share of international trips taken by this age group has increased from 17 per cent in 1994 to 25 per cent in 2005 (Figure 3.7). Moreover, in the future this age group is likely to become proportionately even more important to tourism because of the growth of this age group within the population, due to people living longer and birth rates falling. This is particularly the case in western economies such as Europe and North America as the result of the baby boomers of the 1950s now reaching this age (Figure 3.8).

There are also a number of social trends which are changing the demand for, and consequently the nature of, travel products. These include a tendency to marry later in life and have smaller families at an older age. This development, combined with an increasing number of couples who are opting to remain childless, means that there are is a rising number of young couples travelling who have less income and time constraints than families with children. In addition, more and more women are working full-time which is increasing the number of double income households. However, at the same time there are a growing number of singles and one-parent families participating in tourism. All these trends are having a significant impact on the volume and nature of demand for tourism products, including air travel, particularly as regards the relative income and time which is available for travel, and the tourism experience which is being sought. A regular survey and forecast of German holidaymaking patterns, the '*Reiseanalyse*', confirms these trends by observing that holidays trips with children under 14 years have decreased from 22 per cent in 1998 to 19 per cent in 2006. Moreover, within this market segment one child families are expected to increase from the current situation of 56 per cent to 64 per cent in 2015, with accompanying adults over 50 years rising from 13 to 18 per cent and single parent families growing from 4 to 5 per cent (Forschungsgemeinschaft Urlaub und Reisen e.V, 2007).

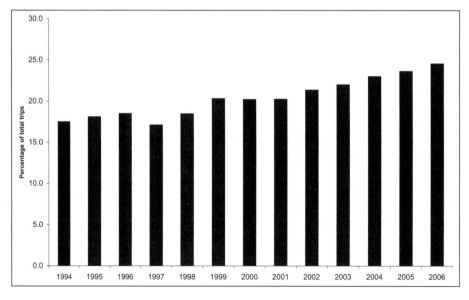

FIGURE 3.7   Share of international trips undertaken by UK residents older than 55 years 1994–2006

Source: IPS.

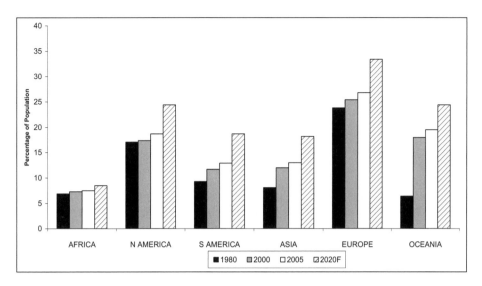

FIGURE 3.8   Share of population older than 55 years (%) 1980–2020
Source: US Census Bureau.

NEW CONSUMER PREFERENCES

These changes in society, combined with greater experience of travel and better education in many developed economies, have meant that there has been a marked broadening of the range of requirements for the leisure travel product and in general tourists have become more sophisticated and demanding. In particular there has been a growth in adventure, cultural and special interest holidays and in the demand for new destinations, especially long-haul. This can be demonstrated by looking at the pattern of international tourist arrivals (Table 3.3). The highest growth rates (of over 7.5 per cent per annum) in the last 10 years or so have been recorded for North East and South Asia, Central America and the Middle East. Whilst some of this has been due to increases in intra-regional travel primarily because of economic growth, it has also been due to the development of long-haul travel from Europe and North America. This is likely to continue into the future with higher annual growth to 2020 being predicted for long-haul travel (5.4 per cent) as opposed to inter-regional travel (3.8 per cent). This is a particularly important trend for aviation, given that there is no alternative mode of transport which can be used here (except perhaps cruising and even then most of these are 'fly-cruises'). There is some evidence to suggest that even the low cost airlines, which to date have focused almost entirely on shorter trips, are beginning to recognise the benefits which long-haul routes could bring because of the potential demand – in spite of some of the economic and operational drawbacks of such services compared to short-haul (Francis *et al.* 2007).

There is also growing demand for a more flexible tourism product. This is increasing the need for holidays of different and shorter lengths rather than the traditional two or three week break. Greater work pressures and fears about job security have meant that the standard long break is either not possible or not very attractive anymore. Instead the current more variable working conditions encourage more participation in shorter holidays and short breaks. As a result for most EU countries, tourist trips of 1–3 days have increased at a higher rate than those of greater than four days in recent years (Figure 3.9).

TABLE 3.3   International tourist arrivals 1996–2020

International Tourist Arrivals	1995	2000	2006	Actual Average Annual Growth (%) 1995–2006	Forecast Average Annual Growth (%) 1995–2020
EUROPE:	315	396	457	3.4	3.0
Northern	40	46	54	2.8	
Western	112	140	150	2.7	
Central/Eastern	60	70	89	3.6	
Southern/Med	103	141	164	4.3	
EAST ASIA/PACIFIC:	78	104	159	6.7	6.5
North-East Asia	41	58	94	7.8	
South-East Asia	29	37	54	5.8	
Oceania	8	9	11	2.9	
SOUTH ASIA	4	6	9	7.7	6.2
AMERICAS:	109	128	136	2.0	3.9
North America	81	91	91	1.1	
Caribbean	14	17	19	2.8	
Central America	3	4	7	8.0	
South America	12	15	19	4.3	
AFRICA:	20	28	41	6.7	5.5
North Africa	7	10	15	7.2	
Sub-Saharan Africa	13	18	26	6.5	
MIDDLE EAST	14	24	41	10.3	7.1
TOTAL:	540	687	842	4.1	4.1

Source: UNWTO.

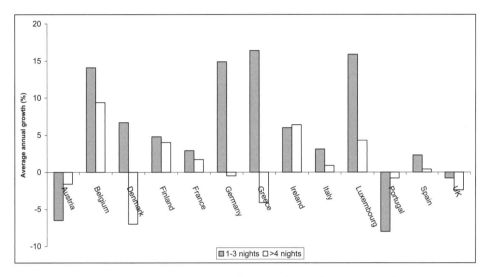

FIGURE 3.9   Growth in tourist trips from selected EU countries 2000–2004

Source: Eurostat.

Moreover particularly within Europe, the need for greater flexibility is encouraging independent travel, the unbundling of package tours and considerable growth in 'dynamic' packaging (when tourists construct their own individual package tour). The lower fares and more adaptable booking arrangements offered by low cost carriers have encouraged this development and consequently the relative role of charter and low cost carriers within the leisure air travel market is a key issue for consideration in the future (see Chapters 8 and 9). This desire for more flexibility, coming at the same time as the emergence of the internet as a major distribution channel for many goods and services, has led to the growth in internet sales of travel products. For example internet sales increased from just 1 per cent in 2000 to 16 per cent in 2006 with air travel (not including packages) accounting for 56 per cent of the sales in 2006. Low cost airlines sales were half of these (Figure 3.10).

The UK is a leading example of a country where these trends are occurring. International activity holidays abroad have grown considerably and now represent 11 per cent of all holidays whilst city/short breaks account for a further 12 per cent. Beach/resort holidays now have a 38 per cent market share, down from 50 per cent in 2002. (Mintel 2005, 2007). The result of this is that the average length of stay has gone down and at the same time the share of holidays which are packaged dropped from 60 per cent in 1990 to just over 40 per cent today (Table 3.4).

Finally, the implications of the growing awareness amongst consumers of the negative environmental and social consequences of tourism need to be considered. The level of response by the industry has been very mixed but there certainly are an expanding proportion of tourists who are seeking more responsible and ethical products – just as with other goods and services. In recent years aviation and its impact on climate change has arguably become the dominant environmental issue related to tourism (see Chapter 18). In 2002 a UK Office of National Statistics omnibus survey found that 62 per cent of the respondents agreed or strongly agreed that air travel harms the environment but by 2006 this figure had risen to 70 per cent. Moreover, in 2006, 55 per cent of the respondents who agreed that air travel harmed the environment said they would be willing to pay at least 15

TABLE 3.4   Characteristics of holidays taken by UK residents 1990–2006

	Average Length of Stay of International Holiday Trips (days)	Package Tours as % Total Air International Holiday Trips
1990	12.0	61
1991	11.9	58
1992	11.8	60
1993	11.6	61
1994	11.3	63
1995	10.9	62
1996	10.9	61
1997	10.4	61
1998	10.4	60
1999	10.5	59
2000	10.5	59
2001	10.3	57
2002	10.1	55
2003	10.2	50
2004	10.0	48
2005	9.8	44
2006	9.8	42

Source: IPS.

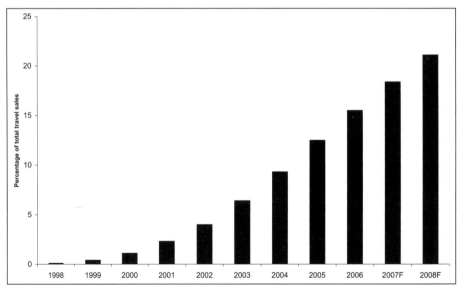

FIGURE 3.10 Share of online Internet travel sales in Europe 1998–2008

Source: CRT.

per cent on the cost of flights to reflect this, compared to just 29 per cent of the respondents in 2002 (Department for Transport 2006a). Whilst the surveys of the two years are not totally comparable, this does suggest that there has been an increase in awareness of the environmental issues related to air and at least some increased willingness to pay for the cost over time – albeit that this has not really been properly tested anywhere. There has also been a growth in the somewhat controversial offsetting schemes which take account of the impact of a flight by supporting the financing of a project elsewhere that is reducing carbon dioxide, but these are still only used by a very small proportion of travellers.

CONCLUSIONS

This chapter has provided an overview of some of the recent key trends and characteristics of air leisure travel demand. Many of the issues mentioned have been expanded in other chapters in this book. It is a matter of little debate that the traditional economic drivers of leisure demand, namely income, cost and leisure time, will continue to play an important role in influencing demand in the future as will the unpredictable external 'shock' factors (at least in the short-term). The rapidly growing economies of countries such as China and India will have a major impact on these countries' ability to both generate and attract leisure tourists. On the other hand, more developed economies with a long history of participation in tourism are likely to find their tourism markets maturing and will begin to see their dominance of world tourism patterns decline somewhat. However, it may be that the demand for air travel will take longer to mature than other travel segments.

As consumer characteristics and preferences continue to evolve through time, they will undoubtedly influence the type of leisure trips undertaken. Currently a combination of changes in society, such as the ageing of the population, more flexible work practices and family structure, life style and life stage changes, together with new consumer preferences are favouring products with greater individuality and flexibility and a shift away from more standardised products. However, it is unclear as to how changes such as growth in long-haul and short break travel can be made compatible with growing concerns about the impact of air travel on the environment, which would actually favour the reverse of these trends, namely less frequent and longer holidays closer to home. This highlights the arguably greatest challenge of the future which is in finding an optimal way in dealing with the undisputable growth in tourism and changing travel preferences, whilst at the same time coping with increased concerns for the environment.

4

Aviation Marketing and the Leisure Market

Stephen Shaw

INTRODUCTION

The final chapter in this section focuses on marketing and further develops the theme of leisure travel demand by exploring the marketing strategies which can be adopted by the airline industry to cope with the changing nature of this demand. In general, critics of the science of marketing might suggest that it is essentially a dishonest and amoral activity. At its worst, it can be based on the meeting of frivolous 'needs' and the exploitation of gullible and naïve consumers. However, it will be demonstrated that it should be neither of these things.[1] First of all, to apply marketing principles to the leisure air travel market requires a great deal of effort to be expended in obtaining a full understanding of the needs of customers in the main segments of the market. Alongside this, knowledge must be accumulated about the so-called marketing environment – the background against which marketing activities take place.

When these essential building blocks are established, the application of marketing principles can move onto the formulation of a marketing strategy. As this chapter will illustrate, there are different strategic routes to success in today's airline industry, but it is essential that one of these routes should be selected and pursued on a long-term, stable, basis. Once a strategy has been defined, the next three stages in the application of marketing principles to leisure air travel marketing should follow on logically. Airlines must define appropriate product, pricing and distribution policies to ensure that their chosen strategy is implemented successfully. When they have done so, the final and vital stage of the marketing process must be implemented. Carriers must find ways of selling hard and effectively to ensure that the potential demand for their services actually materialises and that customers choose them rather than the services of a competitor.

In all industries marketing is a dynamic and changing subject. Customer needs do not remain static – rather they change and evolve over time. This is particularly the case with the marketing of leisure air travel. Going back just ten years, the marketing of leisure travel was a very different challenge from the one facing airlines today. The market was much smaller in size. Moreover, for European airlines, for example, overwhelmingly the

---

1   For a fuller description of the application of marketing principles to the airline industry, see Chapter 1 of Shaw (2007). A recommended general textbook on marketing is Brassington and Pettit (2007).

product they supplied was a wholesale one, with the retail market largely in the hands of tour operators and consolidators who produced the packaged holidays which were the common way that the product was put together and sold to customers. The destination choices available were limited with long-haul travel still the reserve of a wealthy and privileged elite. Distribution of the packaged product was carried out by an army of high street travel agents, who were either part of large, vertically integrated chains, or small-scale 'mom-and-pop' operators.

Thus the question which this chapter is firstly seeking to answer is what have been the main drivers that account for this rapid pace of change. Then there will be an examination of the implications that these drivers have had for marketing strategies, in order that the airlines can successfully exploit the opportunities that the leisure market has provided for them.

DRIVERS OF CHANGE IN THE MARKETING OF LEISURE AIR TRAVEL

Regulatory Liberalisation

There are many dates that stand out in aviation history, from the Wright Brothers first flight onwards. Few though in Europe have been of greater significance than 1st April 1997. This was the day when, after many years of argument and slow evolution, the Single Aviation Market of the European Union finally came into existence. From that day onwards, European airlines have been able to operate in a market characterised by almost complete freedom from constraints in the areas of market entry, capacity and pricing. This has been a political change of great significance, particularly in comparison to the old system of tight regulatory interference in airlines' commercial freedom of action (see Chapter 5 for a fuller discussion of air transport regulation and liberalisation).

It is almost impossible to exaggerate the significance of this change from the point-of-view of the marketing of leisure air travel. At a stroke, charter airlines were freed from the straightjacket that had previously confined them to the role of only producing what were known as 'inclusive tour' charters. For the first time, they could sell openly on a 'seat-only' basis. New airlines such as easyJet grew up and older-established ones (Ryanair) were able to completely change their business strategy. A new kind of airline appeared for the first time, a one which offered much reduced fares in exchange for a more basic air transport product. This has been a trade-off that many leisure passengers have embraced with enthusiasm.

The consequence has been nothing short of a strategic revolution in the marketing of leisure air travel. Fuelled by a long period of economic growth and stability that has produced rises in real incomes, demand has grown substantially. New markets have appeared, for weekend breaks and for stag and hen parties in European cities. Foreign property ownership has boomed, stimulated by cheaper air travel, low interest rates and a buoyant property market. For airlines, there has been a mixture of opportunities but also significant challenges that have resulted in new marketing strategies appearing and in a need to modify long-established and hitherto successful strategies (Williams 2002).

Low cost carriers have expanded in a way that few would have predicted, in terms of both growth and, more importantly, profitability. For charter airlines, on the other hand, things have become more difficult. The charter carriers had proved themselves to be experts in the production of the cheap seats that were needed to underpin the market of one-week and two-week packaged holidays. They have been exposed as the combination of lower fares and, increasingly, ownership of villas and apartments has meant that demand has changed. The most attractive product is now often the one that allows for flexible long weekends rather than two-week holidays. It is a need that the low cost carrier business model has proved more effective in meeting than the model employed by traditional charter airlines (Lawton 2002).

In consequence, many charter airlines have had to re-work their way of doing business. Some have essentially changed themselves into low cost carriers. The German airline Air Berlin is a good example (Pilling 2007). These carriers have launched their own websites to carry out their own retail marketing and now use the smaller aircraft that the low cost carrier model requires. Others, such as the UK-based First Choice Airways have successfully moved their product up-market, and have increasingly concentrated on long-haul routes. (This discussion is expanded in Chapters 8 and 9 when Williams and Barrett consider the specific development of the charter and low cost sector respectively).

For the so-called 'legacy' sector of the industry, many of these traditional airlines had built up ways of working and cost structures, in times when regulatory conditions were different and provided an effective cushion for carriers who did not adequately control their costs. The setting up of the Single Aviation Market removed this cushion. Many legacy carriers have been shown to have cost structures which are inappropriate for today's competitive conditions and for a market which has become much more price-sensitive in many of its segments. The better managed of these airlines have made at least a start in taking the necessary steps to change. Others, such as Alitalia, seem wedded to the past and to be incapable of doing so.

Political Instability and the Terrorism Threat

Another recent change in the marketing of leisure air travel that can be related to political considerations is a difficult and depressing one to address. Today, anyone concerned with the marketing of leisure air travel has to accept that the world political situation is unstable and that wars and 'terrorism' constitute a continuing threat. The industry has to accept that when a war breaks out in a tourism-receiving area, or a major terrorism incident occurs in such an area, demand will fall away almost instantly and may take some time to recover. When terrorism is related to the aviation industry, as the September 11 2001 attacks tragically were, the downturn in traffic can be massive (see Chapter 3 for further details).

The other marketing effect of the world political situation can be seen at airports around the world and especially in the UK and the USA. Passengers are being subjected to ever more onerous security procedures at the beginning of their journeys. Business air travellers perhaps have little choice but to accept this, at least on long-haul routes where train and car journeys do not provide an alternative. Leisure passengers certainly do. They can holiday at home, or indeed not holiday at all, if the hassles associated with travelling by air simply become too frustrating.

The message is all too apparent – airline marketeers must do all they can to work with airports and security agencies to minimise disruption at airports and to move ahead as fast as possible with the new technologies that might make airport security screening less onerous and annoying than it is currently. (Sigala in Chapter 16 provides a detailed discussion of these new technologies).

Economic Factors in Leisure Air Travel Marketing

In Chapter 2, Li has provided a detailed discussion of the impact of economic factors on aviation. Basically aviation always has been, and always will be, a cyclical industry. When GDP grows, disposable incomes increase and demand for air travel shows a corresponding rise. Over recent years, the leisure side of the air transport industry has in many ways been fortunate in that many countries have seen a long period of economic growth. This has in turn led to a strong pattern of rising demand, fuelled still further by falling real prices for air travel. At the same time, the benefits of growth have been unevenly distributed. Generally, the already wealthy have become more so, especially so in the United States and in emerging economies such as India and Brazil.

Such growth has been of substantial benefit to airlines, in that the market for air travel has grown consistently. Better still, rising real disposable incomes have begun to change the nature of what airlines see as their 'premium traffic' – passengers using high fares to travel in the comfort of the first, business and the various 'premium economy' cabins which different airlines are now offering. Ten years ago, the conventional wisdom was that these cabins were only likely to be used on a significant scale by high status business travellers using expense accounts to pay the high prices. Today, this is far less true. Some carriers are reporting that as much as around 40 per cent of their premium traffic consists of well-off leisure travellers, prepared to pay more for comfort on what are, increasingly, long-haul leisure journeys.

As far as airline strategies are concerned, buoyant economic conditions give carriers valuable opportunities that, of course, should be exploited to the full. They do, however, also point to the need for a sense of proportion. Carriers need to be reminded that buoyant conditions in the world economy always turn out to be transient, and that airline business models have to be capable of dealing both with the good times, but also times of slowdown and recession. The emphasis on travel in the so-called 'premium' cabins of aircraft plus the placing of large numbers of orders for new planes[2] could both turn out to have been extremely unwise, if the world economy enters a significant period of much slower economic growth. Such a period of slower growth could also have a major – and negative – impact on the so-called 'all business class' airlines (such as Silverjet) that have entered transatlantic markets over the last couple of years (Scobie 2007).

Changing Family Structures

It is a very interesting experiment to examine the front covers of still too many travel brochures produced by airlines and tour operators in Europe. They still feature the most perfect 'family' picture. This picture features a handsome man, an attractive woman and two, usually perfectly-behaved, children. By some miracle of family planning, the children are always a boy and a girl.

---

2   Boeing and Airbus have both taken record numbers of orders for new aircraft during the 2005–2007 period.

The problem with such a stereotype is that it no longer reflects the reality of air travel marketing in an increasing number of cases. In many countries in northwest Europe and North America, and certainly in Japan and Australasia, the population is ageing very rapidly. Fewer children are being born – many people elect to remain childless – and older people are living longer. Such trends, which are also discussed by A. Graham in Chapter 3, have resulted in significant sub-segments of the leisure air travel market appearing, which do not reflect the stereotypical 'family' model at all. Young people make up a growing part of the market. Budget travel is now an important part of the planning of almost all those who take a gap year before beginning a university course. Singles and gays constitute a part of the leisure market, as do the so-called 'empty nesters' whose children have left home and who are taking advantage of (for now) generous pension arrangements and perhaps the inheritance of money from a booming property market. Any sensible airline marketing strategy today recognises that there are sub-segments of the leisure market, which need individual and tailored approaches.

Changing Tastes and Fashions in Holidays

As discussed in Chapter 3, alongside the changing demographics of passengers, changing tastes and fashions in holidays give additional challenges but also significant new opportunities. People today expect that their holidays will allow them to pursue hobbies and interests, rather than simply sit beside a hotel swimming pool. This in turn is allowing for greater creativity in the setting up of holidays, with such ingredients as golfing, trekking or the study of history added to them.

Important though these social changes have been, it is the continuing interest of people in new and exotic travel destinations which has probably been the greatest change that social factors have brought about in the marketing of leisure air travel. It is now evident that vacation resorts go though clear product life cycles, which have been discussed by Butler and other tourism researchers. In some cases, these can be surprisingly short. In the UK, for example, until the 1960s, most people took their holidays at a British seaside resort. The 1960s, though, saw the beginnings of the trend towards holidays being taken in continental Europe, especially in Spain. At first, Spain was a different and prestigious resort area, but it did not remain so. Whilst holidays to Spain have remained popular, the status-conscious and adventurous amongst leisure travellers have always shown themselves to be willing to travel to new and ever more exotic holiday destinations. The 1980s saw the beginnings of a boom -which has continued- for holidays to be taken in the United States, whilst resort areas such as Kenya and Thailand have emerged as significant mass-market destinations.

In their strategies for marketing leisure destinations, airlines need to have a clear picture of the stage in the product life cycle that a resort area has reached. Early on, the resort will be of interest to so-called 'innovators' – well-off, adventurous and status-conscious people looking for holidays which will pander to their social status and sense of the unusual. Later, the resort must be made attractive to far more cautious and lower-income consumers.

The Technology of Travel Distribution[3]

Up until the end of the 1990s, there had been little change in the distribution strategies of airlines aiming to penetrate the leisure air travel market for more than a quarter of a century. A single channel of distribution was overwhelmingly dominant. Almost all holidays were sold through what are now called off-line travel agents, with such agents being responsible for more than 90 per cent of the sales of holidays, in almost all countries. Airlines were marketing their seats directly though agents and very commonly in Europe, these seats were also supplied on a wholesale basis to tour operators, who would add in the accommodation and surface transfers to make up packaged holidays.

The cost consequences of this form of distribution were substantial, and by today's standards, unacceptable. Airlines found that travel agents' commissions were a major component of their costs – sometimes as high as around 15 per cent of them – as agents played one carrier off against another in order to raise their commission income. Equally serious, almost all agents were using the technology of the so-called global distribution systems. The GDSs brought huge productivity gains to the travel agency industry, in that GDS technology allowed them to make bookings direct with airlines and other travel suppliers without the need for time-consuming telephone calls. The costs, though, fell almost entirely upon the airlines, with carriers having to pay a fee every time that an agent used a GDS to make a booking on one of its flights.

At the time, there was no doubt that the travel agency industry and the GDS firms thought that they were being very astute in using their strong bargaining position to push up their own profits at the expense of airlines. With the benefit of hindsight, though, it is very clear that they were being the very opposite of astute in that they were digging their own graves.

Today, the booking process for leisure air travel has been revolutionised by the arrival of the internet as a highly significant new channel of distribution. Some low cost airlines have never paid a penny of commission to any travel agent, nor have they ever paid booking fees to any of the major GDSs. Many others have made every effort to build the business that they have done through their own websites, both a direct way of saving money and also as a method of increasing their bargaining power with agents and GDSs. As a result, commission costs have come down. Many airlines have stopped paying commissions to travel agents completely, whilst others only offer what are termed 'task-based payments' – paying the travel agent small amounts for the work actually done, rather than offering lucrative percentage commissions of the fare paid. With the GDSs, airlines have had some successes in renegotiating their business relationships. They have linked reduced payments of booking fees to the granting full access to the different GDSs to the lowest fares they offer, rather than limiting the selling of these fares to their own websites.

The development of the internet has had one further effect on the marketing of leisure air travel. Before its arrival, almost all leisure air travellers in Europe used to rely on the so-called tour operating industry to put together the package holidays which they would then buy on an inclusive tour basis.[4] Today, this is by no means the case. Travellers have discovered that it is often better for them to put together their own packages, by booking an airline seat, accommodation and perhaps car hire as well on-line. The low

---

3   This subject is covered in detail in Chapter 7 of Doganis (2006)
4   As has already been noted, charter airlines were in any case prevented by restrictive regulatory policies from selling on a 'seat only' basis

cost carriers that make it possible for them to book an airline seat are also increasingly including opportunities to book hotels and car rental through their websites – a useful service for their passengers and also a growing source of what is known as 'ancillary revenue', as other firms are charged significant fees to use the airline website as a portal to reach their customers.

Despite the undoubted revolution that the internet has brought to distribution to leisure passengers, major concerns remain about the long-term future of airline distribution in an on-line age. Airline websites have allowed a significant reduction in distribution and selling costs to be achieved. The marketing proposition that underlies them is, though, deficient in one significant area. An airline website will only be an attractive option to a person who has already decided to book with the airline running the site. What it cannot do is provide a survey of the whole market, and show the customer the best value-for-money option available from all the competing airlines on a route.

This has meant that the internet age has seen the rapid development of a large number of new travel agency businesses that operate in an on-line rather than an off-line environment. Travelocity and Expedia are the most commonly-quoted example of these, but there are many others. In one sense, from an airline viewpoint they are a welcome development, in that these new agents have much lower overhead costs than the old off-line companies. They do not have to spend heavily on the large numbers of High Street branches that leisure-orientated offline agents traditionally thought that they needed. The development is still, though, a disturbing one. When a traveller is seeking information on their best-value option, the display offered to them by the on-line travel agent will be highly significant in the choice that they eventually make. The agent is therefore in a strong position to play one airline off against another, in exactly the same way that off-line agents were able to do up to a decade ago. The role that search engines such as Google and MSN could play in travel retailing in the future would be an even more worrying development, for exactly the same reason.

New Aircraft Technology[5]

It has always been the case that the arrival of new aircraft technology drives strategic change in the marketing of leisure air travel and the present time is no exception. There are two areas of innovation that may result in some interesting new developments.

Long-haul leisure air travel has always depended on cost-efficient aircraft technology enabling airlines to charge the fares often price-sensitive customers, paying out of their own pocket, are prepared to pay. Such a requirement has been particularly pressing during recent years as high fuel prices have put pressure on airlines' operating costs. Fortunately, Boeing is working on a new aircraft family – the 787 – that, when it begins to enter service in 2008, will bring significant efficiency advances. The aircraft will feature new, fuel-efficient engines, improved aerodynamics and, an especially, significant advance – will have large amounts of carbon fibre in its primary structure, resulting in reduced weight (giving low landing fees) and lower fuel burn. It will allow airlines to fly longer, thinner routes in a cost-effective way, and should allow for the opening up of new direct services from regional airports to emerging leisure travel destinations. Airbus is working

---

5   For a more detailed discussion, see P. Clark (2007)

on a competitor to the 787, the A350, which should incorporate similar advances. It will, however, be at least five years later in coming to the market.

Important though the arrival of the Boeing 787 will be, it is undoubtedly the new Airbus large aircraft, the A380, which is exciting the most interest at the moment. This aircraft has been promoted by Airbus as having a seating capacity of 525 passengers in a mixed class configuration. However, it is possible to consider an all-economy layout of the aircraft with at least 750 seats, whilst later stretched versions could increase this to over 1000 seats. Such aircraft would pose immense airport handling problems. If these could be overcome, though, they could deliver extremely low seat-kilometre costs, allowing further significant fare reductions to be made available that could in turn spur market growth.

Environmental Factors in Leisure Air Travel Marketing

All the subjects covered so far in this chapter are important ones. However, during the last few years, the environmental issue has risen up the agenda. If this cannot be satisfactorily addressed, arguably it threatens the whole future of the leisure side of the air travel industry.

Airlines have, of course, become used to addressing environmental opposition to their activities. From the advent of jet aircraft in the late 1950s, airlines have been under pressure because of noise nuisance created around airports. Strong environmental opposition has become increasingly apparent whenever proposals are put forward to expand airport capacity. The result has been that in many countries expansion has been slowed or even prevented altogether, with in consequence a growing disparity between the demand for airport takeoff and landing slots and their availability. Difficult though these questions have been, airlines have always been able to argue that almost all the people who live under airport flight paths have moved there knowing about the problem of aircraft noise. They can therefore hardly claim to have been surprised when they discover that they find such noise unpleasant.

No such easy argument is available to airlines as they seek to address the more recent – and still more serious – environmental issue which has arisen during the last few years – that of climate change. Today, few people seriously doubt that the world's climate is warming at an accelerating and alarming rate. Such a development gives airlines a difficult dilemma as they seek to grow and develop. So far, the principal response of the industry has been to mount a major public relations initiative, in which great emphasis has been placed on the small proportion of total greenhouse emissions for which aviation is currently responsible and the progress that has been made in making aircraft more fuel efficient. Some airlines, as discussed by Daley *et al.* in Chapter 18 have also sought to embrace the idea of emissions trading.

Daley *et al.* also discuss that although currently aviation's greenhouse gas emissions are a small part of the total, they will increase rapidly both in absolute quantity and also as a proportion of the total because of aviation's growth, the inability of better fuel efficiency to counter the effects of growth and the improvements which will be achieved in other sectors of the economy. A nightmare scenario could then eventually appear. This will consist firstly of climate change having a significant effect on the rate of growth in the world economy (which will in turn have an impact on airlines). Secondly, tourism development could be hit as extreme weather events become more common and people become reluctant to travel in large numbers to currently prosperous tourism receiving areas. Sea level rise will also cause flooding and inundation of many low lying areas which are currently the foundation of the international leisure air travel industry. Finally, and in some ways worst of all, a major backlash will develop against the airline industry, with airlines being blamed for the problems that the world is experiencing and a strong moral pressure building up against the taking of air trips, for both business and leisure travel.

Because of the risk of such developments occurring, it is clear that the air travel industry will not only be a partial cause of climate change, it will also be a highly significant victim of it. Therefore, it is essential that all possible actions are taken now – while there is still time – to reverse the process of global warming. A number of options are described in Chapter 18. Most importantly, the airline industry must continue and intensify its efforts to improve its own fuel efficiency, and must embrace carbon trading enthusiastically. There is a role to be played by airlines in sponsoring and funding carbon offsetting activities in other industries as a potentially valuable way of altering peoples' perceptions.

IMPLICATIONS FOR AIRLINE MARKETING STRATEGIES[6]

This chapter has so far addressed some of the key changes that are taking place in the market for leisure air travel. It will now consider the airline characteristics which will be needed to successfully exploit this changing market.

Overwhelmingly, carriers will need to achieve and sustain low production costs in order to charge low fares. The leisure air travel market has always been price-sensitive and will remain so. Therefore, airlines with low costs can charge low, attractive fares whilst still finding that such fares generate profits. Higher cost carriers that try to match such prices will find themselves in an unprofitable situation. Alongside the need for low costs, however, will be another, vital area for decision-making. Carriers will have to decide what product features consumers will, and will not, give up to gain access to cheap prices. In setting their strategies, a distinct contrast is now appearing for different carriers.

Some – Ryanair is the best example – appear to have decided the most important need that the majority of customers have is for a bargain fare. In order to keep their costs down, therefore, they offer only a very basic product. Others appear to feel that success is more likely if a so-called 'hybrid' strategy is used, whereby at least some of the frills associated with more traditional airlines are available. Air Berlin, for example, offers complementary meals and a 20 kilo free baggage allowance. It also pre-allocates its seats, presumably to avoid the accusation of 'cattle truck handling' often levelled at some of its competitors.

So far, at least, it appears that the first of these strategies is the more successful one. This is because it allows the airlines using it to fully exploit all opportunities for the generation of the ancillary revenues. It is now clear that carriers can increase their revenues by up to around 15 per cent by the use of such methods as charging for access to their websites, selling food and drink on board their aircraft, and, more controversially, charging for the checking-in of hold baggage.

A further requirement for success may turn out to be the most crucial one in the long term. To be successful in an increasingly volatile leisure market, airlines will have to retain (if they have it already) or develop (in the case of many legacy airlines) the ability to make

---

6   The subject of airline strategies is covered in detail in Shaw (2007), 76–141.

decisions to enter or leave markets in a flexible and speedy way. Expedients, such as the leasing of a proportion of the aircraft that they use, and the buying in of support services on an 'as needed' basis, may both be important in this regard.

The final area for strategic decision-making for the marketing of leisure air travel is perhaps the most interesting. Should airlines adopt a strategy of focusing exclusively on the leisure segment of demand, or should they serve leisure alongside the other core segments of the market-business travel and air freight? There are certainly examples of airlines pursuing each of these strategies. The British airline First Choice (now part of the German-based TUI group), is putting its whole emphasis on the holiday market. It is investing large sums in new Boeing 787 aircraft and engaging in substantial media advertising to promote itself as the quality, up-market choice for long-haul holidays to exotic destinations. Many other airlines are adopting a 'total market' approach. This means having a major commitment to leisure travel, but having this commitment alongside a substantial presence in business air travel and air freight. British Airways, Singapore Airlines and Emirates all illustrate the latter strategy.

There are many advantages of a focusing approach. In particular, managing a single-segment airline should be a straightforward task, with only one product having to be produced and all managers able to work in the same direction. The result should be a high level of expertise in the one product, which should allow the low unit production costs that are so important in the successful marketing of leisure air travel. Decision-making should also be easier and faster, because only one set of constraints will have to be taken into account in deciding, for example, which routes should be included in the carrier's network.

In contrast, the total market airline will be faced with a complex management task, as tradeoffs and compromises will be needed to take account of the different product requirements of the different segments. Decision-making will therefore be slower and – perhaps – costs higher than will be the case for a focused player. Nonetheless, the total market airline may have decisive advantages. In particular, it will have access to important synergies that will not be available to the focusing firm. Year-round cash flows should be better, as business travel, leisure travel and air freight all have different patterns of demand peaking which to a significant degree complement one another. Also, there will be scheduling synergies that will be very important. The total market airline will be able to maintain a wider route network and greater frequencies as a result of serving all segments of the market, something from which all its customers will benefit. It will also, all other things being equal, be able to use larger aircraft, with the result of it having lower seat-kilometre operating costs and the ability to offer cheaper prices to price-sensitive customers. Perhaps the most telling advantage of all will be that in an increasingly unstable industry, it will have a buffer against the shocks that such instability can induce. For example, a broad route network should certainly provide such a buffer as it is unlikely that an economic slowdown will affect all the routes in a network with equal severity at the same time. Equally, a strong presence in air freight will, at least to a degree, protect cash flows against the possibility of a sudden collapse in passenger demand brought about by fears associated with wars and terrorism.

CONCLUSIONS

This chapter has explored the marketing environment of the aviation and tourism industries by identifying some of the key drivers of change which currently exist. These are associated with aviation liberalisation trends; political instability; economic growth; changing family structures and travel fashions; travel distribution and aircraft technology; and very importantly environmental impacts. This discussion has been used to provide much insight into successful airline marketing strategies for the future. Difficult decisions will have to be made regarding cost control and the associated pricing structures. Moreover, airlines will need to become more flexible to cope with the more volatile leisure market and decide whether a focused or total market approach is more suitable.

PART II

Regulation and Government Policy

5

The Impact of Civil Aviation Regimes on Leisure Travel

Andreas Papatheodorou

INTRODUCTION

The previous chapters in this book underlined the complementary nature of the air transport and tourism products focussing primarily on the demand side. This chapter aims at stressing the role of the prevailing institutional economics regimes in the aviation industry and how these may affect the tourism sector. Starting from a highly regulated environment until the late 1970s, civil aviation had been gradually liberalised in the following decades allowing market forces to shape the business environment. This change had major implications for the accessibility of tourism regions; among others, the free operation of charter carriers and the more recent introduction of low cost air services resulted in a substantial increase of traffic and tourist arrivals. This may be welcoming news but on the other hand, tourism destinations should also pay attention to tourism receipts as well as to the impact of increased flows on the natural and built environment. Section two of the chapter studies the rationale and operating principles of aviation regulation while section three elaborates on the advantages but also the potential dangers arising from market liberalisation. The primary focus is on the airline industry but the discussion also addresses issues related to airports, ground handling services and computer reservation systems. Finally, section four summarises and concludes.

AIR TRANSPORT REGULATION

Over the relatively short history of the civil aviation sector, a multitude of technical rules and regulations have been introduced to ensure that safety and security conditions are met. In the post second world war environment, however, technical regulation was accompanied by severe business restrictions. In fact, the Second World War not only bequeathed mutual suspiciousness and protectionism among the countries but also a spirit of strong government intervention in the domestic economic affairs. In particular, the term 'economic regulation' refers to the imposition of specific rules and constraints in business functions aiming at averting the supposed dangers emerging from the free evolution of market mechanisms. Policymakers in the 1950s and 1960s were persuaded that such obstacles are required for the effective and sustainable operation of the air transport sector.

For the airline industry, regulation was deemed necessary to avoid destructive competition and market instability (Papatheodorou 2002). The main problem here arises from a fundamental caveat in the airline business model, namely the potential significant divergence between marginal and average cost and the inability of the carrier to store seats for sale at a later date (Doganis 2002). If a flight is scheduled to depart irrespectively of the actual number of passengers, then its fixed cost effectively becomes sunk as it cannot be recovered; moreover, and to fill any unsold seats the airline may revert to marginal cost pricing: if, however, the additional cost of an extra passenger is very low (related almost exclusively to in-flight catering and the handling of their luggage) and certainly well below the average cost (since this takes into consideration the heavy fixed cost), then hence the airline loses money from the operation. The rationale behind regulation, therefore, suggests that free competition among airlines would initially lead to substantial market entry and subsequently to overcapacity; this would induce airlines to engage in destructive marginal cost pricing and eventually go bankrupt. Market instability would prevail up to the point that the few surviving carriers would then decide to (tacitly or overtly) collude to abandon price wars, share the market and jointly abuse their market power to the detriment of consumer interests. Consequently, regulation of fares and seat capacity was thought to restore market stability enabling the institutionally licensed carriers to grow and prosper by achieving high load factors and economies of scale without yield dilution. At an international level, regulation took the form of restrictive bilateral agreements between countries regarding the exchange of traffic rights, the designation of airlines allowed to fly between the two states, the control of tariffs, frequency and capacity. The International Air Transport Association (IATA) played a particularly important role in tariff setting in this context (Doganis 2002).

The development of the economic regulatory system in air transport became strongly intertwined with the fortification of the flag carrier, which was state-owned and aimed at promoting national interests; in smaller and/or less developed countries the flag carrier was also a symbol of national pride, societal cohesion and modernisation (Raguraman 1997), while infant industry arguments were also used (Krugman 1986). Following heavy initial subsidisation to sustain operations financially when the market is still small as a result of low income, the flag carrier can subsequently develop into a profitable 'national champion' with an extensive route network. The flag carrier was usually granted an institutional monopoly in domestic services: in this way, it could secure super-profits in thick routes (i.e. those with heavy traffic), which could then be partly used to subsidise thin and loss-making itineraries. In other words, this cross-subsidisation policy of the flag carrier was an instrument for the government to exercise regional development policy in the area of transport and accessibility. This could potentially have a positive effect on tourism in peripheral destinations although it could come at a severe financial penalisation of accessibility to major resorts. Still, the idea was that the flag carrier could use part of its profits to finance advertising campaigns and sponsor events aiming to raise the profile of a country and its awareness as a tourism destination. This was especially important at an international level, since incoming tourism was a major source of foreign exchange and receipts and had a boosting impact on the national economy.

This protectionism of the flag carrier should be also understood in a wider effort to insulate scheduled airlines from the threat of charter services. This sounds perhaps as a paradox, given that charter airlines were the engine behind leisure tourism traffic in

Europe (at least until the emergence of low cost carriers) as they ensured cheap flights to a multitude of tourism destinations during the peak seasons (especially in the summer) as part of a holiday package offered by a tour operator at an inclusive price. The argument, however, was that the market participation of these charter airlines on a seasonal basis denied the necessary profits from the scheduled carriers to provide a financially sustainable regular service throughout the year. In other words, as a result of competition from charter carriers in peak periods, scheduled airlines could not finance loss-making operations in the off-peak season and in peripheral destinations (as argued earlier). Following strong lobbying from scheduled airlines, the United Kingdom introduced Standard Provision 1 (SP1) in the mid 1960s: this conditioned the granting of chartered air transport licence to a tour operator on the price of its inclusive tour package not being lower than the cheapest return fare of a scheduled airline flying to the same destination on that particular date and time. SP1 reduced rivalry between the scheduled and the charter carriers but also among the vertically integrated tour operators (Burkart 1975).

Reactions against charter carriers from tourism receiving countries also acknowledged the danger of income leakage: these airlines were almost exclusively based in tourism origin countries hence a potentially significant loss of traffic for the destination's flag carrier could have negative repercussions on the overall level of the tourism multiplier. Moreover, the fact that charter carriers were usually part of a vertically integrated tour operator accentuated the fear of rising external control and exercise of oligopsonistic power to the detriment of a destination's tourism suppliers such as hoteliers (Britton 1991). It was also believed that charter tourism was essentially of low income and quality; on the other hand, a policy of high fares by the destination's national airline in a protected business environment could raise the tourist profile and generate important financial benefits. In this context, various barriers against the free operation of charter airlines were erected: Seychelles did not allow charter carriers, while Cyprus obliged tour operators to meet part of their seat requirements by booking on Cyprus Airways (Wheatcroft 1994); Israel did not license charter airlines to fly to airports at a distance less than 150 km from the points served by scheduled carriers (Haitovsky *et al*. 1987) and Greece requested that incoming charter passengers should bear an accommodation voucher with them. Moreover, only a very limited number of the country's airports were allowed to receive international traffic, effectively obliging charters to fly to Athens and transfer their passengers into a domestic flight operated by Olympic Airways to reach their final destination. Chapters 24 (by Seetaram) and 25 (by Taumoepeau) deal with case studies on Mauritius and South Pacific Islands respectively, showing how airline deregulation has been strategically used as a means of filtering tourism flows in certain countries.

In addition to the airline industry, other parts of the air transport sector were also heavily regulated. More specifically, airports were essentially understood as passive service providers to airlines. They were owned by the state in most cases and their revenue depended almost exclusively on aeronautical sources and subsidies; their tariff policy was usually determined by the government on an ad hoc basis and commercial activities played only a minor role. Likewise, ground handling services were usually institutionally monopolised either by the airport operator or the flag carrier (A. Graham 2003). On the other hand, the regulation of Computer Reservation Systems (CRS) was more detailed and applied both at national and international levels. In particular, from the mid 1960s onwards and until the emergence of the Internet as a feasible alternative in the early 2000s, the CRS played a very important role in the distribution system effectively shaping business transactions between the airlines, the travel agents and the final consumers.

The gradual vertical integration between some carriers and the major CRS raised anti-competitive concerns related to display screen bias (which could effectively prioritise the display of flights operated by the parent airline); architectural software bias (which could provide faster and better quality information on the parent carrier's flights); discriminatory access pricing (which aimed at unfairly raising booking fees on rival airlines) and the subsequent 'halo' effect (which induced travel agents to direct their sales in favour of the airlines that provided the CRS in their offices). To address these issues, which could also have an adverse impact on tourism destinations mainly served by smaller airlines) the European Commission established a relevant Code of Conduct with the adoption of Regulation 2299/89 (European Commission 2007a).

It seems, therefore, that the economic regulation of the air transport sector had an interesting rationale behind it. In practice, however, the strict regulatory regime created more problems than it actually solved. In most cases, flag carriers became spoiled infants, which either never grew up and/or lobbied for the continuation of government subsidies to cover their loss-making and inefficient operations. This inevitably raised public concerns and created a negative sentiment about whether the taxpayers' resources were well spent: evidence from deregulated airline markets such as the state of Texas in the early 1970s showed that competition from Southwest Airlines could in fact result in lower fares and better service (Doganis 2002). Moreover, the practice of temporal and spatial cross-subsidisation of routes was non-transparent from an accounting perspective and it would be easier for the government to follow a direct regional development policy (based on solid criteria for intervention) instead of using such tools. In addition, the policy of high fares proved detrimental for tourism development in most cases as it was not accompanied by the delivery of an equally high quality service either onboard or at the destination: hence, tourists were discouraged from visiting countries, which followed such protectionist policies and preferred to spend their holidays in charter-friendly destinations, such as Spain. Eventually, it became clear that regulation was not a panacea and voices that advocated market deregulation and liberalisation were gradually becoming stronger.

AIR TRANSPORT DEREGULATION

In contrast to the supporters of regulation, the proponents of market liberalisation believed that competition would prove beneficial for air transport. Free market entry and corporate rivalry in thick markets would ensure lower fares, higher frequency and/or better quality of service. Benefits would also extend to peripheral routes as the prevalence of contestability conditions (Baumol 1982) would deter a monopolist from abusing their market power; more specifically, even if the market size can at best support one or two carriers, these will still behave competitively and engage in limit pricing to discourage potential entry by a hit-and-run carrier: what matters in this case is potential and not actual competition. Advocates of market liberalisation also argued against hidden subsidies to airlines and were in favour of a transparent system of state-aid to be provided only in exceptional cases. They also called for gradual privatisation of airlines and commercialisation of airports, intensification of competition in ground handling services and more recently in favour of the removal of restrictions in the management of CRS.

Having the above in mind, the Carter Administration deregulated the domestic USA airline market in 1978 and pursued an active policy of liberalisation through the so-called 'open skies' agreements at an international level. On the other hand, Europe followed a stepwise approach implementing Three Packages between 1988 and 1997 to establish a European Common Aviation Area (ECAA) among the European Union (EU) and the European Economic Area (EEA) countries (i.e. Norway, Iceland, Switzerland and Liechtenstein). Since 1997, carriers registered in a ECAA country have full traffic rights within the ECAA including cabotage: for example, British Airways is allowed to fly between Rome and Milan. Fares, frequencies and capacity are freely determined by the airlines although the European Commission retains the right to intervene against predatory pricing, excessive fares and seat dumping. Legal distinction between charter and scheduled carriers has also been abandoned (Doganis 2002). Following the June 2006 decision of the European Council on the external aviation policy of the EU, Member States are required to renegotiate and align their existing bilateral agreements (with third countries) with the Community Law through horizontal agreements. In April 2007, the EU and the USA agreed to establish an Open Aviation Area: this transatlantic collaboration is expected to boost traffic by more than 25 million passengers in the following five years, generating up to 12 billion euros in consumer benefits and 80,000 new jobs (European Commission 2007b). Leisure tourism will undoubtedly play a major role in this context.

As a result of market deregulation and liberalisation and the emergence of new competitive dynamics, the contemporary airline corporate environment is characterised by the co-existence of four business models. First, traditional carriers such as British Airways, American Airlines and Qantas still play a very important role. They operate in both short and long haul routes actively seeking cost reduction in the former and merely emphasising service quality in the latter. Second, charter airlines still exist: as discussed by Williams in Chapter 8, these keep their affiliations with the travel distribution system (being part of vertically integrated groups) but they have also introduced substantial elements of flexibility enabling them to offer e.g. seat-only, one-way packages. Both types of airlines (traditional and charter) had to change their business model to face competition from the low cost carriers (LCC) – a genuine product of the market deregulation process. These airlines have experienced phenomenal growth since the mid-1990s initially in Europe and the USA but increasingly throughout the world. Chapters 9 (by Barrett) and 14 (by Echevarne) in this book deal extensively with LCC so there is no need to replicate this material here. What is important to note, however, is that LCC seem to be built both for economic recession and recovery: in the former case, people switch from traditional airlines to LCC while in the latter, LCC meet the increased travel demand for leisure purposes. So far, LCC engage predominantly in short-haul routes; nonetheless, Ryanair and other airlines have already made plans to shortly expand into the long-haul market (McGrath 2007). Finally, the fourth business model has only emerged recently and refers to all business-class carriers, such as Silverjet. These carriers are unlikely to directly affect leisure travel; by competing, however, into a so far safe territory of traditional airlines, they may indirectly reshape the latter's business model with inevitable repercussions for all market segments.

To fully assess the impact of air transport deregulation on leisure travel, one should analyse various aspects including pricing, service quality and accessibility, environment and travel distribution. Overall, the liberalisation of the market has resulted in a dramatic reduction of fares, especially on routes where LCC operate, with an undoubtedly positive effect on leisure tourism. Nonetheless, the failure of contestability conditions (Borenstein 1992) in conjunction with the rise in market concentration ratios (Goetz and Sutton 1997) may lead to an effective oligopolisation and tacit cartelisation of the airline sector to the detriment of the consumer including the leisure tourist. For this reason, competition authorities should be alert and impose heavy fines where applicable; illustratively, British Airways was imposed a penalty of £121.5 million by the Office of Fair Trading in August 2007 for price fixing in long-haul passenger fuel surcharges (Office of Fair Trading 2007). Traditional airlines may also use their frequent flyer programmes (FFP) as an effective marketing tool to command a fare premium and discourage passengers from switching to other airlines. The FFP may be particularly valuable in the context of airline alliances, as argued by Iatrou in Chapter 11, since business passengers can redeem their miles for leisure travel on an extended network of routes.

Service quality is essentially related to facilities and scheduling/routing. Onboard and airport amenities for leisure passengers travelling on economy class have rather deteriorated since the liberalisation of the market as the need to cut costs have induced a number of airlines to remove frills from their service especially in short-haul routes. Still, the Internet revolution and the introduction of e-ticketing and e-check-in enable the leisure passenger to expedite various processes and avoid long queues as argued by Sigala in Chapter 16. On the other hand, scheduling and routing are mainly associated with frequency, reliability and punctuality of services, direct or indirect flights and airport choice. As a result of market deregulation in the USA, traditional carriers such as American, United and Delta decided to develop a hub-and-spoke network, which increased load factors and sustained regular services to a multitude of routes including popular tourist destinations such as Florida or Las Vegas. Major carriers in Europe follow the same practice: Lufthansa, for example, uses Frankfurt Airport and especially Munich Airport Terminal 2, as its major hubs. Nonetheless, the hub-and-spoke system puts great pressure on airport infrastructure: delays with a domino effect and missing luggage are just some of the emerging problems. Given the substantial rise of air traffic in the last thirty years (as noted by Anne Graham in Chapter 3) and the seasonal nature of leisure travel, it may be concluded that leisure passengers may receive a poor and unreliable airline service, especially in periods of demand peaks. The European Commission introduced Regulation 261/2004 to penalise airlines for serious delays, amongst other problems (see Chapter 6 for a thorough discussion of the issue by Vasiliadou). To counter hub problems from a market perspective, however, some traditional carriers are seriously thinking of 'de-hubbing' either in terms of spreading arrivals and departures more equally within the day and/or reverting back to a system of direct point-to-point services (Boston Consulting Group 2006). This is essentially, what the LCC do: even if the large ones among them (such as Ryanair, Southwest and easyJet) operate a system of multiple quasi-hubs (e.g. at London Stansted or Luton), their refusal to offer online or interline connections keeps the whole operation relatively simple.

In fact, by offering point-to-point services and using secondary airports, the LCC have managed to redefine the geography of air transport dramatically improving accessibility to a number of previously remote destinations in Europe and the USA. This has important implications for economic and tourism development of those regions as argued by Brian Graham in Chapter 17. For example, the use of Carcassonne Airport in Southwest France by Ryanair as a proxy for Toulouse has added significant value to its existing cultural and religious tourism product (Palaskas, Papatheodorou and Tsampra 2006). As a result of the tourism boom, not only new relevant infrastructure has been built but also the price of real estate has gone up. Illustratively, a recent Mintel study shows that 800,000 households in Britain owned a second home abroad in 2006, i.e. an increase of 45 per cent compared to June 2004 (Kirby 2006). The LCC, however, are aware of these impacts of improved accessibility and usually demand heavy concessions from local airports and authorities:

the latter may then enter into a beggar-thy-neighbour policy against other airports, which results into a zero-sum game to the sole benefit of the LCC. In response to this and in an effort to introduce transparency into the system, the European Commission issued some guidelines regarding aid offered by regional airports to start-up airline operations (European Commission 2005). Echevarne extensively discusses the impact on airports of attracting LCC in Chapter 14.

Airline deregulation became also associated with the establishment of the Essential Air Service (EAS) and Public Service Obligations (PSO) programmes in the USA and the EU respectively. Both initiatives refer to a framework of subsidising certain routes. These are regarded as important for economic and strategic reasons; nonetheless, and due to the small size of the respective markets, commercial air services are financially unsustainable. In 2007, the EU had more than 220 PSO services (European Commission 2007e) while the USA supported approximately 140 rural communities under the EAS programme (Department of Transport 2007). Following an infant industry argumentation, this state intervention may prove beneficial for leisure travel to remote tourism destinations. In fact, the introduction of PSO or EAS flights may induce tourists to visit resorts, which are still in the exploration stage of their life cycle. Subsequently, these areas can capitalise on this initial boost in accessibility to properly enter the tourism market; beyond a certain level of popularity, charter or even scheduled flights may become commercially profitable enabling the suspension of air subsidies. In any case, however, care should be taken by the authorities not to use the PSO/EAS regimes as an excuse for indirect protectionism of certain carriers. Halpern and Niskala elaborate further on the issue of leisure air travel in remote regions in Chapter 15.

The rise of air traffic in the post-liberalisation period has also raised environmental concerns. These are mainly related to aircraft fuel emissions, which may expedite the emergence of the greenhouse phenomenon, but also to congestion, noise and other problems created in areas surrounding airports. While flying for business purposes may escape direct criticism as it is deemed necessary for the economy, the discretionary nature of leisure air travel may induce environmentally sensitive people to react. Interestingly, a 2005 survey undertaken by the European Union Directorate General for the Environment (EUDGE) shows that 68 per cent of the interviewees fully agree and another 17 per cent rather agree that the cost of climate change should be incorporated in the air transport fares (Cairns and Newson 2006). Ironically perhaps, some British hoteliers support the environmental lobby to encourage domestic tourism (Milmo 2007)! In any case, the European Commission is in train to take relevant policy measures such as aircraft fuel taxes, inclusion of air transport in the EU emissions trading scheme, en-route charges or taxes on aircraft emissions and impacts, departure and/or arrival taxes as well as VAT on air transport. Some airlines (and especially LCC) have also decided to voluntarily participate in Carbon Offsetting schemes: Virgin Blue, the Australian LCC, for example, offers its customers the ability to offset their flights by buying carbon credits online (Virgin Blue 2007). Similarly, to counter any Not-In-My-Back-Yard (NIMBY) problems emerging in the airport neighbourhoods, airlines engage in corporate social responsibility programmes aiming to assist the local community. Daley et al. extensively discuss the relationship between the environment and leisure travel in Chapter 18.

With respect to travel distribution issues emerging in the post-deregulation environment, it is evident that the airlines enthusiastically embraced the Internet in their effort to reduce their cost basis. More specifically, the Internet endowed airlines with a powerful channel of direct sales to the customer and subsequently enabled them to exercise substantial pressure on both the CRS and the travel agents to reduce their subscription fees and travel commissions respectively. By sharing the arising cost savings with their customers and guaranteeing that the best deals are found online, the airlines have deeply impacted on the booking behaviour of leisure tourists who are by definition more sensitive to fare changes than business travellers. More recently, LCC but increasingly traditional airlines too, have realised the usefulness of their websites in raising ancillary revenue from selling complementary products such as hotel accommodation, travel insurance, car rental etc. According to a 2003 IT survey undertaken by the Airline Business magazine, 33 per cent of interviewed carriers offered hotels, 32 per cent excursions and 24 per cent car hire (Airline Business 2003) while many other airlines planned to introduce such services in the forthcoming years. This trend has effectively facilitated the creation of the so-called dynamic packaging, which enables the traveller to build their own holiday by putting together the individual components of a package based on pricing and constraints determined by a real-time inventory. Nonetheless, unlike traditional packaging offered by tour operators at an inclusive price, customers building a dynamic package remain unprotected in case of financial insolvency of one of their service providers; hence and unless they had already bought special travel insurance, they may be left stranded in a foreign country incurring heavy repatriation costs. The Civil Aviation Authority (CAA) in Britain operates a bonding-system called ATOL to protect holidaymakers flying on inclusive packages, however, this is not applicable in the case of dynamic packagers (using traditional or LCC carriers) or travellers booking seat-only packages of charter airlines. Illustratively, the CAA projects that less than 20 per cent of holidaymakers will be ATOL-protected by 2008 compared to 98 per cent in 1997 (Civil Aviation Authority 2005b).

The advancement of the Internet as an alternative distribution channel had also important implications for the regulatory system prevailing in the CRS market. At present, this is highly concentrated as it is effectively controlled by four major companies, i.e. Amadeus, Sabre, Galileo and Worldspan (the last two are now part of the Travelport group). Still, it is believed that the Internet now poses a sufficient threat on CRS providers to deter the latter from exercising their oligopsonistic power on airlines and travel agencies. In this context, the USA decided to deregulate the CRS market in July 2004 (Ioannides and Petridou-Daughtrey 2006), while the EU recently issued a proposal for a regulation to revise the 1989 Code of Conduct (as modified by Regulations 3089/93 and 323/99) in a more liberal direction (European Commission 2007d). More specifically, policymakers seem to expect that CRS deregulation will result in lower booking fees and the introduction of incentive payments rather than 'content fragmentation', i.e. airlines offering different content to different CRS. This is especially important for leisure travellers who are price sensitive yet for some reason decide to use traditional travel agents. The latter wish to secure that low web fares will also be available on CRS (European Commission 2007a).

To conclude this discussion on the impacts of air transport deregulation on leisure travel, it is also important to briefly look at developments in the airport and the ground handling sector. In particular and over the last twenty years, gales of airport commercialisation have started blowing especially in Europe and Asia as airports have gradually understood the importance of non-aeronautical revenue for their finances. Although the abolition of duty-free sales in intra-EU flights in the late 1990s had negative effects (A. Graham 2003), these proved only transitory as the current trend is to build shopping malls within airport terminals. Leisure passengers who fly infrequently are likely to be excited when found in the airport and may, therefore, be induced to spend considerable amounts of money on shopping. Moreover, those travelling on LCC may also consume food and drinks in the airport restaurants given that LCC do not offer complimentary in-flight catering (Papatheodorou and Lei 2006). This airport commercialisation is also welcomed by airlines, as they expect that this ancillary revenue may partly be used to reduce aeronautical charges; still, this issue remains rather controversial. In most countries, airport tariff policy is still highly regulated to avoid any potential abuse of infrastructural monopoly, especially in the cases of major hubs (A. Graham 2003); yet, problems with pricing transparency have recently led the European Commission to propose a new directive on airport charges (European Commission 2007c). As for ground handling services, their market was gradually liberalised in the EU in 1996; Directive 96/97/EC gave the right of carriers to self-handling and conditioned competition among handlers on the airports' passenger traffic (A. Graham 2003). This partial liberalisation aimed at reducing operating costs and improving service quality. Leisure passengers would also be expected to benefit from this regime change. Still, the European Commission now believes that it is time to revise this Directive to face recent developments in the airport sector.

CONCLUSIONS

This chapter aimed at exploring the impact of alternative civil aviation regimes on leisure travel. While there was an interesting rationale behind the introduction of regulation, in practice there were serious implementation problems. The transition into a liberal civil aviation regime had important implications for leisure travel. Overall, the assessment is rather positive; nonetheless, deregulation is not a panacea either: among others, competition authorities should be alert to intervene in cases of market abuse; moreover, tourism destinations should pay attention so that increased traffic as a result of airline liberalisation does not reach unsustainable levels beyond their carrying capacity. This is especially important for small island states such as Malta and Cyprus, where environmental constraints may be seriously binding (Papatheodorou and Busuttil 2003). In other words, the public authorities should understand the highly complementary nature of the air transport and tourism products and therefore design integrated policies, which internalise any possible adverse effects.

6

Leisure Travel and Legal Issues in Aviation

Anastasia Vasiliadou

INTRODUCTION

An examination of the legal position of air transport could not be seriously undertaken without taking due account of the particularities that distinguish air transport in comparison to other forms of passenger transport. Its intensive international character, which is demonstrated by the many international agreements and international organisations of civil aviation that coordinate air transport, alongside with its equally intensive national character, arising from the recognition of territorial air space and connected to governmental interests and involvement, form a complex legal frame (Chatzinikolaou 2005; Dagtoglou 1994). Even in cases where there is a common air traffic market as in the EU, there is also (the "fiction" of) nationality, because air transport, notwithstanding its liberalisation and privatisation is still a national public utility for which governments carry a heavy responsibility towards the public (Wassenbergh 2000).

Having said that, and considering the limitations that this issue imposes, it is important to clarify that the present chapter is not intended to serve as an analysis and commentary of aviation law but merely as a brief presentation of the current legislation regulating air transport to the degree that it affects leisure travel. In the following sections an attempt is made to introduce the framework of international conventions that regulate aviation in public as well as private international aviation law, and also to briefly present current developments in EU policies to the extend that they reflect on travel for leisure purposes.

INTERNATIONAL CONVENTIONS AND THE LEGAL FRAMEWORK IN AVIATION

Public International Aviation Law

The first international multilateral Convention on the "Regulation of Aerial Navigation", signed in Paris in 1919, recognised the principle of air-space sovereignty, until then customarily enforced by states, according to which member states have complete and exclusive sovereignty over the air space above their territory. Aiming mainly at defending the security of member states and protecting their national air space, due to the post–war circumstances, the Paris Convention recognised the freedom to over-fly and land in the territory of member states, only for technical reasons (e.g. refueling, maintenance), without transferring passengers.

The tremendous development of aviation during World War II demonstrated the need for an international organisation to assist and regulate international flights for peaceful purposes, covering all aspects of flying, including technical, economic, and legal issues. For these reasons, the Paris Convention, already whittled down by successive amendments, was replaced by the "Convention on International Civil Aviation" signed in Chicago in 1944, which established the International Civil Aviation Organisation (ICAO), a specialised agency of the United Nations, charged with coordinating and regulating international air travel. The "Convention on International Civil Aviation", also known as the "Chicago Convention", affirmed the principle of air- space sovereignty and raised for the first time issues concerning exchange of commercial rights in international civil aviation. Since it was not possible to reach an agreement on the exchange of commercial rights satisfactory to all states attending the conference, the Chigaco Convention's two supplementary treaties[1], which are binding only on the ICAO member states that have ratified them, established the frame of the "five freedoms of the air", formulated as a result of disagreements over the extent of aviation liberalisation (see Cheng 1962). Nevertheless, free competition in international civil aviation, and consequently in passenger transport for leisure purposes, was not facilitated by freedoms of the air, since they all are subject to negotiations and bilateral air transport agreements (BATA).

It was in the framework of such bilateral agreements between the USA and European countries though, that the "deregulation" of US civil aviation was partly transferred to Europe, contributing to the development of commercial aviation. The nationally regulated and mutually supported protectionism that had served as a basis for the Chicago Convention, favoured a policy of high prices and created, through International Air Transport Association (IATA), a highly developed and reliable air transport system which was only accessible to a relatively small number of people. The competition between scheduled airlines (restricted by the trading agreements with IATA) and charter operators, which entered the scene in the early 1960s, led to "illegal" though widespread practices through which unofficially cheap scheduled air fares were offered "under the counter". A successful law suit of a British air operator against the British Government[2] was a considerably important step for the development of commercial aviation, since for the first time no conditions (advance booking; minimal stay in the destination; flight only on certain days or hours) were attached to scheduled low fares. Eventually, liberal pricing features were introduced to the very protectionist BATA between the USA and Britain (the so called Bermuda II) and liberal agreements were signed between the USA and European countries such as Belgium, Netherlands or Germany. In this way, the USA exported "deregulation" policy to Europe (Dagtoglou 1994) and travel for leisure purposes was further facilitated.

---

1   The International Air Services Transit Agreement and the International Air Transport Agreement.
2   Laker Airways Ltd. V. Department of Trade [1977] Q.B. 643. Sir Freddie Laker secured the license to start a scheduled "Skytrain" between London and New York at a drastically reduced fare. 500,000 passengers flew in 1978 with Laker Airways between London and New York (Dagtoglou 1994).

Private International Aviation Law – Air Carrier Liability

The main legal issue that arises in passenger air transport is that of carrier's liability in a field where conflict of law could constitute a major problem. The necessity of international uniformity in the rules governing carrier's liability so that both carrier and passenger could foresee the risks and insure themselves against possible losses, emerged when aviation industry was still in its infancy.

Until recently, most of international air transport was governed by the first international Convention on air carrier's liability, the "Warsaw Convention for the Unification of Certain Rules Relating to International Carriage by Air", adopted in 1929, as amended and supplemented by the Hague Protocol of 1955, the Guadalajara Convention of 1961, the Guatemala City Protocol of 1971 and the additional Montreal Protocols Nos. 1, 2, 3 and 4 of 1975 (Whalen 2000). The above Conventions and Protocols form a legal frame known as "Warsaw System". The purpose of the Convention was the creation of a certain degree of uniformity in the rules of international air carriage of persons, baggage or goods for reward (Art.1) and also the protection, at that time, of the financially weak aviation industry, creating an incentive for further development. It provided a world–wide system of standard rules, establishing and elaborating air carrier's liability arising out of the death, wounding and other bodily injury of passengers caused by an event that occurs on board the carrier's aircraft or in the course of embarking or disembarking (Art. 17), and out of destruction, loss of or damage to registered luggage caused by an occurrence on their aircraft during international carriage.

The legal basis of the carrier's liability, which represents the core subject of the Warsaw Convention, is fault/negligence but with a reversed burden of proof (Art. 20(1)). That is, instead of the claimant having to prove fault on the part of the carrier, the carrier has to disprove fault in order to avoid paying compensation[3]. The carrier is liable according to the limit fixed by the Convention. Only when a claimant could demonstrate in court that the basis of the claim was the result of carrier's "wilful misconduct" – an allegation difficult to prove -, is it possible to recover damages in excess of the Warsaw system's prescribed limit? However, the carrier is not liable if it can prove that it took all necessary measures to avoid the damage, or that it was impossible to take such measures. Uniformity was also reached in the format and the legal significance of the carriage documents, whereas the possible conflicts of both laws and jurisdictions have been reduced by providing for four different fora in the territory of one of the High Contracting Parties where the claimant can sue.

Drafted at a time when carriage by air was a dangerous adventure and when most airlines were government owned, the Convention contributed significantly to avoiding complex conflicts of laws and unpredictable, costly and possibly uninsurable settlement of claims. Although it was the cornerstone of private international air law for almost a century, its rules have long been viewed as outdated and unjust. The limits of air carrier liability had become outdated and unreasonably low, different limits would apply to passengers travelling on the same aircraft but to different destinations (Diederiks-Verschoor 2001), the attempts to update the Convention had all led to dis-unification of law and some of the terms used in the Convention had caused difficulties of interpretation and application.

---

3   The reason behind this regime was the necessity of certainty, as well as the reduction of legal costs that would burden the claimant. This arrangement also prevented the claimant from the difficulty to provide the necessary evidence in a field of technical complexity. The reversed burden of proof reflected a quid pro quo, since it was placed on the carrier to counterbalance the monetary limit of liability in Art. 22 (see Larsen 2002: 7).

In addition, international agreements and private voluntary arrangements among airlines had been developed, particularly by IATA and EU (Diederiks-Verschoor 2001) increasing or waiving the compensation limit and further complicating the carrier liability system (Hermida 2001).

The relative disorder created by the Warsaw system and the need for modernisation, resulted in an attempt to reform the system. In May 1999 a Diplomatic Conference was held in Montreal with the ambition to adopt a new Convention recognizing the importance of protecting the interests of passengers in international carriage by air and the need for equitable compensation based on the principle of restitution. 121 states attended the Conference, which resulted in the adoption of a new "Montreal Convention for the Unification of Certain Rules for International Carriage by Air". The Montreal Convention stands on its own and is not another amendment to the Warsaw Convention. It prevails over the whole Warsaw System between States Parties to the Montreal Convention but is only valid between states that have both ratified it. In cases between non-signatory states, the amended Warsaw Convention 1929 still remains in force. However, the high rate of ratifications of the Montreal Convention, despite the initially expressed doubts (Diederiks-Verschoor 2001) indicates that it will gradually become the worldwide norm, eliminating uniformity problems.

The new Convention preserves many aspects of the Warsaw System but features many significant advances over the existing system. According to its provisions:

- In the case of injury or death resulting from an air accident the carrier is liable:
    a) For claims up to a first tier of 100,000 Special Drawing Rights (1 SDR = €1.05 in May 08) per passenger, regardless of fault, unless the carrier proves that the damage was caused by the negligence of the claimant.
    b) For a second tier of claims in excess of 100,000 SDRs per passenger, the carrier is liable without limit, unless it proves that it was not at fault for the accident (reversed burden of proof).

- For damage sustained in case of destruction or loss of or damage to checked baggage, the carrier is liable unless it proves that the damage resulted from an inherent defect of the baggage. In the case of unchecked baggage the carrier is liable only if the damage resulted from its fault. In both cases the carrier's liability is limited to 1,000 SDRs per passenger unless the passenger has made a special declaration of interest or it is proved that the damage resulted from an act or omission of the carrier, done with intent to cause damage.

- In case of damage caused by delay:
    a) In the carriage of passengers, the carrier is liable up to 4,150 SDRs.
    b) In the carriage of baggage, the carrier is liable up to 1,000 SDRs unless it proves that it took all measures that could reasonably be required to avoid the damage or that it was impossible for it to take such measures. Carrier's liability is unlimited if it is proved that the damage resulted from its act or omission, done with intent to cause damage.

However, the term "delay" is not defined, thus allowing airlines to continue their practice of stating in their contracts of carriage that their schedule as set out in the timetables is not guaranteed (Hermida 2001).

- An additional "fifth jurisdiction" is inserted, enabling claimants to bring an action in the permanent and principal place of their residence, provided that the airline operates services and conducts business from that place.

- Documents of carriage are modernised and updated, making the use of electronic ticketing possible and thus enabling airlines to reduce their operation costs.

- A distinction between contracting carrier and actual carrier is inserted.

- Carriers shall maintain adequate insurance coverage to cover potential liability. Though consumers would certainly benefit if insurance companies were forced by law to issue policies without limits (Whalen 2000), it has been argued, that this provision might result in passing on to the passengers any increase in insurance. Instead, alternative risk management techniques (such as loss control, risk transfer guarantees or risk retention) could be contemplated for the airlines (Hermida 2001).

- Provision is made for advance payments by carriers to persons entitled to claim compensation in case of death or injury, in order to meet their immediate economic needs. The amount of the advance payment will be subject to national law and deductible from the final settlement.

- Liability limits shall be reviewed at five – year intervals to take account of inflation.

The Convention is undoubtedly an improvement from the Warsaw system, providing major benefits to the passenger and updating the system of settlement of issues that affect leisure travel. It has unified and modernised private international law, conforming with the principle of restitution and with the focus that today's society puts on consumer protection instead of the protection of the carrier (Diederiks-Verschoor 2001). Moreover, it recognises to the claimant the most logical jurisdiction, the place of their residence. In this framework passengers would find it easier to claim compensation, whereas a significant number of claims will be settled without the need for lengthy and costly litigation. Nevertheless, the Montreal Convention does not specifically address issues related to liability arising from code-sharing, franchising and other forms of airline cooperation, since they were not considered of high priority (Hermida 2001).

The European Community ratified the Montreal Convention with Council Decision 2001/539/EC[4]. Accordingly, Regulation No 2027/97[5], which defined the obligations of community air carriers in the event of injury to passengers imposing unlimited liability on them, was amended by Regulation No 889/2002[6] which applied the rules of the Montreal Convention to all flights, whether domestic or international, operated by Community air carriers.

---

4   Official Journal L 194 of 18.7.2001.
5   Official Journal L 285 of 17.10.1997.
6   Official Journal L 140 of 30.5.2002.

RECENT DEVELOPMENTS IN THE EU AND IMPLICATIONS FOR LEISURE TRAVEL

The above mentioned Regulation 2027/97 is closely connected to a broader frame of European Union legislation through which the traditional bilateral way of organising intra-Community air transport was replaced with the Community policy of gradual liberalisation of air transport (Manuhatu 2000: 265). This development was made possible firstly through the application of the principles of freedom to provide services and freedom of establishment for any airline established in a Member State, secondly through harmonisation measures in the most important areas of the aviation sector and finally through strict controls on State aid. The main purpose of this policy, which has been implemented in three successive stages, was to provide the user of air transport, and consequently the leisure traveller, with a better product, expand the choice of products and reduce tariffs (Wassenbergh 2000).

Though it has been argued that reduced airline regulation poses a threat to tourism because of the short term risk of instability of services (Shaw 1982) and while it is true that transport market is still in transition – with the results of competition between different modes of transport still to be examined (Sambracos and Rigas 2007) – it is generally accepted that aviation liberalisation has contributed significantly, along with improvements in aviation technology, to the worldwide "boom" in tourism (Forsyth 2006).

However, the "boom" in air travel exacerbated problems relating to the saturation levels reached at airports or to the overloaded air traffic control system. These problems apart from leading to inefficiency and major delays, also limited access to the new companies wishing to compete with the well established carriers. In addition, code-sharing, franchising and other forms of airline cooperation, along with the so-called "open skies agreements" raised significant safety, passenger protection and personal data protection issues. The Commission's work in the field of air transport and the Community legislative frame is intended to tackle issues such as fragmentation of air traffic control (ATC), physical access to the market (allocation of slots), costs of infrastructure, the absence of an external dimension to aviation, the fragmentation of safety rules[7] as well as to ensure protection of passenger rights.

A brief presentation of the main legislative texts of the EU relating to air transport is attempted in the following paragraphs, aiming to outline the current framework of interconnected Regulations and Directives to the degree that EU policies affect, directly or indirectly transport for leisure purposes. To show the evolution of legislation, the order of the presentation is, in general, chronological irrespective of the subject of the legislative measure. Exceptions were made for reasons of consistency when the legislative measures should be examined as a group due to their common objectives.

Council Regulations 2407/92[8] on licensing of air carriers, 2408/92[9] on access for Community air carriers to intra-Community air routes and 2409/92[10] on passenger fares and air cargo rates were part of the so-called "third aviation package". They laid down the criteria which must be met by air carriers to obtain or maintain an operating licence,

---

7   See COM (2000) 595 final.
8   Official Journal L 240 of 24.08.1992.
9   Official Journal L 240 of 24.08.1992.
10   Official Journal L 240 of 24.08.1992.

covered access for air carriers to scheduled and non-scheduled intra – Community air services and set out to liberalise price formation for Community air services.

The Community policy to facilitate competition and to encourage entry into the aviation market, as provided for in Regulation 2408/92 requires strong support for air carriers intending to operate intra-Community routes. The provisions of the Council Regulation No 95/93[11] on common rules for the allocation of slots at Community airports, as amended by Regulation 793/2004[12] attempts to strike a balance between the interests of incumbent air carriers and new entrants to the market who need to establish a competitive intra-Community network, enhancing competition (Frühling and Eyskens 2004). The Regulation aims to ensure that available landing and take-off slots are used efficiently and distributed in an equitable, non–discriminatory and transparent way, despite scarce airport capacity.

The objective to eliminate the restrictions on freedom to provide services in the Community, as attained with regard to air transport service through Council Regulations 2407/92, 2408/92 and 2409/92, was further pursued through the implementation of Council Directive 96/67/EC[13] on "access to the ground handling market at Community airports". The Directive aims at reducing the operating costs of airline companies in order to improve the quality of service provided to airport users.

The "third package" of aviation measures created an internal aviation market where the need of harmonisation of the rules on the nature and limitation of liability was obvious[14]. Member States had variously increased the liability limit set by the Warsaw Convention, thereby leading to different terms and conditions of carriage in the Community. Council Regulation No 2027/97[15] on "air carrier liability in respect of the carriage of passengers and their baggage by air" which defined and harmonised the obligations of Community air carriers in case of accidents to passengers, was amended by Regulation 889/2002 of the European Parliament and the Council[16]. The amended Regulation brought Community arrangements fully into line with the Montreal Convention signed in May 1999 in order to harmonise liability limits and legal defences irrespective of the route on which the accident occurs.

The need for protection of the travelling public had already emerged in 1988, when the Commission submitted the proposal[17] for the Council Regulation 2299/89 on "a code of conduct for computerised reservation systems"[18]. As discussed by Papatheodorou in Chapter 5, the problem of limited number of options usually displayed on CRS, precludes the options offered by airlines enjoying less priority than others, from being made known to the prospective airline customer (Abeyratne 2001: 10). The Regulation, which contributed significantly to ensuring easy access to updated and accurate flight and fare information through computerised reservation systems, protecting air carriers, travel agents and thereby consumers, was amended for the second time by Council Regulation 323/1999[19]. Thus its scope was extended and its provisions clarified so that its objectives are met in all Member States[20].

---

11   Official Journal L 14 of 21.02.1993.
12   Official Journal L 138 of 30.04.2004.
13   Official Journal L 272 of 25.10.1996.
14   See COM/95/0724 final.
15   Official Journal L 285 of 17.10.1997.
16   Official Journal L 140 of 30.05.2002.
17   COM/88/447 final Official Journal C 294, 18.11.1988.
18   Official Journal L 220 of 29.07.1989.
19   Official Journal L 40 of 13.02.1999.
20   The changes were related to subscriber obligations, charging policy, display of code – share flights, ticketing arrangements for flights carrying the same flight number operated by the same carrier, security package, right of

In the light of the radically changing environment in which air carriers have to operate, the need for common action to protect consumer interests was further met with Regulation 295/91[21] "establishing common rules for a denied-boarding compensation system in scheduled air transport". The numerous changes that the air transport sector had seen since the implementation of Regulation 295/91 (emergence of low cost airlines, restructuring of other airlines, opening up of new routes, availability of information or tickets on the Internet with a general reduction in fares) were not accompanied by sufficient measures to protect passengers' rights. Considering the fact that an increasing number of passengers that have already paid for their travel arrangements faces situations such as cancellations, overbooking, loss of luggage, delays etc. while being at the same time subject to certain very strict formalities (controls, registration, reservation), the Community adopted Regulation 261/2004[22] "establishing common rules on compensation and assistance to passengers in the event of denied boarding and of cancellation or long delay of flights"[23].

A few months before the Regulation's implementation, IATA, ELFAA and Hapag Lloyd Express submitted an application for judicial review of the Regulation to the High Court of Justice of England and Wales, claiming that Regulation 261/2004 was invalid on several grounds including: inconsistency with the Montreal Convention of 1999; lack of legal certainty; inadequate reasoning; lack of proportionality; discrimination and breach of certain procedural requirements. The High Court later referred the case for a preliminary ruling to the European Court of Justice[24]. On 10 January 2006, the European Court of Justice rendered its judgment on the validity of Regulation 261/2004, holding that the articles in question are valid in the light of the mentioned provisions of international air law. However, it is still argued that Regulation 261/2004 appears to be inconsistent with the purpose and scope of the Montreal Convention 1999 (see Wegter 2006)[25].

Vasiliadou (2006) examined the implementation of Regulation 261/2004 in Greece (a major leisure tourism destination in the Mediterranean Region) by analysing the database of passenger complaints made to the Hellenic Civil Aviation Authority. According to her research, the Regulation contributed significantly into satisfying claims of passengers who would otherwise be compelled to resort to judicial action (which is usually costly and not worth the time and expenses in cases of passenger rights violation). Moreover, and despite carriers' initial fears about their obligation to compensate passengers even in case of cancellation for reasons outside their control, the proven existence of extraordinary circumstances constitutes a significant exemption factor. Still, there is an increased possibility that an incident of flight cancellation is "labelled" by the carrier as "delay" so as for it to avoid its increased obligations. The need for a preset time limit in the case of flight delay is therefore apparent. Furthermore, it became apparent that a document proving the passenger's belated appearance for check-in should be provided, in case of

---

a defendant to be heard, inclusion of information systems within the scope of the code, ranking of flights, billing information on magnetic media.

21   Official Journal L 36 of 8.02.1991.
22   Official Journal L 46 of 17.02.2004.
23   Regulation 261/2004 repealed Regulation (EEC) 295/91.
24   Case C-344/04.
25   Regulation's Art. 6.1.iii as combined to Art. 8.1.a, which when the delay is at least five hours provide for reimbursement within seven days of the full cost of the ticket, for the part or parts of the journey not made, and for the part or parts already made if the flight is no longer serving any purpose in relation to the passenger's original travel plan, is in breach with Art. 19 of the Montreal Convention, according to which "… the carrier shall not be liable for damage occasioned by delay if it proves that it and its servants and agents took all measures that could reasonably be required to avoid the damage or that it was impossible for it or them to take such measures".

boarding denial, so that no doubts arise concerning the truthfulness of the carrier's claim. Finally, Vasiliadou (2006) argues that the provision of a common form of complaint filing across all EU member states would facilitate the necessary collection and analysis of relevant information at a European level.

A further important initiative on travellers' rights was recently taken by the EU with Regulation 1107/2006[26] "concerning the rights of disabled persons and persons with reduced mobility when travelling by air"[27]. This regulation aims to ensure that disabled people and people with reduced mobility are given equal opportunities for air travel. It provides for assistance to meet their particular needs at the airport as well as on board. Member States should supervise and ensure compliance with this Regulation and designate an appropriate body to carry out enforcement tasks.

Safety Issues[28]

Air transport liberalisation process which began in 1988, gradually transformed a market based on bilateral agreements, with virtually no competition, into a genuine open market based on the Treaty principles. As soon as this process started, the aviation community realised that a genuine air transport single market required also the establishment and uniform application of common rules in the fields of aviation safety and environmental protection in order to ensure a high level of protection for the European citizen, and consequently the leisure traveller, and to provide a level playing field for Community air operators[29].

In this perspective the Community has proposed a number of legislative measures. Council Directive 94/56/EC[30] establishing the fundamental principles governing the investigation of civil aviation accidents and incidents is one of them. It aims at improving air safety by facilitating the expeditious holding of investigations. The same objective was further pursued, following the events of 11 September 2001, with Directive 2003/42/EC[31] on occurrence reporting in civil aviation, which set out to improve air safety by ensuring that safety-critical information is reported, collected, stored, protected and disseminated in order to facilitate its effective analysis and follow-up, with a view to preventing future accidents and incidents.

Regulation 1592/2002[32] on common rules in the field of civil aviation and the establishment of the European Aviation Safety Agency (EASA), as amended by Regulation 1643/2003[33], set out the responsibilities of EASA in the respect of establishing a uniformly high level of civil aviation safety in Europe, responding to increasing concerns over the health[34] and welfare of passengers during flights. According to the Regulation, operation

---

26   Official Journal L 204 of 26.07.2006.
27   Regulation (EC) No 1107/2006 of the European Parliament and of the Council of 5 July 2006 concerning the rights of disabled persons and persons with reduced mobility when travelling by air.
28   In civil aviation, a distinction has to be made between aviation security aimed at preventing any unlawful acts in the aviation field and aviation safety concerning the rules on the construction and operation of aircraft.
29   COM(2000) 595 final.
30   Official Journal L 319 of 12.12.1994.
31   Official Journal L 167 of 04.07.2003.
32   Official Journal L 240 of 07.09.2002.
33   Official Journal L 245 of 22.07.2003.
34   A current relevant topic among airlines and insurers is the "Deep Vein Thrombosis" (DVT) or "Economy Class" Syndrome, which causes the threat of legal liability claims being pursued against airlines for disabling injury or death of passengers (see Tompkins 2001; Meyer 2001; Clark and Fulena 2001). Despite the fact that

of the EASA aims to harmonise technical rules and, in particular, to ensure their uniform application.

The realisation that third-county carriers using Community airports do not always comply with international minimum safety standards, a fact that could place Community citizens travelling with these carriers in danger, led to the implementation of Directive 2004/36/EC[35] on the safety of third-country aircraft using Community airports. The Directive establishes a harmonised approach to the effective enforcement of international safety standards in the Community by harmonising the rules and procedures for ramp inspections of third-country aircraft landing at airports located in the Member States. This Directive provides for the exchange of information between the Member States and the possibility to extend to the whole Community measures taken by one Member State against a third country aircraft or operator not complying with international safety standards[36].

Despite the fact that, according to statistics, air transport accidents have become extremely rare in Europe[37], the accident involving leisure passengers in Sharm-el-Sheikh[38] indicated that more stringent rules than the existing ones are needed to make ramp inspections obligatory and to oblige Member States to participate in a wider exchange of information and apply common measures decided on the results of these checks. To this aim, Regulation 2111/2005[39] on "the establishment of a Community list of air carriers subject to an operating ban within the Community and on informing air transport passengers of the identity of the operating air carrier" was adopted. According to the Regulation, a list of air carriers that are subject to an operating ban in the Community was established and each Member State enforces within its territory the operating bans included in this list. Moreover, an obligation of the air carriage contractor to inform the passenger of the identity of the operating air carrier, whatever the means used to make the reservation improves the position of the travelling public vis-à-vis the air transport industry. Passenger's right to be informed on the identity of the carrier gains an increasing importance due to the emergence of practices such as code–sharing, and merger politics such as alliances etc, that might mislead the passenger about the identity of the operating carrier. Further to Regulation 2111/2005, the Commission adopted Regulation 474/2006[40] banning certain named carriers from flying passengers in the EU or operate within European airspace.

---

popular media and the medical press are constantly publishing anecdote and preliminary studies on the phenomenon of non – accidental death on the air, serious science, reliable statistics and careful epidemiological studies have yet to be developed to assess the statistical significance of death in the cabin as compared with similar non flying incidents. One probable reason for the deficiency of serious studies is that the subject of air passenger's health "has fallen through the regulatory cracks". (Caplan 2001). Nevertheless, passenger's health might be affected by a number of factors, such as turbulence (Abeyratne 2001), low oxygen levels, low air pressure or insufficient air filtering which might cause the spread of infectious diseases such as tuberculosis (Abeyratne 2001).

35   Official Journal L 143 of 30.04.2004.
36   Art. 5.
37   COM(2005) 48 final.
38   On 3 January 2004 a passenger jet carrying 148 people to Paris crashed shortly after take-off at the Egyptian resort of Sharm-El-Sheikh, killing everyone on board. It emerged after the accident that this operating carrier was, at the time of the accident, banned from flying to Switzerland because of concerns about its safety level, but authorised in certain Member States.
39   Official Journal L 344 of 27.12.2005.
40   Official Journal L 84, 23.3.2006.

Security

Following the criminal acts of 11 September 2001, the Commission took an interest in restoring the confidence of travellers in international air transport which was devastated by a 5 per cent drop in traffic in 2001 and an 8 billion loss euros for carriers[41]. Aviation security standards were revised and minimum insurance requirements covering carrier liability were introduced in order to foster traveller protection and avoid distortion of competition between air carriers.

Regulation No 785/2004[42] on "insurance requirements for air carriers and aircraft operators" requires air carriers and aircraft operators to be insured, in particular with respect to passengers, baggage, cargo and third parties, to cover the risks associated with aviation–specific liability, including acts of war, terrorism, hijacking, acts of sabotage, unlawful seizure of aircraft and civil commotion[43].

The EU's effort to revise all aviation security standards in order to correct shortcomings and take account of any terrorist threats, commenced with Regulation 2320/2002[44] "establishing common rules in the field of civil aviation security" which was amended by Regulation 849/2004[45]. The Commission presented a Regulation requiring the EU to implement the security measures defined by the European Civil Aviation Conference (ECAC) and aimed at setting up a system of unannounced inspections, introducing more rigorous screening of passengers, luggage and staff and requiring Member States to introduce national security programmes and common standards for equipment. Regulation 2320/2002 is backed up by implementing Regulations with detailed measures. The first act laying down such measures was Commission Regulation 622/2003[46] which aimed at laying down the necessary measures for the implementation and technical adaptation of common basic standards regarding aviation security to be incorporated into national civil aviation security programmes[47]. This Regulation was first amended by Regulation 68/2004[48] which contains a list of objects which may not be carried on board by passengers. The currently increased risk of liquid explosives being introduced onto aircraft was addressed by the recent Regulation 1546/2006[49]. Its confidential Annex amended the Annex of Regulation 622/2003 with measures that should be reviewed every six months in the light of technical developments, operational implications at airports and the impact on passengers.

---

41   http://europa.eu/scadplus/leg/en/lvb/l24253.htm 20.3.2007.
42   Official Journal L 138 of 30.04.2004.
43   For liability in respect of passengers, the minimum insurance cover must be 250 000 SDRs per passenger. However, in respect of non-commercial operations by aircraft with a MTOM of 2 700 kg or less, Member States may set a lower level of minimum insurance cover, provided that such cover is at least 100 000 SDRs per passenger. For liability in respect of baggage, the minimum insurance cover must be 1 000 SDRs per passenger in commercial operations.
44   Official Journal L 355 of 30.12.2002.
45   Official Journal L 158 of 30.04.2004.
46   Official Journal L 89 of 05.04.2003. With the aim of preventing unlawful acts, the annex to the Regulation is classified for security reasons as an "EU restricted" document, which is not for the public domain.
47   Art. 1.
48   Official Journal L 10 of 16.01.2004.
49   Official Journal L 286 of 17.10.2006.

Single European Sky

The term "Single European Sky" means a package of measures to meet future capacity and air safety needs. They apply to both civilian and military sectors and cover the regulatory, economic, safety, environmental, technological and institutional aspects of aviation. The objective is to put an end to a way of organising air traffic management which had remained unchanged since the '60s and is one of the main reasons of air traffic congestion in the EU[50].

Regulation 549/2004[51] of the European Parliament and the Council forms the first part of the legislation package on air traffic management designed to create a Single European Sky by 31 December 2004. Implementation of the common transport policy requires an efficient air transport system allowing safe and regular operation of air transport services[52], thus facilitating the free movement of goods, persons and services, with beneficial consequences as regards air traffic delays and growth. The objective of the Single European Sky initiative is to enhance current safety standards and overall efficiency for general air traffic in Europe, to optimise capacity meeting the requirements of all airspace users and to minimise delays[53]. The "Single European Sky" package consists of this Framework Regulation plus three technical regulations on the provision of air navigation services (Regulation 550/2004[54]), organisation and use of the airspace (Regulation 551/2004[55]) and the interoperability of the European air traffic management network Regulation 552/2004[56]. These Regulations are designed, in particular, to improve and reinforce safety and to restructure the airspace on the basis of traffic instead of national frontiers.

Open Skies Agreements

The Commission has adopted a package of measures aimed at creating a legal framework for all bilateral relations between the EU and third countries in air transport. These measures aim to put an end to the uncertainty that prevails in the air transport sector following the judgment of the Court of Justice of the European Communities which declared the bilateral ("open skies") agreements between the United States and eight Member States to be incompatible with EU law[57]. Regulation 847/2004[58] forms part of the abovementioned

---

50   http://europa.eu/scadplus/leg/en/lvb/l24020.htm 20.3.2007.
51   Official Journal L 96 of 31.3.2004.
52   Preamble to the Regulation (1).
53   Art. 1.
54   Official Journal L 96 of 31.3.2004.
55   Official Journal L 96 of 31.3.2004.
56   Official Journal L 96 of 31.3.2004.
57   Cases C-466/98, C-467/98, C-468/98, C-469/98, C-471/98, C-472/98, C-475/98 and C-476/98. These agreements were concluded by Sweden, Finland, Belgium, Luxembourg, Austria, the Netherlands, Denmark and the United Kingdom after the Second World War. They authorise the United States to withdraw, suspend or limit the traffic rights of air carriers designated by the signatory States. According to the Court of Justice of the European Communities, these agreements infringe EU law in two respects. On the one hand, the presence of nationality clauses infringes the right of European airlines to non-discriminatory market access to routes between all Member States and third countries. On the other hand, only the EU has the authority to sign up to this type of commitment where agreements affect the exercise of EU competence, i.e. involve an area covered by EU legislation. The Court held that since the United States has the right to refuse a carrier, these agreements therefore constitute an obstacle to the freedom of establishment and freedom to provide services, as the opening of European skies to American companies is not reciprocal for all EU airlines. (http://europa.eu/scadplus/leg/en/lvb/l24260.htm 30.3.2007).
58   Official Journal L 157 of 30.04.2004.

proposed package of measures, laying down a set of principles designed to ensure an adequate exchange of information within the EU, so that Member States, in their bilateral relations with third countries in the area of air service, do not risk infringing EU law.

An effort to liberalise transatlantic air travel, has concluded in the recent approval of an Open Skies agreement between the EU and the United States by the EU Transport Commissioner. The agreement is set to come into effect in March 2008 promising to increase competition, though sceptic voices have been raised on the forthcoming conflict of interests and the long-term benefits if a second stage of negotiations on further liberalisation by 2010 is not achieved.

Data Protection

Since the events of 11 September 2001, airlines flying from and into US airports and also through US airspace must submit Passenger Name Records (PNR) available to Customs and Border Protection upon request. Next to the standard information such as name, address, date of birth, address, itinerary etc, PNR data contain additional information which the US authorities determine as being reasonable and necessary to ensure aviation safety. This information has been the subject of consideration in the light of EU concerns regarding the safeguarding of human rights, Community law procedures and international air law provisions, since it pertains to personal data revealing racial or ethnic origin, political opinions, religious or philosophical beliefs, trade union membership and information regarding the health or sex life of the passenger (Mendes 2006: 320–1).

Several European airlines contended that disclosing sensitive PNR data would violate EU data protection rules and human rights[59]. If the airlines did not transfer the said data to public authorities, they would face fines, and could lose landing or even transit rights, whereas if they did transfer such data, they would be violating European Human rights conventions and face fines. Directive 95/46[60] as amended by Regulation 1882/2003[61] further protects the rights and freedoms of individuals, obliging Member States to limit the freedom to process personal data. However, the mentioned Directive does not apply to the processing of personal data in the course of activities falling outside the scope of Community law, including 'in any case the processing operations concerning public security, defence and State security ... and the activities of the State in areas of criminal law[62]. This provision caused a controversy between the European Parliament and the European Council and Commission[63], which was resolved by the European Court of Justice which annulled in a ruling on 30 May 2006[64] the Commission's adequacy decision

---

59   Namely, the right of privacy (Article 7 of the European Union Charter of Fundamental Rights: "Everyone has the right to respect for his or her private and family life" – Official Journal C 364 of 18.12.2000) and protection of personal data (Art. 8 of Council of Europe Convention for the Protection of Human Rights and Fundamental Freedoms).

60   Directive 95/46/EC of the European Parliament and of the Council of 24 October 1995 on the protection of individuals with regard to the processing of personal data and on the free movement of such data, Official Journal L 281 of 23.11.1995.

61   Official Journal L 284 of 31.10.2003.

62   Art. 3.

63   The European Community and the United States signed an International Agreement on 28 May 2004 that made possible the transfer of air passenger data to the US, under certain conditions. It entered into force with immediate effect. This agreement was closely related to the Decision previously adopted by the European Commission, establishing the adequacy of US Bureau of Customs and Border Protection's personal data protection.

64   Case C – 317/04.

and the Council decision concerning the conclusion of the above mentioned international agreement (Mendes 2006). The need for prompt and adequate action during negotiations between the EU and US is necessary to ensure the protection of fundamental human rights, without posing any threats to leisure travel and tourism transactions.

CONCLUSIONS

This chapter explored legal issues in aviation with primary emphasis on the implications for leisure passengers. It should be apparent by the previous analysis that the prevailing legal framework is complex and occasionally contradictory raising serious and important debates about the effectiveness of consumer protection. The emergence of leisure tourism as a global phenomenon structurally intertwined with developments in the aviation sector will undoubtedly put serious pressures on the existing legal system; in fact, unless the latter is further simplified and homogenised across countries, this may become a significant impediment to further tourism growth. Therefore and although the need to carefully balance consumer welfare, producer and national (or even regional) interests is acknowledged and required, policymakers are urged to work towards this direction in collaboration with all the involved stakeholders in the air transport and tourism sectors.

7

Tourism and Aviation Policy: Exploring the Links

Peter Forsyth

INTRODUCTION

The links between tourism and aviation are becoming more explicitly recognised, and these links are having a role in governments' aviation policy formation. This is particularly so when it comes to international aviation, which, in many countries, remains a relatively tightly regulated industry. For most of its history, international aviation has been treated separately from other industries. International aviation agreements were negotiated between countries with no reference to any impacts they might have on other industries, especially tourism. However, the importance of international aviation for tourism and how restrictive aviation policies can limit tourism are being increasingly recognised, and many countries are revising their international aviation policies to take explicit recognition of tourism benefits.

The problem is a relevant one because of the ways in which international aviation has been regulated. Most international aviation routes were regulated very tightly, and strict limits were placed on the number of flights and seats that could be offered. Not surprisingly, this restricted tourism flows. Over the past two decades, many international routes have been liberalised, and one major region, Europe, was liberalised on a regional basis. Greater capacity and more competition led to lower fares and increased tourism flows. However, elsewhere, many routes remain restrictive, and limit tourism development. Progress towards liberalisation is slow because regulation is on a bilateral basis – the two countries at either end of a route determine the regulation which is applied to it. Thus two countries need to decide to liberalise a route, not just one.

With many countries nowadays, tourism benefits are becoming much more important as a factor influencing their international aviation policies. They realise that if they are to grow their tourism industries, lower international air fares are needed. Several countries now explicitly take tourism impacts into account when undertaking international aviation negotiations. A few countries have sought to measure how large tourism benefits might be, and to compare these benefits against impacts on home country airlines, and benefits to home country travellers. This tourism – aviation policy trade-off forms the focus of this chapter.

It begins with a review of aviation policy, and how it can impact on tourism flows. The next section looks at tourism benefits – what they consist of and how they might be measured. How the aviation–tourism trade-off has been handled in a number of cases around the world is reviewed in the following section. Finally, some conclusions are drawn.

TOURISM–AVIATION POLICY LINKS

Aviation is the preferred form of transport for much of tourism, especially long haul tourism and tourism to islands. It is particularly important for international tourism. Aviation is important in some countries for domestic tourism, especially for difficult to access regions. Unlike most other components of the tourism industry, it is an industry which has been subjected to extensive regulation, though this regulation has become much less restrictive than in the past. Most countries now have deregulated their domestic airline industries, and regulation is no longer a constraint on tourism flows. This is not the case with international tourism, where, despite considerable changes in many markets over the past four decades, several countries still regulate aviation tightly. The liberalisation which has taken place has led to the rapid growth in international tourism. As also argued by Papatheodorou in Chapter 5, for many countries, aviation policy is tourism policy – if they wish to stimulate the growth of tourism, the most effective single measure they can take is to liberalise their international aviation arrangements, if they can.

International aviation regulation has grown up as a web of bilateral agreements between countries. Ever since the end of the Second World War, countries have regulated air routes between themselves and partner countries. Thus, air travel between the UK and the US is governed by the air services agreements (ASAs) which the governments have put in place. These agreements specify which airlines (from which countries) can fly on the route, how many flights the airlines are permitted to operate, and which cities they may fly between (Doganis 2006). This is in marked contrast to international shipping, which is much more open.

In earlier post war years, regulation was invariably restrictive. Typically, only two airlines, one from each country, were permitted to operate. The number of flights or seats they were permitted to offer was limited, and mostly they were only allowed to fly to a small number of cities in the destination country. Other airlines from other countries were normally not permitted to offer seats on the route, though in some cases they were allowed to sell a small number of seats (thus a Singaporean airline flying to New York via Frankfurt might be able to pick up some Frankfurt–New York passengers). Very often, the seat capacity which was permitted to be offered was kept low relative to demand, resulting in high air fares. Naturally, this meant that international tourism, especially long haul tourism, was only accessible by the well off.

Over the years, there has been a gradual process of liberalisation of aviation. A number of countries took the step of opening up their domestic aviation markets to competition – the most significant example was when the US moved to deregulate in the late 1970s (Morrison and Winston 1986). International liberalisation has been a much more gradual process, with changes taking place on a country-by-country, route-by-route basis. Some countries, like the US and Singapore, decided to seek to liberalise most of their international routes, where their country partners were in agreement- often they were not (Oum and Yu 2000). Thus, US–Singapore aviation has been relatively unrestrictive for a long time, though Singapore–UK and US–UK markets have been less open, and are currently being further liberalised. This liberalisation has sometimes, though not always been linked to tourism development; Singapore saw easy access via air as being essential to its development as a tourism destination, though the US probably did not consider tourism objectives into its decisions to any great extent.

The process of liberalisation is the outcome of pressures from different interests in economies. Consumer interests support liberalisation, to encourage lower fares. As against this, airlines often oppose liberalisation, since more competition means lower market shares and less profit from them. Airlines are, however, keen to break into markets dominated by other airlines. Labour interests usually oppose concessions being granted to foreign airlines, since this may lead to less employment in the airline industry at home. Finally, tourism interests are beginning to assert themselves. The home tourism industry will often see its development as being constrained by highly regulated airline markets, and it will push for opening up the market to stimulate the flow of inbound tourism.

Thus, in some cases, the pressure for opening up aviation markets has been from tourism industries. A good example was the air charter boom to Spain from the 1960s on. The Spanish government realised that, if its potential as a tourism destination for holidaymakers from Northern Europe were to be realised, tourists would need to have access to low fares. Thus, it was prepared to open up air routes in to Spain to charter airlines, most of which were foreign owned, operating a lower cost basis than normal scheduled airlines, to enable lower fares to become a reality. Some South East Asian countries, such as Singapore and Thailand, sought to encourage tourists to visit them, and they were prepared to open up their air routes to achieve this. By contrast, most countries of South America have been avowedly keen to attract tourism, but they have been unwilling to take the step of liberalising their air routes- the result is that tourists do not come.

Countries vary in their attitudes towards liberalisation, and it is this that makes progress towards a more liberal environment slow. When countries disagree about regulation on a route, the status quo tends to prevail, and this usually means that restrictions remain. Some countries are explicitly liberal, and seek to open up their airline markets wherever their partners agree. These countries include the US, Singapore, New Zealand, the United Arab Emirates and Chile. Often these countries see a liberal environment as being helpful to the development of their aviation and tourism industries. Other countries are traditionally more restrictive – these include Italy, Japan, China, the Philippines and African and South American countries. In between the extremes, there are a number of countries which might be described as pragmatic – willing to liberalise, but only if they see advantage in so doing. These include the UK, Australia, Canada and several European and South East Asian countries.

These countries are likely to look at liberalisation on a case by case basis, and to make an assessment whether a proposal to open up a particular route will be in their overall interests. Sometimes countries explicitly recognise tourism benefits, and they make a judgmental assessment of this, but increasingly lately, these countries have made quantitative assessments of the costs and benefits of proposals.

Liberalisation which enables airlines to operate more capacity on the market, and which allows more airlines to serve it, will lead to stronger competition between airlines, and lower fares. Outbound travellers from the home country will gain from the lower fares. The home country airlines will normally lose, at least in the short run, since they will face lower profit margins and individual airlines could well suffer a reduction in their market share (though the market share of all of a country's airlines on the route could also rise). There is often scope for the airlines to reduce their costs, in the medium to longer term, and this limits the cost to them. The balance of gains and losses to a country could go either way – for example, if a country's airlines have a large market share, but few of the country's residents travel on it, liberalisation may result in a larger loss to airlines than gain to consumers. However, in addition to these costs and benefits, there will be an impact on tourism to the country. If tourism brings economic benefits, then additional tourism stimulated by liberalisation will be a factor in favour of liberalisation. Countries are now attempting to assess how large the impacts on tourism will be, and how much they might gain from increased inbound tourism.

While regulatory arrangements represent the most important way in which aviation impacts on tourism flows, countries sometimes impose other aviation level policies which impact on tourism. In particular, several countries are now imposing taxes on air travel. In some cases, these take the form of charges for services, such as those at airports, which are in excess of the costs of supplying the services – some governments see tourism as a cash cow. In other cases, there are explicit aviation taxes being levied. Controversial examples of these are the UK Air Passenger Duty (APD), and the French anti-poverty tax levied on air passengers. Both taxes are explicitly revenue raising taxes, though the UK APD is claimed by the government to be an environmental levy. Taxes at the aviation level are not very widespread, though they are perhaps becoming more so, as governments realise that they can get foreign tourists to pay part of the tax. The downside is that these taxes are reducing tourism, and thus the gains that countries are enjoying from it.

MEASURING TOURISM BENEFITS

Most countries regard an increase in inbound tourism expenditure as being positive for their economies. In spite of this, there has been little by way of rigorous assessment of the economic benefits of tourism.

An increase in inbound tourism expenditure is an increase in exports of a country. While popular opinion still probably regards additional exports as desirable, most economists would regard this view as a throwback to the days of mercantilism. Increased exports are neither particularly positive nor negative for the economy. It is possible that increased exports of a particular kind, for example, of tourism services, could be positive for the economy, but the case needs to be made.

One possibility is that inbound tourism stimulates economic activity in the economy (Forsyth 2006). For this to happen, it would be necessary that the economy has some slack – if there is full employment, the scope for increasing output is limited (though there will be some scope for using additional capital and substituting capital for labour). This stimulatory effect is more likely to be strong if the economy has a fixed exchange rate, which is no longer the case for most or all developed countries. With a flexible exchange rate, the tourism export boom will lead to upward pressure on the exchange rate, which discourages other exports, and encourages imports. Developing countries would be most likely to enjoy a positive stimulus from additional inbound tourism expenditure – they often have fixed or managed exchange rates, and often have a slack labour market.

The other main possibility is that a country gains through selling tourism services at prices which are above the cost of supplying them. Most tourism industries are fairly competitive, and prices are close to cost. However, some taxes are levied on tourism products, both directly and indirectly. Unlike most exports, tourism is usually subject to taxes like the Value Added Tax (VAT) or Goods and Services Tax (GST) levied in most developed countries. While tourists can sometimes obtain rebates of VAT/GST for some of their purchases, much of what they buy is still taxed- thus tourism as an export industry is relatively highly taxed. This means that, in a sense, the economy makes a profit from selling to tourists. The extent to which this is the case depends on how taxes are levied both directly and indirectly on tourism – on the pattern of distortions (including taxes, subsidies and high profit margins in less competitive markets) in the economy which result in prices not being equal to costs. If there is no macro economic stimulation of the economy or increase in overall output of the economy, a country can still gain from additional tourism exports. The net gain to the economy might be of the order of 5–20 per cent of the additional expenditure (see below), depending on the taxes and other distortions present.

In addition to these possibilities, tourism expenditure may be positive for the economy in other ways. One is through the terms of trade effect. An increase in export demand can push up export prices, if resources are in limited supply. Many specific tourism resources are limited – for example, beaches or ski fields. As demand for them increases, the prices for the preferred locations grow. As a result, a country will gain increased revenues from its tourism exports. This will be benefit to the economy. Another source of benefit could be through agglomeration economies. As tourism to a district grows, the quality of the product may increase. The range of attractions provided will increase, and a greater variety of tastes can be catered for. Transport services in and to the district become more frequent and convenient. Measuring such economies would be difficult, and it is not clear that they would be large relative to expenditure. In addition, they need to be set against additional costs resulting from congestion. Additional tourism, especially to crowded locations, leads to delays and discomfort, along with less reliable services.

The benefits of additional tourism expenditure are likely to be greater, proportionally, at the regional than the national level. When tourism is stimulated into a region, for example by new low cost carrier (LCC) services to a regional airport, economic activity in the region will be stimulated. It is easy for economic activity to expand, because it can attract resources, such as labour, from other regions of the economy. A boom in one region will lead to a reduction in economic activity in other regions, unless there are slack resources, such as unemployment of labour. Thus the addition to economic activity in the region will almost always be well in excess of the impact on the country as a whole. It is important to distinguish between the impact on economic activity, for example as measured by change in GDP at the regional level, and the net benefit to the region – as always, additional production relies on additional inputs, which have a cost. Nonetheless, additional economic activity will normally bring positive economic benefit to a region.

If increased inbound tourism to a country or region is to be regarded as a positive economic benefit, what of additional outbound tourism? Lower air fares stimulate additional outbound tourism as well as inbound tourism- this will be particularly so for tourism source markets such as the UK and Germany. Additional outbound tourism from an economy could lead to negative macroeconomic impacts – if the economy is slack, a reduction in domestic spending could be negative for the economy. When there is no macroeconomic problem- there is reasonably full employment, additional outbound tourism will lead to a change in composition of expenditure which could be negative for the economy. Tourists switch from spending on goods and services which are taxed in the home economy to foreign travel, which is not taxed by the home government. Just as inbound tourism expenditure can bring economic benefits, outbound tourism can have economic costs. As against this, however, there will be gains to the outbound tourists themselves – they will gain from lower cost trips, and as long as the costs to the economy of outbound tourism are proportionally not large (as will be argued to be the case below), the gains to travellers will normally outweigh other costs to the economy.

Thus, overall, there are sound reasons for believing that additional inbound tourism expenditure will be positive for an economy. Many countries act as though they believe this- they promote tourism extensively, and many tailor their aviation policies so as to attract tourism. From a policy perspective, the critical question is how large these benefits from tourism are. In determining a policy stance, for example, whether to liberalise an air route, tourism benefits must be set against other costs. While other costs and benefits of liberalisation have been quantified (e.g. see Gillen, Harris and Oum 1996), tourism benefits have not. How large tourism benefits are will determine which policies should be pursued.

There has been relatively little rigorous attempt to measure the economic benefits of tourism. Many consider these benefits to be large, especially in relation to expenditure. This perception has often been gained from the use of Input Output models, which usually indicate that the impact on output will be considerably greater than the change in expenditure – proponents of tourism developments typically claim large "benefits" from additional tourism. However Input Output techniques grossly overstate the impacts on output, because they only account for the positive effects, and ignore the negative effects, which are of a comparable size. Furthermore, as noted above, the net benefits to the economy will normally be much less than the changes in the value of the output. Recently there have been some attempts to measure tourism benefits more rigorously (Forsyth 2006).

One approach is the partial equilibrium one. This involves comparing the revenues that an economy gains from tourism with the costs of providing for it. If, for example, the goods and services purchased by tourism are taxed, the cost is less than the revenues gained – the country makes a profit out of selling to tourists. Economists have used rules of thumb to obtain measures of the benefits from additional tourism expenditure (for an example, see Victorian Auditor General's Office 2007).

This approach is limited in that it can focus on some of the benefits and costs of tourism. It does not pick up any benefits from macroeconomic stimulation of the economy, nor does it pick up any terms of trade effects. Recently, economists have been using computable general equilibrium (CGE) models of economies to explore tourism questions (Adams and Parmenter 1995). CGE models are complete models of the economy, with resource constraints, factor and product markets, and consumer and government behaviour built in. They are now extensively used in policy analysis in many countries (Dixon and Parmenter 1996). They provide a good way of measuring how tourism changes, such as additional inbound tourism due to air transport liberalisation, can affect the economy in terms of GDP and employment. Typically they find that the impacts on GDP are very much smaller than those estimated using the more popular Input Output approach. Moreover, impacts on GDP are not the same as net economic benefits, since the costs of producing the extra GDP are not taken into account. However, economic benefit measures can be developed using the CGE model framework.

Thus, rigorous work on measuring the economic benefits of tourism is only beginning and it is showing the way to developing measures which are of use in policy decisions. In economies with full employment, the net economic gains from additional inbound tourism expenditure are likely to be small, say around 10 per cent of the initial expenditure change, but positive. While further work is needed to produce more reliable estimates, the large economic benefits which are sometimes claimed for tourism must be treated with suspicion.

AVIATION–TOURISM POLICY TRADE-OFFS: SOME EXAMPLES

Countries face trade-offs when setting their aviation and tourism policies. They are under pressure from their airlines to expand their opportunities or to protect them from competition, but most countries also wish to develop their tourism industries. For some countries the trade-offs are quite stark. For example, in the South Pacific, aviation is critical to tourism, but long thin routes and small home country airlines make provision of competitive services difficult (see Chapter 25 by Taumoepeau), and several countries have chosen to rely on services provided by foreign countries' airlines. On the other hand, aviation and tourism policies have not conflicted much for a country like Mauritius, which has chosen to go for smaller numbers of high yield tourists, and this has not necessitated airline liberalisation (see Chapter 24 by Seetaram). Here, a number of situations where countries have had to balance aviation with tourism interests in determining their aviation policies.

The European Charter Boom

The European charter boom of the 1960s and 1970s is an early example of where countries were prepared to trade off advantages for their airlines against tourism development. Countries such as Spain realised that they could access Northern European tourists seeking beach holidays, but only if air fares were lower than those offered by scheduled airlines. By opening up their routes to charter airlines they were able to achieve this. Charter airlines operated under restrictive conditions, which limited the extent to which they competed with the existing scheduled airlines, and they were able to achieve high load factors and offer low fares (Doganis 2006). Relatively free entry into the charter segment meant that the market was competitive and costs were kept low. The consequence of this was a boom in tourism from Northern to Southern Europe, especially Spain. Most of the charter airlines were owned in the origin countries, such as the UK and Germany. Thus Spain was prepared to sacrifice its aviation interests, since its airlines had only a relatively small share of the traffic into Spain, but it succeeded in stimulating its tourism industry. With European liberalisation, and the growth of LCCs, charter airlines are only now losing their rationale and market share.

South East Asian Airlines and Sixth Freedom Routes

Another early example of where a country had to choose between protecting its airline or allowing tourism development arose with the long haul route between Australia and Europe in the late 1970s and early 1980s (Findlay 1985). Up to this time, flights on this route had been dominated by the European and Australian airlines. However, the airlines of the South East Asian countries, such as Singapore Airlines, gradually had become larger and more competitive, and they sought to break into the Europe–Australia market. They could do this on a sixth freedom basis – they had rights to fly from Australia to SE Asia, and rights to fly from SE Asia to Europe, and putting these together, they could fly passengers from Europe to Australia. However, their entry would undercut the European and Australian airlines, making it difficult for them to survive. Initially, the Australian government tried to restrict their access to the Europe route, by limiting capacity from SE Asia to Australia to the amount of demand for this route, thereby giving them limited scope to carry Australia–Europe travellers. However, the government was also under pressure from Australian travellers, who wanted cheap flights to Europe. Eventually, the Australian government decided that cheap fares for outbound Australian tourists, and for inbound European tourism to Australia was more important than protecting the home airline and it ceased to control capacity on the SE Asia Australia routes. After this, European travel to Australia began to grow significantly. The Australian carrier was able to adapt and it survives on the route, though the majority of traffic now between Europe and Australia is carried by sixth freedom carriers, especially those from S E Asia and from the Middle East as argued by O' Connell in Chapter 22.

The Australia–US/Singapore Airlines Case

In 2005, Singapore Airlines, which has extensive services to Australia, sought permission from the Australian government to operate services between Australia and the US (Forsyth 2006). Currently, this route is dominated by Qantas and United Airlines, and is highly profitable. The request was unusual in that it is very rare for an airline to be allowed to fly directly between two foreign countries except perhaps on a very limited basis (e.g. within Europe since liberalisation). The case is interesting because it is one of the first examples of where quantitative estimates of tourism benefits were used in the evaluation of the proposition. If Singapore Airlines were allowed to fly the route, the Australian airline would lose market share and profits. As against this, air fares would fall, and this would be of benefit to Australian travellers, and tourism flows in both directions would increase (in this situation, it was likely that the growth of inbound tourism to Australia would exceed the outbound to the US). Both the Australian government and Singapore Airlines commissioned modelling work to estimate how large the tourism benefits to Australia would be. In the end, the government refused permission, partly because it was not convinced that the tourism benefits would be sufficient to offset the costs to the Australian airline.

ASEAN Aviation Liberalisation

The dilemmas facing the ASEAN community are a good example of the conflicts between aviation and tourism policy (See Oum and Yu 2000; Forsyth, King and Rodolfo 2006). The Association of South East Asian Nations (ASEAN) is an economic community of ten nations. These countries are of different sizes and levels of development. Overall, they are growing rapidly, though performance is mixed. Aviation policies are set by the individual countries, though the community is trying to move towards European style regional open skies.

The aviation policies of the ASEAN countries are mixed. Some countries, like Singapore and Thailand, have pursued generally liberal policies. Some countries, such as Vietnam, have had restrictive policies, though they are liberalising. Malaysia and Indonesia are sometimes liberal, and sometimes restrictive. Singapore's liberal policies have allowed Singapore to develop as a major aviation hub, and they have fostered the growth of short stay stopover tourism. The tourism boom in Thailand has been made possible by its liberal aviation policies. By contrast, tourism in the Philippines has been relatively stagnant, in spite of the country having great tourism potential. Restrictive aviation policies have made the country relatively expensive to visit, and services are less frequent and convenient than those to competitor destinations. The fortunes of the countries' tourism industries depend a lot on how open the countries' aviation policies are.

Intra ASEAN liberalisation is a major issue for the community. ASEAN would like to move to internal open skies, along the lines of the European model. However, progress has been very slow, and established airline interests have opposed change. Within ASEAN, there has been a LCC boom, with several successful airlines such as AirAsia becoming established. These airlines would like to fly freely within ASEAN, but their aspirations on many routes have been blocked. With rising real incomes, the prospects for intra ASEAN tourism are very good, however this potential is not being realised because of slow progress towards aviation liberalisation.

Regional Tourism and Airport Policy

Tourism–aviation trade-offs do not just arise at the national level – they can be quite evident at the regional level. Regional airport policies can be important in stimulating tourism growth in a region. With the opening up of the European aviation market, regional airports have taken on a more important role. LCCs have grown rapidly, but often they find it difficult to gain access to the major city airports. In addition, they are quite price-sensitive to airport charges, and their passengers are willing to travel further to an airport to get a low fare. Thus, several LCCs have been willing to shop around amongst the regional airports for a good deal. Regional governments have realised that this presents an opportunity to stimulate tourism. If their airports can attract services by LCCs, the passengers will spend some of their time within the region, thereby creating tourism benefits (Barrett 2004a).

As a consequence, many regional governments have a policy of attracting LCCs to their airports, as also argued by Echevarne in Chapter 14. To win services, some are willing to subsidise their airports. From the perspective of the regional government, the issues that need to be resolved include how large the tourism benefits will be, and what the cost of attracting LCCs will be. The policy issue goes beyond the regional government. More flights to a regional airport, and more tourism expenditure in the region, come, at least to some extent, at a cost of less traffic to other airports, and less tourism expenditure in other regions. Where city airports are already very busy, and cities are congested, this presents no problem. However, when it leads to a subsidy war between regional governments to win footloose tourists, there can be a loss to the nation as a whole. Hence, bodies such as the European Commission are concerned about the regional airport subsidy issue (Barbot 2006).

Aviation, Environmental Policies and Tourism

The recognition of the environmental costs of aviation is posing new policy trade-offs for governments. It is recognised that aviation does create environmental externalities, especially greenhouse gas emissions, and that policies to control for these will increase the costs of aviation. This in turn will lead to increases in air fares, and a reduction in tourism flows. Both short haul and long haul aviation will be affected, though the absolute price increases for long haul flights could be significant and there are few substitutes for aviation in long haul tourism. Some governments have imposed taxes on aviation, ostensibly linked to its environmental costs – an example of this is the UK's Air Passenger Duty (APD), which many regard as primarily a revenue raising duty. Both Europe and Australia are proposing to incorporate aviation within an emissions trading scheme. Doing so could be an efficient way of meeting greenhouse gas reduction targets, though it has a cost in terms of reduced tourism. In particular, countries like Australia are concerned that they will lose tourists to other countries which do not impose climate change policies. The tourism costs of such measures, which come about to a significant though not exclusive extent because of their impacts on aviation, are an issue with which countries have yet to come to terms with as also discussed by Daley *et al.* in Chapter 18.

CONCLUSIONS

While the links between aviation and tourism are obvious, they have not been given much attention. Countries are more aware of their tourism industries, and they are keen to promote tourism, which they see as a source of economic benefits. Quite often, tourism is constrained by restrictive international aviation regulation. There has been a gradual trend towards liberalisation, and this has stimulated tourism, but this regulation still acts as a constraint.

Countries too are becoming more aware of the tourism and aviation trade-offs. Opening up markets is generally good for tourism, but home country airlines are likely to suffer, especially in the short term. Thus, countries have to strike a balance between the home country airline industries, benefits to home country travellers, and benefits from increased inbound tourism. Nowadays, several countries are trying to quantify the costs and benefits of aviation liberalisation. While the costs and benefits to airlines and home country passengers are readily estimated, the size of the economic benefits from increased inbound tourism is less well documented. This is an area in which research is beginning to produce results, and it has the potential to enable international aviation policy choices to be made on a much better informed basis.

PART III

Airline Issues

8

The Future of Charter Operations

George Williams

INTRODUCTION

This is the first in a series of five chapters dealing with airline issues in the context of leisure travel. In particular, the present chapter focuses on charter services, which are gradually being replaced by scheduled operations in many parts of the world as a result of air transport liberalisation. The same has occurred in Europe, but the sheer scale of the continent's charter market has meant that this remains large.[1] Much of the European charter market involves short to medium distance journeys, with the average sector flown by the larger charter carriers being typically around 2,500 km. Low cost scheduled airlines not surprisingly have taken the opportunity to enter the shorter distanced routes and have been able to capture many of these passengers. The greater flexibility offered to the traveller by low cost airlines particularly in respect of service frequency, their easily accessed fares and their success at convincing customers that they offer the lowest prices have been the key factors in bringing about this transformation (Williams 2001).

Section two of the chapter discusses the serious threat posed by the LCC to charter operators and how the latter reacted against this offensive. Section three then analyses the implications of consolidation in the European tour operations industry and section four identifies Europe's charter airlines and their main markets. This is followed by section five which examines the factors influencing the operating and economic performance of charter carriers. Finally, section six summarises and concludes with the way forward for these airline operations.

CHARTER RESPONSE TO THE LCC OFFENSIVE

A good example of the targeting of charter passengers by low cost carriers is shown by what has happened in respect of traffic to the UK's largest short-haul holiday destination, Malaga in southern Spain. Figure 8.1 shows the traffic split between scheduled and charter carriers between UK airports and Malaga between 1990 and 2006. Charter traffic peaked in 2000 with 2.4 million passenger journeys undertaken, but by 2006 this had fallen to less than 900,000. By contrast, scheduled traffic had quadrupled over the same period to over 4 million, nearly all of the increase attributable to low cost airlines.

---

1   Europe accounts for over 90 per cent of the world's non-scheduled passenger traffic, the majority of this being holiday travellers carried by subsidiaries of the large tour operating companies.

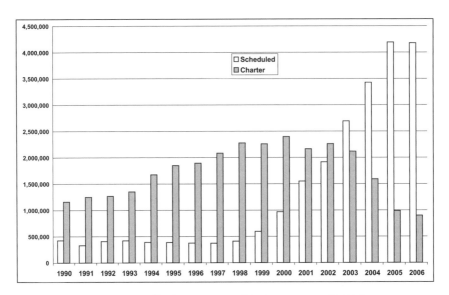

FIGURE 8.1   Passenger traffic between UK airports and Malaga
Source: UK CAA, 1990–2006.

In response to this encroachment of their traditional short haul markets charter operators have responded in different ways, as is apparent from the changes between 2000 and 2006 in the charter/scheduled traffic mix of the UK's five largest charter operators shown in Figure 8.2. While First Choice and Thomas Cook have steered clear of operating scheduled services[2], Monarch, MyTravel and Thomson have done so with varying degrees of success. Monarch has undergone the largest transformation, with more half of its passengers now carried on its scheduled services. The airline had begun operating scheduled services to a small number of its traditional holiday charter destinations in Spain and Portugal back in 1983, but has considerably expanded its scheduled offerings since 2000. While the other four carriers were mainly engaged in carrying their tour operating parents' clientele, Monarch provided charter flights for many tour operators. As the demand for short haul charter services declined, the large, vertically integrated tour operators reduced capacity, resulting in them carrying a much higher proportion of their customers on in-house airlines (*Airfinance Journal* 2005). While Monarch simply expanded its scheduled operations, MyTravel and Thomson opted to establish subsidiary companies to operate low cost, scheduled services.

MyTravel's incursion into the low cost scheduled market began in October 2002 in the guise of MyTravelLite and lasted three years before being subsumed into the charter airline, at a time when the MyTravel Goup was experiencing severe financial difficulties. Thomsonfly emerged two years later, the scheduled low cost arm of the Thomson Group, in effect a subsidiary of its charter carrier, Britannia Airways[3].

First Choice's strategy of reducing its dependence on short haul mainstream holiday destinations, developing a better quality long haul product, and acquiring specialist niche market tour operators has proved successful (Air Transport World 2005). Table 8.1 gives details of the company's share of passengers by length of haul between 2003 and 2006.

---

2   Aside that is from operating to a small number of destinations for regulatory reasons.
3   The charter airline Britannia adopted the Thomsonfly name in 2005.

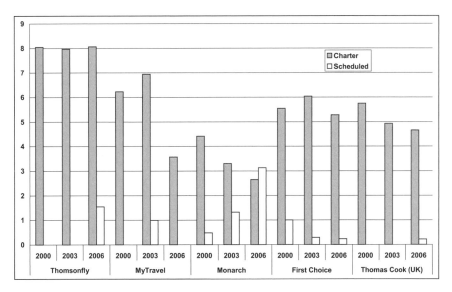

FIGURE 8.2   Charter/scheduled passenger traffic mix (millions)

Source: UK CAA, 2000, 2003, 2006.

TABLE 8.1   Split of First Choice passengers by length of haul

	Short-haul (%)	Medium-haul (%)	Long-haul (%)	Total (000)
2003	44.6	49.8	5.6	2,906
2004	41.0	52.8	6.2	2,809
2005	36.5	56.4	7.1	2,703
2006	34.4	55.3	10.3	2,542

Source: First Choice Annual Reports.

CONSOLIDATION OF EUROPEAN TOUR OPERATORS

Consolidation of the tour operating market in Europe in order to take advantage of scale economies and to attempt to control supply has been evident since the 1980s, with cross-border mergers and acquisitions becoming a regular feature in the 1990s. It has been in the very recent past however that the more substantial phase of this industry restructuring has taken place, with the emergence of two tour operating pan-European giants, TUI and Thomas Cook. At the end of the 1990s four tour operating organisations accounted for over 80 per cent of demand in Germany and the UK, the largest markets in Europe (Table 8.2). A major development in 2000 was the acquisition by TUI of the UK's Thomson Group, followed a year later by C&N's purchase of Thomas Cook. On completion of these mergers, the largest tour operators and their charter airline subsidiaries were as shown in Table 8.3. The turnover in 2004 of the largest ten travel groups in Europe is shown in Figure 8.3.

TABLE 8.2   Europe's major tour operating markets in the late 1990s

UK		Germany	
Tour Operator	Market Share	Tour Operator	Market Share
Airtours*	25%	TUI	27%
Thomson	23%	C&N	23%
Thomas Cook	18%	LTU	20%
First Choice	15%	Frosch Touristik	6%

Source: Williams (2001). * Renamed MyTravel in 2002.

TABLE 8.3   Charter airline subsidiaries of Europe's largest tour operators in 2004

TUI	Thomas Cook	MyTravel	REWE*	First Choice	Iberostar	Kuoni
Britannia	Condor	MyTravel	LTU**	First Choice	Iberworld	Edelweiss
Britannia Nordic	Condor Berlin	MyTravel A/S				Novair
Corsair	SunExpress					
Hapag-Lloyd	Thomas Cook (Belgium)					
	Thomas Cook (UK)					

* REWE sold its 40% shareholding in 2006. ** LTU was acquired by Air Berlin in 2007.

The policy of tour operating groups adopting common branding for the various elements of their businesses became evident in respect to their charter subsidiaries from 2004, with TUI for example appending the word "fly" to the names of its airlines. Most recently, TUI has announced that all of its airline subsidiaries will adopt the name TUIfly from 2008 (Flight International 2007a).

A further round of consolidation has occurred in 2007 with the mergers of TUI and First Choice and that of Thomas Cook and MyTravel. The merged companies are adopting the names TUI Travel and Thomas Cook respectively, with the MyTravel Airways fleet being subsumed into Thomas Cook Airlines. It has yet to be announced whether the First Choice fleet will adopt the TUIfly name. In the case of the Thomas Cook merger with MyTravel, Thomas Cook's owner, retailer KarstadtQuelle, will hold 52 per cent of the shares and MyTravel 48 per cent. Since these developments took place in the early part of 2007, a yet further round of consolidation involving the charter sector in Germany has occurred with Air Berlin acquiring LTU[4] and most recently with Thomas Cook announcing the sale of its 75 per cent shareholding in Condor also to Air Berlin (to be completed in 2009). The 25 per cent shareholding in Condor held by Lufthansa will be acquired by Thomas Cook

---

4   The integration of LTU into the Air Berlin group is expected to yield synergy savings of €70–100m (Low Fare and Regional Airlines 2007).

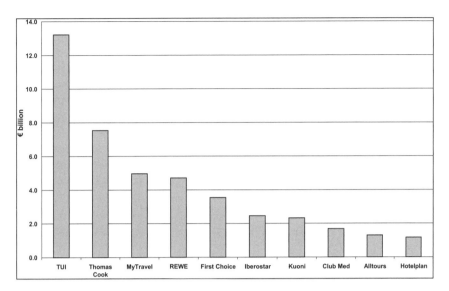

FIGURE 8.3   Europe's top ten travel groups' turnover in 2004

Source: Kuoni Annual Report, 2005.

during 2009 and sold on to Air Berlin in 2010. In exchange, Thomas Cook will hold up to a 30 per cent shareholding in Air Berlin. This major restructuring of Europe's large tour operators and their charter flight suppliers results, in large measure, from the activities of low cost scheduled carriers.

The financial performances of the major tour operating groups reveal the difficult trading conditions that several have faced since 2000 and provide the reasoning behind the continuing trend of supplier concentration. The aim of the latest mergers is to achieve annual cost synergies totalling €140 million in the case of the Thomas Cook Group and €146 million for TUI Travel. The recent financial performance of the leading tour operating groups is shown in Table 8.4. TUI Group's Tourism division earnings increased substantially in 2004 and have continued to grow since then, albeit by more modest amounts. Earnings in 2006 yielded an operating margin of 2.8 per cent. While earnings in 2006 increased by 36 per cent to €89.5 million in the Central Europe division, TUI recorded a loss of €53.7 million in its Western division and a reduction in its Northern Europe division earnings of €21.9 million.

The Thomas Cook Group returned to profit in 2005 after incurring losses over the previous four years. In 2006, the group increased its earnings to €205.8 million, up by over €50 million compared to the previous year. Its improved financial performance was due to a major restructuring involving a continued reduction in staffing (down from 23,306 in 2005 to 19,775 in 2006).

Of the three largest tour operators, MyTravel has performed the worst over the past five years (Aviation Strategy 2004). However, since 2004 as a result of significant downsizing it has managed to improve its financial performance. Overall, the group's turnover has fallen by 36 per cent since 2002. By contrast, First Choice has continued to increase its earnings over the five years from 2002 to 2006, achieving an operating margin of 4.3 per cent in 2006.

TABLE 8.4   Financial performance of major tour operating groups

	TUI Tourism		Thomas Cook Group		MyTravel		First Choice	
	Earnings (€m)	Turnover (€m)	Earnings (€m)	Turnover (€m)	Earnings (£m)	Turnover (£m)	Earnings (£m)	Turnover (£m)
2002	336	12416	(26.8)	8059	(11.9)	4379	75.7	2183
2003	208	12671	(151.0)	7242	(411.3)	4190	90.7	2249
2004	353	13319	(34.5)	7479	(47.1)	3204	98.6	2318
2005	365	14097	154.4	7661	50.2	2910	115.0	2442
2006	394	14084	205.8	7780	61.6	2797	117.4	2715

Sources: Annual Reports of TUI Group, Thomas Cook Group, MyTravel, and First Choice.

EUROPE'S CHARTER AIRLINES AND MAIN CHARTER MARKETS

At the beginning of 2007, there were 97 charter airlines based in Europe[5] operating commercial services with aircraft seating over 50 passengers[6]. The average length of time these carriers have been in existence is 11 years. Table 8.5 provides a listing of the 97 carriers; indicating country of registration, date established, fleet size and ownership. As may be seen, the countries with the largest number of passenger charter airlines are Turkey (13), Spain (12) and the UK (11). The fleets operated by the 97 airlines totalled 795 aircraft, of which 208 were flown by UK carriers, 128 by German carriers, 103 by Turkish carriers and 71 by Spanish companies. The charter airlines owned by tour operators accounted for 42 per cent of these aircraft.

As is apparent from Figure 8.4, demand for short haul charter flights from the UK has fallen by 20 per cent between 2003 and 2006 resulting from the dramatic growth in services offered by low cost scheduled airlines. This decrease has been partly offset by a 58 per cent increase in passengers flying to longer haul destinations from the UK over the same period. It is apparent from Figure 8.5 that the bulk of the decline in short haul charter flying has occurred on routes to Spanish and Portuguese holiday destinations. Of the nearly 20 million passenger trips made between the UK and Spain in 2003, some 8 million were to and from the Canary islands (4–5 hours flying time from the UK). The decrease to less than 14 million journeys in 2006 has nearly all involved shorter distance trips to mainland Spain and the Balearic islands in the Mediterranean. The same trend is apparent in traffic between the UK and Portugal, albeit involving much smaller numbers of passengers. The decline in charter traffic between the UK and Greece is more likely to be the result of passengers switching to other holiday destinations rather than them transferring to scheduled services provided by low cost airlines given the small number of LCC operations between the two countries.

The provision of long haul services by low cost scheduled airlines from the UK is a very recent phenomenon. Figure 8.6 shows the changes in traffic to long haul destinations from

---

5   Europe here includes the 27 EU Member States, Croatia, Iceland, Norway, Switzerland and Turkey.
6   Air Berlin is excluded from this listing, given its low cost scheduled services focus. It does, however, continue to operate a significant number of charter services.

TABLE 8.5   Europe's passenger charter airlines in 2007

		Established	Fleet	Ownership
Austria	LTU Austria	2004	1	Air Berlin
	MAP	2002	9	Independent
Belgium	Jetairfly	2004	9	TUI
	Thomas Cook (Belgium)	2002	6	Thomas Cook
Bulgaria	BHAir	2001	7	Balkan Holidays
	Bulgarian Air Charter	2000	11	Independent
	VIA	1990	3	Independent
Croatia	Air Adriatic	2000	6	Independent
	Dubrovnik Airline	2005	5	Independent
	Trade Air	1994	2	Independent
Cyprus	Eurocypria	1990	4	Cyprus Airways
Czech	Travel Service Czech	1997	7	Canaria Travel
Denmark	MyTravel A/S	1994	11	Thomas Cook
Finland	Air Finland	2002	3	Independent
France	Aigle Azur	1970	9	Independent
	Air Mediterranee	1997	9	Independent
	Axis Airways	2001	4	Independent
	Blue Line	2002	4	Independent
	Corsairfly	1981	11	TUI
	Eagle Aviation	1999	4	Independent
	XL Airways France	1995	5	XL Leisure Group
Germany	Blue Wings	2002	5	Independent
	Condor	1955	22	Thomas Cook
	Condor Berlin	1997	14	Thomas Cook
	Hamburg Int'al	1998	7	Independent
	LTU	1955	27	Air Berlin
	TUIfly.com	1972	50	TUI
	XL Airways Germany	2006	3	XL Leisure Group
Greece	Alexandair	2005	1	Independent
	Hellas Jet	2002	1	Independent
	Hellenic Imperial A/ways	2006	1	Independent
	Sky Wings	2004	1	Independent
Hungary	Travel Service Hungary	2001	1	Travel Service

TABLE 8.5 (continued)

Iceland	Air Atlanta Icelandic	1986	23	Avion Group
	Jet X	2004	3	Independent
Italy	Air Europe	1989	1	Volare Group
	Air Italy	2005	4	Independent
	Blue Panorama	1998	6	Independent
	Eurofly	1989	13	Independent
	Itali Airlines	2003	3	Independent
	Livingston	2003	6	Gruppo Ventaglio
	Neos	2001	6	AlpiTour Group
Latvia	LAT Charter	1993	2	Independent
Lithuania	Aurela	1996	2	Independent
Netherlands	Arkefly	2004	5	TUI
	Interstate Airlines	2005	1	Independent
	Martinair	1958	15	KLM 50%
	Transavia	1966	27	KLM
Poland	Prima	2005	1	Independent
	White Eagle	1992	3	Independent
Portugal	EuroAtlantic	1993	7	Independent
	Luzair	2000	2	Independent
	White	2000	1	TAP
Romania	Jetran Air	2005	6	Independent
	Romavia	1991	5	Independent
Spain	Airclass Airways	2003	2	Independent
	Audeli	2006	7	Group Gestair
	Flightline SL	2006	2	Flightline
	Futura	1989	23	Independent
	Girjet	2002	7	Independent
	Hola	2002	4	Independent
	Iberworld	1998	10	Grupo Iberostar
	LTE	1987	5	Independent
	Privilege Style	2003	1	Independent
	Pullmantur Air	2003	3	Groupo Marsans
	Swiftair	1986	7	Independent

TABLE 8.5 (continued)

Sweden	Fly Nordic	2004	9	Independent
	Novair	1997	5	Kuoni
	TUIfly Nordic	1997	5	TUI
	Viking	2003	4	Independent
Switzerland	Belair	2001	3	Hotelplan/Air Berlin
	Edelweiss Air	1995	4	Kuoni
	Hello	2004	6	Independent
Turkey	Atlasjet International	2001	17	Independent
	Best Air	2006	2	Independent
	Corendon	2004	4	Independent
	Freebird	2001	5	Independent
	Golden International	2005	1	Independent
	Inter Airlines	2002	4	Independent
	Onur Air	1992	29	Ten Tour International
	Pegasus	1990	15	Independent
	Saga Airlines	2004	3	Independent
	Sky Airlines	2001	6	Independent
	Sunexpress	1990	12	Condor/Turkish
	Tarhan Tower Airlines	2005	2	Independent
	World Focus Airline	2004	3	Independent
UK	Astraeus	2001	10	Independent
	European Air Charter	1993	6	Independent
	First Choice	1986	31	TUI
	Flightline	1989	7	Independent
	FlyJet	2002	2	Independent
	Monarch	1967	28	Globus Group
	MyTravel	1986	21	Thomas Cook
	Thomas Cook (UK)	1998	24	Thomas Cook
	Thomsonfly	1962	47	TUI
	Titan	1988	9	Independent
	XL Airways	1994	19	XL Leisure Group

Sources: JP Airline-Fleets International, ICAO, IATA, ATI, Airline Business, DGAC France, UK CAA.

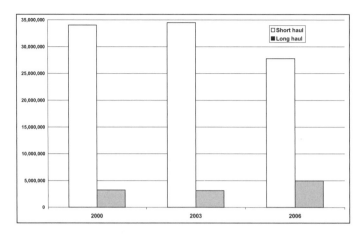

FIGURE 8.4 UK long and short haul charter demand 2000–2006

Source: UK CAA, 2000, 2003, 2006.

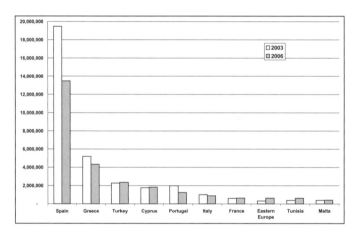

FIGURE 8.5 Changes in UK short haul charter demand 2003–2006

Source: UK CAA, 2003, 2006.

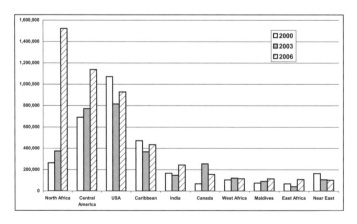

FIGURE 8.6 Changes in UK long haul charter demand 2000–2006

Source: UK CAA, 2000, 2003, 2006.

the UK between 2000 and 2006. Charter flights to North Africa, predominantly Egypt, and Central America, mainly Cuba, the Dominican Republic and Mexico, have increased substantially. The impact of the terrorist events of 9/11 is clearly evident in the traffic fall off to the US and the Caribbean between 2000 and 2003. Nearly all of the charter traffic to the US is to Florida. The impact of liberalising the UK–Canada bilateral is evident in the drop in charter passengers between 2003 and 2006, with Air Transat transferring its former charter operations into scheduled services.

A major feature affecting European charter airlines is the seasonality of their traffic. Demand is high during summer months, but during the winter season demand is much reduced. Finding new activity for their aircraft during the low season is therefore a priority for charter companies. Two examples of these 'new' markets are cited here. The first involves long haul operations to Australia and New Zealand, and the second, short haul flights to a remote part of northern Europe with little daylight and very cold temperatures. While the latter continues to thrive, the former has all but disappeared as a result of the large growth in sixth freedom capacity between Europe and Australasia. Figure 8.7 shows the demand for these long haul flights from the late 1980s until 2006. An alternative activity for charter aircraft capable of long haul flying has been the carriage of pilgrims to Mecca for the annual Hajj, but as the date of this religious event varies this does not always provide a low season opportunity for Europe's operators.

More unusually perhaps has been the success of the flights to Finnish Lapland providing families with an opportunity to visit Santa Claus at home. Five regional airports in northern Finland have benefited from this winter traffic, as have most UK regional airports. Day trips involving a three hours flight in each direction typically cost around £300. Most of these flights take place in the month before Christmas, providing much needed work for charter fleets at a time of traditionally lowest demand. Figure 8.8 shows the growth of this charter traffic from UK airports between 1992 and 2004.

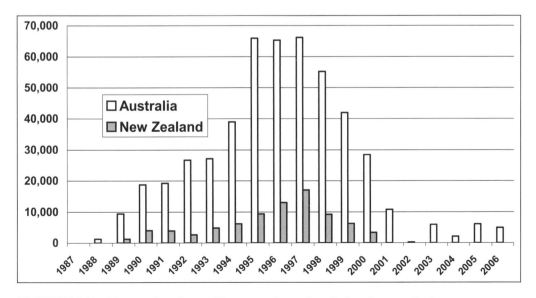

FIGURE 8.7   Example of an off-season long haul charter market
Source: UK CAA, 1987–2006.

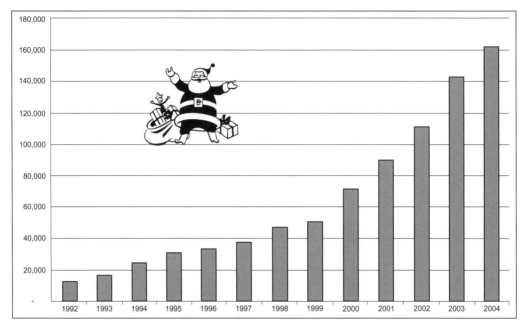

FIGURE 8.8   Santa Claus traffic from the UK to Finnish Lapland
Source: UK CAA, 1992–2004.

FACTORS INFLUENCING THE OPERATING AND ECONOMIC PERFORMANCE OF CHARTER AIRLINES

It is apparent that the combination of larger aircraft, longer flight sectors, greater aircraft and crew utilisation, high seating configurations and higher load factors provides the typical charter airline with significantly lower costs per passenger carried than scheduled airlines (Williams, Mason and Turner 2003). Figure 8.9 reveals that easyJet, one of the largest "no-frills" scheduled operators in Europe, had unit operating costs close to double those of the largest UK charter airlines in 2006. This cost difference mostly results though from the larger aircraft used by charter carriers and the longer sectors they fly. When these factors are taken into account, much of the cost difference disappears and in the case of Ryanair, the largest European LCC, it is the latter that has the lowest unit costs.

It is readily apparent that aircraft size has a profound effect on an airline's unit costs. It is usually the case that the larger an aircraft, the lower will be its direct operating costs per passenger kilometre. The flying costs per block hour of a large aircraft are, of course, greater than those of a small aeroplane, but when this cost is divided by the corresponding total output of each aircraft a lower unit cost is produced. This situation occurs because the hourly productivity of a larger aircraft increases more rapidly with size than does its hourly operating cost. Other characteristics of an aircraft affecting operating costs include range, fuel consumption, leasing costs, capital charges and maintenance requirements.

In 2006, the average seating capacity of the UK's largest charter airlines was 230. For short and medium haul charter operations the Airbus 321 (with 220 seats) and Boeing 757 (with 235 seats) are typical, whilst for long haul flights the Boeing 767-300 (with 328 seats)

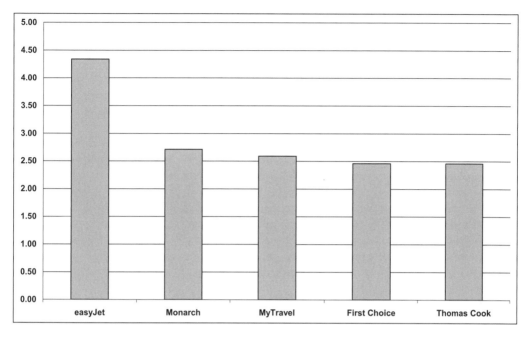

FIGURE 8.9   Unit operating costs in 2005–6 (pence per ASK)
Source: UK CAA, 2006.

and Airbus 330-200 (with 360 seats) predominate.[7] By comparison, most scheduled carriers in Europe use Airbus 319/320 or Boeing 737NG aircraft seating no more 150 passengers for their short haul services. On long haul flights charter airlines squeeze in many more seats than their scheduled counterparts. For example, British Airways configures its three class Boeing 767-300 aircraft with 181 seats, in sharp contrast to the 328 seats that are fitted to the same aircraft type used by Thomsonfly. Even where charter airlines offer a two class service on their long haul operations, many more seats feature than on the same type of aircraft operated by scheduled carriers. Monarch, for example, has 323 economy and 51 premium economy seats on its Airbus 330-200 aircraft. The same aircraft type operated by Air France in a two class configuration features 40 business and 179 economy seats.[8]

The longer sectors flown by charter airlines raise the utilisation of their aircraft and crew, and reduces the amount of fuel they use per block hour, the relative size of their station costs and part of their maintenance expenses. Europe's charter airlines typically fly average sectors of 2000–3000 kms, in marked contrast to the 1000 kms average flown by the low cost scheduled companies, as Figure 8.10 reveals.

High load factor has long been a feature of the charter sector. The aircraft size advantage of the non-scheduled carriers is enhanced by the high load factors that most achieve. In 2006, aircraft operated by First Choice flew with on average 90.7 per cent of their seats occupied. During the same year, easyJet achieved an average load factor of 81.5 per cent.

---

7   UK charter carriers pack more seats into their aircraft than their German and Scandinavian counterparts. For example, LTU configures its Boeing 757 aircraft with 210 seats and Condor its Boeing 767-300s with 269 seats.
8   First Choice has reduced the number of seats fitted to its Boeing 767-300 aircraft, resulting in its economy class seat pitch being raised to 33 inches.

This figure though is high in comparison with the achievements of scheduled network carriers, as may be seen in Figure 8.11.

Aircraft utilisation for short to medium haul scheduled carriers is with few exceptions lower than that achieved by charter airlines. Figure 8.12 contrasts the daily utilisation rates of the Airbus 319/320 fleets operated by British Airways, easyJet and First Choice. The seasonal nature of the charter business is immediately apparent, with First Choice aircraft operating close to twice as many flying hours during the third quarter of 2004 compared to the first quarter of 2005.[9] Despite the large seasonal variation however, each of the charter carrier's aircraft is in the air annually for significantly longer than the amount of time of the BA Airbus 320 fleet. The shorter turnaround times achieved by the new low cost carriers, however, has reduced the gap that has traditionally existed. LCCs operating between the hours of 22.00 and 06.00 during the summer months to holiday destinations have also helped to reduce the difference. The differences in aircraft utilisation rates are considerably reduced however when long haul services are being operated, as may be seen in Figure 8.13.

Labour productivity is considerably influenced by the extent to which a carrier outsources its activities and by the nature of the product it offers to its customers. The low cost scheduled and charter airlines have much in common in terms of the products they supply, but wide differences are apparent with respect to the degree of outsourcing that occurs. For example, the long established charter operators often undertake their maintenance in-house, whereas the low cost scheduled companies have in the main outsourced this activity. Figure 8.14 contrasts the levels of output per employee that were achieved by a selection of UK charter and scheduled carriers in 2006. As may be seen, the productivity of easyJet employees matches that of the UK's largest charter airlines.

Distribution costs are virtually non-existent for the vertically integrated charter airlines, as sales and promotion activities are undertaken by the tour operator parent companies.[10] However, in the cases of those charter airlines that now operate scheduled services, such as Monarch and Thomsonfly, they have had to cover this item of cost in respect of their scheduled operations themselves.

Landing fees are lower on average for charter carriers than for scheduled airlines due to their greater use of secondary airports and avoidance of peak time operations at primary airports. LCC are generally exceptions to this however, owing to their policy of flying mostly to under-utilised airports[11], at which landing charges are low, as argued by Echevarne in Chapter 14.

Administration and finance expenses are also usually low for charter airlines, as many of the tasks usually included under this category are undertaken by the tour operator parent company.

With their low operating costs and yields, most charter airlines face relatively high break-even load factors. As Figure 8.15 shows, the largest UK charter carriers typically require passenger load factors above 80 per cent to break-even. Despite this however, most of the large integrated carriers have over many years experienced a healthy gap between their actual load factors and that needed to balance the books.

---

9   The utilisation rate for easyJet in Q4 2004 is clearly incorrect and should be around 11 hours.
10   A similar situation applies with regards to ticketing.
11   These airports are often located a long distance away from the cities they purport to serve.

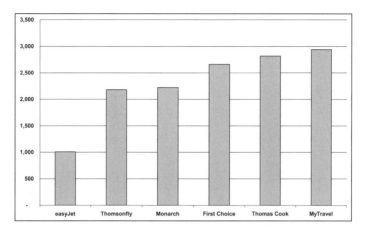

FIGURE 8.10 Average stage lengths (kms) flown in 2006
Source: UK CAA, 2006.

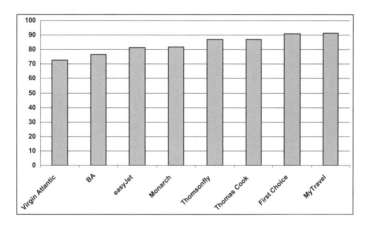

FIGURE 8.11 Passenger load factors (%) in 2006
Source: UK CAA, 2006.

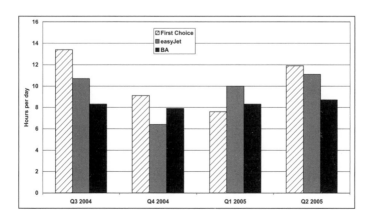

FIGURE 8.12 Short haul aircraft utilisation rate comparison
Source: UK CAA, 2004, 2005.

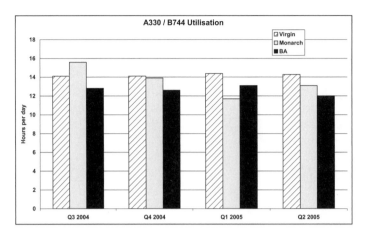

FIGURE 8.13 Long haul aircraft utilisation rate comparison
Source: UK CAA, 2004, 2005.

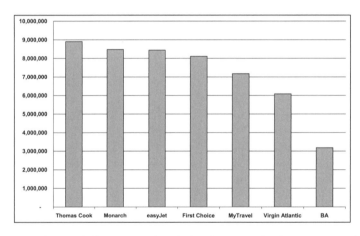

FIGURE 8.14 Airlines' labour productivity in 2006 (ASK per employee)
Source: UK CAA, 2006.

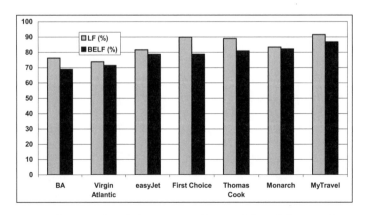

FIGURE 8.15 Break-even load factors and actual load factors in 2005–6
Source: UK CAA, 2006.

CONCLUSIONS

Judging by the relatively small number of aircraft on order by Europe's charter airlines, it is clear that the sector will continue to decline. Aside from a small number intended as short haul fleet replacements, the only significant development is the ordering of the Boeing 787 by Air Berlin, Blue Panorama, First Choice, Monarch and TUI. A few of the UK charter airlines have also been re-configuring their existing long haul fleets with fewer seats, offering their customers a better quality of service. Reducing the dependence on traditional short haul markets and concentrating instead on markets that the LCC have not encroached has been the strategy pursued by these carriers. Most other charter operators though have pursued a very different strategic response. Thomson and MyTravel each established LCC subsidiaries, while Monarch has rapidly expanded its scheduled flights as demand for its charter operations have declined. Thomas Cook, like First Choice, has decided not to go down the LCC route. While the UK charter fleet has contracted only by some 10 per cent to date, with the only significant downsizing involving MyTravel, the charter fleets of German companies have been reduced significantly (Aviation Strategy 2005).

Most European countries have experienced a decline in passenger demand for charter flights. This has been more marked in countries that have had economic downturns, such as Germany and Sweden. In these countries, charter traffic has fallen by more than 25 per cent over the past three years. The UK, the largest charter traffic generating country, has also seen demand falling but to date by only 10 per cent over the same period. Further decline is inevitable, as LCC expand their networks across Europe and further afield.

Over the next decade it would seem probable that in most short haul markets the services provided by LCC will replace package tour charter flights. With ever increasing market transparency, only if tour operators can offer their clientele lower overall prices and the flexibility of self-assembled holidays, and be perceived by consumers as doing so, will they be able to prevent this from happening. This seems unlikely, however. The natural choice of younger generation, computer-literate consumers will not be the traditional package holiday.

Further market liberalisation (e.g. EU-North Africa) and the accession of additional countries to the EU (particularly, Turkey) will lead to further erosion of the charter sector. The addition of Moroccan cities to the route networks of easyJet and Ryanair has already occurred.

Competitive pressures on vertically integrated tour operating organisations will increase, leading some to fail or merge, and others to re-organise their assets, which may involve the sale of their charter airline subsidiaries. The strategy of concentrating on longer haul markets that are not subject to the attentions of LCC will prove increasingly attractive. Downsizing will be an inevitable outcome of this policy, however. The extent to which the new generation of long haul LCC will target the more distant markets served by charter airlines is as yet unclear. It is likely though that richer picking will come from competing in the markets of scheduled carriers.

Overall, Europe's charter sector is likely to contract to only half its present size within ten years. Its focus will be increasingly on medium to long haul operations, with much emphasis on seeking out niche markets. The break-up of some long established, vertically integrated tour operating organisations is also likely to occur, with fewer charter airline subsidiaries in existence. The possibility of TUIfly, when fully formed in 2008, being sold has already been mooted (Aviation Strategy 2007a). The business model being pursued by Air

Berlin may provide the best guide as to what is the best strategy to follow. The alternative is invariably going to be on a smaller scale and feature niche market operations.

9

The Emergence of the Low Cost Carrier Sector

Sean Barrett

INTRODUCTION

The emergence of the low cost airline has had massive implications for the growth of tourism. Low cost airlines have brought large reductions in price and large increases in the number of seats available. The UK Civil Aviation Authority (2006a) found that between 1996 and 2005 international passenger numbers between the UK and the EU by low cost airlines increased from 3.1m to 51.5m. Full service airline passengers increased from 42.2m to 47.2m and charter passengers grew from 23.8m to 25m. 89 per cent of the growth of 54.6m passengers in this market was on no frills airlines. Full service and charter shares of the growth were 9 per cent and 2 per cent respectively. The CAA also noted (2006b: 3.3) that "since 2000, both charter and full-service carriers have seen flat or declining demand" as the market share of low cost airlines has increased more rapidly in the new millennium. A regulatory system based on the exclusion of new entrants, non-price competition and capacity sharing between monopolistic national airlines has been replaced by a competitive market with significant benefits to the wider economy in terms of lower prices, a better range of services in the market and large increases in productivity in the aviation sector.

Section two complements the analysis undertaken on charter carriers by Williams in Chapter 8 by focusing on their cost structure and advantages over full service airlines. Section three then explicitly focuses on low cost operations while section four argues that the differences between full service, low cost and charter airlines are gradually becoming blurred. Sections five and six assess the consumer benefits arising from the emergence of low cost airlines and the implications for leisure travel in a deregulated aviation environment whereas section seven provides some examples of LCC growth in the European context. Finally, section eight summarises and concludes.

THE CHARTER SECTOR – EUROPE'S FIRST LOW COST AIRLINES

The charter sector grew up serving sun destinations where the regulating governments sought to develop tourism while reserving access to capital, hub and main city airports for designated national airlines. The charter airlines dominated sun destination markets from Northern Europe to the Mediterranean basin, for example, 96.3 per cent of the market between the United Kingdom and the Canary Islands and 86.8 per cent of the market between the United Kingdom and Spain in 1982 (Barrett 1987). Gimeno *et al.* (2003) estimated that in 2001 charter airlines accounted for 44 per cent of passenger miles flown in Europe and for 27 per cent of passengers. The average length of a charter flight within the European Union is 1,323 km compared to 808 km for the average of all carriers, a 64 per cent longer stage length. 'Compared to scheduled services, European charter airlines experienced higher, more stable growth: between 1994 and 2001 the average annual growth of revenues was 4 per cent compared to 0.6 per cent of scheduled carriers.

The International Air Carrier Association (IACA) reported that in 2005 Europe accounted for 88 per cent of charter passengers worldwide. The European share is in fact higher if one includes the Canary Islands in Europe rather than in the Africa region as in the IACA data. High charter shares at leisure destinations were 68 per cent at Tenerife and 61 per cent at Palma, and Zakinthos. Luxor, Lanzarote and Paphos had charter shares of over 50 per cent. IACA carried 120m passengers worldwide to 650 airports in 130 countries. IACA also reports fast charter growth in markets such as Egypt, Turkey, Croatia and Tunisia in 2005.

In early cascade studies which compared the costs of full service and charter airlines, the charter product's costs were estimated to range between 32 per cent and 37 per cent of the cost of the traditional scheduled airline product. The savings which reduced the costs of the charter per seat mile compared to a scheduled seat mile by two-thirds are shown in Table 9.1. The various sources of saving listed in Table 9.1 combine to give a saving of 66 per cent off the traditional scheduled airline product in Europe.

The early cascade studies such as shown in Table 9.1 indicated that within Europe large cost reductions in aviation were available by adopting a different aviation product, the

TABLE 9.1   Decomposition of savings of charter airline operation over scheduled full service airlines, 1981

Source of Saving	Share of Scheduled Cost (%)
Higher load factor	21
Factors not applicable to charter flights	14
Lower standard	9
Lower agent commission	8
Single class cabin	8
Higher seat density	4
Higher aircraft utilisation	2
Total savings	**66**

Source: European Community, 1981. Table based on cascade study route B.

charter model, instead of the traditional scheduled airline product. The cascade studies were important in indicating that the traditional scheduled airline in Europe could reduce its cost base by changing any combination of the factors shown in Table 9.1. The cascade studies quantified for regulators the high costs of protectionism in European aviation. The traditional airline product in Europe was protected by government regulation from both unbundled product competition and from new market entrants. The cascade studies also provided information for the new market entrants on the extent to which they could undercut the fares charged by traditional scheduled airlines and achieve higher profitability.

The cascade studies were therefore significant in influencing policy change towards a contestable market in European aviation. Since a cascade study describes costs in a particular time frame it is subject to change over time. For example many full service airlines eliminated first class cabins on short haul flights in the 1980s and Table 9.1 estimates a potential saving of 8 per cent from the operation of a single cabin flight. Doganis (2002) in a cascade analysis of the London-Athens route estimated larger savings of 69 per cent for charter operation over scheduled services compared to the 66 per cent two decades earlier in Table 9.1. Despite many attempts by the scheduled airlines in the 1980s and 1990s to reduce costs the Doganis data indicate that the cost disadvantage of the scheduled airlines over charter airlines increased slightly over the two decades.

The major cost advantages of charters in the 2002 analysis were higher seat occupancy which gave charters a 26 per cent cost advantage, higher seat density (generating a 17 per cent cost advantage), and lower ticketing, sales, promotion and commissions costs (generating a 15 per cent cost advantage). These three factors generated 58 of the 69 points of cost savings of the charters over scheduled operators. The smaller cost savings were higher aircraft utilisation, outsourcing at airports, fewer cabin attendants, economies in passenger services and lower administration costs. The charter airlines generated a mass tourist market to the Mediterranean basin which the high cost scheduled airlines did not seek to serve. The savings of two-thirds of the cost of the scheduled product, as shown in Table 9.1, were generated by selling a higher proportion of the seats on each flight, selling direct to the public rather than through agents, not operating first and business class cabins, having more seats per aircraft and flying more hours per aircraft per day.

In the evolution of aviation policy in Europe away from bilateral aviation agreements between governments based on one airline per country, and predetermined allocations of market capacity with bans on new entrants to the market and on price competition, the existence of the charter sector was influential. The charter airline success on markets between northern Europe and the Mediterranean showed that a low cost aviation product could be provided profitably within Europe. This was important in rebutting the case made by incumbent scheduled airlines in Europe that the American style of deregulation could not succeed in Europe because of differences in workplace culture and economic policy. On the contrary the success of charter airlines showed that Europe already had a vibrant low cost aviation sector providing flights at fares some two-thirds lower than the favoured national airlines operating in markets between the same countries.

The success of charter airlines paved the way for low cost airlines when European markets were deregulated. The charter airlines proved to investors that low cost airlines could be profitable in a Europe in which the profit margins of the protected national airlines were low. The main requirement for Europe's low cost airlines to bring their model to travel within northern Europe and to city rather then resort destinations was regulatory change to permit market access. The regulatory change which allowed Ryanair to enter the Dublin–London route in 1986 brought the low cost model to intercity international air travel in Europe based on the success of the charter low cost model combined with product changes compared to both the scheduled airline product and the charter airline product. Deregulation allowed the new low cost airlines to emulate the low costs of the charter airlines already in the market and also to unbundle from the charter product restrictions such as a requirement to purchase an accommodation package with the flight and the restriction of charter flights to holiday resorts in the Mediterranean basin only in order to protect national airlines at hubs. Deregulation also allowed the new low cost airlines to unbundle many of services included by full service airlines in their ticket prices as indicated in Table 9.4.

THE LOW COST SCHEDULED AIRLINE

A cascade analysis showing the cost advantages of low cost airlines over full service airlines on short-haul routes was estimated by Doganis (2006). It shows that low cost carriers have a cost per seat of 49 per cent compared to an index of 100 for conventional short-haul carriers. Three cost headings account for 55 per cent of the savings. These are higher seat density which reduces the low cost airline costs per passenger by 16 per cent, a reduction more than twice as important as the next saving (7 per cent) on station costs and outsourced handling. The third category is a 6 per cent saving on agents and global distribution costs.

In another cost comparison, Doganis (2006) presents cost data for seven full service and two low cost airlines. The cost index ranges from Austrian Airlines at 129 down to Ryanair at 38, i.e. 29 per cent of the Austrian cost base. Table 9.2 shows cost, fare and net margin information for seven European airlines with Ryanair having the lowest costs and fares and the highest net margin.

Table 9.3 presents a cascade analysis of the Ryanair cost savings over its nearest low cost rival easyJet. Almost four-fifths of the Ryanair cost savings over easyJet arise under three headings. These are staff costs, aircraft ownership and maintenance costs and other costs including fuel. The staff cost differences are due to higher productivity, a lower number of staff per aircraft, higher seating density and the absence of staff overnight costs in the Ryanair model. The lower aircraft costs are due to the volume and other discounts achieved by Ryanair from Boeing and financial assistance from the Export-Import Bank of the United States on aircraft purchases as Ireland does not have an aircraft manufacturing sector. The third major cost saving under the heading of other costs including fuel reflects fuel price hedging and tight control on overheads.

The fare and cost differences between the airlines in Table 9.2 reflect differences in networks and services provided and individual route and service comparisons are required in order to ascertain the options available on specific routes. In addition to prices the product differences between full service, charter and low cost airlines should be examined when comparing different airlines. Table 9.4 shows the product differences between full service, low cost and charter airlines.

TABLE 9.2   Revenue and cost per passenger and net margin, 2005/6

	Revenue Per Pax (€)	Cost Per Pax (€)	Net Margin (%)
Ryanair	49	40	18
Aer Lingus	125	114	9
Southwest	72	66	7
British Airways	351	332	6
Air France	306	293	4
Lufthansa	352	341	3
easyJet	67	65	3

Source: Ryanair Investor Roadshow presentation, September 2006.

TABLE 9.3   Cost advantages of Ryanair over easyJet – a cascade study showing cumulative cost advantage, 2003

easyJet cost per passenger (€)	61.96	Index 100
Ryanair savings – lower staff costs	-7.90	87
Secondary airport/handling	-4.07	80
Route charges	-0.52	79
Aircraft ownership/maintenance	-5.81	70
Advertising/selling costs	-1.09	68
Other costs including fuel	-6.64	58
Ryanair cost per passenger (€)	35.92	58

Source: Ryanair Investor Roadshow presentation, September 2006.

FULL SERVICE, LOW COST AND CHARTER AIRLINES IN DEREGULATED MARKETS – A HYBRID PRODUCT?

The three segments of Europe's aviation markets, full service, low cost and charter airlines are based on regulatory policy. This contrasts with most other consumer product markets where the trade-off between price and perceived quality is made by consumers themselves.

In a deregulated market, such as Europe since 1997, the distinctions between the three airline types shown in Table 9.4 have been eroded. For example on Europe's longest deregulated major intercity route, Dublin-London, the busiest route in Europe, two full service airlines, Aer Lingus and British Midland, have adopted the Ryanair low cost model but retained seat allocation, leaving only Cityjet, a subsidiary of Air France, the only full service airline serving the route. It has a market share of only 3.3 per cent. The adoption

TABLE 9.4   The low cost airline product compared with full service and charter airlines

Full Service Airlines	Charter	Low Cost
Free newspapers, food, drinks	Free food/drinks	For sale
Seat allocation	Seat allocation	Free seating
Business class	One class operation	One class
Low seat density	High set density	High seat density
Low load factor	High load factor	High load factor
Hub city airports	Resort airports	Secondary airports
Day flights	Some night flights	Day flights
Interlining available	Point to point	Point to point
Business lounges at airports	No lounges	No lounges
Ticket brought near flight date	Advance purchase	Near flight date
Ticket sales at own shops	Tour operators	Internet
Ticket sales at travel agents	No	No
Flexible one way tickets	No	Yes
Unbundled tickets	Package holiday	Unbundled
Frequent flyer programme	No	No
High frequency service	One/two week trip	High frequency
Nil no show penalty on higher fares	No show penalty	No show penalty

Sources: Barrett (2004b), Doganis (2002).

of the low cost model by previously full service airlines such as Aer Lingus and British Midland is replicated in a changing charter sector. The traditional identification of charter airlines with bundled accommodation packages has also been eroded. Doganis (2002: 155) notes that "German charter airlines sell around 20 per cent of their total capacity to seat only passengers" in contrast to the United Kingdom where 95 per cent of passengers on charter flights in 2000 were on inclusive tour or package charters.

Scheduled airlines too carry large numbers of leisure passengers notwithstanding their traditional emphasis on business travellers. The Civil Aviation Authority survey of 14 United Kingdom airports in 2005, covering 125.1m scheduled airline passengers, found that 68.6 per cent were on leisure trips. Of the 31.4 per cent on business trips 20.1 per cent were on international and 11.3 per cent on domestic trips. On the other hand, the business use of charter airlines was minimal at only 1.3 per cent of 24.2m passengers surveyed. Table 9.5 shows the data from the surveys of both charter and scheduled airline passengers. Table 9.5 indicates that the charter flight business in the United Kingdom is 97.9 per cent based on passengers residing in the United Kingdom whereas the scheduled airlines passengers are 44 per cent foreign based in the case of international business passengers and 34 per cent in the case of international leisure passengers.

TABLE 9.5   Characteristics of terminating passengers at 14 United Kingdom airports, 2005

Scheduled Traffic (Percentage of Those Surveyed)			
	UK	Foreign	Total
International Business	11.2	8.9	20.1
International Leisure	37.5	19.5	57.0
Domestic Business	10.6	0.7	11.3
Domestic Leisure	10.3	1.3	11.6
Total	**69.6**	**30.4**	**100.0**
Charter Traffic (Percentage of Those Surveyed)			
	UK	Foreign	Total
International Business	0.8	0.2	1.0
International Leisure	96.5	2.0	98.5
Domestic Business	0.3	0.0	0.3
Domestic Leisure	0.3	0.0	0.3
Total	**97.9**	**2.2**	**100.0**

Airports surveyed; Aberdeen, Bournemouth, Durham Tees Valley, Edinburgh, Gatwick, Glasgow, Heathrow, Inverness, Leeds Bradford, Luton, Manchester, Newcastle, Prestwick and Stansted. The fourteen airports in the survey had 125.1m scheduled and 24.2m charter passengers.

The CAA survey did not distinguish between full service and low cost airlines within the category of scheduled airline passengers. The characteristics of full service and low cost airline passengers can be seen however by contrasting the survey results at London Heathrow and Stansted. The former is a traditional hub airport served by full service airlines while the latter is used mainly by low cost airlines. Table 9.6 shows that at Heathrow 61.7 per cent of passengers are on leisure trips on traditional full service airlines while the low cost airlines at Stansted have 19.1 per cent of their passengers on business trips.

A survey of Ryanair passengers by Davy found that 23 per cent were on business trips, 37.6 per cent were on leisure trips and 39.3 per cent were visiting friends and relatives. 24.1 per cent of passengers purchased food on board the aircraft compared to 36.3 per cent who purchased food or drink at the airport. 83.2 per cent of those surveyed had flown with Ryanair before, indicating that the low cost product has bedded in and attracts a high level of repeat business.

THE CONSUMER BENEFITS OF LOW COST AIRLINES

The low cost airline offers large fare reductions and point to point flights from local airports rather than routing over hubs compared to the traditional full service airlines. Compared to the traditional charter airline bundled service of two weeks at a seaside sun destination the low cost airline offers flexible tickets to a wider choice of destinations with

TABLE 9.6   Characteristics of terminating passengers at Heathrow and Stansted, 2005

Heathrow (Percentage of Those Surveyed)			
	UK	Foreign	Total
International Business	17.6	15.3	32.9
International Leisure	36.0	22.9	58.9
Domestic Business	5.3	0.3	5.6
Domestic Leisure	2.5	0.3	2.8
Total	**61.4**	**38.8**	**100.0**
Stansted (Percentage of Those Surveyed)			
International Business	9.1	5.5	14.6
International Leisure	46.6	26.9	73.3
Domestic Business	4.4	0.1	4.5
Domestic Leisure	6.8	0.6	7.4
Total	**66.9**	**33.1**	**100.0**

Note; Heathrow had 43.6m passengers and Stansted had 19.2m. The Heathrow survey contains 0.3 per cent charter passengers and the Stansted survey contains 4.3 per cent charter passengers. The dominant product at Heathrow is the full service airline and at Stansted the low cost airline.

short break city tourism as an alternative to the traditional two weeks at the seaside. The low cost airline caters for the independent traveller seeking to enjoy the culture, museums, theatres, galleries, architecture plus some experience of the diversity of European cities. The low cost airline also served the growing market of those who owned properties abroad and thus did not require accommodation at their destination. The growth of independent travellers contrasted with the traditional charter package product based on large scale movement of passengers to seaside and sun destinations rather than venturing further afield in the destination country.

In addition to significant fare savings and a more individualised holiday low cost airlines have generated some consumer service improvements such as avoiding congested hub airports, better punctuality at non-congested secondary airports with less walking distances and less time waiting for baggage. Fewer bags are lost because of the simple point to point product. There is no risk of denied boarding on overbooked flights compared to the traditional airlines whose overbooking policy imposed the cost of no show passengers on overbooked passengers rather than on the no show passengers themselves. The low cost point to point model benefited second cities by providing direct service rather than routing these passengers through hubs. The low cost airline model made viable routes which high cost airlines were unable to serve operate.

Regulatory change permitting low cost airlines to enter the previously closed market was facilitated by the development of the internet and the growth of airport competition. Travel agents had an income incentive to support high air fares since they were paid a percentage commission on the ticket price. They faced a financial loss if passengers changed from high cost to low cost airlines. The agents also had long-established business relationships with full service airlines over many decades. The Internet allowed passengers to bypass travel agents and seek for themselves fare options over many airlines and destinations.

Since the grandfather rights system of slot allocation at hub airports was a barrier to new entrant airlines secondary airports were vital to market access by low cost airlines. Since low cost airlines sought both internal and external cost reductions secondary airports offered lower charges in order to attract these airlines. The non-congested secondary airports allowed low cost airlines to turn planes around in 25 minutes compared to as much as 75 minutes at congested hubs. Low cost airlines at low cost secondary airports were thus able to operate more flights per plane per day.

CAP 771 suggests that the savings from low cost operation on long haul 'would not be as pronounced as for short haul' (5.11). The estimates of the long haul savings is 15 per cent compared to 45 per cent savings from no frills operation on short haul routes. The main potential savings were in passenger and distribution costs. European air fares were the highest in the world before deregulation and the scope for cost and fare reductions was therefore greater.

THE EUROPEAN AVIATION LEISURE MARKET SINCE DEREGULATION

The Association of European Airlines representing the legacy full service airlines in Europe Yearbook states that the Association's thirty reporting members carried 320m passengers in 2005. The six largest member airlines carried 67 per cent of the passengers on AEA member airlines in 2004 and shown in Table 9.7. The large carriers were Lufthansa (48.3m passengers), Air France (45.4m), British Airways (35.5m), Iberia (25.8m), Alitalia (22.0m), and SAS and KLM, both 20.4m. Based on the CAA survey at Heathrow, shown in Table 9.6, some 61 per cent of scheduled airline passengers were leisure passengers. In a total of 320m passengers this implies some 195m leisure passengers on full service airlines in Europe in 2005.

The charter sector in Europe, according to IACA data, is some 108m passengers. This is based on a 90 per cent share of charter passenger numbers worldwide of 120m plus an adjustment for the designation of Canary Island flights in the Africa region. All but 1 per cent of these passengers are on leisure trips, according to the survey data in Table 9.5.

In the European low cost sector leisure passengers are 81 per cent of total passengers, as indicated in the survey data at Stansted in Table 9.6. Davy estimated the European low cost airline sector at 117m passengers in 2006. The sector is dominated by Ryanair with 35m passengers and a 30 per cent market share and easyJet with 30m passengers and a 26 per cent market share. Air Berlin at 11.8 per cent is the only other low cost airline with a market share in excess of 5 per cent. Table 9.8 shows the European low cost airline passenger numbers and market shares in 2006. The growth of the sector has been very rapid. Ryanair, the oldest surviving low cost airline in Europe, was founded in 1986 and exceeded 1m passengers for the first time in 1993. It is guiding 52m passengers in 2007. easyJet was founded in 1995 and is anticipated to have 34m passengers in 2007, based on an 11 per cent growth rate. The two leading low cost airlines will have a combined total of 86m passengers in 2007 from virtual start-up operations a dozen years before when easyJet was founded and Ryanair had 2.2m passengers. The remaining seventeen low cost airlines in Table 9.8 had 52m passengers in 2006. A 5 per cent growth in passenger

TABLE 9.7   **Passengers carried by member airlines of the Association of European Airlines, 2004 (m)**

Adria	0.8
Aer Lingus	6.0
Air France	45.4
Air Malta	1.4
Alitalia	22.0
Austrian	7.6
BMI	6.9
British Airways	35.5
Croatia Airlines	1.4
CSA	4.0
Cyprus Airways	1.7
Finnair	6.0
Iberia	25.8
Icelandair	1.4
Jat Airways	1.1
KLM	20.4
LOT	3.5
Lufthansa	48.3
Luxair	0.9
Malev	2.5
Meridiana	3.6
Olympic Airlines	5.8
SAS	20.4
SN Brussels	3.2
Spanair	5.6
Swiss	9.3
TAP	6.0
Tarom	1.1
Turkish	11.4
Virgin Atlantic	4.3
Total	313.3

Source: Association of European Airlines, Yearbook 2005, 57; Aer Lingus Annual Accounts.
Note: Passengers carried in 2005 increased to 320m. (AEA Yearbook 2006, 6).

TABLE 9.8   **European low cost airline passenger numbers and market shares, 2006**

	Passengers (m)	Low Cost Market Share (%)
Ryanair	34.9	29.9
easyJet	30.3	25.9
Air Berlin/Niki	13.8	11.8
Flybe	5.5	4.7
Germanwings	5.5	4.7
Sterling/Maersk	3.8	3.3
bmibaby	3.5	3.0
dba	3.0	2.6
Hapag Lloyd Express	2.7	2.3
Vueling	2.5	2.1
Norwegian Air Shuttle	2.1	1.8
Virgin Express	2.0	1.7
Sky Europe	1.9	1.6
Wizz	1.9	1.6
Wind Jet	1.0	0.9
Air Baltic	1.0	0.9
Fly Me	0.5	0.4
Jet2	0.5	0.4
Monarch scheduled	0.5	0.4
Total	**116.9**	**100.0**

Source: Davy, 2006.

numbers for this disparate group in 2005 when added to the 86m passengers on the "big two" low cost carriers, Ryanair and easyJet, would bring the low cost sector's passenger numbers in 2007 to over 140m.

The passenger data for Europe in 2007 suggest a market of 600m passengers. The projected market shares are 55 per cent on full service airlines, 25 per cent on low cost airlines and 20 per cent on charters. Of the 600m total passengers an estimated 440m are leisure passengers. The leisure passengers comprise 61 per cent of the scheduled airline passengers, 81 per cent of low cost airline passengers and 99 per cent of charter passengers. The fastest growing segment of the European aviation industry is the low cost sector and its potential to further attract market share from full service and charter airlines is examined next.

EXAMPLES OF THE GROWTH OF LOW COST AIRLINE MARKETS IN EUROPE

Dublin–London

This is the busiest international route in Europe and was deregulated in 1986. In 2007 it has four competing airlines, i.e. Ryanair, the market leader, Aer Lingus, British Midland and Cityjet. The low cost airlines have 96.7 per cent of the market with only Cityjet operating the full service model. Cityjet is a subsidiary of Air France which is a full service airline. It operates to London City airport which is close to the City of London financial services centre and both the airline and airport serve the business market segment. The runway at London City is restricted in the size of aircraft it can handle and the smaller aircraft thus required at the airport require higher yields to make the service viable. In competition with Ryanair's low cost model, British Airways withdrew from the market in 1991 in order to use its slots at Heathrow on higher yield routes. British Midland and Aer Lingus later adopted the low cost model, dropping Diamond Class and Business Class service respectively. Aer Lingus found that, on the unbundling of ticket prices from service levels, the large majority of passengers were unwilling to pay for meal and drink service previously included in the air fare.

In the five years 1980 to 1985 before deregulation passenger numbers on the Dublin-London route increased by a cumulative 2.8 per cent with a fare increase of 72.6 per cent. On deregulation in May 1986 the unrestricted fare fell from £208 to £95, a reduction of 54 per cent. In the first full year of deregulation between London and Dublin passenger numbers were 64.9 per cent higher than in 1985, the last full year of pre-deregulation policies. The largest increase in monthly travel was in August 1987 with volumes up 92 per cent over August 1985.

The features of the Dublin–London route are its large size, at 4.3 million passengers in 2006, the linking to two popular city tourism destinations and the choice of five competing airports in London. Heathrow is the main international airport and before deregulation was the only airport offering service to Dublin. Stansted was largely pioneered by Ryanair's Dublin service and is now the airline's largest base with 45 routes throughout Europe. Gatwick serves the area south of London. Luton serves the northern part of London while the City airport serves the business market. The route is a short one at 279 miles and passengers have voted overwhelmingly for the low cost model. The success of the low cost model on this route in Europe calls into question whether the traditional full service model can survive low cost competition on a short haul route. It is also to be questioned whether "business class" in the past was a premium product requested by passengers or owed more to rent-seeking and monopolistic pricing by airlines operating in a non-competitive market.

In the twenty years before airline deregulation inward tourism to Ireland was showed no increase from 2m visitors per year. After airline deregulation visitor numbers increased to over 7m and in the Dublin area alone over sixty new hotels were built. Tourism became a major sector of the rapidly growing Irish economy with more employees than either multinational or indigenous manufacturing. The number of passengers at Irish airports increased from 3.5m in 1986 to 28.6m in 2005 while the increase in sea passengers was from 2.9m to 3.3m. The impact of airline deregulation in Ireland, an outer offshore island, was dramatic because access by sea was slow and aviation policy was extreme in excluding charter airlines and independent airlines from Irish airports. The protectionist policy towards Aer Lingus was extraordinary even compared to other "old" EU countries with a strong protectionist tradition such as France, Germany, and Spain. The decision to move to the low cost competitive aviation model was taken because of a parliamentary revolt in 1984 against legislation to further protect Aer Lingus. Irish airline deregulation in 1986 was part of a wider change in economic policy towards open markets and a reduced share of government in GDP. The policy changes in the mid to late 1980s led in turn to the Celtic Tiger era in the 1990s. In 2006 Irish GDP per head was 139 per cent of the EU average and exceeded only by Luxembourg. The Dublin-London route indicates a high preference for low cost aviation in a high GDP per head economy with competition on price rather than on in-flight services.

The Ireland–United Kingdom routes' overwhelming dominance by the low cost model contrasts with the experience of US airline deregulation eight years earlier in 1978. ELFAA estimates that the low cost share of the US domestic market in 2004 was 25 per cent compared to 99 per cent on Ireland-UK routes over a period since deregulation. The factors which made the Ireland-UK deregulation result more dramatic than in the US include shorter journey lengths where any loss of service on low cost airlines was more acceptable, the ready availability in the UK of competing low cost airports close to hub airports controlled by incumbent airlines and government policies in both the UK and Ireland that British Airways and Aer Lingus should operate to a strict commercial mandate. British Airways withdrew from Ireland and Aer Lingus reinvented itself as a low cost airline because both were denied subsidies by their government. By contrast the US airlines have avoided market exit and the adoption of the low cost model by a combination of government subsidy and Chapter 11 bankruptcy. In the US fares are 50 per cent lower on routes where Southwest is present. Due to the grandfather rights allocation of capacity at hub airports low cost airlines cannot access all markets and competing airports are less readily available in the US than in Europe where population density is higher and there is a stock of underutilised airport capacity built up for past military purposes and by regional and local governments.

London–Italy

Doganis (2006) examined thirteen routes between London and Italy in 2003 with 6.5m passengers. The previous dominance of full service national airlines, British Airways and Alitalia, saw their market shares fall to between 58 per cent (on London–Rome) and 32 per cent (on London-Genoa). On London–Rome Ryanair, at 33 per cent, and easyJet, at 9 per cent, gave the low cost new entrants a market share of 42 per cent or 790,000 passengers. On London–Milan the low cost share was higher still at 36 per cent for Ryanair and 11 per cent for easyJet, a combined total of 47 per cent of the market and 650,000 passengers travelling low cost. On London–Venice the low cost shares were 43 per cent for Ryanair and 20 per cent for easyJet. Williams et al (2003) note that the low cost share was only 20 per cent in 1998. On London–Turin the low cost airline share was 94 per cent compared to 57 per cent on London–Bologna and 68 per cent on London-Genoa. In addition low cost airlines operated four routes, London to Alghero, Trieste, Palermo and Pescara, where there was no full service airline presence in the market.

Second City Routes

In addition to large fare reductions the low cost airlines the low cost airline is able to enter routes which were not served by full service airlines. The four Italian routes ex London which were not viable for full service airlines but are now served by low cost airlines have many parallels at airports such as Prestwick, Skavsta, Nottingham East Midlands, Liverpool, Frankfurt Hahn, Charleroi, Kerry, Knock, Girona, Katowice, Bratislava, Carcassone, Tempe and many other cities. The full service airlines in the era of national carriers typically routed regional passengers through hubs at which these airlines coordinated their services, facilitated interlining trips, and accepted the tickets of other member airline's tickets. The high cost of full service airlines made it expensive to start new direct services at acceptable fares between secondary airports. There was also little incentive to launch such routes because their passenger numbers would have been deducted from the agreed market shares between the national airlines. The low cost airlines brought to second city markets direct services with significant fare and time savings over previous high cost time consuming routings over hub airports. For example, the Frankfurt Hahn–Kerry route introduced a direct low fare service from Germany to the southwest of Ireland compared to alternative indirect routings over Dublin with a flight connection or a routing over London Heathrow and Cork with a road or rail onward connection at Cork.

A study on the impact of Ryanair on the Ayrshire Tourism Economy in 2003 found that Ryanair's inbound passengers spent 2.4m bednights in Scotland in 2002–2003. The added output in the Scottish economy was estimated in the range of £13.8m and £18.4m with additional employment in the range of 1,300 and 1,800. In addition there were benefits such as greater access to people that previously could not afford to fly; the greater attractiveness of Scotland as a tourist destination; increased capacity to several key destinations, in particular, London; and savings for residents, for businesses and for visitors (SQW and NFO 2003).

According to ELFAA (2004), there were nineteen European second cities to which low cost airlines brought direct international services in 2004. Air travel between the UK and the eastern European countries in the EU increased by 25 per cent in 2006 from 6.3m to 7.9m. The routes to Poland grew by 80 per cent from 1.8m to 3.3m. Charter passengers to Poland were under 4,000 and for the full region were fewer than 15,000. The market shares for charter airlines were 0.2 per cent for the Eastern Europe EU countries and 0.1 per cent for Poland indicating that in this extension of the deregulated European aviation market low cost scheduled airlines have achieved dominance over the charter model.

CONCLUSIONS

The airline sector has three main types of product provider- the full service, low cost and charter airlines. Full service and charter airlines are both a legacy from the traditional restrictive regulation of the sector. The full service airline is based on the old non-competing national airlines model adopted by governments in 1944 as the provider model in international aviation. The charter airline sector was the chosen policy instrument chosen by governments seeking to develop inbound tourism to resort destinations but serving markets which were restricted in order that full service national airlines would not be undermined.

The low cost airline model was chosen in the United States in 1978, between Ireland and the United Kingdom in 1986, and in the EU mostly between 1993 and 1997. The model was chosen because of consumer opposition to the high fares charged by non-competing airlines and their high operating costs. The low cost airline's product is simpler and much less expensive to produce. Fares have fallen steadily and staff productivity has increased while non-core functions have been outsourced. The case studies cited here indicate that consumer preference strongly favours the low cost model over both full service and charter airlines.

The inherited cost disadvantages of full service airlines in a deregulated market with consumer preference for low cost airlines are illustrated by the productivity differences in Europe between the full service airline members of the Association of European Airlines (AEA) and the members of the European Low Fares Airlines Association (ELFAA). The thirty member airlines reporting in the Association of European Airlines 2005 Yearbook had 339,000 employees and 316m passengers, an average of 932 passengers per year per staff member. The 2006 Yearbook reported 320m passengers and 378,000 employees, an average of 847 passengers per employee. The main influence on the changing productivity over the two years has been the net addition of 39,000 staff and 4m passengers, a ratio of only 103 extra passengers per additional staff member employed in 2005. While there are likely to be data problems of comparability over thirty airlines and two years there has been a productivity problem at European national airlines inherited from the era of non-competing airlines. It has also been difficult to sustain productivity increase programmes at Europe's legacy airlines as staff numbers increase after the initial productivity programmes expire.

The eleven low fare airlines in the European Low Fares Airlines Association have an average of 6,000 passengers per employee with Ryanair, the lowest cost airline, having 11,100 passengers per airline staff member. (ELFAA 2004; Ryanair 2006). The advantages of the low cost airlines in terms of labour productivity are based on fewer bundled services included in the fare, thus requiring fewer staff; the recruitment of new start-up staff and management compared to inherited management and staff structures in full service airlines from the era before deregulation in aviation, and the advantage of a deregulated market in services bought in such as maintenance, catering, passenger and baggage handling, information technology and ticketing, sales and promotion services, all traditionally provided in-house by the legacy airlines. The legacy airlines face transition costs in replacing in-house provision of services by external provision unlike new and start-up airlines.

While Ireland's average annual real GDP growth rate of 7.9 per cent makes it the only OECD country to rank in the top twenty over the decade 1994–2004 there are several Asian tiger economies in this category. These include China, India, Vietnam, Laos and Cambodia. The low cost airline model, based on the Irish precedent, is likely to succeed in an economic environment of free trade and high growth rates as in the Asia-Pacific region, and to be opposed in less dynamic markets with protectionist economic policies, strong national airlines and low growth rates.

The ultimate goal of all economic activity is to satisfy consumer wants. There is no evidence that consumers do not wish to continue to purchase low cost airline tickets. The consumer preference has been to respond to low air fares by increasing the number of trips. The EU estimates that the number of scheduled airlines in Europe increased from 77 in 1992 to 139 in 2000. In a deregulated market with 80 per cent more producers any significant demand from consumers for a return to a full service product would be reflected on the supply side. The evidence is, however, those low cost airlines are growing much faster than either full service airlines or charter airlines which in the past both provided a higher standard of in-flight service. The price and productivity advantages of low cost airlines over full service airlines indicate increased market share for the low cost sector in scheduled services. The flexibility of low cost airlines and their wider range of destinations and greater frequency of service, combined with changes in tastes in the leisure market indicate that the low cost airline share will increase also on routes dominated in the past by charter airlines. Once, they were the only element of competition in a protected regulatory world dominated by national airlines but in the deregulated market the low cost airlines have taken on that role throughout the full aviation network.

10

From a National Airline to an EU Leisure-Based Carrier

John Zammit

INTRODUCTION

Malta is the smallest EU Member State with a population of 400,000.[1] Its economy has the highest level of reliance on Travel & Tourism (T&T) among EU countries as tourism accounts for 26.1 per cent of Gross Domestic Product (GDP) and 31.9 per cent of employment (World Economic Forum 2007). For its tourism intake, Malta competes with better resourced EU countries such as Italy, Spain, Portugal and Greece, as well as with other non-EU Mediterranean countries like Tunisia, Turkey and Morocco which have significantly lower per capita income and consequently lower cost. Cyprus is the closest country which compares with Malta in terms of size, accessibility, level of economic activity and the importance of T&T to the overall economy[2].

Air Malta originated as the national airline of Malta. Its evolution is intricately intertwined with the development of Malta's tourism and travel industry. Malta's accession to the EU marks a turning point for Air Malta as a tourism-based airline set in an island economy. This chapter explores how Air Malta transcended from a national carrier into an EU community carrier. Section two discusses the relationship between Air Malta and tourism development on the island and section three identifies major tourism issues in Malta. Section four focuses on the implications of the changing business environment for Air Malta and section five assesses the efforts undertaken to turn around the Mediterranean carrier. Finally, section six summarises and concludes highlighting the future challenges.

---

1   Malta acceded to the EU on 1 May 2004.
2   More comprehensive comparative statistics are given in Table 10.1. The Travel & Tourism Competitiveness Report 2007 gives the 2006 estimated economic contribution of Travel & Tourism (T&T) in terms of an economy's GDP and employment using the Tourism Satellite Accounting approach. The 'T&T industry' indicator is defined as the narrow perspective of T&T activity that captures the production-side industry contribution (that is, direct impact only). The 'T&T economy' indicator gives a broader perspective that takes into account the direct as well as the indirect contributions by traditional travel service providers and industry suppliers with the resident economy. This indicator shows the total impact of T&T on the resident economy.

TABLE 10.1   Travel & tourism indicators – small EU economies

Country	Population (2005 in millions)	Population Density (pop/sq km)	Area (1,000 sq kms)	GDP/Capita (2005 PPP, US$)	T&T Industry 2006 Estimates GDP (US$ m)	% of Total	Employment (1,000 Jobs)	% of Total	T&T Economy 2006 Estimates GDP (US$ m)	% of Total	Employment (1,000 Jobs)	% of Total
Cyprus	0.8	86	9.3	21,177	1,844	10.7%	57	15.0%	4,021	23.3%	113	29.7%
Estonia	1.3	29	45.2	16,414	479	3.5%	22	3.1%	2,199	16.0%	97	13.9%
Latvia	2.3	36	64.6	12,666	235	1.3%	12	1.2%	1,021	5.8%	51	5.0%
Lithuania	3.4	52	65.3	14,158	424	1.6%	21	1.4%	2,282	8.8%	112	7.5%
Luxembourg	0.5	192	2.6	69,800	1,001	2.9%	7	3.9%	3,315	9.4%	24	13.4%
Malta	0.4	1,333	0.3	19,739	743	13.2%	28	18.4%	1,474	26.1%	48	31.9%
Slovenia	2.0	99	20.3	21,808	1,207	3.4%	38	4.6%	5,209	14.6%	140	16.9%

Size (row group label)

Source: World Economic Forum (2007).

AIR MALTA AND TOURISM DEVELOPMENT

Since its initiation as a national carrier, Air Malta was responsible to develop air services connectivity between Malta and the rest of the world for the benefit of Malta's island economy (tourism, industry and services) and the resident population. It started flying on 1 April 1974 with two Boeing 720B aircraft operating scheduled services to London, Birmingham, Manchester, Rome, Frankfurt, Paris and Tripoli.[3] The airline had a clear mandate to achieve its mission without recourse to a single Lira of taxpayers' money.

On a span of 33 years, Air Malta clearly made its imprint on air services in and out of Malta – see Figure 10.1. Air Malta developed Malta's air transport connectivity within the framework of bilateral air services agreements (ASA), modelled on the Chicago Convention, which was protective (limited competition to designated carriers) as much as it was restrictive (limited services to designated airports, with defined levels of frequency and/or capacity).

From the start, Air Malta proved to be a resilient airline competing within the prevailing regulatory framework, each year turning out a modest profit, handsomely fulfilling its national carrier obligations – providing substantial air passenger and cargo connectivity to Europe, N. Africa, Middle East and globally through interline agreements, promoting tourism to Malta, earning foreign exchange, providing employment, creating new opportunities for Maltese to become pilots and airline engineers – a national asset fulfilling a key objective of Malta's tourism policy, that is to 'Sustain existing jobs and create more and better jobs' (Ministry for Tourism and Culture 2006: 5).

Local legislation, prevailing until Malta's accession to the EU in May 2004, made it mandatory that Air Malta makes an annual financial contribution to the Malta Tourism Authority (MTA) budget – the only airline to do so. Nonetheless, Air Malta was more than proactive in its support of the MTA mission. Air Malta sought to pool resources with MTA seeking win-win opportunities to develop Malta's tourism industry. This included co-operation to bring tour operators, travel agents, travel journalists and television crews to Malta on educational trips and joint participation in all key tourism travel fairs in European tourism source markets.

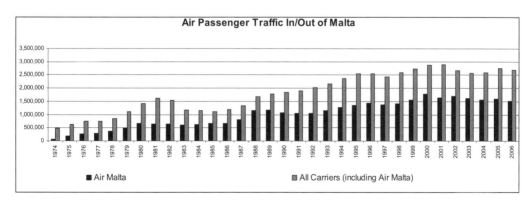

FIGURE 10.1 Development of Malta's air passenger traffic

Source: Air Malta data.

---

3   Competing airlines at the time included: scheduled airlines – Alitalia, British Airways, Libyan Arab Airlines, U.T.A. and other airlines – Austrian Airlines, Bavaria, British Airtours, British Caledonian, Britannia Airways, Condor Air Services, Dan Air, Finnair, Hapag Lloyd, Laker Airways, Sollair, Sterling Airways.

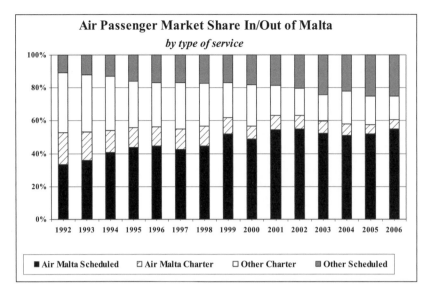

FIGURE 10.2 Development of scheduled and charter services
Source: Air Malta data.

Air Malta led the local tourism industry along the path of growth and also spearheaded the market diversification process to reduce the overdependence on the British market (dependence on British tourists peaked at 77 per cent in 1980). In the late seventies and early eighties, Air Malta took the bold decision of going into the accommodation business which was specifically oriented to and exclusively marketed for the continental tourist. This initiative together with the introduction of business class on its own flights met with success. The diversification process was triggered and took off in the late 1980s as the private accommodation sector followed suit.[4] While the UK became less important as a source market, British tourism to Malta still grew and maintained its level at just below half a million annual arrivals (see Figure 10.3).

The German, Italian, French, Dutch and other source markets developed faster than the British market (see Table 10.2) giving Malta's tourism industry a more diversified market mix.

Over the last five years, 80 per cent of Air Malta's passengers came from 8 different countries (the UK accounting for 36 per cent of the country mix). On the other hand, 80 per cent of the passengers flying to Malta on the other remaining airlines put together came from only four different countries, with a significant dependence on the UK, 48 per cent. Air Malta's sustained commitment to a diversified tourism market base is undisputed.

Tourism seasonality is characteristic to many Mediterranean holiday destinations. As clearly indicated in Figure 10.4, Malta is no exception. Nonetheless, Malta's tourism infrastructure, including hotels, operates year round. 'Reduce seasonality' and 'Manage tourism in Malta and Gozo on the principles of sustained development', are two other stated objectives of Malta's tourism policy (Ministry for Tourism and Culture 2006, 5–6)

---

4   In January 2007 the bed-places in tourist collective accommodation establishments in Malta were distributed in the following proportions: 5-star hotels 15 per cent, 4-star 40 per cent, 3-star 27 per cent, 2-star 2 per cent,
other accommodation (aparthotel, tourist village, guesthouse, hostel) 17 per cent. Source: National Statistics
Office (2007).

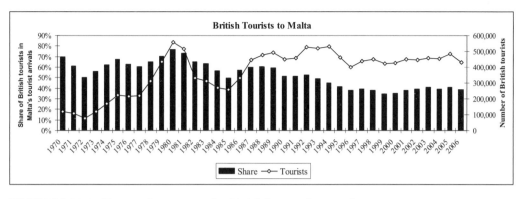

FIGURE 10.3 Dependency on the British tourist market

Source: National Statistics Office – Malta.

TABLE 10.2   Country share of tourist arrivals to Malta

1970		1980		1990		2000		2006	
UK	70%	UK	77%	UK	52%	U K	35%	UK	38%
Italy	8%	Italy	4%	Germany	15%	Germany	17%	Germany	11%
USA	7%	Germany	3%	Italy	7%	Italy	8%	Italy	10%
Sweden	3%	Libya	2%	Libya	4%	France	6%	France	7%
Germany	2%	Denmark	2%	France	4%	Netherlands	5%	Netherlands	3%
Other	10%	Other	13%	Other	18%	Other	29%	Other	31%

Source: National Statistics Office – Malta.

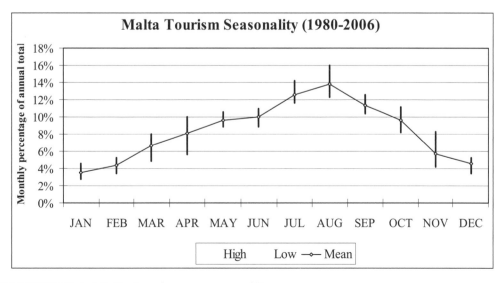

FIGURE 10.4 Malta tourism – seasonality

Source: National Statistics Office – Malta.

Air Malta strives to create business in both summer and winter by promoting different types of tourists and tourism interests – MICE[5], culture, sports (especially diving), health (spa and medical) and English language. Together with MTA, Air Malta often sponsors major international sports events held in Malta, such as the Powerboat P1 World Championship, Middle Sea Race and the Malta Open Snooker Competition. Air Malta's seasonality factor[6] was 0.35 over the last five years against 0.38 for all the other carriers flying to Malta.

Air Malta is committed to the stated objective of Malta's tourism policy, 'to increase accessibility to and from Malta' (Ministry for Tourism and Culture 2006: 6). As a full service carrier, through code-share and interline agreements with other carriers, flying to major hub airports (not regional), Air Malta offers secure flight connections to its passengers. Combined with a business Club Class service on-board, this specifically addresses the transcontinental travel needs of the more affluent tourist and business traveller.

Over the years, Air Malta pioneered the development of new international services, often followed by competition when the new markets reached viable levels of activity. This is how Air Malta developed its route network of 50 or so scheduled destinations, an air transport network supporting the tourism sector, the resident population and business community.

In the early 1990s, Air Malta experimented with the concept of hubbing through Malta, building on passenger flows between Egypt and Libya when the borders of the two N. African countries were closed. Sicily was also targeted as an important source of traffic for a Trans-Mediterranean hub. However, conflict in the Middle East and the eventual UN embargo on Libya severely restricted the scope for such a hub.[7] Moreover, on the economic side the hub concept proved difficult to develop due to the airport charges incurred by transferring passengers in Malta, who pay the same level of charges as Malta departing passengers.

In the late 1990s, Air Malta was actively considering going into the home-port cruise liner business, generating passengers that fly-cruise in and out of Malta to join Mediterranean cruises. Air Malta came close to getting into this business but finally decided that it was too risky for it to enter into such non-core activity. In hindsight, 9/11 events and the escalation of fuel prices proved that the airline took the right decision. Nonetheless, it remains a good prospect for another entity with the right resources and expertise.

Air Malta regularly invests heavily in aircraft fleet resources to remain ahead in its aviation and tourism business. The last wave of fleet renewal comprised the rollover of its entire fleet to a single type of Airbus A320/A319 aircraft, delivering the latest in aircraft passenger comfort and technology, a good match for the investment which Malta has made in top class hotel accommodation and other tourism amenities.

Air Malta's new aircraft fleet also confirms the airline's commitment to the global environment. Consider that Malta is an island covering only 316 square kilometres with a population density of 1,333 persons per square kilometre, increasing by a further 12–18 per cent in the peak summer months due to tourist intake. The new Airbus fleet ensures that the 80-dBA aircraft noise footprint on take-off is mostly contained within the airport perimeter. The 65-dBA noise footprint, equivalent to that generated by normal road traffic flow, affects only 17.5 per cent of Malta's land mass (see Zammit 2003). Air Malta is a friendly neighbour to the resident population and visiting community.

---

5   Meetings, Incentives, Conferencing and Exhibitions (MICE).
6   Measured as the ratio of the standard deviation and the monthly mean of tourism flows.
7   Due to the UN embargo, Air Malta ceased operating air services to Libya in March 1992, then resumed in April 1999.

Another stated objective of Malta's tourism policy is, 'to increase tourism earnings and tourism value-added' (Ministry for Tourism and Culture 2006, 5). The Air Malta Group generates 24 per cent of the total expenditure by tourists visiting Malta (Air Malta 1999). Moreover, the Group accounts for 7 per cent of the Maltese GNP, generates 5 per cent of the Malta Government income and is responsible for 5 per cent of national employment on a full-time equivalent basis. These parameters take into account the full multiplier effect of the Group's economic activity.

Every Lm1 million tourists spend in Malta leads to an increase of Lm0.62 million in GNP and 61 workers being employed (Blake *et al.* 2003)[8]. The Air Malta multipliers are shown in Table 10.3. Considering the import leakage inherent in the airline business, resulting from the purchase or lease of aircraft, purchase of aircraft components, expenses covering engine overhaul, fuel, landing and handling charges at foreign airports, navigation and en-route charges, Air Malta still has relatively significant multipliers for GNP and employment. This arises as Air Malta's aviation activity primarily takes place in Malta – employment of flight crew, engineers, all supporting operational, commercial, managerial and administrative staff together with locally contracted work such as part of aircraft maintenance, in-flight catering, ICT and general purchases. On the contrary, the business activity of all the other airlines flying into Malta occurs overseas. This means that the air transport element of the expenditure made by tourists flown to Malta by foreign airlines generates economic activity in the tourists' country of origin rather than in Malta. Indeed, Air Malta is a key and integral player in Malta's stated objective of increasing value-added from its tourism economic activity.

TABLE 10.3   Multipliers

GNP and employment multipliers for tourism sectors in Malta (direct & indirect effect only)		
Sector	GNP Maltese Liri (million)	Employment Full time equivalent
Accommodation	0.75	85.86
Restaurants	0.64	77.93
Car Hire	0.68	79.20
Air Malta	0.41	48.08
Other Services	0.47	53.52
Goods	0.53	47.29
Total	0.62	61.29

Source: Blake *et al.* (2003).

---

8   Exchange rate in 2007 was fixed at €1=Lm0.4293. Malta's entry in the euro-zone took place on the 1st January 2008.

KEY MALTA TOURISM ISSUES

Due to its size and finite carrying capacity, Malta cannot effectively compete with other Mediterranean resorts on the basis of 'mass tourism'. Malta encounters its capacity limits in the months of July and August when resources such as water, beach space, road network, waste management are stretched to capacity (Mangion 2001). Unlike many other countries, Malta's tourism is not confined to specific enclaves. When the leisure infrastructure (beaches, the capital city of Valletta as well as hotel and restaurant zones) becomes crowded, it negatively impinges on the quality of life of the visiting and resident population alike.

The thrust of Malta's tourism development has to maintain a quality product; reduce the negative social impact of tourism on a high population density; better utilise available resources, emphasising the country's history and culture together with its climate; minimise the increased demand on scarce resources (water, energy and space); and focus on higher value-added tourism in the peak months and on growing both volume and value tourism during the rest of the year.

At the same time, certain key issues have to be addressed, including: adjusting and repositioning accommodation capacity to capitalise on higher value-added demand; striving away from overdependence on any single source or type of tourism; moving towards a better mix between tourists generated by large volume operators (be they tour operators or LCC that push for the lowest airfare and accommodation rates and press the authorities for tourism support) and individual or group travellers (that tend to generate higher value-added); and repositioning the destination to attract the high daily spend, short-breaks segments.

Tourism and air transport policy need to be synchronised to guide future tourism development in a sustainable manner giving priority to the social, cultural, environmental and economic needs of the host country.

WINDS OF CHANGE

Malta's Accession to the EU

Under the ASA regime and the Malta Government Charter Policy, the small Malta market was not accessible to foreign charter carriers, but reserved for all scheduled carriers and for any Maltese charter operator. Price elasticity for air travel tends to be lower for passengers originating in an island market. The Charter Policy acted on the supply side of the market, maintaining a relatively higher price for air travel originating in Malta. However, Maltese residents enjoyed and still maintain a higher level of direct international air transport connectivity than for example Sicily.[9] Most often Sicilians have to fly via another Italian airport (Rome, Milan) to reach an international destination.

Nonetheless, before Malta's accession to the EU, Air Malta was exposed indirectly to the market pressures created by multilateral competition in Europe, since the battle waged by LCC on the traditional scheduled and charter carriers was mainly focused between

---

9   80 per cent of passengers at Catania and Palermo airports are directed to another Italian airport. 50 per cent of passengers at Catania and Palermo airports fly to either Rome or Milan – Italy's main hub airports.

the UK and Germany, prime tourism source markets, and the Iberian Peninsula, a major holiday destination. This exerted a gravitational pull on all the air travel markets and tourism flows across Europe, also affecting Malta's tourism industry and Air Malta.

Malta became an EU Member State in 2004 and simultaneously Air Malta had to rapidly adjust to a liberalised European air transport market recently characterised by the continuing rapid growth of LCC, a process that evolved in Europe over a span of 20 years.[10]

Ryanair started flying to Malta from Pisa and Luton on 31 October 2006, two and a half years after Malta's accession to the EU. Essentially, LCC broke into the Malta market not after a change in regulatory regime but after the Malta Government offered airlines a financial package for marketing assistance to operate selected 'underserved routes'.

The government's proactive policy of promoting LCC on the Malta market increased the urgency for Air Malta to adjust from national carrier to an EU community carrier. While the technical (regulatory) transition was so to speak instantaneous, the physical transition reflected by the adjustments in the expectations of all the airline's stakeholders is a long process.

Full Service/Low-Cost – A Balancing Act?

The paradigm shift in the European air transport regulatory regime, brought to the fore the 'Third Way' of doing airline business –the new LCC formula– which focuses on low-cost, low-fare, no frills segment of the market, characterised also by marketing and distribution of low-fares directly on the Internet. The implications of LCC development on the Malta aviation scene must be analysed in the context of the size of the Malta market, its finite carrying capacity as a tourist destination and the inherent value which a full service air transport system (with global connectivity) has for high value-added export manufacturing, the financial and ICT services sector, as well as the resident island population.

LCC entry in the Malta market is also viewed in the context of Ryanair's sustained proposal to base six aircraft[11] in Malta and carry 2 million passengers (maximum 1 million tourists) on condition that Malta airport costs per passenger are brought down from €25 to €7. The Malta Government responded with a 'service concession', a scheme based on the Community guidelines on financing of airports and start-up aid to airlines departing from regional airports (Department of Information Malta 2006). Ryanair initiated services under this scheme from Pisa, Luton and Dublin also adding Bremen, Valencia, Girona and Stockholm under a subsequent scheme. easyJet did not take up the first offer, although initially interested as the scheme specified Mulhouse-Basel as an underserved route. Discussions continue however to interest easyJet in destinations like Geneva, Basle, Madrid and Belfast.

---

10   For a succinct exposition of this process the reader is referred to Chapter 1 of CAA (2006a).
11   This is a significantly large base considering that Ryanair's bases outside its home bases of Stansted and Dublin featured the following deployment of aircraft: Frankfurt 9, Liverpool and Barcelona 7 each, Rome 5, Stockholm, Milan, Brussels, Luton, Glasgow 4 each, Pisa and Shannon 3 each, Bremen, Nottingham and Marseille 2 each and Cork 1 aircraft (Ryanair 2006).

Successful LCC operations are critically dependent on a formula which focuses heavily on costs even at the expense of sidetracking certain full service transportation needs demanded by the wider spectrum of economic activity that goes beyond tourism.

By design, LCC do not carry cargo and mail as this would negatively impinge on the turnaround times of aircraft, aircraft utilisation and subsequently on the overall cost of operation. As an island economy, Malta's air transport system cannot disregard the air freight requirements of the export-manufacturing sector (electronics, pharmaceuticals, fish-farming and other high value-added time-sensitive industries). Market requirements show that high frequency air freight capacity as provided by traditional scheduled passenger flights to a multiplicity of destinations, rather than infrequent dedicated freighter services, is critical in order to sustain such a key economic activity.

Air transport connectivity is critical for increased productivity and economic growth generated by all the sectors of the economy – tourism as well as manufacturing, financial services, ICT – more so for an island economy like Malta (Pearce 2007). Connectivity facilitates world trade (indispensable for high-tech and knowledge-based sectors, and just-in-time production), lubricating investment flows and spurring innovation. Connectivity is determined by the number of operated destinations, the frequency and capacity offered, and the number of onward connections available at each destination. Two key elements of the LCC formula which supports their low-cost base but only at the expense of connectivity are: (i) their concentration on secondary regional airports rather than the prime hubs, (ii) their strict adherence to point-to-point flying – no interlining even with their own flights. In contrast full service carriers align their flights into a network, connecting with their own services as well as with other full service carriers, and operate code-share agreements to further facilitate connectivity and seamless travel with comparable service levels on board. Malta's economy currently enjoys the benefit of such tangible investment in connectivity which Air Malta and other traditional scheduled carriers have made to effectively give global market reach to the island economy, whether for business, leisure and other travel.

Earlier, reference was made to Air Malta's niche marketing activity (special interest travel and MICE) jointly with the MTA and other stakeholders in tourism, to promote tourism flows in the off season and to further increase GNP via multipliers, so critical to an island economy facing operating limits in its carrying capacity. This specialised business differentiates in the market on the basis of product, price and promotion. To counter seasonality, LCC primarily act on price, which limits the scope of maximising value-added for the economy.

LCC and/or Distribution Power

As discussed by Barrett in Chapter 9, LCC flourished in Europe riding on three key factors: (i) a liberalised Single Market, (ii) a low-cost formula, (iii) low-cost distribution on the Internet combined with the low-fare brand promise.

For Air Malta and Malta's tourism industry, the evolution of how air travel is marketed, bundled, distributed and sold has more far reaching implications than balancing the mix between scheduled, charter and LCC airlines. Tourism marketing is strategically vital, especially for a small economy, as it determines the negotiating and market power of the stakeholders in the destination and source markets.

Corrodi (2007) succinctly addresses a common weakness experienced by many governments of small economies and local suppliers of tourism services. To counter insufficient 'critical mass', lack of 'resonance' and inability to 'convert' interest into sales, they often outsource the responsibility to position their tourism destination to foreign tour operators, through deeply discounted 'net rates' and brochure contributions. This still leaves open the issue of misalignment with the 'promise' – how the tour operator positions the destination vis-à-vis its customers and to what extent the destination delivers to the promised level. Such a situation can also develop if responsibility to position the tourism destination is left in the hands of LCC. It is therefore, critical that the prime focus of the tourism authorities is put on striving for a transparent and open market for tourism investment and checking the heavier-weight stakeholders from attempting to mop up all the profits generated by the industry. The authorities' policies and strategic (longer term) decisions on where and how they channel their tourism investment, and their ability to integrate, harmonise and synergise the local stakeholders of the tourism industry, determines the collective bargaining strength of the destination's local suppliers vis-à-vis their overseas counterparts. This role of the Tourism Ministry and the Malta Tourism Authority is crucial in promoting tourism's GDP growth and employment in a socially and environmentally sustained manner.

It is not an easy role as evidenced in recent years. The duress of stagnation in Malta's tourism industry since 2001 has put this collaborative process to a serious test, epitomised by the diverse positions taken by the different stakeholders in the industry on the question of whether, to what extent and who should give incentives to LCC to operate to Malta. To leverage the industry out of stagnation, also in the face of weak tour operator support, the accommodation and restaurant sector has been all out to turn tourism investment funds into incentives for LCC. The established air travel sector – traditional airlines and travel agents– have obviously been concerned by such incentives as they disturb a level playing field. The privatised airport company would do better with more passenger throughput and more airlines operating to Malta, but can ill afford having its airport charges pared across the board to the level demanded by LCC. Malta International Airport is Malta's only airport, operating with a single terminal geared to international standards, deriving 70 per cent of its revenue directly from aviation related activity (Malta International Airport 2007a).

While *prima face* the issue in the Malta scenario has been whether Malta should use tourism investment funds to tap into the growing LCC segment of the market, the real issue transcends this realm and implicates the wider air transport needs of the economy as a whole.

Shifting custom from tour operators to LCC can boost tourism flows in the short term but does not solve the problem of dependency on how the foreign tour operators and LCC sell Malta (Corrodi 2007). Tourism investment needs to be ultimately channelled into consumer research, destination marketing and a dynamic programme of direct marketing and selling co-ordinated by the local tourism stakeholders. Only then, would Malta gain the necessary leverage and reigns to drive its tourism industry into a sustainable growth mode, with emphasis placed on GDP growth rather than just more visitors or tourist nights.

This discussion centres only on Air Malta, especially since it is the major airline (accounting for 55 per cent of passenger movement in 2006) (Malta International Airport 2007b) and the key local aviation stakeholder in the tourism industry. Although Air Malta is substantially government owned, even though as a national airline it has had the role of a policy tool for the development of tourism and the economy, state aid has never been part of its economic equation, even more so now as an EU community carrier. Indeed, Air Malta is a financial asset to government as shareholder, but more importantly a national asset of intrinsic value to Malta's tourism industry, the local economy and resident population. Nonetheless, Air Malta has to sustain its competitiveness and seek its own path leading to its financial turnaround, drawing on its own internal resources. Financial incentives aimed primarily at attracting LCC to Malta, albeit offered to all interested airlines, makes Air Malta's turnaround process harder to achieve.

TURNING AROUND AIR MALTA

Air Malta's break in positive financial performance is illustrated in Figure 10.5.[12] In 1995 it became apparent that it could not sustain the level of operating profit that prevailed in the previous eight years. Eight years (1995–2002) where operating profit staggered just above break-even preceded the plunge into the red in 2003.

Air Malta's significant break in profitability came about for several reasons: (i) losses incurred in core airline operations, (ii) losses incurred by Air Malta's investment in AZZURRAair[13], (iii) losses incurred on the purchased fleet of seven BAE RJ70/85 aircraft[14], and (iv) ongoing sustained losses from subsidiary companies. As it entered the new millennium with such excess baggage and riding into unprecedented turbulence experienced by the global aviation industry (war, terrorism, epidemics, fluctuating currencies and spiralling fuel prices), it became more than clear that Air Malta could not sustain itself in its previous shape and size. Timely action had to be taken to sustain its balance sheet and maintain its cash-flow. Air Malta as a group of companies implemented a succession of initiatives in a wide ranging restructuring programme.

Fleet Restructuring

Valuable aircraft assets were capitalised upon to strengthen the balance sheet and cash flow. Risk exposure on less valuable aircraft assets was eliminated or capped. The core aircraft fleet was transformed into a single type capable of delivering to Air Malta's needs in the market. The transformed aircraft fleet became a key strength for the airline.

---

12   Note the following atypical financial years:
          2002*   is 16 months 1/4/2001 to 31/7/2002;
          2003#   is 12 months 1/8/2002 to 31/7/2003;
          2004**   is 12 months 1/8/2003 to 31/7/2004;
          2005~   is 8 months 1/8/2004 to 31/3/2005.
       The remaining years all run from April to March.
13   AZZURRAair's activity spanned the period 1994 to 2004, but its financial impact on Air Malta survived this period up to 2006.
14   Air Malta's commitment to the RJ fleet of aircraft spanned the period 1994 to 2008; however, losses were reported between 2001 and 2003 by way of impairment charges on the book value of aircraft and provisions against losses on their lease up to 2008.

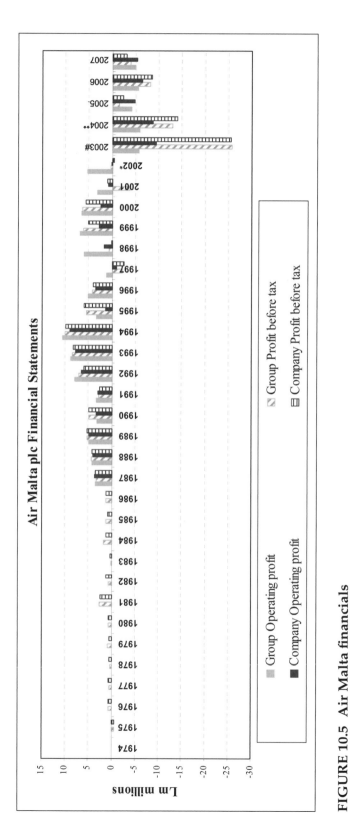

FIGURE 10.5 Air Malta financials

Sources: Air Malta annual reports and financial statements.

Associate and Subsidiary Companies

The Air Malta Group portfolio of investments was rationalised. Decisions were taken on each business unit based on profitability and core operation criteria. Care was also taken to capitalise on asset value of investments to the benefit of the holding company.

Core Operation

The whole airline operation was X-rayed in the context of a first and second business plan. The airline was repositioned in the market, the route network redesigned, costs benchmarked and reduced across the board, processes reviewed, fresh investment made to support the airline's revenue earning capability as well as its sales and distribution capacity.

Human Resources

The airline business, like tourism, is a people's industry. None of the initiatives mentioned so far could or would have ever been successful without addressing the employees' needs, concerns and expectations. After all, employees represent a significant part of the airline's value-added. The collaboration under the Rescue Plan agreement, the open book communication policy implemented through the Works Council, the safeguarding of the employees interests (no forced redundancies) and judicious decisions with regards to outsourcing (aimed only at increasing efficiency, reducing costs and raising quality of service and at the same time safeguarding employment), were the underlying elements driving the success of Air Malta's turnaround. Over a three year period staff numbers engaged directly by Air Malta were reduced by 20 per cent.

These initiatives were undertaken in earnest, striving for a balance between financial exigencies and the capacity of the organisation to absorb the accelerated rate of change. The balance had to be achieved as the airline walked a tight rope that was tensed up by escalating competition in the market and inclined ever more steeply by breathtaking escalation in fuel prices. Essentially, the savings in non-fuel costs achieved during the term of the Rescue Plan were countervailed by escalation in fuel prices. Investments made in the revenue management system narrowed the profitability gap, albeit significantly mitigated by heavy fare discounting in response to higher levels of competition. Against these odds, the airline managed to cut its operating losses from Lm7.9 million (financial year March 2004) to Lm3.2 million (financial year March 2007), before accounting for terminal benefits paid to employees under the Voluntary Redundancy Scheme.

In any business, unit cost has to relate to unit revenue. Unit revenue is an indication of the level of service or value-added generated by the business. The relationship between costs and revenues is illustrated in Figure 10.6. Four possibilities arise from this Relative Unit Cost/Unit Revenue ('RUCUR' Box) analysis. The High-Cost/Low-Fare option runs out of business in no time. A Low-Cost/High-Fare oasis turns out to be a mirage on the landscape of a competitive airline market. In airline business, market forces allow possibilities only along a value-added scale that slides down from full business class service (high-cost/high-fare), down to economy/leisure based service (low-cost/low-fare).

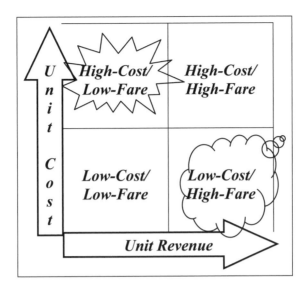

FIGURE 10.6 Relative unit cost/unit revenue – 'RUCUR' box

In practical terms, this model translates in what is shown in Figure 10.7 where different airlines are positioned relative to one another according to their total operating cost per available seat kilometre (CASK) and their relative passenger revenue per available seat kilometre (RASK). Air Malta is identified. The position of the two major LCC is approximated, bearing in mind limitations inherent in source data.

The global full service network carriers, with high business to leisure traffic ratios, would gravitate towards the top end of the trend line – in the high value-added/high cost quadrant. Leisure based scheduled carriers, like Air Malta, are positioned at the bottom end – in the low-fare/low-cost quadrant. An airline positioned on the lower-right side of the trend line has a competitive edge over others positioned on the higher-left side of the trend line. Moreover, to become profitable an airline's RASK has to exceed CASK, that is, it has to traverse over to the bottom-right side of the diagonal that cuts across the graph.

This 2005 snapshot highlights a number of points: (i) Air Malta compares well with industry trends, (ii) Air Malta is positioned in the predominantly leisure based end of the market, (iii) Air Malta's RASK was still lower than its CASK meaning that it was still not profitable as evidenced by the airline's financial results.

Since 2005, Air Malta has moved further along the roadmap outlined in its Rescue Plan. Suffice it to say that a proportion of the restructuring and turnaround initiatives mentioned earlier materialised post 2005. Consider also the time lag between implementing initiatives and achievement of results. Moreover, the airline has not run out of initiatives and is still writing its story. Nevertheless, the economic assumption of *ceteris paribus* does not hold in the dynamic airline industry as the competitive scenario evolves by the day.

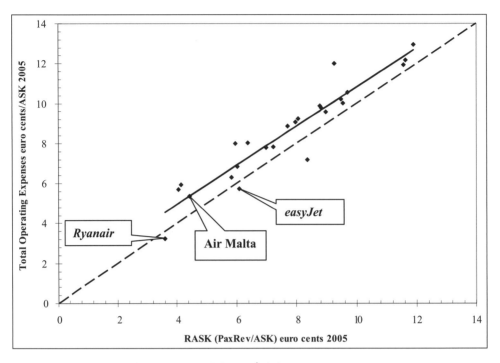

FIGURE 10.7 Air Malta's competitive position – 2005

Note: Data source is AEA for geographic Europe, that is intra-European operations excluding domestic flights. Data for Ryanair and easyJet is sourced from their published financial statements.
Source: AEA.

CHALLENGES AHEAD

It is always risky to prognosticate about issues that will challenge the business in the years ahead. There will always be exogenous factors that strike unexpectedly. However, there are a number of issues and developing trends that are relevant to Air Malta's future:

- Proliferation of LCC in Europe is an established trend. The extent to which LCC will penetrate the Malta market, their impact on the incumbent airlines, and their specific impact on Air Malta's route network development and profitability, are difficult to estimate in a competitively dynamic scenario.

- The development of intra-EU operations by Air Malta and the further establishment of its secondary bases in the EU can be partly driven by developments in the Malta market (emphasising the need for network diversification) and partly the result of the airline's success in flexing its wings as an EU community carrier.

- Point-to-point leisure passengers, full service premium and connecting global travellers as well as air freight and fast courier services, all combine and synergise together on a full service airline like Air Malta flying to a network of prime airports. Some of these elements of air travel demand cannot be as effectively supported independently – hence, it is important that local air transport and tourism authorities recognise the real value which a full service airline like Air Malta has to the island's economy.

- The hubbing concept that did not meet with success in the past, may still offer opportunity to a full service carrier based in Malta. Depending on the level of airport charges levied on transfer passengers relative to departing passengers in Malta and relative to alternate neighbouring airports, this passenger hub concept may be developed at MIA by Air Malta as the home carrier, before the lead is taken up in a neighbouring airport.

- The fly-cruise concept can take off in Malta. Air Malta has an established route network which through its synergies and agreements with other global carriers goes far beyond its direct reach. The new cruise liner terminal is operative. The next stage is for one of the many cruise lining companies that regularly calls at Malta's magnificent Grand Harbour, to make Malta its home-port.

- At the turn of the next decade, the EU is setting itself to include aviation in its Emissions Trading Scheme (ETS) as discussed by Daley *et al.* in Chapter 18. This will certainly impact tourism especially in island economies like Malta (due to the nearly absolute dependence of tourism on air travel) and consequently Air Malta, depending on how ETS is implemented and whether a derogation or abatement for small island economies will be permitted.

This is by no means an exhaustive list. It is just to illustrate the evolving environment in which Air Malta together with all other airlines operates.

Air Malta embarked on this change process of transiting from a national carrier to a EU leisure based carrier, on an agreed platform – the Rescue Plan. It is the spirit of collaboration of the key stakeholders participating in this plan (whether it is maintained in the framework of the formal Rescue Plan or exercised under other alternatives) that makes the turnaround process of Air Malta possible and successful. Air Malta's future rests on being a value focused airline, operating at the highly competitive edge of the leisure travel market, however still maintaining its full service concept that is of critical value in the wider context of the Maltese island economy. A local air transport policy that is cognizant of this reality would complement Air Malta's efforts to realise its plan. The evolution of the EU air transport policy (including aviation ETS) too will leave its mark on the future of Air Malta.

As a national airline, operating under the bilateral ASA regime, Air Malta had an element of protection but was also restricted in its potential for business development. The liberalised Single Market exposed Air Malta to both new business opportunities and higher levels of competition. The 'metamorphosis of a national airline' is a very apt way of describing Air Malta's evolving strategy to meet its new challenges. Metamorphosis is a complex and delicate process that transports an entity into a new existence. This transformation process bears high risks but the rewards of success are survival and growth. The future belongs not to the biggest or strongest as much as to the most flexible and adaptable to new realities. To the extent that Air Malta embraces this Darwinian principle it will first secure its future and then its role of serving the country of which it bears its name.

11

Leisure Travel, Network Carriers and Alliances

Kostas Iatrou and Elena Tsitsiragou

INTRODUCTION

Air transport and leisure tourism have developed in the last decades of the 20th century on parallel interdependent courses. The two have a symbiotic relationship inextricably linked by mutual dependence with the one fostering the development of the other. A survey of international arrivals in a group of twenty major countries indicates that over 70 per cent of international tourists arrive by air (UNWTO 2000). Catalysts for these changes were globalisation, the deregulation/liberalisation of the air transport and the concomitant increased use of information and communication technologies. Section two of this chapter highlights the role of network carriers in serving leisure and travel demand. Section three then discusses changes in leisure travel patterns and the impact of airline alliances. Subsequently, section four presents business challenges in the airline industry and the arising implications for alliances; finally, section five concludes.

THE ROLE OF NETWORK CARRIERS IN SERVING LEISURE AND TRAVEL DEMAND

Until the early 1990s and in terms of air transport, the leisure traveller market was dominated by the traditional scheduled legacy or network carriers – partly or completely government owned – and also in Europe charter or non-scheduled carriers. The network carriers have played a major role in tourism and its growth by providing the most easily accessible, secure, standard and reliable transport service. They flew on domestic and international routes providing full on board and ground services covering as many demand categories as possible and offering several classes of services. National carriers were often projected as "ambassadors" of their countries promoting tourism abroad and bringing tourists into the country. With the support of their governments, they built connections all around the world. Many air routes have been initiated for political reasons but have been sustained by the demand for business tourism and growing leisure markets. In fact, a strong argument in favour of the national character of airlines is the fact they can provide regular air services irrespective of the country's situation, immune to domestic emergencies, crises, health risks or physical catastrophes or even political pressures (e.g. travel warnings issued unilaterally by the governments of the main tourism generating markets which remain in place even after the causes that theoretically justified the warnings have been removed). If because of a potential crisis, air connections are discontinued and leisure traveller flows are redirected to other destinations, it would be extremely difficult to reinstate regular air transport in the absence of national carriers. Without the latter or at least some form of government supported air transport, many developing countries could be marginalised from tourist receiving countries and become dependent on the commercial objectives of mega carriers.

The economic and aviation environment markedly changed in the early 1990s, as globalisation and increased market liberalisation have had an impact on aviation. The concept of a "national carrier" has eroded and financial problems made national airlines too expensive to keep for "national pride" reasons. As argued by Papatheodorou in Chapter 5, the deregulation of the air transport industry first in USA in 1978 and then in Europe in the 1990s tore apart the traditional distribution channels, blurred market boundaries leading to profound structural changes in the whole tourism supply chain forcing all players to rethink and change their business models. In fact, the US market deregulation was followed by industry consolidation producing several carriers with large national networks and a strong commercial orientation. These carriers saw greater opportunities for expansion in international markets than within the more mature US domestic market. In Europe, where international traffic already constituted a substantial part of flag carriers' revenue, the trend toward privatisation and away from state aid was putting increased pressure on carriers to become self-sufficient.

Air transport liberalisation has also led to consumer-friendly developments in the form of a fall in fares, increased and less time-consuming connections and a rise in the number of destinations served. The authorisation of free market access on air routes allowed the development of low-cost no-frills carriers (LCCs) first in the domestic US, then in intra-European flights and lately in Asia. Their success is due to the adoption of an alternative strategy, i.e. focusing on smaller airports outside the metropolitan areas and outside peak times, as well as taking a point-to-point market approach (Papatheodorou and Lei 2006), which allows them to offer frequency at low cost. LCCs have introduced low fares, generating new traffic and winning market share from scheduled and charter airline competitors alike.

To address effectively the emerging challenges in the new competitive environment, the network carriers decided to conclude a number of agreements and form alliances with each other. These are voluntary agreements between airlines to enhance the competitive positions of the allied partners. Members benefit from greater scale and scope economies, lower transaction costs and a sharing of risks while remaining independent. They cooperate on scheduling, frequent flyer programmes (FFP), equipment maintenance and schedule integration. The alliances provide leisure travellers with benefits in spite of not targeting them as their primary customer segment. These benefits range from more convenient and customer-friendly pricing systems (e.g. round the world tickets, the various passes in the USA, Europe and Asia etc.), better travel options and flight coordination (more choices in terms of both destinations and frequencies) and a seamless approach to flying in general (e.g. inter-airline through check-in, interline electronic ticketing, consistent baggage policies etc.). The alliances also offer the ability to redeem points and flights on allied partners and provide lounge access priority boarding and upgrades, etc. At present, the three mega-alliances – Star Alliance (led by Lufthansa and United Airlines), SkyTeam (led by Air France – KLM and Delta Airlines) and oneworld (led by British Airways and American Airlines) – account for more than 60 per cent of world traffic. Each of these major alliances encompasses almost every significant business and leisure market across the globe.

CHANGES IN LEISURE TRAVEL PATTERNS AND THE IMPACT OF AIRLINE ALLIANCES

The reduction in air fares resulting from the LCCs and the greater choice and flexibility offered by Internet have brought about three major irreversible changes in the behaviour of leisure travellers in relation to air transport: disintermediation (that is cutting out middlemen and bypassing the traditional travel agencies and global distribution systems), a reduction in seasonality (as people now take shorter and more frequent breaks to accessible urban destinations) and a strong belief in the commoditisation of the airline product: this means that travellers are convinced that airlines are all basically the same and the only thing that matters, certainly to leisure customers, is price. In a 2006 survey, the majority of non-business surveyed travellers, even in the mature and flying-familiarised market of North America, could not distinguish between the network carriers and low cost carriers for most differentiating items and claimed that they purchased solely on price; likewise, even business travellers are becoming less willing to pay for higher quality services claiming that price is even more important than safety and FFP (Wessels 2006). In an IATA 2007 survey (IATA, 2007), European leisure travellers were asked whether they would fly LCCs or traditional carriers for their leisure trips: the overwhelming majority of travellers answered that they would compare the price and decide based on the price, illustrating once more that the distinction between LCCs and scheduled airlines is now blurred.

The Role of Airlines Alliances

So, now that LCCs have captured the overwhelming majority of leisure travellers on short- and medium-haul markets, what is then the relationship and interaction between the price-sensitive leisure travellers and the airline alliances? No one can deny that deregulation and airline alliances have been consumer-friendly as they have made it possible for the airline industry to provide better quality in the form of more frequency, better connections, integrated route network and lower-priced service around the world. At the same time, the not-so-often-admitted truth is that airline alliances were created to formulate a network of services and incentives that would attract high-yield and high-fare business passengers: features such as a global network, lounge access, FFP, a 'seamless' travel experience with reliable departure times and minimum waiting time all cater for the needs of this particular target group (Iatrou and Oretti 2007). Although these passengers typically represent only around 20 per cent of total traffic, their contribution to total revenue is much higher – about 50 per cent. As they represent a respectable part of the airlines' customer base, particularly in terms of yield, a substantial change in their preferences can strongly impact on a carrier's bottom line. What counts for airline alliances is not simply volume, but 'valuable volume', i.e., which maximises revenues per seat-kilometre.

When airlines speak of 'valuable volume', what they mean is high-yield business class passengers (Iatrou and Oretti 2007), preferably on profitable long-haul routes.

Airline alliances aim at serving and controlling the highly profitable cross-continental, transatlantic and transpacific level. Some European airlines derive more than 30 per cent of their profits from transatlantic services (Egan 2001) with this percentage jumping to 50 per cent in the case of British Airways, as it controls the majority of the highly lucrative landing and takeoff slots at Heathrow, the world's busiest international airport. Growth in the 1990s meant that airlines were expected to access new markets, thus they needed to start building an international route structure. It seems that alliances have been part of a wider move by some carriers to shift resources into the longer haul market. To achieve that purpose, they operate on a hub-and-spoke system and the whole alliance structure aims at increasing hub-to-hub traffic, especially on the high yield and efficient transatlantic and transpacific routes. Airlines ally to link their networks to effectively feed passengers from spokes to hubs and through those networks to transfer these travellers around the globe. Hubs are the centres around which airlines participating in alliances develop their whole strategy, from code share agreements to schedule optimisation and FFP lock-in effects. This becomes even more evident by the fact that some 54 per cent of all European long-distance air traffic is concentrated at the four busiest airports – London–Heathrow, Frankfurt, Paris and Amsterdam – that is, the hubs of the European pillars of the three alliances. Airline alliances have led to network economies in long-haul markets: major carriers have strengthened their position on inter-continental routes, while other airlines previously enjoying a larger market share on short-haul markets have been experiencing financial problems and increased competition from low-cost, no-frills airlines. It has even been argued that the ultimate motive behind the Air France–KLM merger was the desire of the two carriers to become the first 'long-haul network dominators' (Doganis 2006).

Airline Alliances and the Leisure Passenger

Having the above in mind, it could be safely argued that airline alliances are interested in three kinds of leisure travellers: those flying on transatlantic and transpacific routes, business travellers combining business with leisure and some other upmarket passengers. Leisure travellers – or travel agencies designing their itinerary – resort to alliances and allied partners when they have selected a medium or long-haul destination (most of the times with one or more transit stops) that can be reached only by the services of network carriers. The more complex the trip is, the more useful the alliance is likely to be (Papatheodorou and Iatrou 2007). It is in this case that consumers can take advantage of the competition between the three major strategic alliances and that «network» becomes a real competitive advantage.

In fact, prices and the duration of the flight time are inversely related to the decision to fly direct (i.e. shorter flight time) or not. For example, a tourist will be more likely to take an indirect flight if it is significantly cheaper than a direct one and provided that the difference in flight duration is not important. Network carriers and alliances can increase the number of leisure tourist passengers. Competitive pricing is the main leverage in this segment that can be overcome by offering more codeshare and interline agreements and better tailored-made travel packages (Papatheodorou and Iatrou 2007). A point not so often referred to is scheduling in relation to short breaks. Those planning to spend a long weekend in another city would like to be able to make the most out of the time available.

Therefore, the price-sensitive leisure passengers can make their choice based on schedule too. Thus, if the network carrier's timetable gives them the opportunity to spend more valuable time at the destination of their choice, they will opt for this carrier provided of course that the price difference between LCC fares and network carrier tickets is not substantial. Network carriers need to realise that leisure travellers are willing to pay a bit more for travel frills and convenience at "normal" economy class rates.

Unfortunately for network airlines, the typical price-sensitive travellers are not knowledgeable of the value added by airline agreements and alliances in particular. As a result, they may be lured by the promotional fares offered by low cost carriers and charter airlines. A possible strategy for airline alliances would be to extend and diversify their marketing efforts to attract affluent leisure passengers but also to inform business travellers about leisure opportunities offered by alliances especially in long-haul travel. Direct marketing and customer relationship management built on generous loyalty schemes (i.e. FFP) can be of major importance here. In the last years, there have been some attempts to ease the way of accruing frequent flyer miles. In the United Kingdom, AirMiles is a British Airways-led loyalty programme through which points are earned on purchases at participating merchants such as Shell petrol stations and Tesco supermarkets; the points awarded can be redeemed for flights, hotels, travel insurance and package holidays. Strapped for cash consumers are more likely to participate in such schemes. Critics argue that limited availability of flights makes Airmiles almost impossible to use; moreover, large amounts of money need to be spent to be awarded sufficient miles for a flight, which would cost peanuts with a low-cost airline – this contradicts the «democratic» character of such schemes. Others suggest that the real benefit of loyalty schemes is the potential they offer to create a massive database. From a business perspective, the primary goal of a loyalty card scheme is to improve customer relationship management. Companies gather information on customers so that they can target them more effectively with marketing communications. Even LCCs have adopted such loyalty schemes: easyJet teamed up in June 2007 with National Westminster Bank and the online travel agent eBookers to launch the YourPoints programme. The scheme is the first loyalty programme that allows customers to buy easyJet flights with points. It has been argued that in the short-haul and LCC market brand alone conveys any pricing power and thus cannot "lock in" passengers. But in an increasingly competitive, mature and cash strapped air transport environment facing several external threats, carriers, LCCs as well as "legacy carriers", will use any weapon available in their marketing arsenal to create and increase their a pool loyal travellers. LCCs gradually realised that FFPs do help increase loyalty and direct specific buying decisions and so took to the "charm" of establishing FPPs for business travellers. The next step seems to be the establishment of partnerships with banks, hotels etc to allure leisure travellers no matter how "infrequent" they might be.

A possible partnership with specialised tour operators and/or travel agents (both online and offline) could prove necessary as many of these passengers may lack the knowledge or the confidence to book a complex airline product or a long-haul holiday package without the assistance of an intermediary. In this context, it should also be noted that airline alliances have been under pressure to expand vertically into other areas of the travel industry, such as hotels, travel agencies, car hire or tour organisers, to gain better control over the 'total travel product'. The clearest example of vertical alliances in the air transport industry are the collaborative arrangements that exist between airlines and hotels, car hire firms, travel agents and other companies involved in travel and tourism, formed in an attempt to provide total travel products and secure larger consumer expenditure on travel. British Airways for example, is in partnership with a number of hotel chains which include Marriott, Hilton, the Ritz-Carlton Group and the Savoy Group, as well as with Hertz for car rental and Diners Club for credit cards (Iatrou and Oretti 2007). Whether these vertical alliances can lead to tourism/air transport concentration remains to be seen. In the past, there were some diversification efforts from the part of the airlines but this strategy was in many cases abandoned. Air France, for example, sold Méridien Hotels and the tour operators Jet Tour and Go Voyage and focused on its core activities. But in a tourist industry currently found in a state of flux the airlines may again reconsider their options.

In any case, leisure travel may add value and profitability to airline alliances and hence it should be seriously considered in relevant commercial decisions (Papatheodorou and Iatrou 2007). The booming traffic in the US-India market fuelled by the large expatriate population of Indian nationals and families with strong ties to India has been exploited by the US majors, such as American and Continental, providing a good example of an opportunity that network carriers have not let go unexploited. It is widely admitted that the fare gap between legacy and LCC is narrowing as majors are reducing their expenses to match LCC fares. Airlines realise that leisure travellers are willing to pay a little extra for more comfort and do try to simplify fares and pricing on shorter-haul services. It remains to be seen whether airline alliances can really differentiate themselves and convince leisure passengers that they offer a higher-class product and quality of service worthy of this extra cost (Wessels 2006). If they can convince travellers that there is a real differentiation of product at a competitive price then they can influence their choice.

BUSINESS CHALLENGES IN THE AIRLINE INDUSTRY AND IMPLICATIONS FOR ALLIANCES

LCC and All-Business Carriers

New challenges lie ahead for airlines, leisure charter carriers, LCCs and network carriers alike. The shift from traditional airlines to LCCs will continue unabated assisted by the trend towards cheaper, shorter and faster travel. The no-frills airlines will continue to have a strong impact on tourism, especially on the short city-breaks market. The enlargement of the EU in May 2004 to include ten more countries has given LCCs a renewed impetus, with many new services starting in Central and Eastern Europe as a result of the deregulation that EU membership brings. Eastern Europe is also increasing in importance as both a destination and a source market.

On the other hand, there are signs of market maturity in the LCC and short-haul market in both the USA and in Europe, not only because of purely economic and business reasons but also because of the environmental reactions against the growth of short-haul routes. This is forcing carriers to operate at airports that would not normally be associated with the low-cost model. Southwest, for instance, has starting operating out of Denver, where it is going head-to-head with Frontier and United. It is also planning to operate out of Washington Dulles, where again it will come up against United. LCCs, with new market creation reaching saturation at least in North America and in Western Europe- with costs creeping higher, thanks to the fuel price increase and the imposition of environmental taxes, and with few new ways to cut expenses, venture to big markets to boost their revenue. The market trend, perhaps to the point of saturation, is also changing the model in other ways and some low-cost carriers start flying longer sectors; some are even operating hub-and-spoke systems. Jetstar, an Australian, Qantas-backed low-cost carrier has inaugurated low-cost flights from Australia to south-east Asia, later possibly moving to Europe. Canadian Zoom Airlines has followed suit operating year-round scheduled flights to UK and France. None has really developed as a major operator in the same way as the successful short-haul budget carriers. Nonetheless, large aircraft such as the A380 (able to hold up to 853 passengers in an all-economy layout and with fuel-efficient technology reducing the cost per passenger by 20 per cent compared to 747) raise the possibility of cheaper tickets and may enable true low-cost long-haul service.

Moreover, alliances of network carriers face increased competition from the success of all-premium carriers (e.g. Silverjet) that aim at attracting business travellers who want to avoid the hassle of spending two hours in airports before take-off. If the endeavour proves successful, network airlines will have to do some serious thinking in relation to their strategies and operating models.

The Role of High Speed Trains and New Tourism Destinations

Yet, there is another development that may affect mostly LCCs: the high-speed train revolution in Europe. Surface transport could replace transborder air travel over short sectors, at least when there are no other barriers such as mountains and sea. Long-distance high-speed rail links are being pushed hard by European authorities – meaning that, for sectors of less than 3h by train, even LCCs will be unable to compete. In the short term, too, these routes will almost without exception be operated by state-owned and state-subsidised rail companies (Flight International, 2002). Network carriers have already experienced the increasing threat of rail connections. Air France-KLM is planning to reduce the London-Paris flights from 12 to 5 faster due to stiff competition from high-speed rail operator Eurostar (Airline Business, 2007)-this move certainly makes way for more transatlantic traffic. Railways from Germany, France, Switzerland, Austria, the Netherlands and Belgium along with Eurostar are planning to kick off an alliance called "RailTeam" to achieve cost and fare reduction and provide clear information, direct connections and smooth change-overs to win over international travellers by offering a "really attractive and effective alternative to the more environmentally damaging, short-haul airlines" across Western Europe. Concern over climate change, hassles at overcrowded airports, delayed flights and congested roads have conspired with better high-speed rail technology to make the train an increasingly attractive green alternative as also argued by Daley et al. in Chapter 18. About 80 per cent of leisure travellers and 70 per cent of business passengers said they would travel more on trains if fares were slightly cheaper (*The Guardian* 2006). Even in the train-averse United States, Amtrak now competes comfortably with airlines on its Boston–New York–Washington express rail service.

Network airlines rejoice at the prospect of trains making a dent in the market for short-haul flights at the expense of LCCs. Perhaps in anticipation of this development – but most of the times forced by the authorities – European network airlines have concluded intermodal code share agreements with high-speed train services: as rail is taking over shorter-haul feeder services, capacity for more profitable medium and long-haul intercontinental flights at congested hubs would be freed up. It is estimated that extending short-haul routes to rail could free up to 5 per cent of Frankfurt Airport's 460,000 annual flight movements, the equivalent of one year of growth (Airline Business 2001). It is estimated that 10–15 per cent of air traffic in Europe could be absorbed by high-speed train connections (Iatrou 2004). But while airlines may like the idea of securing slots at congested hubs, giving up so many 'spokes' of the hub-and-spoke structure would entail redesigning their whole network structure or even reconsidering their operating model.

Another development favouring network airlines and airline alliances is the continuing geographic spread and diversification of tourist destinations as also discussed by A. Graham in Chapter 3. Although tourist activity is still concentrated in the developed regions of Europe and the Americas, a substantial proliferation of new tourist-receiving markets is emerging in the developing regions. The UNWTO predicts that by 2010 a quarter of all tourist arrivals will be received by countries in the developing world. Alliances are the only ones that can cater for the needs of travellers who want to scout new destinations. LCCs could find it difficult to flourish in such countries because of the protectionist policies of these countries, the restrictive bilateral agreements and the dearth of secondary airports. The very sustainability of the business model of LCCs is based on the use of secondary airports and their reduced cost. Having to use primary airports derives them of the opportunity to offer prices competitive enough to lure leisure passengers away from established carriers.

Hub Strategies and Airline Alliances

Hub-and-spoke operations of the network carriers lower unit costs by increasing load factors. On the other hand, they also increase distances, raising the overall cost and time of a journey, especially since these carriers serve main congested and high fee airports. This simply means that on short-haul routes, network carriers cannot compete with LCCs. Thus, the former have left intra-continental routes to smaller partners and/or LCCs and have concentrated on getting the most out of the intercontinental markets which remain to a significant extent protected by some form of Air Service Agreement. In several cases, network carriers have also opened up new intercontinental services.

The impending consolidation of air transport and the new aircraft technology have triggered a debate over the possible bypassing of certain destinations. The argument over the future airline network configuration centres upon hub concentration and thus the increase of hub-to-hub flights versus hub fragmentation leading to more and more point-to-point flights. Apart from the industry pundits contemplating over the future of the industry, the argument is also kindled by aircraft manufacturers in their effort to support their business choices and of course sell aircraft.

On the one hand, there are those that support that the continuing deregulation will open the possibility of new city pairs, which, together with the preference of passengers for point-to-point flying and the fact that smaller long-haul planes (manufactured mostly by Boeing), make it both possible and financially sustainable to establish such routes. Airline markets naturally evolve toward point-to-point flying over time. In their early stages, hub-and-spoke flying predominates because very few routes have enough demand to warrant direct routes. As a market develops, however, certain routes reach the necessary demand threshold to justify direct daily services (Boston Consulting Group 2006). If there is no need to feed to another partner's hub, alliances will decline in importance. This trend may be reinforced by open skies agreements that may allow airlines to reap the direct benefits of mergers and acquisitions. We may then see airlines bypassing their alliance partners, and/or build code share relationships with low-cost carriers in other airports. Upholders of this view put their money in hub fragmentation supporting growth of point-to-point flying. Others counter-argue that given the enormous capacity and environmental strains of many airports and the continuing urbanisation especially in Asia, very large aircraft (manufactured by Airbus) will be useful in connecting many hub airports especially since they also bring down the cost of such flights. These advocates have their stakes in hub consolidation and hub-to-hub flights. Perhaps the middle ground answer is the correct one: one does not exclude the other and could even prove complementary.

In any case, the inevitable market consolidation in Europe means that certain hubs will be demoted given their geographic proximity and there will be fewer long-haul flights. Proof of this is the reduction in transatlantic city pairs receiving non stop service as a result of the bankruptcies of Swissair and Sabena. Consolidation within Europe will come as network carriers pull off short-haul routes in the face of the low-cost challenge. Instead, they will look to affiliated regional carriers or even LCCs to feed their intercontinental services. This will be particularly relevant with the arrival of the A380 at Europe's airports. An effective feeder system will be essential if such a large aircraft is to be operated profitably from Frankfurt or London or Paris. It does not mean, however, that certain airports will close down as a result of no services. Their demotion will be a blow for the surrounding area and the airport employees but in general air transport services whether operated by network carriers, regional airlines or LCCs will remain as long as there is sufficient demand. At the same time it is true that those cities actually generating enough traffic to support non-stop transatlantic operations in their own right will sustain such services as long as their overall economic environment is sound. Delta Airlines has mounted a major European point-to-point push from the NY city area.

CONCLUSIONS

The very marketing argument of airline alliances, i.e. "getting passengers to all four corners of the world" and the adage "if there is a market need there is someone to satisfy it", may be a guarantee that there will be connections for every destination in the world: these may be cumbersome and time-consuming perhaps, but one way or the other there will be services. When there is a demand or a need for a service between two points, there will be someone to provide this service. But leisure traffic is a market in which the determinant factor is price and the concomitant "value for money". The question is not only what is on offer but whether the passengers are willing to buy it or whether they can be convinced that it is worth buying it.

At the same time, tourism is an unstable industry, as it is highly sensitive to the business cycle, political tensions, health crises and consumer tastes. Leisure air travel is constantly haunted by the threat of economic downturn, which together with the increasing fuel prices and the euro-dollar exchange fluctuations will influence leisure travellers' behaviour and route flow. It is estimated that a 10 per cent increase in the price of a ticket will result in a concomitant 15 per cent fall in the demand for air travel, which could hit LCCs harder than network carriers. (*Flight International*, 2007b)

China and India, as the new economic superpowers, will capture around 15 per cent of the expected global growth of passengers. This will be driven mainly by economic activities, but new inbound and outbound tourism flows will account for a significant slice of the traffic which will bring about a shift in traffic from North to South and from West to East.

The fierce competition between LCCs and traditional carriers and the need for airlines to cut costs has blurred the distinction in product offering and at the same time has led to differentiation of services. Some airlines have abolished their business class on short and medium-haul flights; LCCs have introduced features to attract business clients, such as in-flight entertainment; while some airlines are now offering all business flights air travel, with all its amenities and luxury facilities on intercontinental flights. It seems that air travel is becoming part of the tourism attraction itself. In any way, the future of air transport will depend on product innovation and customer preferences and on the overall economic and political stability.

Airlines need to be ready to assess whether they have a full understanding of these changes, and their impact on the business environment, business practices and models but also be ready for the unexpected. What they can really pray for is the development of world economies because as population grows and as disposable income increases, people undertake more leisure travel preferably by air.

12

Market Power and Vertical (Dis)integration? Airline Networks and Destination Development in the United States and Dubai

Keith G. Debbage and Khaula Alkaabi

INTRODUCTION

The competitive strategies of the airline industry have substantially impacted both overall accessibility levels and the economic performance of major tourist destinations across the world. During the 1970s, the development of the jet engine and wide-bodied aircraft essentially triggered the era of mass tourism in places like Florida, Greece, Hawaii and Spain. In subsequent decades, the airline industry has experienced radical shifts in the regulatory regime that sets airfares and authorises air routes and these major changes have further altered the geography of leisure destinations. For example, the deregulation of airline markets in both the USA and the European Union (EU) increased airline management's freedom to restructure route networks and, thus, substantially altered accessibility levels in certain key leisure markets.

One of the most striking results of airline liberalisation has been the increase in market power on some routes to and from airline hubs and the heightened levels of competition on other routes. The purpose of this chapter is to articulate how the airline industry has utilised market power and scale economies to shape consumer demand and accessibility levels in both major leisure destinations and also in small and emerging destinations. It will be argued that conventional vertical integration has never been particularly widespread in the US travel and tourism industry, although vertical disintegration and vertical alliances have recently emerged as alternative strategic approaches. However, a case study of the rapid growth of Dubai in the United Arab Emirates and its clear links to the emerging market power of Emirates Airlines and the Emirates Group conglomerate will provide an explicit example of a state capitalism model that embraces an alternative perspective of market power and vertical integration. This case study complements very well the analysis undertaken by O'Connell in Chapter 22 on the developments in the Middle Eastern aviation and tourism markets. Finally, the present chapter concludes by analyzing how specific airline business models might fundamentally shape destination development patterns. However, we first begin the chapter with a brief definition of market power and vertical integration.

WHAT IS MARKET POWER AND VERTICAL INTEGRATION?

A key feature of market power is the ability of a firm to control both the quantity of goods and services traded and the price at which they are sold. In the air transportation industry, market power exists if an airline can alter the total quantity of airline seats available and/ or the prevailing airfare in any given city-pair market without a concern for losing a significant number of airline passengers to a competitor (Borenstein 1989, 1990).

By contrast, vertical integration is a more specific form of ownership and market control where airlines might integrate operations with upstream suppliers (backward vertical integration) or downstream buyers (forward vertical integration). For example, an airline may own a tour operating company to help generate a stable supply of airline passengers or inputs (i.e., backward vertical integration). Conversely, an airline might set up a subsidiary to distribute or market products to customers such as buying-out a hotel chain or car rental operation (i.e., forward vertical integration). Part of the logic of vertical integration is to lower transaction costs and uncertainty while simultaneously synchronizing supply and demand along the entire supply chain of products. However, one potential drawback is the organisational complexity of such a move and the inability to innovate as the firm gets larger and becomes less nimble. The evidence on vertically-integrated travel companies is mixed – a point to which we shall return to later in this chapter.

That said, market power and vertical integration have been powerful forces that have substantially shaped the international airline industry and this has, in turn, greatly influenced which major resort destinations will succeed or fail. We now turn to a detailed examination of how airline market power and vertical integration have shaped the accessibility levels of leisure destinations by focusing on the largest air transport market in the world – the United States.

MARKET POWER IN THE U.S. AIRLINE INDUSTRY: CONTESTABILITY, AIRFARES, FORTRESS HUBS AND THE POST-9/11 ERA

During the 1980s, the US legacy carriers (e.g., American, Delta, and United) exercised market power by controlling a large portion of the market through the development of extensive hub-and-spoke systems. The economies of scope and scale generated by major hub operations like American Airlines at Dallas-Fort Worth Airport conferred upon the dominant carrier a sustainable competitive advantage and a geographic monopoly power (Pustay 1993; Debbage 1993, 1994). However, market share alone is not a good indicator of market power. It is possible that highly concentrated markets may be *contestable* if there are no barriers to entry or exit since this may limit the incumbent firm's ability to raise airfares above competitive levels.

The Theory of Contestable Markets

It was the theory of contestable markets that provided the intellectual justification for the US Airline Deregulation Act of 1978 (Baumol *et al.* 1982; Bailey and Baumol 1984; Baumol and Willig 1986). Contestable conditions were theorised to arise not simply through the existence of classical perfect competition but from the *potential threat of competition*. Deregulated airline markets were believed to be contestable and, thus, easy to enter, because aircraft were mobile at a relatively low cost – the "capital on wings" rationalisation. Contestability theorists believed that even city-pair markets with only one airline serving the route would remain competitive simply because airlines not currently in the market might conceivably enter if the incumbent carrier charged too high an airfare on any given route.

Market Power and Airfares

Of course, we now know that the theory of contestable markets did not match up well with an industry where many suppliers are not small and where many routes were most efficiently served by, at best, two different air carriers that often tacitly "price-colluded." One of the first to question the theory of contestable markets was Borenstein (1989, 1990) who analyzed the connections that existed between airline mergers, airport dominance, and market power with a focus on discovering the effect that an airline merger may have on airport dominance and an airline's market power. He focused on two controversial airline mergers (Northwest with Republic Airlines, and Trans World Airlines with Ozark Airlines) that occurred in the fall of 1986. The mergers left the dominant carriers – Northwest Airlines in Minneapolis-St. Paul and TWA in St. Louis – with over 75 per cent of the traffic at each respective hub. According to Borenstein (1990: 400) "one obvious test of the acquisition of market power is a before and after comparison of the merging firms' prices." The evidence on price changes suggested that while Minneapolis-St. Paul, in particular, was one of the least expensive hubs to travel to or from before the merger, it had become as expensive as the other major dominant hubs after the merger. Borenstein did not examine the impact of these price changes on overall accessibility levels for leisure travelers but given the price sensitivity of tourist class passengers it is likely that increased airfares significantly depressed leisure-oriented travel demand in the Minneapolis-St.Paul market in the years immediately after the merger.

Fortress Hubs

Subsequent reports by the US General Accounting Office (1990, 1996, 1999) provided additional rigorous empirical evidence that the enormous market power of the so-called "fortress hubs" – where the dominant carrier controlled 60 per cent or more of all passenger enplanements – had resulted in higher fares than normal and a lack of competition in some markets that was not anticipated by some of the supporters of airline deregulation.

During the 1990s these fortress hubs included American Airlines at Dallas-Fort Worth Airport and Miami Airport, Continental Airlines at Houston Intercontinental Airport, Delta at Atlanta and Cincinnati Airport, Northwest Airlines at Minneapolis-St. Paul and Memphis Airport, US Airways at Charlotte and Pittsburgh Airport, and United Airlines at Denver. By the end of the 1990s, five airlines controlled 74.5 per cent of all Revenue Passenger Miles (RPMs) and these included United (19.2 per cent), American (16.9 per cent), Delta (16.1 per cent), Northwest (11.4 per cent) and Continental (8.9 per cent) (Table 12.1). Debbage (2004) has argued that the economies of scope and scale generated by these large hub operations provided the dominant carriers with a sustainable competitive advantage – through extensive access to a large number of gates and landing slots – that effectively curtailed competition in some markets. All this changed after 9/11.

TABLE 12.1   U.S. airline market share leaders (based on revenue passenger-miles)

1999 Rank	Airline	Market Share (%)	2007[*] Rank	Airline	Market Share (%)
1	United	19.2	1	American	17.8
2	American	16.9	2	United	15.0
3	Delta	16.1	3	Delta	12.2
4	Northwest	11.4	4	Continental	10.5
5	Continental	8.9	5	Northwest	9.7
6	US Airways	6.4	6	Southwest	8.9
7	Southwest	5.6	7	US Airways	7.9
8	TWA	4.0	8	JetBlue	3.2
9	America West	2.7	9	Alaska	2.3
10	Alaska	1.8	10	SkyWest	2.3
	Others	7.0		Others	10.5

[*] In February 2007

Source: Standard and Poor 2007.

The Post-9/11 Era

In the aftermath of the terrorist attacks on New York's World Trade Center and the Pentagon on September 11th, 2001, US airlines laid off over 100,000 airline employees and trimmed seat capacity by 15–20 per cent given the precipitous drop-off in airline travel demand (Debbage 2004). The US airline industry reported net losses of $7 billion for 2001. The entire geography of air transportation underwent a fundamental restructuring as low cost carriers such as JetBlue and Southwest Airlines began to erode the market share of the

Legacy Carriers who were not as nimble and able to respond to the significant changes that played out during the post 9/11 era.

On December 9, 2002, United Airlines filed for Chapter 11 bankruptcy protection – a monumental event in the industry since the airline accounted for about 25 per cent of all revenue passenger miles flown by US scheduled airlines at the time. As US airline financial losses mounted, three other major carriers filed for bankruptcy from 2002 through 2005 including Delta, Northwest, and US Airways. Although the U.S. airline industry incurred the heaviest losses, airlines around the world faced a difficult environment. According to the International Air Transport Association, the global airline industry lost a staggering $48.4 billion between 2001 and 2005.

From 2001 through 2005, the competitive environment in the airline industry was brutal although the low-cost carriers were generally able to cope better than the legacy carriers. Notably, Southwest Airlines posted its 34th consecutive year of net income in 2006. Instead of operating out of a large, connecting hub format, Southwest is a major domestic airline that provides primarily short- haul, high frequency, point-to-point, low-fare service. During the post 9/11 era, Southwest Airlines grew to become the largest airline in the United States in terms of passengers and departures and it is now one of the world's most profitable airlines.

Approximately 80 per cent of Southwest passengers fly nonstop flights and the largest destination in terms of daily departures is Las Vegas where its low-fare operation has attracted a significant number of price-sensitive leisure travellers. Southwest's emphasis on cutting costs and offering low-fares means it can play a key role in shaping the accessibility levels of places like Las Vegas. Partly because of the demand generated by Southwest Airlines, it is no accident that 8 of the 10 largest hotels in the world are located in Las Vegas including the MGM Grand, Luxor and the Mandalay Bay hotels (Table 12.2). Many of the nearly 40 million visitors to Las Vegas are attracted to these hotels, in part, by the competitive fares offered by Southwest Airlines. Southwest Airlines also handles a large amount of tourist traffic at Orlando International Airport – another major leisure destination that includes the Disney theme park and Universal Studios.

MARKET POWER AND THE 2006–2007 RECOVERY: MERGER/ ACQUISITIONS AND THE NORTH ATLANTIC MARKET

If the early 2000s can be characterised as an era of bankruptcies and diminished market power for the legacy carriers, then 2006/7 became a period of sharp financial improvement and profitability – even with the high jet fuel costs. The ten largest U.S. airlines reported a net profit of $1.6 billion in 2006 (excluding bankruptcy reorganisation costs). Between 2005 and mid-2007, the four major carriers that filed for bankruptcy protection during the early 2000s had all come out of bankruptcy (i.e., Delta, Northwest Airlines, United and US Airways.) These reorganised carriers had been able to cut costs and trim unprofitable routes while under bankruptcy protection and were now better positioned to compete with the low cost carriers.

Beginning in 2005, some of these airlines began to recapture lost market share through merger and acquisition activity. The late 2005 merger of US Airways and America West was widely viewed by some Wall Street analysts as the beginning point of a new round of

TABLE 12.2   The largest hotels in the world, 2007

2007	Hotel	Location	Rooms
1	First World Hotel	Malaysia	6,118
2	MGM Grand	Las Vegas	5,690
3	Ambassador City Jomtlen	Thailand	4,631
4	Luxor	Las Vegas	4,408
5	Mandalay Bay	Las Vegas	4,341
6	The Venetian	Las Vegas	4,027
7	Excalibur	Las Vegas	4,008
8	Bellagio	Las Vegas	3,993
9	Circus Circus	Las Vegas	3,774
10	Flamingo Las Vegas	Les Vegas	3,565

Under construction is the Asia Asia Hotel in Dubai. It is scheduled for completion in 2010, and is expected to have 6,500 rooms.

Source: InsiderVLV.com 2007.

mergers and acquisitions. Since 2005, the "new" US Airways has successfully cut costs and integrated a route network that had been widely perceived to be overly locked into the East Coast. By merging with a West Coast-centric airline like America West, US Airways has generated an improved national geographic footprint that has the potential to radically change the accessibility levels of some leisure destinations that feature prominently in the new revamped route network.

Immediately after the America West deal, US Airways proposed a merger deal with Delta in 2006 but was unable to agree an offer price. However, a potential new round of mergers and acquisitions may make it more difficult for low-cost carriers like Southwest Airlines and JetBlue since the legacy airlines are now "leaner and meaner." Low-cost carriers are already feeling the heat with JetBlue posting a small net loss in 2006 and Southwest Airlines reporting reduced profits relative to previous years. Consequently, although the "Big Three" (i.e., American, Delta, and United) had a total market share of 52.2 per cent in 1999 that had dropped to 45 per cent by early 2007 (Table 12.1), it is possible that their market share might rise again through 2010.

According to Brueckner and Pels (2005), airline mergers have also become popular in Europe in order to address the "inefficient excess capacity" problem created by the national flag-carrier system. However, they analyzed the merger between Air France and KLM and argued that the merger had the potential to negatively impact passenger welfare since it may create an anticompetitive environment and lead to airfare increases. In the United States, fares and passenger yields have also begun to rise, although fuel costs remain the biggest uncertainty for airline profits.

On the other hand, the new US–European Union open skies treaty that will become effective in early 2008 also has the potential to radically reconfigure accessibility levels in the North Atlantic market (Aviation Week and Space Technology 2007). The treaty replaces various pre-existing bilateral agreements between US and EU countries with a single pact that extends open-skies provisions to the entire US–EU market. Under the new regime, any US airline will be able to fly from any point in the US to any point in the EU, and vice versa. The deal is likely to open up Heathrow Airport since the current US–UK bilateral restricts travel between the US and Heathrow to just four carriers – American Airlines, British Airways, United Airlines and Virgin.

One end result of the more liberal aviation regime over the North Atlantic is potential new service in many markets and a downward pressure on fares. It is not an understatement to say that the geography of origin-destination tourist flows will be re-configured on a grand scale and the mobility levels of individual tourists could be greatly enhanced. However, the deal may also ultimately trigger international airline industry consolidation as the increased level of competition forces the dominant incumbent carriers to buy-out low-cost, low-fare competitors to mitigate the competitive threat.

VERTICAL INTEGRATION, VERTICAL DISINTEGRATION OR VERTICAL ALLIANCE?

The Follies of Vertical Integration

Although increased market concentration through horizontal integration has been a major trait of the largest airline, hotel and cruise-ship companies (Table 12.3), vertical integration has never been widespread. However, it is true that select examples of large-scale vertical integration exist, particularly in Europe where major tour operating firms operate their own charter airlines and travel agencies. For example, the recent consolidation of Thomas Cook and My Travel as well as that of TUI and First Choice has led to the formation of two large tour operator groups that together account for an "annual turnover approaching $40 billion, 46 million customers and a fleet of around 265 aircraft" (Airline Business 2007: 74). However, although these two new vertically integrated groups will likely exert more control over capacity in the European market, it is also likely that they will continue to rely on third-party flying with other carriers (such as Monarch Airlines) to avoid overcapacity issues during the off-peak winter months.

Unlike many joint business ventures where one component of the production chain might bolster the other during a crisis, the fortunes of airlines, hotels and tour operators tend to rise and fall together, depending on the overall health of the economy. Furthermore, the overall complexity of the amorphous travel industry and the intensely competitive environment mean most US airlines prefer to focus on their own core business. One of the most unsuccessful vertical integration experiments in the United States was the infamous Allegis fiasco – a travel umbrella group assembled by United Airlines in the mid-1980s that included Hertz, Hilton International and Westin Hotels and Resorts – which lasted three years before being disbanded due to poor stock performance. Partly as a consequence of the Allegis experience, only a small number of airlines currently directly own or manage hotel chains, travel agents, or car rental agencies. According to Lafferty and Fossen (2001) attempts at conventional vertical integration within the tourism industry – particularly those centered on the critical airline-hotel connection – have met with very limited success resulting in a more diverse range of alternate management strategies.

TABLE 12.3   The world's largest tourist business operations, 2005

Airlines	Passengers (millions)
American	98.1
Southwest	88.5
Delta	86.1
Air France – KLM	69.2
United	68.8
US Airways – America West	64.0
JAL	58.0
Northwest	56.5
Lufthansa	51.3
ANA	49.6

Hotel Chains	Rooms
Intercontinental Hotels Group	537,533
Wyndham Worldwide	532,284
Marriot International	499,165
Hilton Hotels Corp.	485,356
Choice Hotels International	481,131
Accor	475,433
Best Western International	315,875
Starwood Hotels & Resorts Worldwide	257,889
Carlson Hospitality Worldwide	147,129
Global Hyatt Corp.	134,296

Cruise-ship Companies (North American Market)	Lower Berths
Carnival Cruise Lines	47,908
Royal Caribbean International	45,570
Princess Cruises	28,800
Norwegian Cruise Lines	20,950
Costa Cruise Lines	17,265

Source: Air Transport World 2006b, Hotels 2006, and Cruise Lines International Association 2006.

Vertical Disintegration and Outsourcing

In an attempt to better control and manage origin–destination tourist flows, many airlines are now increasingly participating in two alternative strategic approaches: vertical disintegration and vertical alliances. According to Ioannides and Debbage (1997), vertical disintegration is a process where non-strategic functions are sub-contracted out to other firms. By externalizing certain production functions, airlines can generate significant cost savings through out-sourcing. Airlines can accrue considerable savings by buying these cheaper services (e.g., aircraft maintenance, aircraft leasing, computer reservation systems technology, and in-flight catering) from outside specialist firms which can, in turn, lead to the generation of economies of scale. Vertical disintegration is now viewed as not only an effective way to reduce costs but also as a way to focus on the airline industry's core competencies – which is transporting passengers and freight. Due to the intense competitive pressures of the increasingly deregulated aviation environment and the substantial capital outlays required to effectively compete, more and more airlines are embracing a strategy of vertical disintegration.

Vertical Alliances and Strategic Alliance Networks

At the same time, a complex system of vertical and horizontal alliances have been established in the international travel industry as firms attempt to capture market share and exercise market power while minimizing uncertainty and risk. However, these "new" vertical alliances fall far short of the full ownership and control associated with more traditional forms of vertical integration. Ironically, the increased popularity of sub-contracting or vertical disintegration has served as an enabler for the creation of vertical and horizontal alliances since these strategic networks offer the promise of a more efficient pooling of resources, better marketing coverage, and technology sharing – a particularly attractive feature as the international tourism production chain becomes ever more complex (Mosedale 2006, 2008).

According to Hanlon (1999), the most common goals of any airline alliance arrangement include additional traffic feed, access to new markets, protecting current markets, and economies in marketing. Also, Hanlon (1999) argued that many airlines in alliance markets have focused on code-sharing, block space agreements, franchising, and developing links between frequent flyer programs. By doing all these things, airlines have been able to build economies of scope by extending route networks, thus, manufacturing a sustainable competitive advantage of sorts.

Currently, there are three major alliance groupings including the Star Alliance anchored by United Airlines and Lufthansa, the Sky Team Alliance with Delta and Air France-KLM, and the oneworld alliance including American Airlines and British Airways. Based on 2006 data, these three alliances accounted for nearly 60 per cent of global Available Seat Miles (ASMs) (Aviation Week and Space Technology 2006) and the market share of these three groups has increased over time (Table 12.4).

Hanlon (1999: 241) has argued that these strategic groupings are not just conventional horizontal alliances between carriers but that they "have something of a vertical nature about them" particularly as markets have liberalised. Hanlon points out that unlike the old interline pooling agreements where carriers cooperated on the *same* route, the new strategic alliance networks are largely negotiated between airlines operating on *different*

TABLE 12.4   Market share of major alliance groupings

Alliance Rank	2000 (%)[*]	Alliance Rank	2004 (%)[*]	Alliance Rank	2006 (%)[†]
Star	21.4	Star	22.0	Star	23.1
Oneworld	16.2	Sky	19.0	Sky	18.7
Sky	10.0	Oneworld	15.0	Oneworld	17.0
Total	**47.6**	**Total**	**56.0**	**Total**	**58.8**

[*] Revenue passenger kilometers
[†] Available seat miles

Source: Airline Business 2001, Standard and Poor 2007, Aviation Week and Space Technology 2006.

routes. He suggests that airline partners, therefore, are increasingly supplying each other with traffic while simultaneously negotiating broader collaborative vertical arrangements with hotels, car rentals, travel agents and other companies involved in travel and tourism – although few of these relationships include the direct control or ownership associated with more conventional forms of vertical integration.

Debbage (1994, 2004) has argued that these various quasi-vertical alliances have not included outright mergers or acquisitions, in part, because traditional bilateral air services agreements typically have prohibited majority ownership and/or imposed caps on the extent of equity involvement by foreign airlines in domestic carriers. In this sense, globally-based airline alliance networks seem to be an "end run" around the current regulatory system. Key features of these alliance networks include enhanced global access, complementary route networks, access to crucial runway slots and terminal gates at already gridlocked international hub airports, and the development of a domestic feeder network in another country.

One of the biggest unanswered questions is when, and if, truly independent low-cost and low-fare carriers like Southwest Airlines, JetBlue and Ryanair might join an alliance grouping. Hanlon (1999) has also pointed out that few airlines have been able to integrate vertically with airport authorities due to government restrictions and the fact that most airports are in quasi-public ownership. Finally, it seems clear that the most intense competition for new alliance members is likely to occur in the Middle East and Asia where several large traditional scheduled airlines still remain unaffiliated to a major alliance network. One of the largest carriers currently not linked to a strategic alliance network is Emirates Airlines and we now turn to a detailed analysis of the United Arab Emirates to illustrate the impact of market power and vertical integration on a small and rapidly emerging destination in the Middle East.

CASE STUDY: DUBAI INC. AND EMIRATES AIRLINES

Perhaps one of the most dramatic, contemporary examples of the exercise of market power and vertical integration in the international airline industry today is Dubai-based Emirates Airlines and the larger Emirates Group. The airline began service as a two-airplane, four-city network in 1985 and has grown into the world's eighth-largest international passenger carrier in terms of total passengers carried serving nearly 90 cities in 59 countries with a fleet of 102 aircraft (The Emirates Group 2007)

Emirates Airlines is one of the world's fastest growing long-haul carriers and recently ranked as the world's second most profitable carrier, after Singapore Airlines. In 2005, profits rose 48 per cent to $637 million (on revenues of $4.9 billion) at a time when the international airline industry was accumulating $6 billion in losses (Newsweek 2006). By the end of 2006, Emirates Airlines passenger volume had risen to more than 17.5 million, more than double the 2001 figure (Figure 12.1), in part, reflecting the rapid growth of Dubai as a commercial and tourist hub in the Middle East. The airline has rapidly emerged as one of the most important success stories in the airline industry largely because much of its growth is tied to a broader corporate and government strategy that has built the market power of both the region and the airline.

Emirates Airlines is part of the state-owned Emirates Group – a large, diversified travel umbrella group wholly owned by the state of Dubai. The Emirates Group has rapidly emerged as a globally influential travel and tourism conglomerate that generated record net profits of $762 million in 2006. While Emirates Airlines is the core unit of the Emirates Group other major divisions include:

- Dnata – one of the largest travel management services companies in the Middle East with more than 6,500 employees handling passengers, cargo, ramp and technical services for airlines at Dubai International Airport

- Emirates Hotels and Resorts – the hospitality division of the Emirates Group with properties such as the Al Maha Desert Resort and Spa, and Wolgan Valley Resort and Spa

- Emirates Holidays – the tour operating arm of Emirates Airlines offering packaged vacations to over 100 destinations, and

- Arabian Adventures – offering scheduled overland explorer programs including desert safaris, wadi bashing, deep-sea fishing, and traditional dhow cruises.

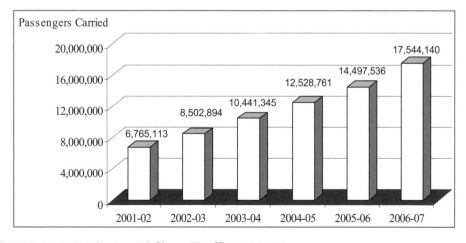

FIGURE 12.1 Emirates Airlines Traffic 2001–07

Source: The Emirates Group (2007).

The Emirates Group is an anomaly regarding the conventional distinction between public and private sectors. For example, although Emirates Airlines operates as a private sector commercial extension of the Dubai government, the chairman of the airline – Sheikh Ahmed– is a member of the ruling Al-Maktoum family. Shiekh Ahmed is also President of Dubai's Department of Civil Aviation which owns and operates Dubai International Airport, and until recently he was also chairman of Dubai's Commerce and Tourism Promotion Board. In late 2005, Qantas Chairman Margaret Jackson tartly observed "life must be wonderfully simple when the airline, government and airport interests are all controlled and run by the same people" (Air Transport World 2006a: 45).

In this sense, the Emirates Group is a sort of "Dubai Inc." where the primary mission is to transform Dubai not merely into a comprehensive long-haul airline hub but also into a major global commercial and tourist center. To that end, Dubai has pursued an "open skies" policy that has allowed over 100 airlines serving over 140 destinations to operate out of Dubai International Airport. The overall goal is to benefit from the major traffic flows by attracting international tourists to the Dubai hub especially since Emirates Airlines is an airline without a sizable domestic market. Dubai's ideal geographic location has allowed the country to effectively link East and West through its international hub and Emirates Airlines has quickly emerged as a major competitor for Singapore Airlines on long-haul routes between Europe and Asia (Map 12.1). For example, Emirates Airlines busiest city-pair markets include Dubai-London and Dubai-Singapore which together accounted for 11 per cent of total services in 2005 although no other route accounted for more than 2.5 per cent (Air Transport World 2006a). By coordinating government aviation policy with the corporate strategy of the largest airline in the country, Dubai Inc. has been able to establish Dubai International Airport as a major global hub. For example, in the early 2000s, approximately 50 per cent of Emirates Airlines passenger traffic was transit traffic beyond Dubai.

However, the country is also emerging as a destination in its own right – part of a broader strategy to develop Dubai as a major international center of commerce and tourism. The United Arab Emirates has now replaced Egypt as the second largest tourist attraction in the Middle East ranking behind only Saudi Arabia's enormous pilgrimage tourism market. In 2003, the entire UAE attracted 5.8 million arrivals well up on the 973,000 visitors in 1990 while Dubai alone attracted 6.1 million visitors in 2005 compared to 1.2 million in neighboring Abu Dhabi. The change in tourist demand has been so rapid that "tourism is now worth more to Dubai than its income from oil" (UAE Yearbook: 126). Some of the largest and most notable tourism development projects include:

- Emirates Mall and Ski Dubai – the world's largest indoor ski slope inside one of the world's largest malls

- Dubailand–a planned Disney – style theme park that will encompass 3 billion square feet and include 50 mega-hotels of 1,000 rooms each upon completion. Dubailand will include: the world's largest shopping mall (the Mall of Arabia) and the $27 billion Bawadi resort and entertainment complex (including the world's largest hotel – the 6,500 room Asia-Asia hotel – and the $2.2 billion Universal Studios Dubai that will supplement the other Universal Studios currently in operation in Los Angeles, Orlando and Japan.)

- Burj Dubai – the world's tallest building that will include the five-star, 250-room Armani Hotel when it opens in 2008

- The Hydropolis Hotel – it will be the world's first luxury underwater hotel upon completion, and

- Attractions and hotels built on vast man-made islands shaped like palm fronds (e.g., the Atlantis Hotel with a total of 2,000 rooms in the Palm Jumeirah).

The overall strategic goal of Dubai Inc. is to attract more visitors to the UAE and Dubai by building mega-projects and, thus, build the passenger traffic for Emirates Airlines and other carriers. For example, the Bawadi project is projected to be a 6-mile long resort strip that resembles Las Vegas without the casinos. Current projections are for Dubai to attract 15 million visitors by 2010. Not surprisingly, the significant increase in tourist traffic has led to a corresponding expansion of both the Emirates Airlines fleet size and airport-related infrastructure capacity. For example, Emirates Airlines current order book stands at 124 aircraft with a total value of approximately $30 billion – it is the main launch customer for the A380 double-decker super-jumbo (45 orders at a cost of $250 million each). The airline anticipates that its fleet will include at least 156 aircraft by 2010 when it is forecast that it will serve 101 destinations and carry 26 million passengers.

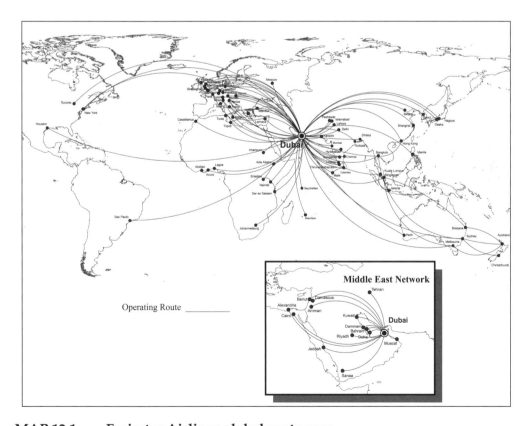

MAP 12.1   Emirates Airlines global route map
Note: This figure is only a graphic illustration, not a complete representation or to scale – Prepared by Obaid Saif Al Dhaheri.

In order to accommodate this growth, Dubai Inc. is currently engaged in a $4.1 billion expansion of Dubai International Airport to build a new double-deck terminal that can handle the A380 super jumbo. Passenger traffic at Dubai International has increased by 248 per cent from 7.1 million passengers in 1995 to 24.7 million in 2005 (Map 12.2) although the new terminals are projected to be at capacity by 2011 based on current growth rates. Given the rapid growth, a second new airport located at Jebel Ali just south of the city of Dubai is being built – the $8.2 billion Dubai World Central Airport – which will feature six runways capable of handling 140 million passengers a year (Air Transport World 2006a). When completed Dubai World Central will be bigger than Atlanta Hartsfield Airport which handled 83.5 million passengers in 2004.

Through meticulous long-range government and airline planning, Dubai Inc. has rapidly emerged as one of the premier examples of the exercise of market power in aviation and tourism. By developing a world-view of the marketplace through a diversified travel and tourism conglomerate like the Emirates Group, it has been possible to substantially enhance accessibility levels and build the United Arab Emirates as a major world destination for both business and leisure tourists.

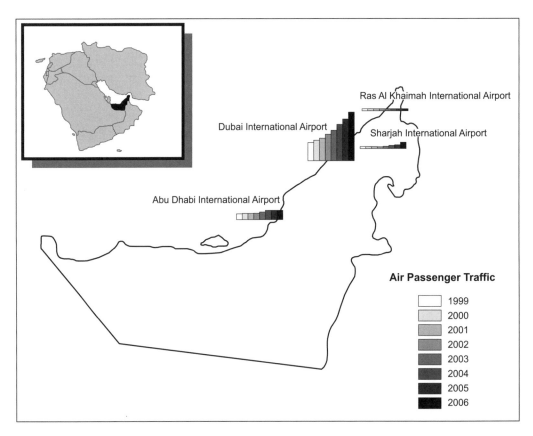

MAP 12.2   Spatial distribution of air passenger traffic by airports in the UAE, 1999–06

Sources: Abu Dhabi, Ras Al Khaimah and Sharjah International Airport Authorities.

Whether this can be replicated elsewhere on the world stage is debatable given the unique circumstances and geography. The level of coordination is unprecedented since it required something as powerful as Dubai Inc. to effectively integrate airline corporate strategy with key public and private investments "on the ground" including substantial airport infrastructure enhancements and massive product development. Some critics have also questioned the fairness of the Dubai state capitalism model since Emirates Airlines is relatively insulated from market risk given the close ties between the state and airline. However, the Emirates Group has insisted that it receives no direct state subsidies and recent audits by PricewaterhouseCoopers and UBS confirmed the claims of financial independence. Still others have suggested that the lack of political stability in the Middle East and recent delays in constructing new hotels may curtail the proposed expansion plans. That said, Air France Chairman/CEO Jean-Cyril Spinetta has recently argued that the emergence of sixth freedom airlines like Emirates and Singapore Airlines represent a more substantive competitive challenge than those previously posed by the low-cost carriers (Aviation Week and Space Technology 2003.) On the other hand, many destinations have benefited from the extensive networks offered by airlines like Emirates since sixth freedom airlines can open up access to a variety of places that have often been underserved in the past.

AIRLINE BUSINESS MODELS AND DESTINATION DEVELOPMENT

Although the Dubai case study vividly demonstrates that Emirates Airlines is an important facilitator of travel and tourism in the United Arab Emirates, little research has been conducted to uncover how specific airline business models might shape destination development patterns. Two recent exceptions to this rule include the work of Bieger and Wittmer (2006) and Papatheodorou and Lei (2006).

Bieger and Wittmer (2006) argued that the strategic development of a destination must be connected to a clear airline policy and air access strategy. According to Bieger and Wittmer (2006: 43), "the network structure of the airlines and especially the position of the destination airport within these networks can influence a market's accessibility and with this the fare structure and the types of tourists who will travel." They argued that destination airports with high-quality infrastructure (e.g., an airstrip over 3000m, easy exit and arrival services, etc.) tended to attract larger airplanes at lower frequencies while smaller airports with lower quality services tended to provide both feeder services to the larger network carriers and point-to-point services from low-cost carriers and charter airlines. Bieger and Wittmer (2006) also suggested that the vitality of an airport largely depends on its location, infrastructure, regulatory environment, and local market. Moreover, they argued that the regulatory strategy regarding strategic alliance networks and global access can also play a significant part in extending airline networks to numerous tourist destinations.

By classifying airline business models into four categories (i.e., low cost carriers, charter airlines, regional carriers, and network carriers), Bieger and Wittmer (2006) very clearly depicted how each airline model can support certain destination typologies. They placed an emphasis on how "different types of airline business models lead to a difference in the traffic carried, and ipso facto to the nature of the visitor stream" (Bieger and Wittmer

2006:45). They also argued that traditional network carriers tended to serve large markets with average-paying customers and a mix of business and leisure passengers, while regional carriers supplied more remote midsize or smaller destinations using smaller aircrafts. Bieger and Wittmer (2006) also suggested that charter airlines operated on largely medium- and long-haul routes with relatively inflexible traffic streams while low-cost carriers tended to operate on short-haul routes. They argued that the low cost carriers appealed to tourists with high price elasticities by offering low fares and they also appealed to business travelers by offering high frequencies in select city-pair markets.

By evaluating the different business models of both destinations and carriers, Bieger and Wittmer (2006) found that specific destinations required very circumscribed air carrier services. For example, they argued that major destinations with a wide variety of natural and man-made attractions are frequently served by large network carriers that provide the mixed traffic streams necessary to sustain demand. On the other hand, they suggested that traditional hotel destinations might provide a good platform of operation for a low-cost carrier (e.g., Las Vegas and Southwest Airlines) or a charter airline. Bieger and Wittmer (2006) concluded by emphasizing that policy makers, airlines, and managers of tourist destinations should spend more time studying each other's needs in order to achieve more effective and cooperative synergies – a point that is well demonstrated in our case study of Dubai and Emirates Airlines.

Papatheodorou and Lei (2006) focused on the impact of three airline business models (i.e., charter airlines, low-cost carriers and traditional scheduled airlines) on regional airport operations in the United Kingdom. They argued that until the early 1990s, charter airlines were the main air service provider of leisure travel in Europe. These airlines acted as the original low-cost carrier by focusing on cutting costs through an emphasis on dense seat configurations and high passenger loads, seasonal schedules and by operating out of secondary airports with lower airport fees. Many charter airlines also simultaneously distributed their travel product as packaged vacations through affiliated tour operators.

Papatheodorou and Lei (2006) also argued that the removal of any legal distinction between EU scheduled and charter carriers in 1997 provided an opening for low-cost carriers to become the leaders in cost reduction. The authors suggested that by the late 1990s the differences in the airline business models had become clear. The traditional scheduled carriers paid more attention to service deliveries offering a network-based product, which could better serve the business traveler as well as the wealthy leisure and VFR customers while the low cost carrier offered affordable point to point travel in specific city-pair markets that had been overlooked by the larger carriers especially at secondary regional airports such as London's Stansted Airport. However, based on an empirical analysis of 21 regional airports in the United Kingdom, Papatheodorou and Lei (2006: 51) concluded that "no matter whether a regional airport operates as an origin or destination gateway, notable improvements in accessibility can play a significant role in economic and/or tourism development" and that low-cost carriers are "not the only way forward for regional airports".

CONCLUSIONS

Airlines have exercised market power in a variety of ways but especially by building market share and dominating specific hub airports. In doing so, the major carriers have been able to control price in some of their most important hub markets while simultaneously warding off any competitive threat by controlling the majority of landing slots and gates at these key airports. For leisure destinations that depend on a large number of tourist arrivals by air, it has become crucial to develop spoke routes to at least one of these so-called fortress hubs.

Low cost airlines like Southwest Airlines and JetBlue altered the calculation by offering point-to-point, low-fare services often to non-traditional destinations. In the aftermath of 9/11, Southwest Airlines emerged as the largest airline in the United States in terms of passengers and other airlines like Ryanair and JetBlue also altered accessibility levels in new secondary airports off the beaten path. However, the 2006–2007 recovery has seen the legacy carriers emerge out of bankruptcy and re-establish a major presence in the market.

For all the competitive turbulence, the airline industry has traditionally tended to focus on its core business rather than attempt to vertically integrate with related suppliers and distributors largely because of the intensely competitive environment. However, the major carriers have embraced alternative management strategies including vertical disintegration and the development of a wide range of quasi-vertical alliances. Vertical disintegration strategies have allowed airlines to effectively cut costs though outsourcing while quasi-vertical alliances like Star and oneworld have allowed airlines to exercise market power and jointly increase revenues without the formal control and ownership of more conventional forms of vertical integration.

A case study of Dubai and Emirates Airlines suggests that a new approach may be emerging that involves developing comprehensive "world-view" strategies that integrate product development "on the ground" with both the market power of the national airline and broader open-skies aviation policies. The Dubai Inc. state capitalism model of broadly coordinated systemic expansion is in sharp contrast to the intensely competitive and chaotic model of vertical disintegration offered up by the American experience. Neither approach is replicated in Europe where package vacations organised by tour operators are the most common type of vacation taken by Europeans when vacationing abroad. The European leisure market is shaped by a more traditional free-market vertical integration model that is now essentially controlled by just two large tour operator groups. The diversity of approaches worldwide may help partly explain why only a limited amount of research has been conducted that attempts to connect the various airline business models with specific destination typologies, even though airline route networks can play a substantive role in shaping accessibility levels particularly in markets that rely on a significant number of arrivals by air.

PART IV

Implications for Airports

13

Airport Requirements for Leisure Travellers

Nuno Mocica Brilha

INTRODUCTION

Having considered the relationship between tourism markets and airlines, this section now investigates the complementary issue concerning the relationship between airports and leisure demand. This first chapter aims to provide a general view of the airport requirements for leisure travellers, and then the other chapters which follow focus on more specific issues such as low cost carriers; peripheral area operations; and information and communication technology developments.

Initially, the airport concept started as a platform associated with processing aircraft, passengers and freight but it has evolved into a key regional infrastructure which is often now described as an 'airport city' or 'aviopolis'. Developing at various stages around the globe, airports have not lost their intrinsic characteristic of intermodal platforms but some have managed to effectively articulate the convergence of interests they encapsulate by converting this transfer between modes of transport into an experience. This experience related to leisure travellers is considered in this chapter.

The chapter begins by investigating the different types of airlines and passengers at airports and assesses the specific characteristics of leisure passengers. It then goes on to examine the important issue of airport security and discusses how the trends to provide a secure environment can be balanced with providing the leisure passengers with a positive travel experience. The focus then shifts to non-aeronautical services which can also contribute to the travel experience. Finally, the challenging issue of coping with the peaks and troughs of traffic which are often associated with leisure demand is considered.

MEETING THE DEMANDS OF DIFFERENT TYPES OF AIRLINES AND PASSENGERS

The airport plays a vital part in the air transport system. It can be described as an intermodal transfer infrastructure where modal transfer from air-mode to land-mode takes place (Ashford *et al.* 2006). It can also be expressed as a complex industrial enterprise because of the large variety of services it provides (Doganis 1992) or finally as a platform for commercial activities and a partner for economic development as defined by Airports

Council International – Europe (York Aviation, 2004). The airport's key function is the provision of infrastructure needed to allow airlines to safely take off and land and to facilitate passenger and freight transfer from surface to air- mode. In order to fulfil their role, airports bring together a wide range of aeronautical and non-aeronautical facilities and services including air traffic control, security, fire and rescue, handling and a diversity of commercial facilities ranging from shops and restaurants to hotels, conference services and business parks. In addition to this central role within the air transport sector, airports hold a strategic importance to the regions they serve due to their interaction with the overall transport system (such as rail and road networks) and the substantial employment opportunities and economic development which they encourage.

Modern airports have an extended customer base which makes huge demands on airport management (Table 13.1). Passengers and airlines have always been the airports' key clients and are thus the main factors affecting airport operations and planning, and influencing decisions on terminal structures, services offered, architectural design, modes of access and so on. However, airlines and passengers view airports from different perspectives.

Basic passenger segmentation considers two main travel purposes, namely business and leisure, and Table 13.2 identifies what were traditionally considered to be the different airport needs of these two core segments. Business passengers were generally thought to be more time conscious, more demanding on facilities and services and more in need of flexible travel arrangements. They would travel for shorter periods and be less sensitive to price fluctuations. On the other hand, the common perception of the leisure passenger was someone who was travelling for longer periods of time, usually in a group of family with children, being very price sensitive but being less demanding for services.

However, air transport industry and tourist profiles have greatly evolved, reflecting increased disposable income, added experience from travel frequency, vast information and social and cultural changes in society. In the early 1990s, Doganis (1991) classified the airline's market segmentation, including already a new leisure segment called 'weekend holiday' commonly known today as 'short-break'. By adding to Doganis' airline features some familiar airport services, it is possible to depict how passengers from different market segments reveal the valuation of their requirements. However, this rather simplistic approach does not take account of important demand trends which are taking place. For instance, low fares are an increasing requirement even for business passengers and leisure passengers are becoming much more demanding for certain services, particularly entertainment and retail. Also, the short-break passengers when compared to the traditional leisure segment tend to be more demanding, experienced and informed with an increased notion of value for money.

This latest major development which has had an impact on passenger profiles has been the emergence of the low cost carriers (LCCs) (see Chapter 9). These LCCs are thought to have created new and induced demand. New demand is achieved by reaching new passengers who can now afford air travel and induced demand by increasing the travel frequency of current passengers that now can travel more often with the same disposable income. In the next Chapter 14, Echevarne considers the issue of low cost carriers and airports in some depth.

Table 13.3 highlights some traditional differences between the airline and passenger view of the airport. Airlines see airports as gateways for business at potential markets. If the market seems profitable, in terms of volume and yield, airlines will then assess the airport's availability of slots and facilities, its operational efficiency and cost effectiveness

TABLE 13.1   The airport's customers

Passengers	Trade	Others
Scheduled – traditional and low-cost	Airlines	Tenants and concessionaires
Charter	Tour Operators	Visitors
Business	Travel Agents	Employees
Leisure	Freight Forwarders	Local Residents
Transfer	General Aviation	Local Businesses

Source: A. Graham (2003).

TABLE 13.2   Needs and characteristics of passengers at airports

	Business	Leisure
Access	Close access to business centres	Bus parking – pickup and delivery
	Easy parking and access to terminal – time	Easy access to terminal – heavy luggage
	Short-term car parking	Long-term car parking
Terminal	Passenger services – baggage services, executive lounges, transport to aircraft	Welcome desks for tour operators or travel agents
	Specialised shops and facilities – gourmet catering, high end brands, executive lounges	Longer dwell time – shopping, catering and entertainment
	Working areas – comfort, connectivity and conferencing	Families with children – entertainment areas, food halls

Source: Compiled by author.

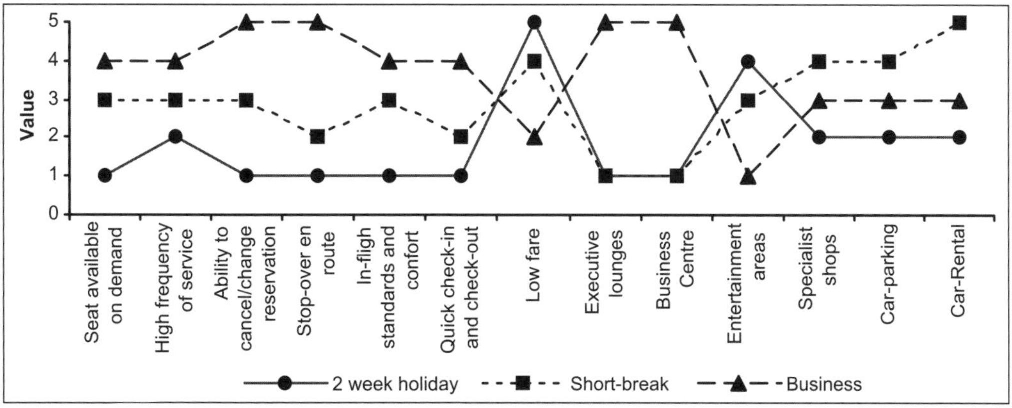

FIGURE 13.1 Segmentation by trip purpose and passenger needs
Source: Doganis (1991). Adapted by author.

of serving this new destination. Crudely, airlines fit into three core profiles of full service, charter and low-cost carriers although airports may also add more niche market players such as regional feeders, general aviation and air-taxis. Moreover, there are other new developments, such as the introduction of the A380, which may require consideration of a 'large aircraft' segment.

Various chapters have discussed how the emergence of the low cost sector has impacted on the operations of both the airline and airport industry. Competing on cost, low fare carriers demand increased operational efficiency and flexible cost structures. This has led many airports to rethink their strategies and carefully balance the opportunities and threats of this new business model. For a busy hub airport lacking capacity, low cost airlines may reveal little bargaining power, thus turning to secondary airports in the vicinity. At these smaller secondary airports, however, low cost airlines may indeed represent vast volumes of passenger traffic but also a low financial return. Forsyth (2007) argues that in the short-term this LCC usage of secondary airports actually lessens the pressure on busy capacity constrained major airports. However, this may not be the case on the long-term, since these small profit margins at airports may not support necessary expansion.

Whereas some airports in Europe have generally followed a focused hub strategy or LCC strategy, Copenhagen airport is an interesting example because it believes in combining LCC and full service airlines in one airport terminal by offering competitive pricing, tariff agreements with bonuses and few delays. Moreover, Copenhagen provides LCCs the same high quality terminal used by full service airlines and easy access for transferring passengers but where possible also tries to maintain a turnaround time of 25 minutes in order to meet their specific needs. Additionally, Copenhagen Airport provides free of charge Common Use and Self-Service (CUSS) check-in machines (see Chapter 16) for all airline customers, enhancing the efficiency of the check-in process and also aiming to increase passenger satisfaction. Besides these adaptive changes, the airport has increased its focus on route development and researching new options for airlines which include the LCCs.

Meeting the changing demands of different types of airlines and passengers often leads airports to rethink their strategic positioning. For example, the business plan for

TABLE 13.3   Factors influencing airport choice for different airport customers

Airlines	Business Passenger	Leisure Passenger
Market potential – volume and mix of passengers	Network – destinations, frequencies, day return flights	Destination attractiveness
Availability of slots	Quality of facilities and services offered	Leisure package components
Availability of facilities – air bridges, CIP lounges	Speed of process – fast track	Package price
Total visiting costs – landing charges, handling, refuelling	Access – road access and parking facilities	Price of facilities and services at the airport
Reliability and quality of service – quick turn-around, baggage handling		

Source: Compiled by author.

Manchester International Airport in the late 1990s forecasted its transformation from a primarily charter market into one of the largest European hubs by 2015, almost as large as Schiphol Amsterdam Airport would be at the same date (Harrop 1999). To cater for this change in profile, it was envisaged that Manchester Airport would have to create major services for business and transfer passengers as well as changing its image accordingly. Another example is BAA's London Stansted Airport which was originally designed for charter traffic but has become one of the fastest growing airports in Europe for scheduled low-cost flights for holidaymakers but a substantial business component as well.

MAINTAINING A SAFE AND SECURE AIRPORT WITHOUT DETERRING TOURISTS

One of the most significant issues facing airports in the twenty first century, and particularly following the events of September 11, 2001, is air transport safety and security. Colloquially these terms may sound synonymous but with regards to airport operations they represent two different airport functions. Airport safety ensures that all airport operations are pursued in a safe and efficient manner minimizing damage to aircraft and injury to people. It comprises requirements and recommendations dealing with a vast number of issues, such as runway safety, bird and wildlife hazards, weather conditions, airfield signing, marking and lighting, aircraft rescue and fire fighting, fueling and pedestrian and ground vehicle control. On the other hand, airport security is responsible for deterring, preventing and responding to criminal acts that may affect the safety and security of the traveling public. These may include activities related to theft, assault or violence against passengers or their property, against aircraft and airport facilities. These criminal behaviors also include the hijacking of aircraft and other forms of terrorism.

In the early days of civil aviation the biggest concerns were, understandably, with the safety of flight and aircraft operation on the ground, with little worry over airport security. Technology and expertise have paved the way to make air travel one of the today's safest modes of transport, from an operational perspective. In contrast air transport security has become more and more important.

Since aviation is an international business, the issue of security is wide in scope, with implications that reach beyond the jurisdictional limits of one airport, as well as spanning to central governments and international organisations. Over time a series of conventions (e.g. Tokyo 1963; Hague 1970; Montreal 1971) have considered the nations' concerns over aviation security. These conventions were followed in 1974 by the adoption by the International Civil Aviation Organisation (ICAO) of Annex 17 to the original Chicago Convention which is the foundation of international civil aviation regulation. Annex 17 establishes international aviation security standards and recommended practices.

After the events of September 11, airport security became a top priority. The United States created the Transport Security Administration (TSA) under the US Department of Transport, whose mission was to co-ordinate with other transport administrations to protect the nation's transportations systems. The TSA has concentrated its efforts on securing passengers on commercial airlines and airports through the implementation of stricter passenger and baggage screening requirements. Also, the European Union worked on formulating a collective response based on common preventive measures. The common rules were uniformly implemented by means of Community law, set out by the European Civil Aviation Conference (ECAC), and were aimed at increased control of domestic and international flights. Subsequently as a result of further terror threats, in October 2006 the European Commission adopted Regulation 1546/2006 which restricted the liquids carried on board aircraft by passengers. This regulation limits the size and amount of liquids carried beyond security control and requires passengers to remove coats and jackets at checkpoints as well as separating laptops and other electrical items.

Security operations at airports are concerned with both airside and landside areas. The airside comprises the aircraft movement area and adjacent infrastructures with controlled access while the landside covers mainly the passenger and cargo terminal infrastructures. However, from a passenger perspective, airport security procedures are only experienced in the terminal. It is here that the escalation of security procedures and additional time needed may deter passengers from flying, especially when competing with other modes of transport. This is particularly the case with domestic routes or short-haul international routes where dwell time, comfort and sense of security may well favour other modes such as the train or private car. Thus the balance between security regulations and customer service is a key modern day challenge for airport management.

Airport management may address this sensitive issue in a number of possible ways. First and foremost, through communication; since security regulations are compulsory and clearly restrictive of tourists' comfort and time, the way for airports to help enforce them is to consider them as an opportunity to communicate with one of their core customers. Traditionally, airports used to limit their relationship with passengers as they viewed them as their airlines' customers. However, with more airport management emphasis on issues such as non-aeronautical revenues, marketing, quality management and customer service, appropriate communication may increase the airport's brand awareness. In spreading the security message widely, by providing advice and supplying information beforehand, airports are able to help minimise travel stress, anxiety and discomfort to passengers. This advisory role expressed through traditional media, airport websites, trade partners, leaflets and staff at the airport, can generate an image of facilitation and assistance to passengers. This role is particularly relevant to leisure tourists and other non-frequent passengers as they may be less familiar with changing security practices due to their scarce use of the airport.

Secondly, technology may also render additional customer service by minimizing valuable time at the airport. For example, airport website reservations, pre-booking of airport services, print at home boarding cards or self check-in facilities allow passengers to take control of procedures, diminishing stress and time on processes not involving security control. Furthermore, technical innovations such as electronic passports, chip cards and biometric media may act as marketing instruments to help segment and value customers by means of alleviated procedures and dedicated processing channels while maintaining security. Sigala discusses these developments in greater detail in Chapter 16.

Finally, the location of security control in the terminal also has to be considered as it can affect passenger comfort and anxiety. Security controls can be centralised, located at pier level or even at gate level. From the passenger point of view centralised security procedures offer less inconvenience quite simply because they alleviate the passenger from that burden earlier. Occurring after check-in, centralised security usually frees the passenger into the airside retail area where they can relax with the commercial services on offer. From the airport perspective there are also advantages since it concentrates staff and equipment in one place, processes large number of passengers at once and encourages more spending in airside retail businesses.

PROVIDING THE RIGHT IMAGE AND NON-AERONAUTICAL FACILITIES TO CONTRIBUTE TO THE LEISURE EXPERIENCE

As discussed in the section 'Meeting the Demands of Different Types of Airlines and Passengers', airports serve a range of different passengers with diverse motivations and needs, from leisure to business, and from transfer to charter or low-cost. Since most airports process more than one of these passenger segments, the non-aeronautical choice of products and services should be adapted to each segment's individual value or share. Moreover, in addition to passenger profiles, the scale and diversity of non-aeronautical activities also derives from the total volume of traffic processed and the airport's strategic positioning as a hub, a feeder or a destination airport. Following this line of thought, the only restriction on non-aeronautical offer should therefore be imagination and availability of space. It is becoming common place to associate airports with non-aviation activities such as hotels, conference centres, office centres, supermarkets, shopping malls, advertising, car-rental, car-parking, valet services, travel agencies or real estate development. Some airports on the cutting edge of non-aeronautical development have also surprised passengers and visitors with casinos, hospitals, art galleries, theme parks, water parks, churches, discos, spas, fitness centres, karting tracks and golf courses.

The airport industry has recognised its role in the tourism value chain and has attempted to contribute to the travel experience of its leisure passengers. This endeavour may be reflected in passenger terminals where architects try to create a sense of place and unique identity which is represented in the design, services and overall ambience of the facilities. For example, by replicating a destination's traits such as sea and sand, golfing, adventure, ecotourism or culture, the airport can convey the same image and message as the destination and conveniently extend the experience to its departure gates. Interesting examples here are Christchurch Airport in New Zealand which has an Antarctic Information Centre and Kansai Airport in Japan which has a multi-themed visitor centre for passengers and visitors.

Leisure passengers are attractive to the airport for non-aeronautical development due to their longer dwell time at the airport, less restricted travel plans and simply their available mindset to experience these services. Therefore they can be some of the highest spenders at the airport although this additionally depends on factors such as country of origin and party size. Moreover, there are significant differences between hub and destination or origin airports when considering leisure passengers. The hub airport's strategy is based on volume which will allow for the development of activities only reachable to these large markets. This is the case for theme parks, fitness centres, casinos or hospitals, where hub airports envisage their high volume of connecting passengers will spend their long dwell time contributing to their overall travel experience.

By contrast, once at the destination airport the tourist's aim is usually to reach and experience the actual destination as soon as possible although there will be scope to expand the leisure travel experience on the return part of the journey until the moment of departure. If the airport is a major origin point for leisure travel such as Manchester airport, there are other commercial opportunities like Manchester Airport Travel Service that acts as a travel agency providing potential passengers with all their travelling arrangements such as holidays, flights, hotels, car rental, car parking, and insurance.

COPING WITH THE PEAKS AND TROUGHS OF LEISURE DEMAND

Airports are first defined through their total numbers of passengers, aircraft and cargo throughput. However, these large numbers are the sum of great variations in demand levels over time, which illustrates the challenge of demand management. As with the rest of the tourism industry, airports experience major demand fluctuations, described in terms of monthly, daily and even hourly demand variations. This raises the important issue of infrastructure under-utilisation since, from the viewpoint of planning and provision of facilities, airport infrastructures are design to handle peak flows. Hence, off-peak periods mean acute infrastructure under-utilisation, resulting in an inefficient operational cost structure.

These demand patterns are an external variable inherent to tourism and airport operations which are directly imposed by its core clients, namely the airlines and passengers. The mix of airline and passenger profiles directly influences peaking, which is illustrated, according to Ashford (1997), by the following characteristics:

- Domestic/international ratio
- Charter/scheduled ratio
- Long-haul/short-haul ratio
- Geographical location
- Nature of catchment-area

Each of these characteristics may impose different restrictions on airport operations resulting in operational and financial inefficiencies. 'Tourist' airports show strong dependence on leisure demand and typically experience stronger differences between peak and off-peak periods. In Europe monthly variations or seasonality reflects the mainstream holiday period from July to September and the traditional holiday movement from north to south. The gap between shorter periods of time such as weekdays or hours of the day are more related to shorter leisure trips and the preferences of leisure tourists to travel at certain times and days of the week.

The issue of seasonality can be clearly illustrated referring to two destination airports, representing respectively a mixed business and leisure passenger profile (airport A) and a full leisure profile (airport B). Comparing both airports' profiles in Table 13.4 the full leisure profile of airport B, distinctly reveals much higher seasonal amplitude, where passenger throughput in the peak month is four times greater than the volume of the trough month. This evidently leads to lower average infrastructure utilisation of only 61 per cent.

Considering that airport infrastructure is designed to handle peak flows there is often much more unused capacity at airports with a stronger leisure passenger share. If passenger demand was more constant over the year the airport B would make full use of its full current capacity, handling an excess of 8 million passengers. In fact, seasonality means that airport B, only handled 5 million passengers, as illustrated by Figure 13.2.

TABLE 13.4   Passenger seasonality by airport passenger mix

	A	B
Total Passengers (millions)	12.00	5.00
Peak month	1.36	0.68
Trough month	0.77	0.16
Monthly Average	1.00	0.42
Seasonality	10.83%	13.53%
Seasonal Amplitude	168.83%	430.67%
Average Utilisation	76.92%	61.64%

Notes:
Seasonality measures peak month or period over total passengers.
Seasonal Amplitude measures the gap between peak and trough month or period.
Average Utilisation measures monthly average against peak month utilisation.

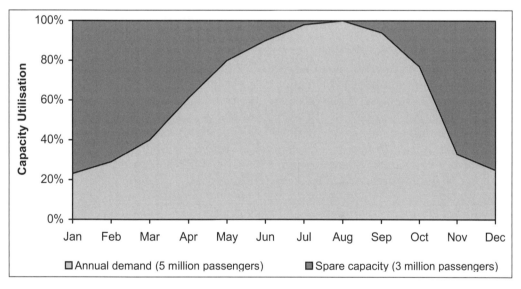

FIGURE 13.2 Capacity utilisation at airport B

Airports may try to cope with fluctuating demand patterns in a number of ways. They may co-operate with regional tourism organisations to increase destination attractiveness, and to spread demand more evenly, by effective promotion, data sharing, trade partnerships and the development of off-season events. Within the scope of airport operations, airports may also deal with peaky leisure demand by peak pricing airport services. The rationale behind this is to encourage airlines to shift their schedules around peak times to more off-peak periods to decrease costs for them. At the same time airlines at peak times will pay more because of the higher costs which they impose on the airport at this peak time. In theory, therefore peak pricing should reduce the congestion at the peak but the topic is complex as many other airline operational and economic factors need to be taken into account. This means that the overall effect of peak pricing, particularly if the differential between the peak and off-peak prices is not substantial, maybe of little inducement for airlines and hence may have very limited effects on airport operations.

Finally, leisure tourist patterns have evolved through time particularly with more short breaks being taken and people travelling more frequently. Low cost carriers have encouraged these developments. The result is that the traditional peaky curve of leisure demand is flattened somewhat. Thus, many European 'tourist' airports often see low-cost carriers as the best answer to absorb leisure demand, at least in the short-term. On the one hand, when compared with traditional scheduled airlines, the aggressive pricing of LCCs stimulates travel, generates new passengers and higher frequencies. On the other hand, the full year operation generally associated with LCCs is more predictable than the seasonal operation of charter airlines which helps to hinder the troughs of traditional leisure demand.

CONCLUSION

This chapter has demonstrated that airports face substantial challenges in meeting the needs of leisure travellers. The types of passengers and airlines and their characteristics are becoming more diverse, which is placing new demands on the airports. Moreover, the increasingly important issue of airport security means that airports, more than ever before, are having to balance the requirements of providing a safe and secure airport without harming the travel experience of leisure passengers at the airport.

This chapter has also discussed the implications of leisure demand for certain areas of airport operations and has highlighted possible strategies which airports may wish to follow. One such area is non-aeronautical services where there is still scope for much innovation, given the fact that the airport visit is often viewed as part of the leisure trip experience. The other issue which has been considered is the variation in demand patterns which is often associated with leisure demand. Although this may result in under-utilisation of resources at certain time and inefficiencies, an indication has also been given of some of the opportunities which exist to lessen these negative impacts.

14

The Impact of Attracting Low Cost Carriers to Airports

Rafael Echevarne

INTRODUCTION

The previous chapter looked at airport requirements for leisure passengers. This chapter now develops this theme further by focusing on low cost carriers (LCCs). The development of these airlines over the last few years, which has been examined by Barrett in Chapter 9, has certainly revolutionised the air transport industry across all its sectors: airlines, aircraft manufacturers, ATC and airports. For airports the impact of attracting low cost carriers can be summarised in four main areas: marketing, finance, operations and capital investments.

The chapter begins by examining the factors which have led to the emergence of the low cost sector and the changing role of airports in dealing with airline customers. It then looks at the financial incentives which airports commonly offer to LCCs and in particular considers the European situation. This leads onto a discussion of the implications of low cost services for airport design and operations and the concept of a low cost terminal is introduced. Finally, the commercial revenue generating opportunities of attracting low cost traffic are assessed.

DEREGULATION, COMPETITION AND THE EMERGENCE OF AIRPORT MARKETING

Airport marketing is a relatively new concept that is becoming increasingly important to airport management. Until the 1980s marketing was not considered a core management activity and airports tended to adopt a reactive attitude to the requests of its clients (airlines, passengers and other users of airport infrastructure) by providing them mainly with statistical information and technical characteristics of the aeronautical infrastructure (A. Graham 2003). The reasons for the change can be traced back to profound changes in key interrelated structural and organisational aspects of the industry: the regulatory framework, the emergence of low cost carriers, the new role of airports as dynamic businesses within the industry, and the competitive nature of the global economy.

Until the 1980s the air transport industry was characterised by heavy regulation and public ownership, with most airlines outside of the United States, and the majority of airports worldwide, in the hands of the public sector (see Chapter 5). Overall, air transport was not seen as a business but more as a necessary tool for development, much like other infrastructure and utilities. Even in the US, until 1978 domestic aviation was heavily regulated.

However, the Airline Deregulation Act of 1978 in the United States sparked a revolution in the air transport industry. It effectively dismantled a comprehensive system of government control as part of a broader movement that, with varying degrees of thoroughness, transformed, among others, such industries as trucking, railroads, buses, telecoms, financial markets and utilities. The success of air transport deregulation in the US triggered change around the world. Europe followed suit and by 1997 the EU air transport market had been fully deregulated, meaning that any EU registered carrier could operate within the internal European market without any restrictions. The trend is being replicated in other parts of the world and the latest development has been the bilateral agreement for open skies between the US and Europe signed in March 2007. This will mean that, from 2008, air services can be established from any European airport to any US airport as long as flights are provided by European or US carriers. This will open-up many opportunities to regional and secondary airports, which, until now, were left out of this market because of bilateral agreement restrictions.

The emergence of low cost airlines has been another major factor contributing to the development of airport marketing. Although not all low cost airlines operate from secondary or remote regional airports, the idea of operating outside main airports has had a fundamental impact on the development of airport marketing. Arguably, when Southwest in the US chose to operate from Houston's Hobby Airport, which is closer to downtown Houston than the new Intercontinental airport, and refused to move out of Dallas Love Field, located 10 minutes from downtown Dallas, to the new Dallas-Fort Worth Regional Airport (35 kms away), the airline established the concept of secondary airport operations (Freiberg K. and Freiberg J.,1996). When Southwest decided to move to Houston's Hobby Airport there were three factors that greatly contributed to the success of the operation from this secondary airport: short distance to downtown Houston, on-time performance and fast check-in times. But not all of Southwest's airports are close to downtown. The airline has also chosen to operate from airports where it does not have direct competitors. For example, in 1999 when it decided to serve the New York market, it chose MacArthur Airport in Islip, Long Island, about 70 kms from Manhattan (Doganis 2001).

However, perhaps the most important factor contributing to the development of air services from regional airports has been the fact that low cost airlines have the power to stimulate the market even from relatively small towns. When Southwest decided to expand its operations in 1973, it thought that it was possible to serve some of Texas' smaller cities profitably. The airline chose a relatively remote area in Texas, the Rio Grande Valley, located at the southernmost point of the state, bordering with Mexico. The airline was right and it managed to almost triple the volume of traffic from 123,000 passengers to 325,000 in just 11 months (Freiberg K. and Freiberg J., 1996). Encouraged by the success on the routes, Southwest decided to expand into other regional airports.

In parallel to all of the above, airports too have undergone important changes as a result of the trend towards commercialisation and, in some instances, privatisation. Indeed, the transformation of the airport scene around the world has been dramatic ever since the privatisation of BAA in 1987. As a result of fundamental changes in policy in many countries, airports have gone from being considered mere public utilities to commercially driven businesses. As such, the role of airports in most parts of the world has evolved from being perceived as purely passive infrastructures serving as points of exchange between transportation modes towards dynamic engines of economic development for the regions they serve and, in some instances, attractive businesses in their own right.

The drive towards a competitive global economy means that regions see airports as tools for their social and economic development and essential for their positioning in the international scene. As a result of the arrival of low cost carriers at regional airports, some regions, particularly in Europe, have experienced a dramatic transformation from being relatively unknown destinations to becoming tourist destinations year round. A good example is the impact that Ryanair has had in the province of Girona in North-eastern Spain. The opening of a base by Ryanair at Girona Airport, originally with the idea of becoming an alternative gateway to Barcelona (Ryanair called Girona "Barcelona North"), has turned the Costa Brava resort region and the Eastern Pyrenees from what used to be just a summer holiday region served mainly by charter carriers, into a year-round destination. The impact on traffic volumes can be dramatic too. In the case of Girona, the airport went from handling half a million passengers in 2002, the year before Ryanair started operations, to 3.5 million in 2005. The success in stimulating the market in Girona is, by no means, a rare example and many other European airports have also experienced similar success stories (Table 14.1).

Consequently, there is increased pressure from the regions and airport companies on airport management to attract carriers and incentivise traffic growth: this justifies the emergence of airport marketing as a fundamental management function. The increasing importance of airport marketing can be seen in the successful development of events that

TABLE 14.1   New international tourism destinations served by LCCs

Country	New International Tourism Destinations
Austria	Graz, Linz, Klagenfurt
Belgium	Charleroi
Denmark	Esbjerg
Finland	Tampere
France	Bergerac, Rodez, Limogez, Carcassonne, Pau, La Rochelle, Nimes, St. Etienne, Tours, Poitiers, Dinard
Germany	Karlsrhue-Baden, Altenburg, Hahn, Tempelhof, Münster (Osnabrück), Erfurt
Ireland	Knock, Derry, Kerry
Italy	Bari, Pescara, Ancona, Brindisi, Palermo, Alghero, Trieste
Norway	Haugesund
Poland	Gdansk, Poznan
Slovakia	Kosice
Spain	Bilbao, Girona, Jerez, Murcia, Santander, Valladolid, Zaragoza
Sweden	Malmo, Nyköping
United Kingdom	Blackpool, Bournemouth, Newquay

Source: ELFAA (2004).

bring together airlines and airports. Examples include Routes, Network USA and French Connect. It is also important to highlight the increasing cooperation between airports and tourism bodies in joint efforts to promote the destinations served by the airports.

AIRPORT FINANCIAL ISSUES

One of the major ways that airports have attracted low cost carriers is by using financial incentives. Within Europe particularly, there have been a number of key developments related to these.

Types of Financial Incentives

The simplest type of incentive is a direct payment to the airline for the purposes of marketing the service. This can be done either by the airport itself or in collaboration with the regional public agency. Generally, these incentives take the form of payments per flight and/or passenger. As an example of a simple payment per passenger, in 2004 Shannon Airport offered a Route Support Scheme whereby it paid EUR 3 per departing passenger, but only on new routes. Many airports, public agencies and tourist boards also offer marketing support through joint marketing budgets (called 'Co-Op Marketing Funds' in North America). The marketing campaigns typically promote the new air service at the same time as the region itself, most commonly with a view to attracting tourists. These campaigns consist largely of advertising, either directly displayed on the aircraft (painted on the fuselage or headrests) or in the airline's media, such as in-flight magazine, website and frequent flier newsletters.

Another form of incentive is through discounts which can be applied to airport charges, the use of airport facilities or even tax discounts. Discounts on airport charges include passenger fees (departing passenger charge, security) and aircraft related fees (landing, parking, aerobridge). These type of discounts are quite common although they vary greatly among airports. Discounts tend to be higher during the initial years of operation and usually decrease over time during a period of three to five years. A good example is Dublin airport's discounts on passenger, landing, security, and aerobridge charges on non-stop routes to non-EU destinations that are not already serviced more than twice a week. The scheme runs for four years starting with a 100 per cent discount on year 1, progressively reducing to 25 per cent on year 4. Some low cost carriers not only ask for reduced charges but also for simplified structures. Consequently, reduced charges often cover passenger charges and landing fees in an inclusive per passenger charge. Although these types of discounts are not normally published, it is clear that they tend to be considerable. For example, Ryanair stated that its airport charges in 2004 (including handling) fell from EUR 7.65 in 2002 to EUR 6.39 in 2004 on a per-passenger basis (Ryanair 2005). Some airports also offer discounts on services and facilities not directly associated with the aeronautical operation. These include, but are not necessarily limited to, the rental of office space, check-in desks, storage rooms, and staff car parking.

ONDA, the Moroccan national airports authority, launched in 2005 a new incentive policy aimed at attracting additional traffic at all its airports, while respecting the principles of non-discrimination. The measures were aimed at increasing air frequencies, creating new domestic and international point-to-point routes to and from Morocco, developing domestic routes and encouraging the development of Casablanca Airport as a regional hub. As a result of the initiative, in 2006, 22 new airlines launched services to Morocco opening 42 new routes. In the case of Rabat Airport, currently underutilised and with just one international route, the discounts for the 2007 season were 100 per cent on passenger fees for increased frequencies and 100 per cent on passenger fees and terminal and landing fees for new destinations.

Risk sharing mechanisms are commonly used in the United States. There are two main types: revenue guarantees and community ticket trusts. With a revenue guarantee, public and private institutions as well as local businesses in a community raise a minimum amount of money as a guarantee to an airline to cover the costs associated with the provision of the service during a limited period of time. A community ticket trust requires the airport operator and/or public institutions to persuade major airline customers in their region to commit to book a minimum number of tickets during the early stages of operation of a new service. Such a travel bank or mileage bank does not necessarily cost the airport or public authorities anything, but reduces the risk of the service for the carrier and thus helps in persuading the airlines to launch the service. Many major companies are prepared to guarantee ticket purchases because they value the connectivity for their own employees and clients, although the success of ticket trusts has been limited by the cumbersome administration required (STRAIR, 2005).

The Charleroi Case

The decision by the European Commission (2004) on the assistance provided by Brussels South Charleroi Airport (Charleroi Airport) and the Walloon Region to Ryanair, established a precedent on the issue of financial assistance for the development of air services. In 2001 a complaint was lodged with the European Commission concerning a number of advantages granted to Ryanair by Charleroi Airport and the Walloon Region in April 2001. Hence, in December 2002 the Commission launched an investigation in order to determine whether the measures taken in favour of Ryanair by the airport and the region were compatible or not with the private market investor principle.

Charleroi Airport is located 46 kms south of Brussels, in a region that had been badly affected by unemployment resulting from the decline of the European steel industry (Sambrinvest 2007). The airport is managed by Brussels South Charleroi Airport (BSCA), a publicly owned company which was set up in 1991 as part of the process of transfer of management of the country's airports from the Belgian State to the regions. There had been several attempts to establish scheduled passenger services from Charleroi, including flights to London. However, none of these succeeded until 1997, when Ryanair decided to develop passenger services at the airport with the launch of the route to Dublin (Deloitte and Touche/ASBL 2003). In April 2001, Ryanair opened its first base in Continental Europe with two aircraft based at Charleroi and the launch of six new routes. As a result, passenger throughput jumped from 200,000 in the year 2000 to 773,431 in 2001. By 2006 Charleroi handled 2.2 million passengers and in 2007 five airlines operated from the airport with 26 daily flights (BSCA 2007). Ryanair continues to be the largest airline at Charleroi.

The aid granted to Ryanair by the airport company and the region in 2001, which no other airline benefited from, was:

- Preferential landing charges of EUR 1 per boarding passenger; about 50 per cent of the standard rate.

- A preferential rate of EUR 1 per passenger for ground handling services, whereas the rates normally charged to other airlines was EUR 8-13.

- A contribution towards promotional activities of EUR 4 per boarding passenger, over 15 years and for up to 26 daily flights.

- Initial incentives amounting to EUR 160,000 per new route opened, for 12 routes, or EUR 1,920,000 in total; EUR 768,000 in reimbursements for pilot training; EUR 250,000 for hotel accommodation costs.

In exchange for all of this, Ryanair agreed to:

- Establish an operational base at Charleroi Airport.

- Base between 2 and 4 aircraft at the airport.

- Operate at least 3 departing daily flights per each aircraft based at the airport over a period of 15 years.

- Return to the airport all financial assistance related to the opening of the operational base as well as the contributions towards promotional activities if it ceased its operations at Charleroi.

The Commission determined that no private operator in the same circumstances as Charleroi Airport would have granted the same advantages to the airline. Since the private market investor principle had not been adhered to, it concluded that the support provided by the airport (and the region) constituted State aid which could distort competition in favour of Ryanair.

However, the Commission took the view that some aspects of the aid could be compatible with European transport policy because it facilitated the development and improved use of a secondary airport infrastructure that was underused and represented a cost to the community as a whole. According to the Commission, such developments benefit the regions by ensuring a better return from existing public goods and facilitate regional economic development, in particular through job creation and tourism. It also encourages the better use of existing airports as opposed to the construction of new infrastructure.

Hence, the Commission allowed Ryanair to keep the aid intended for the launch of new air routes (marketing and publicity) and one-shot incentives, including the airport's contribution to the financing of a joint promotion and publicity company with Ryanair (Promocy), which could be considered to be aid to the start-up of new air routes. In order for such aid to be authorised, the Belgian authorities had to comply with the conditions imposed by the Commission, in particular:

- It must be proportional to the objective pursued, and be granted with due regard for the principles of transparency, equal treatment and non-discrimination between operators. It must be accompanied by a mechanism for imposing penalties should the carrier fail to comply with its commitment and it must not be aggregated with aid which serves a social objective or with public service compensation payments.

- It must be of limited duration (five years in the case of point-to-point European routes, and not 15 years) and correspond to a maximum amount of 50 per cent of the net start-up costs incurred. The airport must have control over such costs and the aid must be available in the future to any airline which is established at Charleroi.

However, the Commission determined that certain forms of aid could not be authorised. In particular:

- Discounts on airport charges, which went beyond the discounts foreseen by the Belgian legislation (which are non-discriminatory and fully transparent).

- Reduced handling fees, which were not offset by possible surpluses from other, purely commercial activities (such as shops and car parking).

- One-shot incentives paid when new routes were launched, where no account was taken of the actual costs of launching such routes.

- Aid provided in respect of the Dublin-Charleroi route, which was not new as it was launched in 1997.

Consequently, in February 2004, the Commission claimed that a portion of the arrangements between Ryanair, the airport and the Walloon Region constituted illegal state aid, and ordered Ryanair to repay the illegally granted benefits. In May 2004, Ryanair appealed against the decision to the European Court of First Instance. Meanwhile in April 2004, in accordance with the Commission's decision, the Walloon Region asked Ryanair for repayment of all illegally granted aid. In September 2004, the Walloon Region issued a formal demand that Ryanair repay a total of approximately EUR 4 million, excluding any interest that may be due. Ryanair believes that no repayment is due when such offsets are taken into account, although it has placed this amount into an escrow account pending the outcome of its appeal to the Court of First Instance. In May 2005, the Walloon Region initiated new proceedings, which are currently pending before the Irish High Court, to recover a further EUR 2.3 million from Ryanair. Ryanair does not believe that any such payment is due pursuant to the Commission's decision and is currently defending the action (Ryanair 2006).

The Strasbourg Case

Although the outcome of the Charleroi case resulted in Ryanair threatening to withdraw some routes from the airport, the airline did not envisage pulling out of the airport entirely (BBC News online 2004). On the contrary, Ryanair's presence in Charleroi has gone from strength to strength. However, a completely different outcome resulted from the dispute between Ryanair and the French authorities in the case of the French airport of Strasbourg.

As a result of a complaint by Air France, in July 2003 the Strasbourg court ruled that marketing support granted by the Strasbourg Chamber of Commerce (owner and operator of Strasbourg Airport) to Ryanair in connection with its launch of services from Strasbourg to London Stansted constituted unlawful state aid. The judgement took effect in September 2003 and effectively annulled Ryanair's contract with Strasbourg Airport. As a result of this, Ryanair decided to close the Strasbourg route and instead opened a route from Baden-Karlsruhe in Germany to London Stansted. Baden airport is located some 40 kms from Strasbourg.

Figure 14.1 shows the evolution of traffic volumes (split between Air France and LCCs) on the London Stansted-Strasbourg route between June 2002 and February 2004. The introduction of LCCs services almost quadrupled passenger throughput on the route but competition was so intense that Air France had to pull out. When Ryanair closed the route, Air France reintroduced its services and volumes returned to pre-LCC levels.

The EU Guidelines on State Aids to Airports and Airlines

Following from the Charleroi case, in September 2006 the European Commission published its "Community guidelines on financing of airports and start-up aid to airlines departing from regional airports". Until then, other than specific cases and general guidelines for the air transport industry, there were no specific guidelines from the Commission on the application of State aid principles to airlines and airports.

By financing of airports, the guidelines refer to State aid related to the development of infrastructure, the operation of the infrastructure and the provision of airport services, such as ground handling. As regards to the latter, the guidelines set the threshold of 2

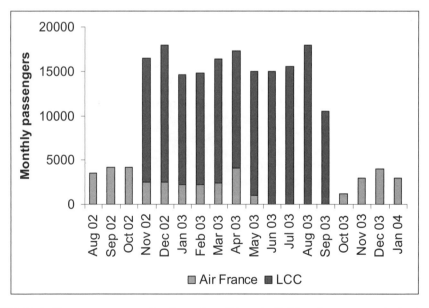

FIGURE 14.1 Passengers on the London Stansted-Strasbourg route between June 2002 and February 2004

Source: Adapted from ELFAA (2004).

million passengers as the point beyond which ground handling services must be self-financing. Airports with a lower volume of throughput, who act as providers of handling services, may offset this activity with other commercial revenue sources.

However, of particular relevance to the discussion in this chapter are the guidelines on start-up aid. By this, the Commission means financial incentives provided by airports to airlines in order to facilitate the establishment of air services. On the basis that the Commission accepts the fact that some airlines are not willing to establish air services from small, unknown or untested airports, it established the following criteria for start-up aid (European Commission 2005):

- The airline must be registered in a Member State of the European Union.

- Routes must be between EU airports of less than 5 million passengers and other EU airports. Only in exceptional circumstances can airports between 5 and 10 million passengers be considered.

- Aid must only apply to new routes or new schedules that lead to an increase to the net volume of passengers.

- The route receiving the aid must ultimately prove profitable for the airline without public funding.

- The amount of aid must be directly linked to the additional start-up costs of the airline in launching the new route or frequency (mainly advertising and marketing) and cost of installing the airline at the airport.

- Digressive aid must be granted for a maximum period of three years. The amount of aid in any one year must not exceed 50 per cent of total eligible costs for that year and total aid must not exceed an average of 30 per cent of eligible costs. Exceptions are made for airports in remote regions.

- Aid must be linked to the net development of the number of passengers carried.

AIRPORT DESIGN AND OPERATIONS

The successful development of low cost carriers has inevitably brought about the concept of low cost airports and low cost terminals. To date, no greenfield airport has been built specifically designed for low cost airlines, but a number of airports that had little or no commercial activity have now been revived by low cost carriers. Also, a number of airports have developed passenger terminals dedicated to handle low cost operations. LCCs aim to maximise productivity and minimise costs and, at airports, this is generally achieved by minimising turnaround times and keeping costs down by not using unnecessary infrastructure and services (see Chapter 9). Hence LCCs tend to be very strict in negotiating with both the airport and handling companies for only the services they require.

However, not all LCCs operate from secondary or regional airports. In Europe, the classic example is the difference between the Ryanair and the easyJet models. Whereas Ryanair favours secondary and regional airports, easyJet prefers to fly to main airports.

Essentially there is a trade-off between the two models. Flying to regional and secondary airports helps in keeping costs down which contributes to low fares and this makes up for the "inconvenience" of travelling to relatively remote airports. By flying to the main airports, however, the higher operational costs are compensated with direct access to more lucrative markets that supposedly are willing to pay higher fares. For example, whereas easyJet flies to the two main Paris airports, Roissy-Charles de Gaulle and Orly, Ryanair operates to Beauvais, a regional airport 80 kms from the French capital. In some cases there is just one airport available for a specific market in which case the LCC has no choice. This is the case with Ryanair in Madrid, where the carrier had to "break" its rule of not operating to main hub airports in order to access this large and growing market. In the US a similar situation occurs between the two largest LCCs, Southwest and JetBlue. However, with the exception of the largest markets, the difference in strategy is not so clear. For example, whereas Southwest operates from Chicago's Midway Airport, JetBlue flies from the main O'Hare Airport. In New York, JetBlue has its main base at JFK Airport, whereas Southwest flies from Long Island. In Southern Florida, however, both airlines avoid Miami and fly instead from Fort Lauderdale.

In terms of runway and taxiway systems and navigational aids, there are no differences between the needs of conventional carriers and low cost airlines, as the design standards and regulations concerning these infrastructures are set by ICAO on the basis of ensuring operational commonality and minimum safety standards. The terminal building and ramp operations, however, are areas where there are significant design and operational differences respectively between the requirements of low cost airlines and those of other carriers, which are fundamental to ensure fast operations and to keep costs down for the LCCs (Table 14.2). In order to accommodate the specific requirements of low cost carriers, some airports have developed the concept of low cost terminals. Marseille (MP2 Terminal), Vienna (Terminal 1A), Kuala Lumpur (LCC Terminal), Singapore (Budget Terminal), and Mexico's Monterrey Airport (Terminal C) are examples of such developments.

In Singapore, the country's Civil Aviation Authority (CAAS), owner and operator of Changi Airport, decided to build a customised terminal (Budget Terminal) for low cost carriers after it received firm commitments from Tiger Airways to use such a terminal. CAAS decided that the operating costs at the Budget Terminal would be kept low to meet the needs and operating models of low cost carriers. In line with this objective, the compact layout of the single-storey terminal has no need for travellators, escalators and aerobridges. The Budget Terminal also offers other services such as a free shuttle bus service to link passengers from the Budget Terminal to Changi Airport's existing terminals. However, services and facilities such as foreign exchange, internet terminals, duty-free shopping, and food and beverage outlets are available at the Budget Terminal. The terminal started operations in March 2006 and the construction costs amounted to SGD45 million. The size of the terminal is 25,000 square metres and its initial capacity is about 2.7 million passengers per annum. In August 2006, Cebu Pacific Air became the second airline to establish operations at the terminal. CAAS applies significantly lower charges at the Budget Terminal as compared to Terminals 1 and 2. The passenger charge is SGD7 which is 50 per cent lower than the SGD15 at Terminals 1 and 2. However, in order to maintain the same security levels, the passenger security service charge is the same as at the other terminals at SGD7.

Marseille Provence Airport was a pioneer in Europe in the provision of low cost facilities, when it decided to develop a dedicated terminal for low cost carriers with a differentiated pricing structure in order to give airlines the choice of service they wanted to offer their

TABLE 14.2 Key passenger terminal requirements and ramp operations

Operational Area	LCCs Requirements	Traditional Airlines	Comments
Access & Car Parking	High demand of car parking facilities at regional and secondary airports	Higher use of taxi	LCCs favour airports with public transportation systems
Check-in	LCCs require fewer check-in desks which usually results in longer queues	Separate check-in desks according to class of travel. Higher number of desks than LCCs to reduce queuing time	LCCs and traditional airlines are enthusiastically embracing web check-in as it reduces the need for check-in desks and hence reduced costs
Security	LCCs demand that procedures do not delay aircraft boarding	Some request separate channels for premium class passengers	
Baggage handling systems	Very simple. No need for sophistication as flights are point-to-point	Airlines that operate hubs require sophisticated and costly baggage handling systems in order to transfer bags between flights at their hub airport	
Boarding bridges	Most prefer not to use them to expedite boarding and unloading of aircraft by using front and back doors	Prefer to use them for the convenience and comfort of passengers	
Ramp operations: aircraft boarding	LCCs prefer passengers to get to the aircraft by foot and avoid using busses to ferry passengers in order to save costs	If possible, passengers are ferried to aircraft by bus for their convenience	Ramp safety issues may arise as a result of passengers walking to/from aircraft
Ramp operations: aircraft push-back	LCCs prefer self-power manoeuvring to reduce costs and expedite operations	Push-back necessary if aircraft connected to boarding bridge	Self-power manoeuvring normally requires more ramp space

Source: Author.

passengers. In order to save costs, the management decided to reconvert the old cargo terminal into a low cost carrier terminal (MP2), which was inaugurated in October 2006. The new terminal has a capacity of 3.7 million passengers and the total investment was EUR16.4 million.

In the words of the airport (Marseille airport 2007):

- "There is no carpet, no marble floors, no flat screen monitors on top of the check-in counters.

- You take your own baggage to the security screening point.

- You walk up stairs instead of escalators.

- You board the airport from the apron, instead of using an aerobridge.

- You contribute to reducing the operational costs of this terminal building which means lower air fares."

The airport company, like most French regional airports, is operated by the Chamber of Commerce, which views its involvement in the airport as a way of helping to achieve wider economic benefits to the region. It is estimated that each flight generates approximately EUR7 million to the region and it is expected that there will be one million additional passengers and almost half a million additional tourists to the region during the first year of operation of the low cost terminal. Ryanair was the first airline to use MP2, when it started operating its first base in France. Ryanair has a 5-year commitment and is expected to have at least four aircraft stationed at Marseille (*Le Figaro* 2006). By 2007 there were four more airlines operating from MP2 (easyJet, myair, jet4you and bmibaby).

In the US, JetBlue is developing its first and main operational base at New York's JFK airport. The airline considers that the future of airport design is about what happens on the other side of security, particularly as increasing numbers of passengers now do their ticketing from home (Blum 2005). According to JetBlue, low cost means putting money in the right place which in the case of the facility at JFK means a practical and efficient building. The new terminal will cost USD875 million and will accommodate 26 gates able to handle 250 flights daily or 20 million passengers per annum. Most of the investment is being made by the Port Authority of New York and New Jersey and JetBlue will make lease payments for the facility. The building incorporates Eero Saarinen's iconic 1962 TWA terminal.

AIRPORT COMMERCIAL REVENUES

Airports worldwide are seeking to optimise their non-aviation revenues. The most successful airports have developed retail strategies that offer attractive shopping opportunities and benefits to passengers and visitors, and are reaping the rewards of satisfying customers through substantial increases in revenues obtained from branded retailing and catering. The vast majority of these revenues are being generated from airside shopping centres where passengers are relaxed, have time to shop, and spend significant amounts of money on an increasingly broad range of targeted merchandise sold from retailers who have developed specific travel retail niche formats.

Airports are successfully stimulating their passengers to become customers of their shops, and a number of research projects undertaken by specialist consultants on behalf of airports, airport retailers and airlines into passengers' views on airport shopping and their shopping needs and expectations, confirm that:

- Airport shopping is an integral part of the airport terminal experience

- Passengers expect good shops and are increasingly arriving earlier in order to shop

- Most passengers will visit the shops and a large proportion plan to buy

- Passengers are easily disappointed if the shopping on offer is limited or of poor quality

- Only a small percentage (less than 5 per cent) of passengers consider shops to be an inconvenience

- Shopping often precedes waiting and seating

- Half of all premium passengers shop before entering their airline lounge.

(Pragma Consulting / ARC Retail Consultants 2006)

The key to developing a successful retailing strategy is a detailed understanding of the potential customer base. Therefore, it is essential to establish who the potential customers are, and how different groups of customers may use the commercial offer. Customers tend to make purchases at airports according to seven different primary motivations. More than one motivation can be applied to each segment, although some motivations are more prevalent amongst certain airport user groups than others (Pragma Consulting / ARC Retail Consultants 2006). These motivations can be classified into three main groups: needs, wants and impulse purchases (Table 14.3).

During the late 1990s, with the advent of low cost airlines, a key concern among airport managers was the impact that these would have on commercial revenues. It was thought that the socio-economic profile of the passengers flying these airlines and, in particular, their buying behaviour, would be different from those on legacy carriers or even charter airlines. The view was that the low fares offered by the low cost carriers would attract

TABLE 14.3   Motivations for airport purchases

Travel necessity/Emergency	Items forgotten, emergency medical/toiletries, things to do/consume during travel (books, toys, music, confectionery etc.)
Destination/Souvenir	Items to remind traveller of the place they are leaving/celebrate that they have been to the destination (e.g. local produce, T-shirt, ornament etc.)
Gift for those at home/destination	Gifts for partner, children, work colleagues etc.
Personal self-treat	Self indulgence (e.g. designer label clothing, watches, jewellery and accessories)
Convenience	Items that would typically be bought in more normal locations, but are bought at the airport because of greater convenience (e.g. tie for executives)
Exclusive opportunity to buy/ price driven	Something only available in Travel Value/Duty Free (current examples: price discounts, unique merchandise to duty free, special packaging, etc.)
Trip enhancement	An impulsive purchase made as part of 'travel feel-good factor' (e.g. sunglasses for holiday)

Source: Pragma Consulting/ARC Retail Consultants (2006).

cost conscious passengers who would not want to spend as much on airport shops as passengers travelling on traditional airlines. Indeed, airports had tended to develop high-end shops and an overall luxury retail experience, particularly at the world's largest hubs. The revenues generated from such activities had been one of the key factors behind the overwhelming success of the airport business.

However, probably to the surprise of many, the buying behaviour of low cost airline passengers at airports did not vary significantly from those flying on legacy carriers. In 2004, Spain's Institute of Tourism Studies (Instituto de Estudios Turísticos 2004) undertook a study on low cost carriers in order to understand the impact that such airlines were having on the tourism industry. The study concluded that, against what was usually perceived, tourists travelling on LCCs to Spain on average income and medium-high income levels represented 65.3 per cent and 20.5 per cent of the total respectively. Surprisingly too, there were more high income passengers on LCCs (5.2 per cent) than on conventional airlines (4.4 per cent). Overall, it could be said that the socio-economic profile of LCC passengers is very similar to those on conventional or legacy carriers.

Consequently, the commercial offer at airports mainly served by low costs carriers, such as Frankfurt-Hahn and low cost terminals, like Marseille's MP2, is very similar as that at conventional airports. In the case of Frankfurt Hahn Airport, in order to cater for the commercial demand generated by LCC passengers, the terminal shopping area underwent a major expansion and development between 2002 and 2005. During that time, the shopping area grew from less than 250 sqm to more than 3,500 sqm.

Commercial activities that have particularly benefited from LCCs are, for example, food and beverage services (bars and restaurants) and car-rental services. Since most LCCs charge for food and beverages served on-board, many passengers tend to eat at the airport or even purchase food and beverage to consume during the flight. This, combined with the fact that passengers are being asked to arrive early at the airport in order to have enough time to complete the increasingly lengthy security measures, has resulted in a significant increase in the average revenue per passenger on these concessions. However, this tendency has also spread to larger airports too, as a result of the increasing numbers of legacy carriers charging for in-flight catering. Consequently, airports have focused on the development of food courts. For example, Marrakech, a popular LCC destination in Morocco, developed a food court following the theme of the rich and varied local gastronomy for which this tourist region is known. Car-rental concessions have also benefited from LCC passengers. This is a direct result of the trend towards independent travel, which sees passengers booking their flights, ground transportation and accommodation themselves using the Internet.

CONCLUSIONS

This chapter has emphasised how airports cannot be passive to the development of low cost carriers. Most large and small airports in regions where LCCs have thrived have had to reconsider their business models in order to accommodate the impact that these new players are having on the air transport industry.

Some large airports have protected their markets by acquiring "secondary" airports and turning these into specialist low-cost airports, such as Frankfurt's investment in Hahn, a former military base. For many regional airports, LCCs are the only option to grow. Some have managed to achieve passenger levels never imagined; many of them easily doubling traffic from one year to the next or even more. Other regional airports that handled little or no commercial traffic or only seasonal traffic, have been given a new lease of life with the arrival of LCCs. Some airports have had to adapt their operational procedures and infrastructure to accommodate the specific requirements of LCCs. Overall, airports have accepted these demands because of the significant increase in passenger levels, which, in turn, have generated additional revenues from commercial concessions.

Regional public and private institutions, particularly in the tourism industry, have played a major role in attracting LCCs, mainly because of the almost immediate benefits resulting from the sudden arrival of considerable numbers of tourists on a year-round basis. According to the European Commission, "the cooperation between low-cost carriers and regions is successful by contributing enormously to [...] regional development. [...] Regions are experiencing increased economic growth in sectors such as tourism and witness the development of small and medium-sized enterprises in a wide range of commercial sectors".(ELFAA 2004, 26). Moreover, the EU's Committee of the Regions observed that "the availability of regional air services and in particular low-cost air services operating from regional airports improves access to the global economy" (ELFAA 2004, 25). For example, in the case Marseille, each daily flight injects 7 million euro to the region and, in terms of employment generation, the overall the development of the LCC terminal has generated 1,000 direct and 2,000 indirect jobs (*Le Figaro* 2006). However, the efforts to attract LCCs must generally be accompanied by generous financial support packages. Under most circumstances, these are generally considered as being reasonable "investments", but in Europe the issue of public finances being used for the benefit of private companies has, in certain cases, resulted in legal challenges. Consequently, the EU determined the guidelines for the award of financial assistance for the establishment of air services.

LCCs have revolutionised the air transport industry and airports have had to react to the new environment. As efforts are currently underway to export the LCC model from short and medium haul sectors to intercontinental services (see Chapter 9), airports should prepare themselves for the potential impact that these new services could have on their business.

15

Airport Marketing and Tourism in Remote Destinations: Exploiting the Potential in Europe's Northern Periphery

Nigel Halpern and Jukka Niskala

INTRODUCTION

In the last two chapters in this airport section general consideration has been given to how both leisure passengers and low cost airlines affect airport operations. An important area which has not been investigated, however, has been issues related to tourism and airports in peripheral or remote regions. Hence, this chapter aims to fill this gap by looking at the situation in Europe's Northern Periphery where deregulation, general economic growth and changes in travel behaviour and motivations have accelerated the growth of tourism and the opportunity for airports to compete in destination markets.

This chapter begins by describing the changes in the business environment which have facilitated greater growth opportunities for airports in Northern Europe, particularly in relation to tourism markets. It then goes on to discuss the specific characteristics of both airport competition and the airport product within the context of airports in peripheral areas. Consideration is made of the implications of these for selecting the most appropriate marketing techniques. This is followed by a detailed case study of Pajala-Ylläs airport in Swedish Lapland to illustrate how marketing practices have been used in practice to exploit its potential for tourism.

THE CHANGING BUSINESS ENVIRONMENT

Halpern (2006) defines and measures Europe's peripheral areas according to inaccessibility to potential markets or the presence of structural handicaps including a sparse population density, island location or mountainous area. NUTS II[1] identified as being peripheral

---

1   The present NUTS system divides the countries of Europe into five levels (three regional and two local), known as NUTS I through to NUTS V'. The study by Halpern (2006) is based on all NUTS II regions of the 19 pre-2004 accession member states of the European Economic Area (EU19).

include large parts of the Nordic countries; parts of the British Isles including the Highlands and Islands and north eastern parts of Scotland, Cornwall and the Isles of Scilly, the Isle of Man, the Channel Islands, Northern Ireland and the Republic of Ireland; alpine regions of Germany, Austria and Switzerland; and, large parts of southern/Mediterranean Europe. The focus of this chapter is on Europe's northern periphery; the most peripheral NUTS II region of each country in northern Europe. This includes a combination of regions (north Norway, north Sweden, north Finland and the Highlands and Islands of Scotland) and countries (Iceland, the Faroe Islands and the Republic of Ireland). The definition and measurement of Europe's northern periphery is limited by a number of factors and readers should refer to Halpern (2006) for further details.

Europe's northern periphery has a relatively good distribution of airports that were developed for military or regional development purposes. This is demonstrated in Table 15.1 where it can be seen that there are 72 airports serving commercial air services and 41,846 inhabitants per airport. This compares to 390 airports and 999,779 inhabitants per airport in the pre-accession European countries (EU19). Table 15.1 also demonstrates the spatial distribution of airports according to surface area per airport and whilst Europe's northern periphery has a favourable spatial distribution of airports compared to the EU19 countries, the advantage is only marginal. This emphasises the vast and sparsely populated nature of Europe's northern periphery.

Before deregulation, the focus of airports in Europe's northern periphery was on providing a public service to the many small and isolated communities by linking them to the main transportation networks (Reynolds-Feighan 1995). Airports were, therefore, dominated by the hub connection of a national airline (or its subsidiary) and tended to offer minimal services with small aircraft and high fares. Most airports were publicly-owned and operated and were largely empty, loss-making and heavily subsidised (Barrett 2004a). This is still the case to some extent as 92 per cent of the airports in Europe's northern

TABLE 15.1   Airport infrastructure in Europe's northern periphery, 2004

Region	Airports	Inhabitants/airport	Surface area (km²) airport
Iceland	7	40,407	14,714
North Norway*	28	17,334	4,008
North Sweden**	10	51,335	15,431
North Finland***	8	78,550	16,037
Faroe Islands	1	46,962	1,399
Highlands & Islands	9	41,111	4,420
Republic of Ireland	9	420,767	7,808
Europe's northern periphery	72	41,846	8,742
EU19****	390	999,779	9,463

*   North Norway (Nord-Norge: Finnmark, Troms and Nordland)
**   North Sweden (Övre Norrland: Norrbotten and Västerbotten)
***   North Finland (Pohjois-Suomi: Keski-Pohjanmaa, Pohjois-Pohjanmaa and Lappi)
****   The 19 pre-2004 accession member states of the European Economic Area

Source: Halpern (2005).

periphery are publicly-owned and 82 per cent have fewer than 250,000 passengers per annum; as many as 61 per cent have fewer than 100,000 passengers per annum (Halpern 2005).

Routes serving airports in Europe's northern periphery were somewhat protected before deregulation because national airlines or their subsidiaries were required to serve lightly populated and unprofitable routes in exchange for monopoly rights on dense and profitable routes. Monopolistic conditions in the airline industry meant that there was minimal competition between airlines but also between airports. There was little incentive for airports to reduce costs and improve efficiency and as discussed by Echevarne in Chapter 14, airport marketing was something of an oxymoron that was limited to passive approaches such as the responsiveness to enquiries and the publication of airport charges, facility literature and an airport timetable (A. Graham 2003).

By 1997, European air transport markets were deregulated and this has created a much more competitive airport environment (see Chapter 5 by Papatheodorou). Deregulation has eliminated the system of cross-subsidy that protected routes serving airports in Europe's northern periphery and has meant that airlines are now less restricted in terms of which airports they can fly to and from. Airlines have become more susceptible to aggressive marketing from airports and the success of an airport is increasingly based on its ability to attract and retain airline customers. As explained by Barrett in Chapter 9, deregulation has also facilitated the emergence of low-cost carriers such as Ryanair, easyJet, Iceland Express, Norwegian and Blue 1, all of which have a presence in Europe's northern periphery.

It is worth noting that despite deregulation a system for subsidising lightly populated and unprofitable routes still exists in Europe. This system is implemented through the Public Service Obligation (PSO) programme. The main objective of the PSO programme is to protect the provision of lifeline air services in remote areas. Lifeline air services are considered to be necessary for social reasons and are not likely to be provided by airlines on a commercial basis. Another objective of the PSO programme is to encourage economic development, with a particular emphasis on stimulating inbound tourism.

Table 15.2 provides a list of all PSO routes in Sweden in 2006. Each PSO route has been introduced by the Swedish government on the basis that it is not considered to be commercially viable but is necessary for social reasons and for the regional development of Sweden's most peripheral areas, thus supporting the main objectives of the PSO programme. Apart from Torsby/Hagfors-Stockholm, each of the routes serves an airport that is located in the north of Sweden and connects the airport to a regional or national hub airport. Airlines tender for each route and are required to provide a certain level of frequency and capacity on the route in exchange for monopoly rights and financial support from the state.

PSOs have a positive impact on the development of tourism because they assure the provision of air services in areas that would otherwise be inaccessible to potential markets. However, PSOs could also be seen as a constraint to the development of tourism because they do not allow competition from non-contract airlines and can result in the provision of minimal services with small aircraft and high fares. This may not be such an issue on thin routes where there is 'no other option'; however, it has become an important point of discussion on dense routes such as those serving established tourism destinations in Europe's southern periphery.

Almost 350,000 passengers used the PSO route between Milan in Italy and Olbia in Sardinia in 2005 (Bacchetta 2007). This compares to less than 150,000 passengers on all of

TABLE 15.2   PSO routes in Sweden, 2006

Route	Airline	Frequency			Aircraft type (seats)
		Weekday	Saturday	Sunday	
Arvidsjaur-Stockholm*	Skyways	2	1	1	SAAB 2000 (50) Avro RJ 100 (112)
Gällivare-Stockholm*	Nordic Regional	2	1	1	MD 87 (135)
Hemavan-Stockholm*	Skyways	1	0	1	Fokker 50 (50)
Lycksele-Stockholm*	Skyways	2	1	1	SAAB 2000 (50) Avro RJ 100 (112)
Pajala-Luleå	Nordkalottflyg	2	0	0	Beechcraft 200 (9)
Storuman-Stockholm*	Skyways	2	0	1	Fokker 50 (50)
Sveg-Stockholm*	Nextjet	2	0	0	Beech 1900 D (19)
Torsby/Hagfors-Stockholm*	Nextjet	2	0	0	Beech 1900 D (19)
Vilhelmina-Stockholm*	Skyways	2	0	1	Fokker 50 (50)
Östersund-Umeå	Nordic Regional	2	0	0	SAAB 340 (33)

*   Stockholm-Arlanda Airport

Source: Adapted from Holmér (2007).

the 10 PSO routes listed in Table 15.2 in Sweden in 2005 (Holmér 2007). European low-cost airline easyJet disputes the importance of PSOs on thick routes such as Milan-Olbia, claiming that the level of demand can be served on a commercial basis. easyJet also claims that competition on such routes is likely to encourage lower fares and increased demand, facilitating the development of tourism (Bacchetta 2007). The European Commission has recently acknowledged this abuse of the PSO programme and has taken action to limit the application of PSOs on thick routes.

Another problem with the PSO programme is that the application and use of PSOs is at the discretion of member states and because of this, major inconsistencies exist in the approach and commitment to PSO's across Europe (Williams and Pagliari 2004). In comparison to the nine PSO routes serving airports in the north of Sweden, 25 are provided in the Highlands and Islands of Scotland, seven are provided in the Republic of Ireland, and none are provided in the north of Finland (European Commission 2007e). This means that many routes serving airports in Europe's northern periphery are entirely exposed to market forces and are susceptible to airport marketing. In addition, the restrictive and non-competitive nature of PSOs means that the main focus for airports involved in the development of tourism is to attract commercial air services, especially those wanting to compete in international markets where PSOs are generally not applied. Again, the attraction and retention of such routes can to a large extent, be driven by airport marketing.

As regards tourism flows, increased competition in air transport and other general factors such as economic growth have encouraged growth in international tourism, especially in non-traditional tourist destinations such as those in Europe's northern periphery. This is being driven by the concept of 'new tourism' (Poon 1993), which is characterised by changing travel behaviour and motivations that are more supportive of the types of tourism that can be offered by Europe's northern periphery such as the opportunity to experience something different and pursue more active, cultural and nature-based interests. This is opposed to traditional types of tourism that are based on the sun, sea and sand combination offered by many southern/Mediterranean destinations (see Chapter 3 by Anne Graham for a discussion relating to how tourism demand is changing).

The growth in international tourism in Europe's northern periphery is highlighted in Table 15.3 where it can be seen that most regions or countries have experienced strong growth in the number of foreign overnights or visitors between 2000 and 2006. The only exception is North Norway, which has experienced an average annual increase of just 0.1 per cent. All other regions or countries have experienced an average annual increase of between 3.6 per cent and 10.5 per cent, which compares well to the average annual increase in Europe of 2.6 per cent. Changes in the business environment have accelerated the growth of tourism and the opportunity for airports in Europe's northern periphery to compete in destination markets based on both packaged and independent travel arrangements.

TABLE 15.3   International tourism in Europe's northern periphery, 2000–2006[†]

Region	2000	2001	2002	2003	2004	2005	2006	Average annual change 00/06
Registered foreign overnights (000)								
North Norway*	424	426	402	392	411	444	427	0.1%
North Sweden**	242	266	291	295	265	275	294	3.6%
North Finland***	539	579	651	727	738	792	826	8.9%
Foreign visitors (000)								
Iceland	303	296	278	320	360	374	422	6.6%
Faroe Islands	86	93	98	107	110	119	140	10.5%
Ireland	6,310	5,990	6,065	6,369	6,574	6,977	7,709	3.7%
Europe (mn)	396	395	407	407	425	442	457	2.6%

*   North Norway (Nord-Norge: Finnmark, Troms and Nordland)
**   North Sweden (Norrbotten)
*** North Finland (Lapland)
†   Readers should not compare data between regions or countries because different methodologies are used by each country to collect data. For instance, data on registered foreign overnights for North Finland includes hotels, motels, hostels, youth hostels, holiday villages and campsites (but does not include establishments with fewer than 10 rooms, cottages or electrical connection points for caravans). In comparison, data for North Norway includes hotels and similar establishments (but not campsites, holiday dwellings and hostels) and data for North Sweden includes hotels, cottages and youth hostels (but not campsites). Data has not been provided for the Highlands and Islands region of Scotland because methodological changes in data collection have affected the ability to compare data between 2000 and 2006.

Sources: National statistics offices; World Tourism Organisation for data on Europe.

AIRPORT COMPETITION

Airports that compete in destination markets based on packaged travel arrangements will typically compete for charter traffic. Lakselv Banak Airport in Norway was developed during the 1990's in order to compete with Ivalo Airport and Rovaniemi Airport (both in Finland) for charter traffic visiting the North Cape (Langedahl 1999). Rovaniemi Airport, Kittilä Airport and Kuusamo Airport (all in Finland) compete for charter traffic seeking Santa-based winter experiences. Kittilä Airport and Kuusamo Airport also compete in ski markets as they serve the ski resorts of Levi/Ylläs and Ruka respectively. In addition, the emergence of low-cost carriers is driving growth in short/city-break and visiting friends and relatives markets based on independent travel arrangements and there are some examples of airports (e.g. in Ireland) in Europe's northern periphery that compete in such markets, although competition is not only between airports but also between airports and other modes of transportation.

Airports seeking to attract charter or low-cost carriers will generally need to offer a high density tourism product as both of these types of carriers depend upon the use of large aircraft such as Boeing 737's and enough demand to maintain high density point-to-point operations that are either seasonal (e.g. for charter carriers) or high frequency (e.g. for low-cost carriers). Airports that are unable to offer a high density tourism product can still compete in destination markets but the low density of demand means that traffic will have to be served by traditional mainline carriers (e.g. SAS and Finnair) or niche regional carriers (e.g. Widerøe and Skyways). These carriers are able to operate smaller aircraft by transferring passengers via hub airports and have traditionally focused on business travellers that were willing to pay a premium for added services. However, in light of growing leisure markets and competition from both charter and low-cost carriers, many traditional mainline and niche regional carriers are increasingly focusing on cost reduction and the attraction of leisure travellers.

A number of airports in Europe's northern periphery compete in low-density destination markets such as those serving special interest markets, where tourists can either book their travel arrangements independently or as a part of a package. The UK tour operator Discover the World offers specialist Arctic Experience package holidays. One of the products is called 'Sleeping on Ice' and allows tourists to choose from a range of ice hotels including the Alta Igloo Hotel in Norway, Jukkasjärvi Icehotel in Sweden, and Kemi Snowcastle in Finland. These destinations are served by Alta Airport, Kiruna Airport and Kemi-Tornio Airport respectively and are served by scheduled flights from London Heathrow Airport with SAS or Finnair. These carriers transfer passengers via their hub airports (in Oslo, Stockholm or Helsinki) and charge higher prices for a premium service.

Of course, most airports try to compete in multiple types of destination market and aim to attract a range of carriers in order to broaden their traffic mix and reduce their reliance on one carrier. Hemavan Airport is located in the Tärna mountain region of Sweden. Skyways (a niche regional carrier) established direct flights to the airport from Stockholm-Arlanda Airport in 1997 and during 2006, offered six scheduled flights between Stockholm and Hemavan each week. The route is operated as a PSO and the flights primarily support the needs of business travellers and the local community; however, they are increasingly used to serve domestic short-break markets such as skiing. Recognising its seasonal frailties, the airport is currently involved in an EU co-funded cross-border INTERREG project involving the Tärna region and its Norwegian neighbours in Helgeland. The project is called Tärna/Helgeland Europort and aims to develop a 'Lakes and

Mountains' product by taking advantage of the lakes of Helgeland and the mountains of Tärna. The project also aims to develop a conference and congress product by targeting markets in both Oslo and Stockholm. The project continues to target scheduled services as they are vital to the development of domestic (and Norwegian) markets. However, it also aims to target international charter markets, which will bring the airport into competition with airports such as Lakselv Banak Airport in Norway and Ivalo Airport and Kittilä Airport in Finland.

Whilst changes in the business environment have provided opportunities for airports to compete in destination markets, they have also meant that the decisions of airlines are increasingly market-driven, especially the decisions of leisure carriers (e.g. charter and low-cost) that are increasingly competing for the same or similar markets. This means that airports wanting to compete in destination markets must adopt more market-driven management practices and must become more proactive in their approach to marketing.

THE AIRPORT PRODUCT

As part of the marketing process, airports need to be aware of the facilitation requirements of leisure carriers. Runway length, terminal capacity and landing systems will all contribute to the decision of whether or not to operate to a particular airport; however, this applies to all types of carrier, not just those that offer opportunities for the development of tourism.

The level of infrastructure available at an airport will to a large extent determine the types of market or carrier that can be targeted. Only airports with adequate runway dimensions, clearance for international flights, and appropriate terminal capacity can realistically target charter or low-cost carriers operating dense intra-European routes with aircraft such as the 189-seat Boeing 737-800 that is currently used by Ryanair on intra-European routes. Airports with smaller runways, domestic clearance only, and limited terminal capacity will need to target traditional mainline carriers or niche regional carriers operating thin routes from a domestic hub with smaller aircraft such as the 50-seat Fokker 50 that is currently used by Skyways on domestic routes in Sweden. The INTERREG project at Hemavan Airport recognises the infrastructure requirements of charter carriers and has supported the extension of the runway at the airport to 1,510 metres so that it is capable of handling aircraft used by charter carriers serving similar markets at competing airports.

The harsh operating conditions that are typically associated with Europe's northern periphery (e.g. frequent adverse weather and permanent obstacles such as mountains) may provide further constraints to some airports, especially those that are not equipped with modern landing systems and accurate real time weather monitoring, both of which have the capacity to improve airport safety and the reliability of flight operations and are of particular importance to leisure carriers seeking minimal delays and a fast turnaround of aircraft. According to Crump (2004), Rovaniemi Airport in Finland has been welcoming Christmas charter flights since 1984. In order to meet increased winter traffic, the airport was upgraded in the early 1990's with the construction of a new terminal building. In 1995, a CAT II landing system was installed to improve the reliability and regularity of air traffic, and the introduction of accurate real time weather monitoring has improved airport safety and flight operations. In 2000, the capacity of the terminal building was doubled in order to accommodate increasing passenger numbers, service and sales facilities, check-in, baggage handling facilities, and transport systems.

Investment in infrastructure is important in meeting capacity needs and facilitating safe and reliable aircraft operations. However, leisure carriers are especially focused on achieving low operating costs and an efficiency of operations and it is here that airports can seek to exploit a competitive advantage over their rivals. In particular leisure carriers will want to see how airports can facilitate cost savings (e.g. by providing simple terminals and minimal services), speed (e.g. by providing fast aircraft turnarounds and an efficient positioning of aircraft), flexibility (e.g. by providing multi-functional and flexible staffing), and access (e.g. by providing longer opening hours and surface transport to the destination).

Associated with the airport product is the idea of the airport brand (A. Graham 2003). Branding has been widely used by airports in Europe's northern periphery and especially by those seeking to attract charter carriers. In this instance, the brand that is developed may be based upon natural or man-made attractions or aspects of historical importance. A few examples include Lakselv Banak Airport in Norway (known as North Cape Airport), Kemi-Tornio Airport in Finland (uses the logo 'For Golf in the Midnight Sun'), and Keflavik International Airport Terminal in Iceland (inaugurated in 1987 under the name of Leifur Eiriksson Air Terminal after the Norwegian navigator who, according to Norse sagas, was the first to discover North America). Airports have also been branded in a way that demonstrates their size or scope of services. For example, Knock Airport in Ireland was branded Knock International Airport in order to emphasise the fact that the airport offered international services. The airport was re-branded in 2005 as Ireland West Airport Knock in order to emphasise its geographical location and its position as the main access hub of the West of Ireland.

Branding creates distinctiveness and adds tangible clues to what is essentially an intangible service. In addition, branding can promote recognition, preference and loyalty amongst target markets. However, branding can have a potentially negative impact by being too distinctive and encouraging aspects such as seasonality. Rovaniemi Airport in Finland was branded as Santa Claus Airport in 1984 in order to contribute to the development of 'Santa-based' tourism in Finnish Lapland. The airport has become a major tourism gateway to the region and during Christmas 2006, the airport attracted over 230 foreign charter flights from 15 different countries carrying over 60,000 international tourists and contributing an estimated 30 million Euros to the local economy (Rovaniemi Tourism and Marketing 2007). The problem is that traffic at the airport is concentrated in the winter months and at certain times of the day and week, leading to seasonal and inefficient airport operations. The winter season, November to April, contributes 60 per cent of the total number of visitors to the region (Rovaniemi Tourism and Marketing 2007). In addition, the dominance of charter traffic, which provided 99 per cent of the airports international passengers in 2006 (Finavia 2007) may be a deterrent to the attraction of low-cost carriers that offer higher frequencies and a scheduled year-round service.

AIRPORT MARKETING TECHNIQUES

In addition to understanding facilitation requirements, airports have a number of marketing techniques at their disposal that can be used to exploit market trends and attract leisure carriers. Advertising is a basic form of marketing that airports can do to create awareness and communicate certain messages to target markets. However, advertising tends to communicate general messages to a general audience and can be very costly. It costs 10,635 Euros for an airport to place a one-page colour advertisement in the publication Airline Business (at 2007 prices). The cost of advertising and the general messages that are communicated means that it is not a particularly cost effective means of communication for airports in Europe's northern periphery.

Attending exhibitions is another basic form of marketing that airports can do to create awareness and communicate certain messages to target markets. Highlands and Islands Airports Limited, operators of the 10 airports in the Scottish Highlands and Islands targeted tour operators at VisitScotland Expo 2004 to promote its airports to around 1,000 buyers from the international travel trade (HIAL 2005). It should be noted that scheduled carriers, especially low-cost carriers increasingly reduce links with the travel trade in order to reduce costs so the effectiveness of attending exhibitions may only be restricted to airports competing in charter markets.

Increasingly, airports adopt a more direct and aggressive means of communicating with target markets. One recent development that has supported this type of marketing is the World Route Development Forum called 'Routes'. This is a type of speed dating for airports and airlines as it provides networking opportunities through one-to-one meetings where airlines will expect to be presented with market research on new route potential. Airlines will also want to know about the tourist appeal of the catchment area for inbound passengers and the purchasing power of residents in the outbound markets (Favotto 1998).

Many smaller airports may not have the financial or human resources to carry out detailed market research and therefore, may find it difficult to target carriers in this way. One way of overcoming this constraint is to develop strategic partnerships with local stakeholders such as tourism and regional development agencies. This enables airports and local stakeholders to pool resources, develop an integrated approach to regional development, and provide airlines or tour operators with a wider overview of the area and its potential. A number of airports in Europe's northern periphery that have developed (or been a part of) strategic partnerships include Highlands and Islands Airports Limited in Scotland (a member of Highlands Loch Ness marketing group), Lakselv Banak Airport in Norway (a member of North Cape Airport Services), Hemavan Airport in Sweden (a member of Tärnafjällen Incoming), and Leifur Eiriksson Air Terminal in Iceland (a member of Iceland Naturally).

When airports promote opportunities for new routes to airlines, the airlines will expect to find out how much it is going to cost them. They will also want to know whether or not the airport is willing to share in the risk associated with establishing a new route. Offering financial incentives has become particularly important at airports wanting to attract low-cost carriers (Francis et al. 2004). Incentives vary greatly between airports but have traditionally included the offer of reduced or discounted airport user charges and/or the provision of marketing support (see Chapter 14 for more details of these incentive schemes).

The final marketing technique to be considered in this chapter is linked to airport distribution channels. Airports sell direct to airlines or tour operators for rights to use the airport. They then rely on intermediaries such as airlines, tour operators, travel agents or travel planning portals to reach end-users. Despite their limited role in reaching the end user, airports are increasingly involved in servicing their needs by providing online travel planning support, which subsequently supports the distribution efforts of their airlines or tour operators. This is particularly important considering that online travel sales in Europe increased by as much as 31 per cent between 2005 and 2006 (Marcussen 2007).

The provision of online timetable services (as provided by companies such as OAG and Innovata) is a basic level of online support but surprisingly, less than 10 per cent of world airports currently buy into online timetable services (Compton 2005). In addition, whilst most airports have an online presence, their support for airlines is fairly limited and especially at airports that belong to large national airport systems where websites tend to be fairly plain and simple. Highlands and Islands Airports Limited maintains a fairly good level of online presence and support. The company provides online timetable services and links to the tourism industry, airline websites, and Expedia (a travel planning portal). Hemavan Airport in Sweden provides another good example of an airport that provides online travel planning support to end-users. In addition to providing timetable information and a link to the online booking system of their niche regional carrier; Skyways, they also provide links to a travel planning portal for the Hemavan/Tärnaby region, where holiday packages can be constructed and purchased online. Servicing the travel planning needs of passengers may be an area that airports increasingly seek to become involved in either as a host agency or as part of website hosted by a tourism or regional development agency. Either way, collaboration with local and regional stakeholders will be vital.

CASE STUDY ON PAJALA-YLLÄS AIRPORT IN SWEDISH LAPLAND

In this next section, a case study is presented to illustrate some of the issues which have been discussed.

Pajala-Ylläs Airport and the Local Tourism Industry

Located 1,173 kilometres north of Stockholm, Pajala is one of the northernmost municipalities in Sweden. Pajala is sparsely populated with just 7,500 inhabitants occupying a surface area of 7,886 square kilometres. A large proportion of the population (roughly 2,100 inhabitants) lives in the main urban centre, the village of Pajala. Pajala is home to Sweden's newest airport, Pajala-Ylläs Airport. The airport is located at 67.14° north and 02.30° east, roughly 100 kilometres north of the Arctic Circle. The airport was built at a cost of 50 million Swedish Kroner and was inaugurated in August 1999. The airport was initially conceived as a means of serving the growing electronics and computer industry in Pajala but is increasingly recognised for its role in facilitating the development of tourism in the region.

The location of the airport provides an ideal gateway to the regions tourism industry. The village of Pajala is just 12 kilometres to the east of the airport and offers attractions such as the world's largest sundial and Pajala church, which dates back to the 18th Century and is one of the largest wooden churches in Sweden. The airport is just a couple of hundred metres away from the Torne River, which is one of the best wild free flowing salmon rivers in the world providing prime opportunities for salmon fishing. Pajala is one large nature reserve with forests, lakes, rivers and a rich abundance of wildlife, flora and fauna providing a range of opportunities for nature-based tourism. It is also blessed by the Northern Lights-a natural light show that appears in the sky on clear winter nights, and the Midnight Sun-a long period of daylight where the sun never actually goes down.

Pajala is the major cultural hub of the Torne Valley with a vibrant drama and music scene. The indigenous Sámi with their unique languages and way of life provide further cultural opportunities for tourists whilst the more active tourist has access to a range of summer and winter-based activities such as canoeing, rafting, fly-fishing, ice-fishing, trekking, snowmobiling, and skiing. Pajala is located in the north-east of the county Norrbotten, bordering Lapland in Finland. Western parts of Norrbotten border Nordland and Troms in Norway and southern parts border Västerbotten County of Sweden. The airport provides good access to tourist destinations in the surrounding areas such as the Lofoten Islands in Nordland, North Cape in Troms, the fells of Ylläs and Ruka in Lapland, and the Gulf of Bothnia.

Tourism in Pajala was in decline until the airport opened. According to unpublished data of the Swedish Statistical Office the total number of guest nights in the region fell from 17,959 in 1996 to 11,989 in 1999 but then increased to 19,478 by 2006. Growth between 1999 and 2006 represents an average annual increase of 8.9 per cent. Figure 15.1 illustrates the number of domestic and foreign guest nights in Pajala between 1996 and 2006 and it is important to note that a decline in the number of domestic guest nights over that period has been compensated for by the steady growth of foreign guest nights. In 1996, there were a total of 3,226 foreign guest nights, contributing just 18 per cent of the total number of guest nights in Pajala. By 2006, this figure had risen to 7,023, contributing 36 per cent of the total number of guest nights in Pajala.

Pajala-Ylläs Airport has experienced modest growth since it opened in August 1999 with the total number of passengers increasing from 2,145 in 2000 to 3,079 in 2006 and aircraft movements increasing from 655 in 2000 to 1,000 in 2006 (see Figure 15.2). The decline in passengers between 2004 and 2006 is attributed, in part, to a reduction in aircraft capacity during mid-2005.

Despite modest growth since opening, the nature of air service provision at the airport has remained relatively unchanged. Initial air services were provided by Barents AirLink (formerly known as Nordkalottflyg) with an 8-seater Piper 31 between Pajala-Ylläs Airport and Luleå-Kallax Airport, which is located approximately 230 kilometres south of Pajala. Flight frequencies have varied little since opening and are limited to two return flights per weekday to Luleå-Kallax Airport, where passengers can then take connecting flights to Stockholm-Arlanda Airport and a number of other airports in Sweden. The route is currently operated by Barents AirLink as a PSO with a 9-seater Beechcraft 200 and serves mainly commuter passengers travelling between Pajala and Stockholm.

The Airport Product at Pajala-Ylläs Airport

Even after the first few years of operations it became clear that Pajala-Ylläs Airport would struggle to meet desired passenger levels. The PSO had been an obstacle for development because it restricts the opportunity for competition and limits the size of aircraft and available passenger capacity on the route. The other major obstacle to development had been the airport's limited runway dimensions of 1,420 x 30 metres. This restricted the types of aircraft that the airport can attract and ruled out the ability for the airport to attract international charter carriers that generally operate aircraft that require a runway

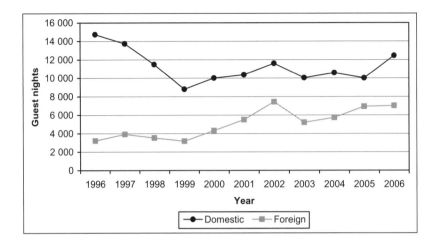

FIGURE 15.1 Guest nights in Pajala, 1996–2006

Source: Swedish Statistical Office (unpublished).

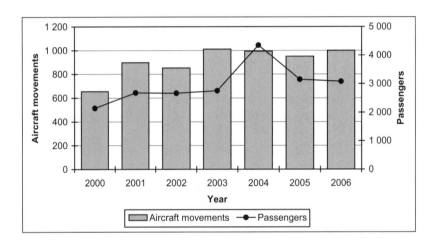

FIGURE 15.2 Passengers and aircraft movements at Pajala-Ylläs Airport,
2000–2006

Source: Swedish Regional Airport Association (unpublished).

length in excess of 1,600 metres, depending on the local operating conditions and technical capabilities of the airport.

In 2005, a process of planning and lobbying, which had previously been successfully carried out by municipal leaders to secure the airport in the first place, began again. This time it was for an extension to the existing airport runway and facilities. This would provide additional opportunities to the current and rather restricted PSO and would cater to the growing demand for tourism in the region. Municipal leaders keen on developing the airport experienced difficulties in securing the necessary funds because different political and interest groups in the region were often competing for the same funds. Success eventually followed after Pajala sought and received a partner in the form of the neighbouring municipality of Kolari in Lapland, Finland. This is where the mountain resort of Ylläs is located, a major destination for Nordic and alpine skiing and other fell-tourism activities.

According to the municipality of Kolari, investments in tourism infrastructure at Ylläs will exceed 650 million Euros for the years 2007–2013 and the provision of capacity for air services is vital to the development of the tourism industry in Ylläs. Most of the demand for air services is seasonal and is concentrated during the Christmas and Easter holiday periods. Ylläs is largely served by Kittilä Airport in Lapland. The airport is about a 40 minute drive from Ylläs and is capable of handling large aircraft that are typically used by international charter carriers. However, airport capacity is under increasing pressure at peak periods and this may constrain the future growth of tourism in the region. Pajala-Ylläs Airport is about a one hour drive from Ylläs and provides a slightly shorter flight time for passengers travelling from the United Kingdom, the main international market for Ylläs. With the appropriate infrastructure, Pajala-Ylläs Airport could provide additional airport capacity for Ylläs. This would allow the airport to gain an international reputation as a gateway to Ylläs and could stimulate demand for tourism in its own municipality where investments in tourism infrastructure are gathering momentum and will help to facilitate future demand. Overall, the municipalities of Pajala and Kolari expect strong future growth in tourism but also recognise that limitations in infrastructure act as a potential constraint to any growth. Limitations in airport capacity are a particular constraint when focusing on the attraction of international tourists because the high distance costs involved mean that tourists have limited alternative means of accessing the region.

Funding for the development of the runway and facilities at Pajala-Ylläs Airport was eventually secured and is being shared by local, regional and central government and the European Union. Total investment is estimated at 50 million Swedish Kroner, the same amount of investment required to develop the airport in the first place. As part of the runway development, there is a recyclable de-icing area which aims to reuse 80 per cent of the liquids used. Construction work began in spring 2007 and was completed in late November 2007. The runway now has the dimensions of 2,300 x 45 metres. This allows movements of all common passenger aircraft including those that are typically operated by international charter carriers.

Target Markets and Airport Marketing Techniques

International charter services are now a key target market for Pajala-Ylläs Airport. Much of the focus is on attracting inbound tourism and it is hoped that the attractiveness of the region, the growing demand for international tourism and the development in airport infrastructure and services will attract the interest of major tour operators operating or intending to operate in the region. Traffic volume for winter 2007 is forecast to reach 30 movements by aircraft such as the Boeing 737 and Airbus 319. Opportunities also exist to serve outbound tourism markets that provide social benefits to local residents in terms of providing them with opportunities to travel abroad. The airport will be targeting outbound as well as inbound services.

In addition to providing opportunities for international air services, the developments in airport infrastructure give way to new, possibly less costly alternative PSO services. One option being studied is the routing of flights to Stockholm-Arlanda Airport via Kemi-Tornio Airport in Finland as opposed to Luleå-Kallax Airport. This would allow the airport to serve the air transport needs of seven Torne Valley Municipalities (Pajala, Övertorneå and Haparanda in Sweden and Kolari, Pello, Ylitornio and Tornio in Finland) as opposed to just serving Pajala. This would provide a much greater catchment area and would therefore create opportunities for the operation of larger aircraft. The operation of larger aircraft would help to reduce the current subsidy level per passenger and would help subdue criticism that the present PSO route is not cost efficient. If the decision is taken to continue operating the PSO to Luleå-Kallax Airport, attention will be focused on attracting larger aircraft on the route. This should be possible under the current PSO framework. However, demand for increased capacity would need to be proven.

Any increases in demand for air services at Pajala-Ylläs Airport may of course give way to domestic routes that can be operated by airlines on a commercial basis. This has been possible at airports in Finnish Lapland and would reduce the tax burden of the existing PSO. However, it will probably take some time before demand for air services becomes commercially viable. Plans for large scale mining operations in the region are developing rapidly and along with the development of tourism, could encourage rapid increases in the demand for air services. This would help broaden the opportunity to develop both public and commercial air services at the airport. General Aviation is another target market for Pajala-Ylläs Airport and the airport received a record number of visitors by private aircraft in 2006, mainly during the summer. The airport generally welcomes between 150–200 visitors by private aircraft each year.

Current marketing activity is concentrated on increasing demand for the scheduled domestic services at Pajala-Ylläs Airport. The main competitors are not other airports because the distance between airports is so great. Instead, the passenger's own vehicle is the main competitor. Local residents that travel for business or pleasure are quite used to travelling long distances by car and a 2–3 hour car journey to them is comparable to a city dweller travelling from one train station to the next. Rail services are fairly limited in northern Sweden and whilst travel by bus is an alternative, it is not viable for longer day trips to destinations such as Luleå or Stockholm. Competition with the car means that it is imperative for the airport to establish air services that are relevant to the needs of local residents and businesses. Maintaining strong working relations with local residents and businesses is an important part of the airport's marketing activities and enables the airport to find out about their travel needs and behaviour.

PSO routes are largely determined by the state so opportunities for airport marketing are fairly limited apart from promoting demand for the route. Airports can, however, adopt techniques to lobby for changes to be made in the PSO framework. Municipal leaders responsible for the airport in Pajala have joined forces with nine other municipalities in northern Sweden to form a working group called Utveckling Flyg i norra Norrlands Inland (UFNI). This group seeks to exert its influence on the framework of the PSOs serving their airports in terms of aspects such as flight schedules and types of aircraft. Financial considerations may mean that these factors are not always a priority for airlines involved in the tendering process. In terms of charter-related marketing activities, Pajala-Ylläs Airport is able to negotiate the charges that it levies to airlines and tour operators (in compliance with European Union legislation and recommended practices), allowing for the provision of incentives and marketing support that can share the start-up cost and marketing of new routes.

With a relatively small budget for marketing it is a constant challenge to find the most cost-effective methods of marketing that maximise the exposure of the airport to its target markets with minimal cost. Passengers are targeted using the airports own website, where flight schedules, online reservations and a range of airport and tourism information is provided. Adverts in General Aviation magazines and attendance at exhibitions such as Aero at Friedrichshafen in Germany and AeroExpo at Wycombe in the United Kingdom have been effective in developing the growth in General Aviation at Pajala-Ylläs Airport and help to further raise awareness of the airport and its region amongst the aviation community. Contributing to the regional economy has been the main motivation behind the development of General Aviation and for this reason the airport has often levied reduced landing fees, which in some instances, have required the purchase of a T-shirt for 200 Swedish Kroner (about 20 Euros). Of course, the opportunity for further publicity has not been lost here as the T-shirts normally feature the airport symbol and logo.

Marketing activities have gathered speed as the current investment in infrastructure is completed. Efforts to contact airlines and tour operators directly have been intensified and in addition to attending travel trade exhibitions such as World Travel Market in London, England and Matka in Helsinki, Finland, the airport made its first appearance at Routes in Stockholm, Sweden in 2007. In addition to directly targeting airlines and tour operators at exhibitions, Pajala-Ylläs Airport is making use of soft sell marketing techniques that target airlines and tour operators but also passengers and General Aviation. Pajala-Ylläs Airport has also used branding techniques to promote recognition, preference and loyalty amongst target markets. The airport uses the logo 'the friendly airport in the middle of Lapland' and has also changed its name. It was previously was known simply as Pajala Airport until February 2007 when the name Ylläs was added. Ylläs is a well-established name in tourism and is already served by a range of tour operators that tend to use Kittilä Airport in Finland. Adding Ylläs to the name of the airport was a rather controversial move considering that Ylläs is in Finland and Pajala is in Sweden. However, it emphasises the good access that Pajala-Ylläs Airport provides to Ylläs.

CONCLUSION

This chapter has demonstrated how changes in the business environment have facilitated the opportunity for airports in Europe's northern periphery to compete in destination markets and contribute to the development of tourism in their region. However, in order for airports to do so, they need to understand the facilitation requirements of their target markets and develop more marketing orientated management practices. In particular, airports should use direct and aggressive means of communication with their target markets, form strategic partnerships in order to pool resources, and consider offering incentives that demonstrate a willingness to share in the risk associated with new routes. Airports should also support the travel planning needs of end-users by providing timetable services and links to the tourism industry, airline websites, tour operators, and travel planning portals.

Whilst airport marketing appears to be effective in exploiting market trends, it should be remembered that it does not prove demand or guarantee success. Therefore, airports must also provide market intelligence and collaborate with local tourism and regional development agencies. This is especially important if airports are to provide an integrated, intelligence-based approach to the development of tourism in their region.

16

Applications and Implications of Information and Communication Technology for Airports and Leisure Travellers

Marianna Sigala

INTRODUCTION

This last chapter in this airport section looks at the issue of information and communication technology (ICT) development. This is very important as airport management involves complex and multifaceted business operations relating to both strategic decisions, such as airport design and capacity levels, and day-to-day operational decisions, such as managing travellers' flows. Airport operations management is further complicated due to the variety of resources processed through the system (e.g. passengers, information, staff, cargo, aircraft, in-flight catering and other materials); the range of airport elements to be managed (e.g. apron areas, terminal buildings, gates, runway systems, security areas, baggage process systems, taxiways and runways); and the numerous stakeholders involved and affected by airport operations (e.g. airlines, airport handling companies, security authorities, retailers) who may have different and even conflicting interests and objectives.

New challenges have also arisen due to the heightened security concerns after September 11th and the increasing volumes of passengers that in some airports are going to mushroom because of the introduction of the A380 aircraft. Unless these growing operational burdens at airports are managed correctly, then the quality of passengers' experiences and the speediness of processes will suffer. Thus the role of ICT development here is key in order to simplify and streamline airport operations to increase efficiency and enhance airport performance as well as satisfying the needs of air travel stakeholders.

Hence this chapter will focus on airport ICT applications that are changing the way travellers are processed and are experiencing air travel. Firstly, critical ICT applications are identified and described along with their operational and customer benefits. Then the overall impact of ICT applications on leisure travellers' air travel experiences, as well as on airport management issues, is analysed by developing and discussing a three dimensional model. Examples of international ICT initiatives and pilot programmes are provided to illustrate the practical application and implications of technology use in airport operations. Moreover, the factors influencing the adoption of technologies by customers, airports and other stakeholders are identified and discussed which provides several practical business implications and suggestions for policy making.

CRITICAL ICT APPLICATIONS: OPERATIONAL BENEFITS AND IMPACTS

ICT is the backbone of the tourism industry (Sheldon 1997) crucially affecting tourism firms' operational efficiency and strategic effectiveness (Sigala 2003). ICT tools and applications feature geographical, analytical, automational, informational, sequential, knowledge management, tracking and disintermediating capabilities. These facilitate and enable airport operations to take place at different geographical places, to become knowledge based and to be managed in real-time and to be streamlined, whilst also providing self-service possibilities to passengers who are simultaneously provided with additional value added personalised services and information. For airport management, ICT fosters and enables major reengineering efforts and the reorganisation of processes which manage passenger flows and airport assets. As illustrated in Figure 16.1, ICT applications enable the merging and integration of the various passengers' processes into three major processes blocks namely, pre-boarding, on board and de-boarding operations. As Doran (from British Airways) concluded (2006) "In future, most customers will only have two direct contact points with BA – online and onboard...".

The following discussion identifies and describes the operational benefits and process reengineering impacts of critical ICT applications for both airports and their travellers. ICT technologies are presented in the sequence required for an air transportation trip. The discussions illustrate how the sequence, the location, the nature as well as the actors undertaking these processes can be transformed into a combined process.

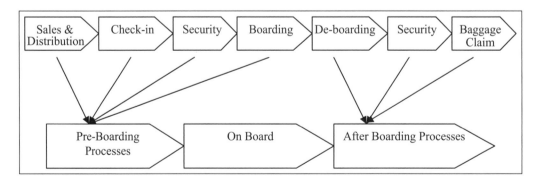

FIGURE 16.1 **Simplifying air travel customer flows and processes: A three step self-service enabled, personalised and streamlined experience**

E-ticketing

Electronic tickets (e-tickets) refer to the first step-process for initiating an airline trip. Passengers are provided with the benefits of place and time convenience of ticket purchases (i.e. Internet based), stress-free ticketing since there is no paper to lose or forget, as well as easier and faster booking changes. Meanwhile, the airlines can substantially reduce their ticket printing and processing costs. An e-ticket saves an average of US $9 per ticket for processing (through elimination of printing, postage, shipping, storage and accounting costs; costs for collateral materials like envelopes and ticket jackets; increased efficiency in revenue accounting) and up to US $3 billion for the industry annually (IATA 2007b).

The informational capabilities of the Internet enable airlines to provide customers with additional personalised value-added services. Most airlines develop and design their websites as a one-stop-travel-shop providing passengers the opportunity to get podcasts downloads of city guides; to design their dynamic package by buying complementary travel products such as accommodation, travel insurance, car rentals, phone cards; and to exchange or buy air-miles for purchasing households products and electronics. For example, Ryanair's website enables dynamic packaging of flights with discounted hotel rooms and bottom of the range car rentals and links to activitybreaks.com for providing additional products. In addition to these features, Lufthansa's website also provides numerous retail shopping experiences through its Lufthansa's WorldShop. Such product diversification enables airlines to enhance not only their revenue opportunities but also their passengers' loyalty.

Although e-tickets do not directly affect airport operations, the availability and use of e-tickets is important, because they substantially influence the way that the remaining passenger oriented airport processes are managed and implemented. This is because e-ticketing does not mean paperless or ticketless travel for the passenger. It only implies that airlines and airports no longer process physical tickets, but instead coupon status, in their information systems. Consequently, due to their increased informational capabilities, ICT applications can further enable numerous knowledge based airline and airport operations. For example, e-tickets provide possibilities of online check-in and printing of boarding passes, which in turn affects the real time management of passenger flows at airports. So, if an airport and airline knows how many connecting passengers are in an incoming flight, real-time gate management would direct an aircraft to a geographically nearby gate of the next flight, or airline staff would be alerted to provide a fast transit passenger service. Airports also benefit from e-tickets enabled check-in, since the need for counter based check-ins is reduced and space can be provided for more profitable activities, such as retailing.

IATA has been a strong industry stakeholder supporting, pushing and lobbying for, the industry wide adoption of e-tickets. Indeed, IATA has taken a leading role in developing industry standards and providing education opportunities for the expansion of electronic ticketing and specifically interline electronic tickets. Although IATA launched an initiative for "100% e-ticketing by the end of 2007", this deadline was extended to a more achievable date, 31 May 2008, whereby e-ticketing interlining complexities and other problems with smaller airlines could be solved.

Electronic Check-in: CUSS, Online and Mobile Check-in

Self-service kiosks have been used at airports for passenger self check-in for more than ten years now. Traditionally, airlines (and later on airline alliances) developed such proprietary systems for achieving a competitive advantage through the provision of a service differentiation to their frequent flyers and business travellers looking for time convenience. However, as the development and maintenance of many system variants proved too expensive industry wide to operate, IATA members decided to create and adopt a common standard. This was to ensure a more cost competitive service offering to their customers, as it has reduced airport counter requirements and economies of scale benefits. Specifically, Frankl calculated average industry savings of US $2.50 per check-in at a self-service kiosk (eBusiness W@tch 2006). Moreover Forrester (Bodine 2005) estimated that the average cost for a network-airline passenger to check-in through a human agent is $3.02, versus a range of $0.14 to $0.32 for kiosk check-in. In this vein, IATA acted again as the lobbying and developing agent for establishing the CUSS (Common Use Self-Service) standard and allowing industry wide savings.

CUSS is a shared kiosk offering convenient passenger check-in whilst allowing multiple airlines to maintain branding and functionality (IATA 2007b). Since many airlines can share the CUSS, such kiosks save a lot of space expansion, whilst they also provide operational flexibility, since they can be located anywhere at airports, their car parks, train stations, hotel lobbies etc. Las Vegas McCarran International Airport is the best known implementer of CUSS (Anonymous 2006b). There are over 80 CUSS kiosks installed in the airport with 15 airline logos sharing the Common Launch Screen, and in addition there are kiosks in the Las Vegas Convention Centre and soon they will also be installed in the local Las Vegas hotels.

Overall, the benefits of CUSS to passengers include faster check-in, avoidance of queues, faster and smoothest passage through airports, and remote check-in capabilities. For airports, they can improve their space and infrastructure capacity redesign and utilisation, as well as enhancing revenues by renting the no longer needed terminal real-estate to more profitable retail businesses. Space savings through CUSS at airports may also be a strategic necessity for their existence. For example, British Airways intends to have 80 per cent of its customers using self-service check-in (and 95 per cent using e-ticketing) at Heathrow Terminal 5, since the biggest single constraint in Heathrow is terminal capacity (eBusiness W@tch 2006). As Heathrow is the world's busiest international airport, but occupying a very small space, the check-in kiosks are a strategic development needed for saving terminal space and increasing the throughput and flow of the numerous travellers in the limited space.

According to IATA (2007b) CUSS check-in is 30 per cent faster and reduces costs and staff requirements, saving up to US $2.5 on each check-in in airline operations. CUSS adoption levels are increasing with IATA forecasting that the number of airports worldwide offering CUSS compliant kiosks will increase from 49 airports in 2006 to 143 in 2008. Any airport planning new terminal buildings must incorporate the growing use of self-service into its architectural brief. Rows of traditional check-in desks may be replaced by clusters of check-in kiosks around baggage reception and security points. Current CUSS developments encourage the concurrent provision of additional optional services such as passport scanners, biometric identification, baggage tag printers, personalised service and wireless connection possibilities for mobiles. Some airlines have already expanded the functionality of their own self-service options. For example, Northwest's and Delta's kiosks can scan passports for international check-in, and United and American Airlines have enabled kiosk and online check-in for return flights that are within 24 hours of departing flights.

The CUSS at Amsterdam Airport Schiphol compares personal details in the passenger's passport, credit card or frequent flyer card with the information on the confirmed reservation. The passenger can then personalise their travel experience by selecting a seat on the aircraft by using a real-time plan, after which a boarding card is printed automatically. The waiting time at the kiosks is less than a minute for 99 per cent of passengers. The average processing time averages 90 seconds, but 20 seconds is not uncommon. When travelling with check-in baggage, passengers hand in their baggage at the relevant baggage drop-off points. At the baggage drop off points, the passengers hand their boarding pass to agents, who scan or swipe them to pull up the passengers' records. The agents weigh and label their baggage and check passengers' travel documents. Then passengers can head to their departure gates. If CUSS at Schiphol was also able to weigh and print baggage tags, then the travellers' flow and processes would be streamlined which would save customer time and increase satisfaction. In other words, the more CUSS becomes integrated with other operational technologies, the more passengers' flow management is streamlined and smoothed, and the more security and control is enhanced because of the ICT informational capabilities processes which are monitored and managed in real-time (Sigala 2004). Thus, kiosks alone provide little value. Only by integrating kiosks and CUSS with a range of business process and IT changes can airlines and airports get the full benefit of technology investments.

Several airlines are also experimenting and trying to spread the use of online check-in, either through a PC or other mobile device. Online check-in costs even less because the airline does not have to install kiosks and/or use CUSS, whilst passengers print their boarding passes using their own paper. DBA (now part of Air Berlin) provides a mobile check-in service, whereby passengers can check-in by using their mobile phone and receive a bar-coded boarding pass in form of a MMS (Multimedia Message Service) on the display of their mobile phone (Harteveldt and Epps 2007). Currently, this is provided in the form of a pilot project on a single domestic route within Germany, but DBA plans to extend this service to further routes (eBusiness W@tch 2006).

Ryanair also offers an "e-Ticketing Check'N'Go" solution. It was initially offered on the Dublin–Cork route, but this has been extended to all routes from Shannon and Cork Airports and on all European routes from Dublin. This service enables passengers to check-in online within three days prior to the proposed flight and up to 4 hours before take-off. The procedure has been approved by the air-travel security authorities. Passengers self-print their boarding passes and can go directly to the security gates by avoiding the airport check-in desk. There security staff scan a bar code printed on the ticket – to eliminate possibility of duplication and multiple uses of the ticket – before passengers can proceed to the various departure gates. However, this process requires passengers to be flying with no check-in luggage. However, bar-coded boarding passes require the appropriate technology at the airport gates (e.g. readers of two dimensional boarding passes), placing additional requirements for airport infrastructure, as well as the acceptance and co-ordination of several other stakeholders, such as security authorities. Overall, operational benefits of self-service check-in increase not only the firms' operational efficiency but also their operational effectiveness in terms of enhanced customer service and revenue opportunities (Table 16.1).

TABLE 16.1   Operational benefits of self-service check-in

Cost Savings	Improved Customer Service	Revenue Opportunities
Less staff needed to handle the same amount of passengers	Reduce need for queuing	Possibilities to sell and promote complementary travel products
Less staff needed to manage irregular operations	Place and time convenience and savings (check in wherever and whenever passengers wish and can)	Release of terminal space for its rental for more profitable retail space
Faster passenger throughput in terminals and lobbies	Improved consistency in applying policies, e.g. upgrades	Sales of promotional and advertising opportunities to different airlines or airport operators, e.g. cafés, duty free shops etc.
Reduced requirements for terminal space	Irregular operations such as technical problems and bad weather are managed in a more efficient, consistent and customer-perceived fair way	
Streamlining of processes and saving from process integration or disintermediation	Provision of personalised information and services, e.g. select seat, in-flight services etc.	
Collection of customer data and intelligence for improving operations	Less crowding and chaotic situations	
	Allow and release staff time for more personalised and customised customer service	
	Conduction of market research	
	Greater customer privacy	

Source: Author.

Bar Coded Boarding Pass (BCBP)

Bar coded documents relative to traditional boarding passes enable cost savings, greater reliability and fewer mechanical problems that may arise with the magnetic strip readers at the gate. Bar coded boarding pass (BCBP) use IATA industry standard two dimensional bar codes in order to include an entire itinerary on one boarding document and link it to an e-ticket, which further enables streamlined interline journeys and thus boosts the efficiencies of electronic ticketing. The new two-dimension system of bar-coding allows barcodes to hold more data than the traditional barcode method (Figure 16.2). Passenger and itinerary data is encoded in both horizontal and vertical dimensions and, as more data is encoded, the size of the barcode is increased in both the horizontal and vertical directions so that a manageable shape is maintained for allowing easy scanning and data inclusion specifications. BCBP allows fast and convenient check-in by enabling the passenger to print the boarding pass on a home printer and/or check-in using a CUSS and proceed directly to the gate. The goal is to reduce queues at airports and reduce airline costs

Conventional 1D barcode

2D Barcode

FIGURE 16.2 **Traditional one-dimensional barcode versus 2D barcode**

associated with check-in processes, whilst offering more convenience to the passenger. Nowadays, it is possible not only to print boarding passes at the passenger's home, but also to place bar codes on the passenger's mobile phones which further eliminates paper costs and increases security (IATA 2007b).

By using BCBP, airports can further improve their use of airport space, lower their equipment related costs and increase throughput of constrained areas. BCBP enables US$3.58 savings per home check-in with baggage and US$5.34 without baggage, meaning that 100 per cent BCBP usage can bring annual industry savings of US$0.8 billion (IATA 2007b). In this vein, IATA has facilitated the dialogue between airlines and airports as the use of BCBP requires the development and existence of appropriate infrastructure. There are currently 80 BCBP capable IATA airlines, but the IATA mandate requires 100 per cent BCBP usage by 2010. However, the European airline industry is lagging behind its US counterparts, whereby air travel has already largely migrated online with about 56 per cent of flight check-ins being conducted at kiosks and with bar-coded boarding passes having become mainstream (eBusiness W@tch 2006).

Radio Frequency ID (RFID)

Radio Frequency Identification is heavily used for enhancing baggage logistics, as well as customer service and satisfaction with baggage handling. RFID is a technology incorporated into a silicon chip embedded in a tag which emits a radio signal that can be read at a distance even if the item is concealed, vision is obscured or the RFID becomes soiled. Thus RFID reading is easier and more reliable than barcodes (Wyld *et al.* 2005). Tags are more flexible and can carry much more information than bar codes, and they can be written and unwritten as many times as is required so that they can be updated to reflect itinerary changes while a passenger is flying. In general, RFID has several benefits compared to barcodes, because it is faster (as multiple RFIDs are read concurrently), more accurate and less prone to human error (Wyld 2006). However, the most important attribute of RFID is its proactive nature, since through RFID airport personnel can quickly become aware if luggage has gone astray and is not uploaded onto an aircraft as well as locating its exact positioning within the airport. In this vein, airlines and airports can rectify potential problems, without the passenger ever knowing that they existed, or minimise any inconvenience, such as the time needed to off load a bag of the passenger who has not boarded a flight (IATA 2007a). Through RFID, airports and airlines can provide passengers with more reliable and timely information about their baggage handling problems.

Overall, RFID has many advantages such as allowing a considerable reduction in mishandled baggage and meeting new security requirements; increasing the load of baggage handling; reducing interline baggage tag read errors (as RFID technology does not require contact or direct line-of-sight as with current optical read technology); allowing the identification of bags in a baggage container that cannot be scanned by an optical scanner; and reducing the costs of manual encoding of interline baggage tags as the result of tags that have failed to be scanned automatically by the system. These benefits are translated into airport operational benefits such as improved capacity utilisation, improved baggage service and improved efficiency.

IATA has calculated that RFID read rates average 95–99 per cent, while for the barcode this is 80–90 per cent. This reduces the 20 pieces of baggage per 1000 passengers mishandled each year and with full RFID implementation US$760 million per year in industry savings (based on US$ 0.10/tag cost) will be made. Heathrow airport is currently experimenting with RFID technology for increasing its efficiency. As a BAA spokesman declared (eBusiness W@tch 2006, p. 136):

> "…we are always looking for new ways to improve the customer experience at our airport and luggage is one of the areas we are looking at. Although baggage handling is not BAA's responsibility – airlines hire firms to manage luggage or do it themselves – but as the airport owner it is in charge of installing RFID technology".

However, as RFID baggage tags induces a complete change of airport infrastructure, the success in the baggage handling process relies on whether airlines and airports agree on a common worldwide investment strategy, specifically as air travel and interlining involves many different airlines, airports, security authorities etc.

So far, the higher cost of the RFID tags has prevented airlines and airports from moving to RFID systems, but after September 11th requirements in the United States to screen all bags for explosives, together with the falling price of RFID tags, has changed the economics. Airlines and airports also need to consider that RFID leads to reduced operating costs in the long term due to its reduced maintenance costs relative to barcodes. Moreover, airports are facing more challenges which are encouraging them to consider RFID adoption as a strategic necessity for survival. For example, the arrival of the A380 will mean not only more passengers, but also more cargo and baggage, have to be managed. Airports also have to meet demands for increased safety and security and are being required to develop fast, cheap, inspection processes whilst simultaneously reducing time and cost. In this case, the introduction of a real control mechanism would allow better delivery of the process through improved efficiency in resource usage and perhaps also improve working conditions as mundane and repetitive tasks could be reduced. Other factors being considered are that some airlines require and pay for extra security services to limit baggage pilferage. Finally, some airports which have lost airlines to other airports have decided to get better baggage handling process performances for their transfer flights in order to reduce passenger claims; moreover, passengers are becoming more aware of the airport baggage performance and include this in their travel purchase decision.

Biometrics

Biometrics involve the authentication or the identification of individuals based on physical characteristics (e.g. fingerprints, facial recognition, hand geometry or iris configuration or traits) or traits (e.g. signature formation, keystroke patterns or voice recognition) (Heracleous and Wirtz 2006). Using biometrics for airport security checks increases efficiency and security of operations, saves time, and enhances customer service since there is no risk of forgetting, losing, copying, loaning, or getting your biometrics stolen (Anonymous 2007). For example, Siemens, a leader in developing security biometrics is testing a setup that transfers fingerprint information into two dimensional BCBP, which gets scanned at the gate and so travellers can avoid the queuing and process of the security checks.

At Changi Airport in Singapore, the FAST (Fully Automated Seamless Travel) process that is based on a biometrics technology integrates three processes, namely airline check-in, pre-immigration security checks, and immigration clearance (Heracleous and Wirtz 2006). In other words, as with other technologies, the maximum benefits of biometrics are realised, when these are integrated with other passengers' flow management operations. As a result, FAST operational benefits include not only improved security and reduced errors, but also reduced airline and airport operational costs and greater customer service and convenience due to the simplified procedures. These benefits have provided Changi airport with a distinctive competitive advantage for its services (Heracleous and Wirtz 2006).

Biometrics are used for developing ePassports (that incorporate chips including physical information) and Registered Travellers Programmes (RTP) (International Biometric Group 2005). RTPs are currently in pilot programmes and they lack interoperability standards for international travel. Although there are no international specifications for the type of biometric used in an RTP, iris and fingerprint recognition have taken a lead as they are more accurate, fast and cost effective. By contrast, ePassports are used in more than 40 states such as the US Visa Waiver Program (VWP) nations (e.g. Germany and France) or established tourist destinations such as Maldives, which began issuing the documents in July 2007.

It should be highlighted that although RTPs are considered and developed as a business tool, ePassports represent government-driven initiatives aiming to conform with the International Civil Aviation Organisation's (ICAO) guidelines, and – in the case of VWP countries – to comply with US requirements. This significantly affects the way RTPs are marketed and designed to their target market, mainly frequent flyers and business travellers. For example, Hong Kong's SPEED programme offers additional benefits such as enhanced Internet check-in, dedicated baggage drop and designated channels for restricted area access, immigration control, security clearance and aircraft boarding. The Dutch Privium scheme offers three types of membership and equivalent business services. There is Privium Plus (including benefits such as access priority parking in two airport car parks, check-in at the business class desk of 19 airlines, and Schiphol valet parking), Privium Basic and Privium Partner. However, Heracleous and Wirtz (2006) have advocated that the winning technology and player will be the one who will manage to harness the power of biometrics for combining the security and authority requirements with enhanced customer service.

For RTPs, more and faster progress is also needed in terms of interoperability among biometrics and data registration. In the US, the Registered Traveller Interoperability Consortium (RTIC) was established to develop common business rules and technical standards to create a permanent, interoperable and vendor-neutral RTP. In the European Union (EU), the responsible body is the European Commission (EC), which first proposed RTPs as a long-term possibility in its November 2005 'Synergies Communication'. RTPs are also a debate item in transatlantic dialogues. More interoperability is also required within EU, whereby many isolated RTPs programmes have been developed and piloted (see examples in Table 16.2), and consequently, only the border police for each specific airport can access their proprietary register. However, as each register has a different structure and content, it is evident that RTPs interoperability refers not only to technical but also process challenges. Therefore, there is a need for an EU-wide central register or data bank which border police of all 27 member states can access to read and change data in order to allow fast and accurate cross-border data exchange.

TABLE 16.2   RTP programmes

Country	Programme Name	Biometrics	Smart Card Solution	Total Cycle Time
Europe				
France	P.E.G.A.S.E.	Fingerprint	Yes	15 seconds
UK	miSENSE	Fingerprint, iris	Yes	10 – 12 seconds
Netherlands	Privium	Iris	Yes	
Germany	ABG	Iris	No	20 seconds
USA				
RTPs for domestic travelling featuring an expedited secure lane and a registered traveller card price of around US$100 at the following airports: Orlando, Los Angeles, Minneapolis-St Paul, Boston Logan, Washington Reagan National, Cincinnati/Northern Kentucky, Indianapolis, Norman Mineta San Jose, JFK New York, San Francisco and George Bush Intercontinental Houston CLEAR and the NEXUS programmes for cross-border travelling: low-risk, pre-approved passengers can enjoy faster border clearance				
San Francisco International Airport: 59 000 USA travellers (2007)	CLEAR	Fingerprint, iris	yes	
Jointly established by Canada's Border Services Agency and US Customs & Border Protection	NEXUS	Iris		
ASIA: RTPs exist between Tokyo and Seoul, and between major airports and Europe, e.g. Hong Kong and the UK or Indonesia and the Netherlands.				

Source: (International Biometric Group, 2005).

The development of the FAST pilot technology also illustrates the requirements for technical and organisational interoperability and compliance (Heracleous and Wirtz 2006). FAST is integrated with several other information systems including: Singapore Airlines' booking system for seating preferences and real-time seat allocation and confirmation; Singapore's current IACS (Immigration Automated Clearance System), used for speedy immigration processes at the border between Singapore and Malaysia; and the SVIP card including biometric passengers' data, which is an initiative by the Ministry of Home Affairs to meet US immigration requirements. FAST also requires co-operation of five organisations which have their own priorities, concerns, and systems namely Singapore Airlines, the Civil Aviation Authority of Singapore, the Immigration and Checkpoints Authority, the Singapore Police Force, and the Ministry of Home Affairs. FAST combines facial recognition (preferred by the EU), and fingerprinting (preferred by Singapore's authorities and currently employed in the Immigration Automated Clearance System at the Singapore-Malaysian border). The FAST design also aims to meet the requirements of the US Enhanced Border Security and Visa Entry Reform Act of 2002.

MODELLING ICT IMPACT ON AIRPORT OPERATIONS AND LEISURE TRAVELLERS' EXPERIENCES

It has become evident that airport ICT applications crucially affect the way airport operations are managed in terms of their nature, location and stakeholders involved. Sigala (2002, 2003) provided evidence that the maximum performance potential of ICT is materialised when, according to Groth (1999) and Zuboff (1988), firms reorganise and reengineer their operations and processes for capturing the three clusters of technology impacts, namely automation, hyperautomation (integration) and informate (providing a personalised and humanised air travel experience). In this vein, the following section summarises the ICT impact on airport operations and leisure travellers' experiences based on this three cluster framework.

Automation Effects: Self-service Operations Boosting Efficiency

First of all, ICT applications enable the automation of a significant number of routine tasks, such as ticket sales, check-in procedures and the printing of luggage tags. Automation decreases not only the level but also the skills of employment requirements. Overall, automation enables airports to manage the same level of passengers with less resources or a greater number of passengers with the same resources. The use of technology for managing the increasing number of travellers' worldwide is a major challenge for all airports. Moreover, based on Amadeus' report about the Air Travellers Tribes of 2020 (Anonymous 2006a), technology has been identified as a major airport asset for handling and serving the particular needs of two specific, lucrative and growing leisure market segments that are continuously rising, namely the active seniors and the global clans. By scanning major macro-trends (such as the aging of the population and the increased globalisation and immigration of populations) this report has identified changes in consumer behaviour and associated technology developments.

Active seniors are wealthy, healthy but frequently with hearing, mobility or other problems, aged between 50–75, and will travel for cultural and leisure pursuits. This market segment requires comfort for money. Automation provides them the location and time convenience of airport–travel operations, such as avoidance of queues and waiting time and the avoidance of the need to walk through great geographical distances between airport elements, for example to change gate for a connecting flight (as gate management systems will be looking for such information and adapting resource management on real time needs). However, for this segment to use automation technology, the latter has to be humanised and become more accessible to them. To address this, technology design needs to be adapted to this market's needs, such as the location of CUSS in easily acceptable and visible places, the adoption of software that caters for visual problems (maybe including voice recognition systems as well), and easy to use and emotional appealing software (e.g. navigation, presentation) and hardware design (Forrester Research 2007; Tunnacliffe 2003).

Global Clans represent the second fast growing leisure air travel market segment referring to people that will travel to visit globally dispersed extended family members. This segment is more price sensitive, tends to travel during specific periods (e.g. holidays, festivities), organises trips at the last minute and usually travels together with several other family members. Air travel will be considered as a commodity purchase for this segment, whilst dealing with easy and fast immigration procedures, and the logistics of the several pieces of baggage, will be the major concerns of their air travel experience. Their needs can be straightforwardly addressed through the increased adoption and use of biometrics, RFID and the digitisation of the booking and distribution of discounted travel packages and offers.

Integration and Hyper-automation Effects

Groth (1999) argued that rather than marking the end of straightforward automation, the technology inaugurates the age of hyper-automation. Hyper-automation makes it possible to integrate a much greater span of organisational activities into one coordinated process, not least because it allows the automation or elimination of significant administrative processes. In principle, hyper-automation effects are based on the coordinative effects of a common and unified database with the value of the integrity of the information it delivers. In this vein, the integration – hyper-automation effects of airport technologies have been illustrated in the previous discussion whereby it was demonstrated that various ICT applications are integrated together in order to provide a holistic, seamless, non-stop (ground) passenger flow management, such as the integration of document check, border control and boarding. Overall, ICT applications are envisioned to create three air travel phases namely the pre-boarding, on board and de-boarding phases. The pre-boarding phase aims to identify the passenger for their eligibility to join a flight by combining operations including check-in, security control of hand baggage, boarding pass and passport control at the gate. For example, a passenger will check-in at home PC, and a SMS with a 2D bar code will be delivered to their mobile device along with additional information and alerts (about gate, boarding time, delay, etc.). Biometric information will be integrated in the mobile device and so the passenger proceeds to the gate whereby the required controls are done in one step. For a more detailed analysis of this non-stop procedure there are examples of the Siemens' mock operated airport and/or the TINA (The

INtelligent Airport) – project taking place at Heathrow which aim to provide seamless passenger experiences by integrating all the disparate information systems of the airport (Table 16.3).

However, the vision of a "non-stop (ground) travel" requires a complete reorganisation of the passenger process such as elimination of check-in desks; centralisation of control procedures at the boarding area (this physical merge of operations are also helpful for elderly travelers) (Pitt *et al.* 2002); creation of more retail and leisure opportunities at the airport terminals; development of health care services for the active seniors market; and the provision of rental handheld devices specially designed for elderly people and available at airports so leisure travellers can be provided with localised and personalised information, services and alerts wherever they are at the airport. Technology applications can also facilitate air travel for those that want to address their luggage logistics problems. Door-to-door luggage services are to be developed in order to cater for the limited physical

TABLE 16.3   Hyper-automating airport processes for providing non-stop air travel experiences

Name of project	Description
Siemens mock airport, Germany	Siemens operates a mock airport, looking a lot like a real airport but without the gates and planes. Siemens aims to demonstrate automation technologies for integrating nearly every aspect of airport operations — from baggage handling and fleet management to passenger check-in and screening. On the passenger side of the airport, a prototype system allows passengers to check in using their mobile phones. Passengers simply make a quick phone call to check in, and the system then sends back a 2D bar code that displays on the mobile phone's screen. At the airport, special readers scan in the bar code and print out boarding passes. Also on display on the passenger side of the mock airport were new fingerprint and facial recognition systems.
TINA (The INtelligent Airport) – Heathrow	The TINA system aims to integrate all disparate airport ICT communications systems and networks applications into a single ICT infrastructure system to handle all electronic communications throughout airport terminals. TINA will manage a wide range of fixed and mobile equipment, including passenger information and entertainment services, security cameras, biometric sensors and explosive and chemical detectors, as well as providing logistical support for airport retailers, transport services and runway operations. TINA's aim is to streamline the airport's operations, reduce its network costs, while also providing a more seamless and convenient air traveller experience.

Source: Author.

capabilities of the active seniors and/or the huge number of pieces and weight of luggage of global clans (Anonymous 2006a). RFID technologies are to be exploited for offering such services, since they allow baggage allocation even without the check-in procedure.

Informative Effects: Informationalising Airport Operation into Providing a Personalised and Humanised Air Travel Experience

Zuboff (1988) argues that ICT goes beyond traditional automation and coins the word "informate" to describe this capacity. This is because while the activities of classical machines only result in concrete products, ICT in addition to this "… simultaneously generates information about the underlying productive and administrative processes through which an organisation accomplishes its work. It provides a deeper level of transparency to activities that had been either partially or completely opaque", (Zuboff 1988: 280). To Zuboff (1988), automation and informating form a hierarchy, where informating derives from and builds upon automation. The informating aspect of the technology is for Zuboff the real revolutionary one, the one that will cause most of the organisational changes in the future.

However, not everybody shares Zuboff's (1988) argument. Others argue that automation and use of ICT for other purposes than informating does not necessarily imply a decreasing dependence on human skills: on the contrary, it entails an increasing dependence on knowledge. Thus, the collection of "know what", (i.e. the gathered information), entails enhanced "know how" skills, (i.e. staff should be able to know how to exploit the collected information from the automated operations for producing knowledge). Indeed, nowadays, the concept of informalisation is linked to the notion of the intelligent enterprise (Quinn 1992). The Unisys Central Integrated Information Management System (CIIMS) is an ICT application established and operated at Guangzhou Balyun International Airport that clearly shows how the system enables the airport to automate and integrate several processes for collecting and sharing real time information and intelligence from disparate internal and external operations. Hence, this enables knowledge based and real time airport management. The applications' benefits for travellers are also identified.

The Amadeus Air Traveller report (Anonymous 2006a) has also identified the following key technology applications with a human-centric design that are going to have a significant impact on personalizing the travel experience of the active seniors and the global clan market segments:

- Digital personal identities (detailed customer information held digitally and therefore easily and quickly accessible) which will enable a far more personalised service. Automated adaptable bookings based on passenger profiles can be very helpful to elderly people who do not have the capacities to go through the booking process again and again.

- Integrated Information systems that combine information from a variety of sources which will enable leisure travellers to easily navigate and find their way to airports and procedures.

- Real-time information delivered to individuals based on need and location. Mobile devices will be the key tools for providing services such as mobile travel guides, SIM card identification, personalised destination information, digital concierge for special needs (e.g. mobility problems), digital memories RFID for both people and baggage security and logistics and humanoid check-in kiosks.

- Virtual reality applications for providing "walk through" to familiarise travellers with the airport before they leave home, to the use of "sensing" technologies to tell if customers are anxious at check-in.

CONCLUSIONS

This chapter aimed to identify and then discuss the implications of ICT applications on airport operations management and air travel experiences of leisure travellers. In reviewing the literature, it was illustrated that ICT applications derive crucial operational (e.g. efficiency, time and space savings, flow management) as well as strategic benefits (e.g. reliability, security, customer service) for airport operators. The analysis of the ICT applications also demonstrated that the full potential of ICT materialises when technologies do not solely automate existing airport operations, but when technologies' integration and informate capabilities are exploited for delivering a non-stop seamless and personalised travel experience to passengers.

Certain technology applications are also envisaged to be able to address the specific needs and requirements of the two lucrative and growing leisure air travel market segments, namely the active seniors and the global clan markets. There is a strategic imperative for airport operators to further support the adoption and integration of new technologies within their business model.

However, the successful adoption of new technologies does not only depend on the airport operator's internal capabilities to redesign and reengineer its own processes, but also on several other equally important but external factors such as the user friendliness of the technology; its emotional appeal and value added services provided to the passengers (which in turn determine the degree of customer adoption of invested technologies); the inter-firm collaboration and organisational aspects with external partners and authorities, regulations and legislation in different countries; and the social and cultural aspects such as the rising privacy public concerns (e.g regarding the use of RFIDs and the location of people and items) (Teufel et al. 2007). In other words, ICT adoption and its impact on air travel is such a perplex and complicated process which requires an in-depth consideration of the inter-relationships of the different issues and organisations involved.

PART V

Economic and Environmental Impacts

17

New Air Services: Tourism and Economic Development

Brian Graham

INTRODUCTION

This next section adopts a broader view of the links between aviation and tourism by considering the resulting impacts that occur on the economy, community and the environment. The aim of this chapter is to discuss the relationships between air transport provision, tourism and economic development, and then the next chapter focuses on the environmental impacts.

The geographical context of the present discussion is largely that of the European Union (EU) although the general points being made are more widely applicable. The conflicting priorities that emanate from these different policy arenas produce contradictions and tensions that are not easily reconciled. There is, for example, the incompatibility of 'squaring' environmental sustainability with business models – especially the low-cost carrier (LCC) variant – that promote rapid growth in air travel without meeting external costs generated principally by noise and atmospheric emissions. These are not internalised and are 'thus excessive in terms of what might be anticipated if a sustainable environment is to be attained' (Button 2001: 70). Simultaneously, however, air transport contributes to regional and urban development and regeneration while, particularly in its low-cost form, claiming to be socially and geographically inclusive.

Black (1996: 151) defines sustainable transport as 'satisfying current transport and mobility needs without compromising the ability of future generations to meet these needs', a definition that conflates environmental objectives with economic and social goals. A report produced for Airports Council International Europe (ACI Europe) (York Aviation 2004) draws upon United Kingdom (UK) government data to define sustainability as comprising: the maintenance of high and stable levels of employment; social progress which recognises the needs of everyone; effective protection of the environment; and prudent use of natural resources. Aviation offers direct employment, catalytic spin-offs, contributes to trade and tourism and is a significant tax-payer (ATAG 2005). It is estimated that every one million air passengers support almost 6,500 people in air-travel related work, including direct, indirect, induced and catalytic effects (York Aviation 2004). A report by Oxford Economic Forecasting (OEF 2006) calculates that in the UK, aviation contributed 1.0 per cent of the overall economy in 2004, directly employed 186,000 people and supported, in total 520,000 jobs.

Given this broader context, it is apparent from the outset that the interrelationships between new air services, tourism and economic development are complex and often contradictory. The chapter consciously does not address environmental issues *per se* (see Chapter 18) but focuses on the nexus of issues linking air transport, economic development and environmental sustainability through the medium of tourism and, more generally, the cultural economy. The discussion demonstrates how this brings together overlapping networks and geographies of problematical categories, processes and practices. These are: culture and the cultural economy; tourism and, in particular, cultural or heritage tourism; accessibility and mobility; and sustainability. Following an introductory contextual discussion, the chapter engages successively with three such overlapping networks and the interconnections between them: heritage and cultural tourism; accessibility, mobility and air services; and the cultural economy, air services and sustainability.

THE CONTEXT

There is ample evidence that cultural innovation and the production and consumption of cultural goods and commodities by creative and cultural industries can be linked to urban and regional development. These commodities, however, are very often not 'neutral', as is signalled by the concept of heritage which can be defined as the meanings and socio-political values attached to the (highly selective) past in the present. In an 'external' sense, it is used to create both a sense of place that links a dynamic present into a beneficial past and to differentiate cities and regions from their competitors (B. Graham 2002). Thus, as a crucial resource for place-marketing, tourism and the cultural economy, heritage, which takes both material and intangible forms, is constructionist, present-centred and quite distinct from history. It is, however, also an 'internal' knowledge in the sense that it is not culturally free but functions as a critical element in questions of identity and identity politics (Ashworth, Graham and Tunbridge 2007). These latter have been of growing importance during the last two decades (and most especially since 2001) and are manifested in, for example, the resurgence of interest in criteria defining national identities. The dissonance between the economic and social/cultural/political uses of heritage is a constant one (Graham, Ashworth and Tunbridge 2000; Smith 2006).

While by no means all tourism can be classified as 'cultural' in the sense that it consumes heritage (both human and natural), the arts or the creative industries (Smith 2003), it is difficult to consider any form of tourism utterly devoid of culture in the wider sense of the representation and imaging used to sell tourism destinations. In this sense, place is a meaningful segment of space, a location 'imbued with meaning and power' (Cresswell 2006: 3). While the recent growth of heritage and culture-based tourism represents a 'major shift in … tourism demand' (Timothy and Boyd 2003: 10), the cause-and-effect relationships between the cultural economy, tourism and regional or city growth are, however, ambiguous and difficult to measure. Moreover, in addition to the very slippery nature of key terms such as the 'cultural economy' or 'cultural tourism', the use of culture in tourism and economic development inevitably leads to a suite of interlinked conflicts and tensions, often framed through an indigenous/tourist binary.

The exploitation of culture as an economic good for tourism also demands access strategies and, increasingly, these are dependent on the mobilities created by air travel. In this regard, the dynamic growth of LCCs, first in North America, then in Europe and now globally (Francis *et al.* 2006) and the market responses by 'legacy' carriers to this form of market entry has transformed the geography of accessibility by opening up many more city- and airport-pairs (see Chapter 9). Consequently, the cultural economy is thus dependent on two industries – transport, especially by air, and tourism – which have extensive environmental externalities that again point to the internal tensions between the economic and environmental dimensions to the holistic concept of sustainability.

It is readily apparent that the idea of interconnections between places, processes and practices that shape international tourism, and the differential geographies which these linkages create, are largely elided from policies that are generally framed with respect to single fields of interest. Thus this chapter seeks to 'put the pieces together in different ways'. As Keeling (2007: 219) argues, theories about transport for example, must move beyond 'the strictly utilitarian … and challenge the very essence of the social processes that take place in myriad social milieus.' Implicit here, too, is the dichotomy between intended or advertent outcomes in one policy agenda and those which are unintended or inadvertent in others.

HERITAGE AND CULTURAL TOURISM

The realms of culture are increasingly 'economised' and whereas economy and culture were once regarded as 'self' and 'other', 'they are now seen to be linked, co-constitutive or seamlessly intertwined' (Castree 2004: 206). Meanwhile, modern economies increasingly produce, circulate and consume cultural commodities. There is ample evidence that cultural innovation and the promotion of cultural industries can be linked to the growth of creative cities and to wider regional development. Rather curiously, however, tourism is essentially elided from Richard Florida's highly influential concept of the 'creative city' and, by extension, region. He focuses instead on the competitive capacities of cities and regions to attract highly mobile creative capital, the basis of the knowledge economy, arguing that 'place is the key economic and social organizing unit of our time' (Florida 2002: xix) while: 'Tolerance and diversity clearly matter to high-technology concentration and growth' (Florida 2005a: 137).

Yet tourism is one of the primary markets for the production of this economy while it, too, depends on marketing one place and its culture to the disadvantage of another. The concept of the creative city overlaps with, but is separate from, that of the 'tourist-historic' city (Ashworth and Tunbridge 2000). Florida argues for cosmopolitanism and tolerance as the cornerstones of the creative city while the tourist-historic city is the ultimate beneficiary of diversifying both the pasts it can sell and the workforce collectively motivated to sell them. The cause-and-effect relationships between the cultural economy and regional or city innovation and growth are, however, ambiguous and difficult to measure, particularly when similar strategies are employed by multiple cities and regions to achieve similar ends.

Conservation of heritage at whatever scale has always been motivated by the desire to enhance distinctive identity at the local scale and to further distinguish one place from another. The more conservation is practised, however, the less locally distinctive identity is likely to become. Widespread attempts to emulate San Francisco's Fisherman's Wharf mean that heritage waterfronts, for example, have become a global cliché as restaurants, craft shops and leisure spaces replace working harbours. European medieval city centres, often partially or even completely rebuilt as a result of war damage, fulfil a similar role as 'old towns' and the generic models are thus replicated over and over again, leading, arguably, to a similarity of experience irrespective of location. Everywhere, cities strive to recreate Bilbao's 'Guggenheim effect', the regeneration and transformation (including Santiago Calatrava's dramatic terminal at the city's airport) of a grim, decayed industrial city around the catalyst of an internationally recognisable signature building, the Guggenheim Museum (Woodworth 2007). European Capitals of Culture may be simply another example of repackaging generic plans.

Beyond this external role of heritage, however, but obviously overlapping with it are the 'internal' or physic functions that relate to identity, including: social inclusion and exclusion; lifestyle; diversity; and multiculturalism/pluralism (Smith 2006). This is a place of complex, overlapping and ambiguous messages, not least because most European cities, for instance, 'were plurally encoded by socially pluralist societies and are now also decoded pluralistically' (Ashworth 1998: 69). Much of the iconography is not decoded at all, less because it is intelligible but because of its irrelevance to contemporary multicultural urban societies. This official heritage will be constructed by agencies of the state, region and city. However, if the representations and narratives created by this official heritage prove inadequate, people will create their own unofficial heritage identity and territorial claims through various acts of cultural 'resistance', including: marching; spectacles; carnivals; and the erection of monuments and other visual representations. Some of this unofficial heritage may even be overtly violent but, nevertheless – as is true of Northern Ireland and other conflicts – can still be sold as 'dark' or 'difficult' tourism' (Lennon and Foley 2000).

The result of the internal/external dialectic is that heritage itself is a contested concept that is often – even always – characterised by the concept of dissonance (Tunbridge and Ashworth 1996), which means that the same heritage can carry different and often contradictory meanings and at a variety of geographical scales – local, regional, national, European, even world. Dissonance reflects the zero-sum nature of heritage in that what is mine (meaning) cannot be yours. The most common sources of dissonance stem: first, from identity politics and second, from the economic commodification of sacred or iconic identity markers as tourism artefacts and imagery. In sum, contested heritage is simultaneously multi-commodified and multi-sold as cultural and economic capital.

Among the most potent examples of the ensuing potential for contestation are UNESCO World Heritage Sites (Harrison and Hitchcock 2005), especially those in developing countries, which are increasingly part of international tourism networks served by air transport. Typically, tourists are flown in and out, often by foreign carriers, while accommodation provision is monopolised by western hotel chains. Thus, for example, the temple landscape at Angkor, Cambodia is a 'form of "living heritage" pivotal in the articulation of cultural, ethnic and national identities' in a country with a recent and terrible past' (Winter 2007a: 134: 2007b). Traffic at Siem Reap International Airport, which serves the complex, increased by 216 per cent from 2001–06 (from 428,000 to 1,354,000 passengers), traffic dominated by international tourism arrivals (Cambodia Airports 2007). As Winter (2005) argues, this arrival of large-scale international tourism and the strategy of developing the Angkor heritage landscape for this market means that the practices and values of domestic visitors – much more likely to be identity related – are downplayed. This is but one example among many where sites of major domestic cultural significance become the objects of superficial external tourism consumption facilitated by air service provision. For example, international heritage tourism at the iconic Peruvian site of Machu Picchu is almost entirely dependent on air services to Cuzco, itself another World Heritage Site, while, in Australia, the Uluru-Kata Tjuta National Park is equally reliant on air access. At such places, the values, expectations and demands of indigenous peoples and tourist consumers may be markedly dissonant, not least because of overlays of colonialism, neo-colonialism and racism.

ACCESSIBILITY, MOBILITY AND AIR SERVICES

Although the cultural economy requires accessibility for people and finance and societies that value mobility, both for economic reasons but also for personal gratification, access and transport infrastructure tends to be very much assumed in the creative and tourism literature. Yet various studies suggest that in terms of the aggregate relationship between aviation and national, regional and urban economies, the sectors most likely to contribute to economic growth – principally those involved in the knowledge and cultural economies – are typically those most dependent on aviation and the enhanced accessibility which it offers (B. Graham 2003). But an understanding of the interrelationships between air transport, tourism and economic development also depends on another set of practices and processes.

Mobility is a fundamental human activity and need but, equally, a behavioural factor being promoted by changes in spatially dispersed social networks and consumer practices (Donaghy *et al.* 2004) and, moreover, readily manipulated by price. Cresswell (2006: 3) identifies three interpretations to mobility. First, it is 'a brute fact'. Secondly, it conveys meaning as in, for example, freedom, transgression and creativity, although Sager (2006), while endorsing the idea of mobility as 'freedom', as the opportunity to travel when and where one might please, acknowledges that these rights may be problematic in that they have to be balanced against other democratic aims. Finally, mobility is something that is practiced, experienced and embodied so that 'mobility is a way of being in the world'. Cresswell argues for a stratification of global society marked by the dichotomy between a mobile, kinetic elite for whom 'space is less and less of a constraint' and a kinetic underclass thrown into a mobile world for whom 'space ... is not disappearing but has to be transcended painfully' (Cresswell 2006: 255). This reflects Bauman's ideas (1998) that the two mobile figures who mark the end point of a scale of mobilities are the 'tourist' and the 'vagabond': 'There are no tourists without [the] vagabonds' who serve them (Cresswell 2006: 256).

While there has been some research on the roles of airports as sites of the production of mobilities, air transport is again largely relegated to being an assumption in this literature. But its material provision is actually a prime means of articulating mobilities. Effective April 1997, all EU airlines have had open access to virtually all routes within the then 15 Member States (followed by Iceland, Norway and Switzerland in 1998: see Chapter 5 by Papatheodorou). The subsequent enlargements of the Union in 2004 and 2007 have added a further 12 states, largely in Central and Eastern Europe, to the Single Aviation Market. According to a spokesperson for the European Low Fares Airline Association (ELFAA):

> The whole air transport deregulation process was aimed at granting EU citizens the *right* to air mobility, lowering the cost of air transport and extending it to a wider share of the population (Pilling 2005: 19; author's emphasis).

While it may not reflect the original intentions behind the Single Aviation Market, ELFAA's contention that EU citizenship includes the *right* to air mobility chimes with Adams's

(1999) concept of hyper-mobile societies with a-spatial communities of interest in which we spend more of our time among strangers. Urry (2000, 2002), for example, sees 'hyper-mobility' as a function of the importance of networks, not least of families in transnational communities, and the nature of 'meetingness' and 'co-presence', terms which refer, essentially, to the value of face-to-face meeting compared to electronic communication. Thus the motivations for travel are less rooted in the individual *per se* as in the properties of social relations between people, institutions and culture:

> Mobility is vital to human existence. It contributes to defining the fabric of our lives and is quickly becoming a formative element of existence (Flamm and Kaufmann 2006: 167).

Furthermore, as in the EU, mobility may also be seen as a highly beneficial force in promoting social and possibly political understanding and integration.

The evolution of a hyper-mobile society is increasingly dependent on air transport which is instrumental within the EU – and elsewhere – in the development of weekend, city or short-break tourism and, especially because of LCC market entry, in effecting a radical expansion of potential destinations and routes (Dobruszkes 2006; Fan 2006). One important study by the UK Civil Aviation Authority (CAA 2006b) has challenged several common assumptions concerning LCCs, finding little evidence that, in aggregate terms, they have 'significantly affected overall rates of traffic growth' which have remained fairly constant at 5–6 per cent per annum since the mid-1990s (CAA 2006b: 3). Individual airports may show very high percentage increases in traffic (often from low bases) but, overall, LCC growth has been at the expense of the full service/legacy carriers and, even more so, of the charter airlines.

The European legacy carriers, for example, have been forced to exit markets or reconfigure their short-haul route systems and fare structures so that they can compete more effectively with the LCCs. Increasingly, too, they have been forced to retrench and focus on their higher-yield long-haul hub operations. In protecting their remaining core short-haul markets, one strategy has been to try and 'ring-fence' leisure operations from higher-yield business routes. This can be done either through using different airports – as in British Airways' Gatwick operation – or through the creation of 'carriers within carriers' (CWCs) (Graham and Vowles 2006). Despite the attendant risks of an airline simply cannibalising its own traffic, the CWC has become an increasingly common strategy worldwide, one of the best example being provided by Qantas' Jetstar subsidiaries which operate leisure routes in Australasia. The latest such venture in Europe has been the repositioning of Transavia and the creation of Transavia France as the low-cost subsidiaries of Air France/KLM.

Charter carriers have responded to LCC competition through considerable retrenchment and industry consolidation and by opening up longer-distance leisure routes although there are markedly increased environmental externalities to long-haul leisure (see Chapter 8). Long-haul will account for about 25 per cent of air travel by 2020 (Hunter and Shaw 2006), although the growth is as much from mass-market charter operators serving 'exotic' destinations as from the growth of what is claimed to be more responsible 'green' or ecotourism. There is also some movement towards long-haul low-cost services with airlines such as Zoom, flyglobespan and Air Transat. While these may be largely serving the 'visiting friends and relations' (VFR) markets, increased availability of such services, combined with those ensuing, for example, from the dynamic growth of Middle Eastern carriers like Emirates, will increase the environmental damage incurred by taking long-haul short breaks in, for example, New York or Dubai, or owning second homes in locations that can be reached only by long-haul services.

In sum, therefore, whether it be the LCCs, legacy or charter carriers, the key recent 'step-change' is not growth *per se* but the availability of low and unrestricted fares which reduce travel costs (A. Graham 2006) and a very considerable increase in the choice of destinations and airports. In the EU, as elsewhere, LCCs, both in their own right and through their impact on the marketing strategies of the legacy and charter carriers, are extending the range of motivations and frequency of travel for private leisure reasons and targeting an eclectic range of overlapping niche markets, ranging from cultural tourism through the second home market, pensioners wintering abroad to 'stag' and 'hen' parties. Some of this traffic may be less than desirable for the destination cities as witnessed by a succession of lurid press stories about the behaviour of British travellers abroad. (See examples of the 'new' genre of low-cost travel literature, for instance: Jones 2006; Chesshyre 2007; Nolan 2007: and specialist websites such as www.praguepissup.com.) LCCs also serve the VFR market while the increasing number of destinations served, especially in Central and Eastern Europe, also points to wider socio-economic changes promoted by EU enlargement. Obviously, these are facilitating the movement of migrant labour and the CAA (2006b) found significant evidence that in-bound traffic to the UK has increased. Its study shows that migration is followed by VFR traffic which is the fastest growing segment of inbound traffic at both Luton and Stansted in recent years, accounting for almost 50 per cent of inbound trips.

Although it is claimed that LCCs are promoting social inclusion in allowing more people to fly, there is little evidence that the 'LCCs are appealing to the less wealthy ... [but] seem to be encouraging more frequent flying ... in some cases influenced by the existence of a second home' (A. Graham 2006: 19–20). The CAA (2006b) found no real 'democratisation' effect, there being little evidence of any major change, especially in the leisure market, in the type of people flying compared to the mid-1990s. While this finding challenges popular perceptions (and even 'empirical experience') of low-cost air travel and despite the significant increase in the total number of people flying, it is the middle and higher-income socio-economic groups who are 'flying more often than in the past, and often on shorter trips' (CAA 2006b: 5).

There are limitations to the geography of LCC networks as, ultimately, there is an inertia created by the geography of demand and also by expanding terrestrial competition, not least from high-speed trains. Inevitably, therefore, the route maps of various operators show a considerable duplication of the same city-pairs although they may often be served by different airport-pairings. In the EU, the focus is very much on historic cities (or in Ryanair's case, somewhere within *c.*120kms of the historic city in question) and traditional hotel (now as much second home) destinations formerly served by the charter carriers, but also on some decentralised markets like rural Spain and France (Bieger and Wittmer 2006). Thus European LCC routes can be classified into three principal types. First, are domestic services (including UK-island of Ireland) which often provide the backbone of the LCC route systems. Secondly, there are numerous essentially leisure-oriented north-south routes, the key markets being the principal Mediterranean city and 'sun' destinations, such as Venice, Nice, Barcelona, Malaga, Alicante and Faro, and winter ski destinations, most notably Geneva. The second home market is especially strong in France, Spain and Portugal and helps support, for example, a number of routes between the UK and small French regional airports. North-south leisure-oriented routes from Scandinavia, Germany and Central Europe also serve the Mediterranean littoral and major inland tourism and leisure destinations.

Finally, west-east routes, combining leisure, migrant labour and VFR traffic, have grown significantly with the 2004 and 2007 expansions of the EU. German-based carriers are particularly well placed to capitalise on this market and there has been a wave of start-up LCCs based in the accession countries. Prague, widely regarded as the 'new Paris', was already well-served, partly because the Czech government had allowed LCC access prior to 2004. Budapest, Kraków, Tallinn and Riga are among those cities being tipped as the 'new Pragues' on the back of the enlargement of the EU single aviation market.

Thus geography matters as region and city 'chances' in tourism and economic development are to some extent dependent on this pattern of accessibility. Everywhere in Europe, regional, city and airport authorities are signing what may very well be Faustian pacts with LCCs in order to attract this sort of traffic at expense of other locations (B. Graham, forthcoming; Graham and Shaw, forthcoming). More commercial and often privatised airports essentially attempt to emulate what the CAA (2005c) terms the 'virtuous airport model' in which they actively seek additional carriers so that non-aeronautical income is increased and the cycle of air transport growth continues.

CULTURAL ECONOMY, AIR SERVICES AND SUSTAINABILITY

However there is one final and very difficult dimension to this set of interconnecting processes and practices. The consensus into what some commentators regard as the oxymoron of 'sustainable aviation' is that, at best, the environmental sustainability of the air transport industry is in doubt, although, conversely, aviation is delivering social and economic goods (Upham *et al.* 2003). Air transport policy-making has been driven by the concern to introduce, implement and protect the competitive marketplace. Nevertheless, as is characteristic of all transport modes, such policies do not encourage individual restraint in the use of environmental resources on the part of any one airline. Air travel can be viewed as another 'tragedy of the commons', the situation in which people believe that any individual sacrifice for the greater good (in this case, the environment) would have no value unless followed by all others (Shaw and Thomas 2006). One recent Scandinavian study (Holden 2007: 189) demonstrates that a green attitude is 'a better predictor of sustainable everyday mobility than of leisure-time mobility', even to the extent that, in the study, membership of an environmental organisation correlated positively (and significantly) with energy consumption for long-distance leisure travel by plane.' Holden attributes this surprising result, perhaps to a sense of powerlessness but also to a desire for personal indulgence.

Air transport makes possible human geographies of interaction. But studies into the mode's impact on tourism and economic development more generally often ignore the problem that this is a two-way process. For example, UK investments overseas between 1997 and 2001 were almost twice incoming FDI (Hacan ClearSkies 2003). York Aviation (2004) also stresses the role of tourism which accounts for 5 per cent of total employment and of GDP in the EU, in addition to accounting for 30 per cent of total external trade in services. Forsyth (2006: 7) points out, however, that tourism benefits may be surprisingly low because they ignore 'the costs of the factors used in producing the goods and services that tourists buy.' Again, crucially, these benefits are not offset against losses incurred from the expenditure of discretionary income on outbound tourism facilitated by the provision of air services. Drawing on Department for Transport statistics which show that UK residents will make a predicted 88m overseas visits by air in 2020, compared to 54m visits by foreign residents to the UK, the pressure group Hacan ClearSkies (2003) estimates that a total expenditure deficit to the UK of £11.1b plus £1.7b VAT loss in 2001 will rise to £14.2b plus £2.1b VAT loss in 2020. It is estimated that 75 per cent of inbound visitors to the UK arrive by air and contribute 1.1 per cent of GDP and support 170,000 jobs. But 'the flow of UK citizens in the other direction is even more substantial' (OEF 2006: 27). Residents of the UK made 66.5m trips abroad in 2005, representing a 61 per cent increase since 1995; two-thirds of these visits were for leisure reasons.

Meanwhile air transport is the fastest increasing source of atmospheric emissions and international air travel is not included in, for example, the UK's carbon targets. If growth continues as forecast, Bows and Anderson (2007: 109) estimate that the aviation industry will be 'likely emitting in the region of a quarter of the UK's 2050 carbon target by 2012', the result being that: 'All other sectors of the economy will need to significantly, possibly completely, decarbonise by 2050 if the [UK] … carbon-reduction target is not to be exceeded'. Moreover, air travel compounds tourism's dubious sustainability record. Thus in their analysis of the ecological footprint of ecotourism, Hunter and Shaw (2006: 302) argue that 'it is the apparently inexorable growth in international tourism involving air transport that is the fundamental problem.' For Hickman (2007: xv), 'tourism is currently one of the most unregulated industries in the world, largely controlled by a relatively small number of western corporations.' But it also one of key industries for nations, regions and cities in promoting economic development, irrespective of whether or not they are located in the First or Third Worlds. So, mirroring the debate on the ethics of air freighting foodstuffs and other Third World products to Europe, Hickman points to the double-bind involved: going on holiday by air can help to impoverish other people, but not flying can have precisely the same result.

Thus enhanced mobility is both proclaimed a human right and seen as fundamental to economic development at national and regional scales because of its input to increased tourism/leisure consumption. OEF (2006: 30) justifies the UK's tourism deficit by stressing the positive role of tourism in 'cultural exchange and education'; it argues that 'virtually all tourism broadens the mind' and even identifies a trend towards ecotourism. The marketing strategies of airlines, airports and the agencies charged with tourism and economic development strive to achieve precisely the opposite effect to the curbs on the growth of personal mobility inevitably intrinsic to the arguments of the environmental lobby. It can be argued that aviation is 'a prime candidate for demand management precisely because its rate of growth is large enough to cancel out gains from technical improvements' (Whitelegg and Cambridge 2004: 26). Conversely, in the EU, as elsewhere, the European Commission and national and regional governments are 'encouraging continued high levels of growth in aviation, whilst simultaneously asserting that they are committed to a policy of substantially reducing carbon emissions' (Tyndall Centre 2005: 50) through, for example, the European Emissions Trading Scheme for airlines proposed for 2011–2012. This, however, is opposed by the remainder of the world's airline industry which favours a global approach through ICAO.

CONCLUSION

The networks of practices and processes outlined in this chapter by no means exhaust the possible interconnections between, and contestations within, air service provision, tourism and economic development. As Keeling (2007: 218) argues, transport makes possible 'myriad geographies of human interaction' and the key point that comes through here is that initiatives in any one policy context will have unintended or inadvertent outcomes in others and will, in turn, also be compromised by policy discourses in those arenas. In essence, therefore, this chapter is pointing at a research agenda that explores the wider ramifications of the interrelationships between air transport, tourism and economic development. Keeling's (2007: 221) premise that greater focus is required 'on the social and economic implications of air transport' points to a significant number of key questions, important because the literature on the creative city, heritage, tourism and economic development rarely give any cognisance to the provision of air services, that being merely assumed rather than contextualised as an interconnected nexus of social, cultural, political and economic processes.

From the preceding discussion, five key areas of enquiry can be isolated. First, can the concept of the creative class and the creative city be extended to accommodate the ubiquity of heritage in strategies for place-marketing and the cultural industries? In turn, this raises questions as to how one place can be differentiated effectively from another. Secondly, if heritage is simultaneously a key marker of identity and an economic resource intrinsic to international tourism, how does the cultural economy deal with the dissonances between these uses? Thirdly, has the rapid expansion of LCCs and the responses by legacy and charter airlines to this form of market entry in an increasingly globalised air transport industry (Goetz and Graham 2004; Graham and Goetz 2008) both increased the potential for heritage dissonance and also for cultural competition by opening up more and more markets, leaving cities 'competing for smaller and smaller niches' (Florida 2005b: 165). Just as creative people choose regions and cities rather than nations (states) so that there is vicious competition between 'cities of ideas', 'the benefits [of tourism] to a region are likely to be much greater than the benefits to the [national] economy' (Forsyth 2006: 10). Fourthly, there are the contradictions surrounding the problematic 'rights' of mobility and the social inequalities inherent in these processes. Finally, irrespective of the social and economic benefits that stem from both air transport and tourism, neither industry is sustainable in environmental terms in their present and predictable future forms.

This then is a story of conflicting messages, strategies and targets – of policies contradicting each other. On one side is the familiar package of neo-liberal arguments: liberalisation, competition and rational actions by individual stakeholders to increase profits; ideas of choice and the life-enhancing dimensions to mobility; heritage as a driver of the cultural economy and tourism; and national, regional and city governments promoting mobility in the interests of economic development of which tourism is part. On the other, however, we have: the 'tragedy of the commons'; the 'who are we' sort of questions that heritage raises and which keep compromising the economic imperative; and governments, together with the aviation and tourism industries, responding to climate change with mixed and contradictory messages that attract often well-deserved accusations of hypocrisy.

In trying to sort out policy priorities for dealing with global warming, the UK Stern Report (2006) recommended that aviation should pay its full carbon price, either by higher taxes or emissions trading, noting that the choice of instrument would be driven as much by political viability as by economics. This latter point will probably apply overall to the contradictions inherent in the overlapping networks of processes identified here. The present balance is clearly with the neo-liberal side of the argument which means, however, that development policies in the knowledge economy are being driven by localism and short-termism. But identity politics and the macro- and micro-scale implications and effects of environmental change will not disappear. Development strategies need to be focussed on the longer-term repercussions of their immediate actions as well as demonstrate understanding of the constraints imposed on tourism as a mode of economic development by the generic nature, at local, regional, national and global scales, of the overlapping sets of interrelationships discussed here.

18

The Environmental Sustainability of Aviation and Tourism

Ben Daley
Dimitrios Dimitriou
Callum Thomas

INTRODUCTION

The aim of this chapter is to consider the environmental impacts of aviation and tourism. Whilst the impacts of both industries have been widely acknowledged separately, the relationship between the two has received less attention. Given increasing concerns about their sustainability, the aviation and tourism industries are under pressure to demonstrate improved environmental performance. However, this task presents a considerable challenge to both industries since air transport represents a large part of the overall environmental impact of tourism – and because rapid growth of both industries is projected to occur. Nevertheless, the changing preferences of tourists and other stakeholders in favour of sustainable tourism and 'greener' flights have significant implications for tourism products and leisure demand.

In this chapter, firstly the recent calls for sustainable aviation and sustainable tourism that are due, in some way, to greater environmental awareness on the part of consumers, are examined. The potential for air transport to contribute to more sustainable tourism is considered. Next, there is a description of the environmental impacts of tourism and the closely related environmental impacts of air transport. The main implications for tourism products and for leisure demand are identified. There is then an investigation of the synergies between aviation and tourism, and finally various measures to mitigate the environmental impacts of aviation and tourism are discussed.

SUSTAINABLE AVIATION AND SUSTAINABLE TOURISM

Aviation plays a significant role in economic development (see Chapter 17). Although the very rapid expansion of air transport – at around 5 per cent per year – has outpaced the growth of the world economy, both air transport growth and economic growth are closely related (IPCC 1999: 296; OEF 1999: 5–6). Air transport is now regarded as a vital economic generator and as an integral part of business, commerce and trade (Rogers *et al.* 2002:

13). Similarly, tourism is an important economic driver; in Europe, tourism generates over 500 billion Euros annually for host countries through a wide range of direct and indirect services (Cabrini 2005). Globally, tourism, like air transport, is expected to expand rapidly – at an average rate of 4 per cent per year until at least 2020. Projections by the United Nations World Tourism Organisation (UNWTO) indicate that international tourist arrivals (ITAs) will double between 2005 and 2020 and are expected to reach 1.6 billion by the latter year (UNWTO 2007b) (see Chapter 3 for more details).

Whilst important for economic growth, the strong and sustained growth in both industries is anticipated to be accompanied by significant environmental impacts, especially on global climate; the environmental impacts of both tourism and aviation are discussed in the following sections. Given recent concerns about the extent and pace of environmental degradation – and given the need to balance environmental protection with economic and social development – the concept of sustainable development has become a central concept in policy formation (Adams 2001; Baker 2006: 30–31; Elliott 2006: 1–2, 10; WCED 1987: 43). The UK Department for Transport (DfT 2003a: 6), for example, has stated: 'The [UK] Government is committed to ensuring that the long term development of aviation is sustainable. This means striking a balance between the social, economic and environmental aspects of air transport.' Promoting sustainable development is regarded as a cross-cutting issue that affects all economic and social activities; overall, drastic improvements in environmental protection are required if economic growth is not to result in severe environmental degradation (HM Government 2005).

Reflecting public concerns about environmental degradation and the scale of the challenge involved in achieving sustainable development, many consumers now call for improved environmental performance by air transport and tourism operators. Various authors have investigated the demand for sustainable forms of transport generally, including more sustainable air transport (Button and Nijkamp 1997; Greene and Wegener 1997; Gudmundsson and Höjer 1996). Some stakeholders have called for air transport growth to be curtailed for environmental reasons – especially those flights that are made for leisure (Bows et al. 2005; Sewill 2005). Similarly, calls have been expressed for greater sustainability in the development and operation of tourism (Cater and Goodall 1992; Williams 1998). In line with the 'polluter pays' principle – as articulated in recent conceptualisations of sustainable development – some authors have called for tourism transport to be more accountable for its externalities, including its environmental costs (Hall 1999; Shaw and Thomas 2006).

Changing preferences in leisure travel – due in part to greater environmental awareness by consumers – have generated various responses within the aviation and tourism industries. The UK aviation response is summarised in the Sustainable Aviation (2005) strategy; other high-level targets have been set by the EU Strategic Research Agenda (SRA) of the Advisory Council for Aeronautics Research in Europe (ACARE 2004). Some airlines have highlighted their attempts to achieve environmental efficiencies: through aircraft eco-labelling (Flybe 2007), carbon offset schemes (British Airways 2007; Climate Care 2007) and revised aircraft operations (Virgin Atlantic 2007). Airport operators have also attempted to demonstrate environmental sustainability, such as the strategy and target adopted by Manchester Airport to achieve carbon neutrality. These examples represent some of the ways in which the aviation industry can improve its environmental performance and, in turn, can contribute to more sustainable tourism. Whether initiatives of this type are sufficient to offset the significant – and rapidly growing – environmental impacts of both industries, however, is doubtful. Below, the main environmental impacts of each industry and their implications for tourism products and leisure demand are described.

THE ENVIRONMENTAL IMPACTS OF TOURISM

The environmental impacts of tourism have been widely acknowledged (Aronsson 2000; Butler 2000; Hall and Lew 1998; Hall and Page 2006; Holden 2000; Mowforth and Munt 1998; Priestly *et al.* 1996; Williams 1998). Holden (2000: 68–9) argued that the environmental impacts of tourism can be either positive or negative, and that those impacts are sometimes difficult to distinguish from the effects of other economic activities or of natural environmental change (see also Butler 2000: 342–4). Furthermore, it is not always possible to separate the impacts attributed to tourists from those due to local residents. Nonetheless, the negative environmental impacts of tourism frequently outweigh the positive, and many instances of environmental degradation due to tourism have been documented. In general, the impacts of tourism on ecosystems and resources occur in predictable ways: they are common to many forms of human consumption. 'The processes by which tourism can affect the natural environment are almost certainly no different to the ways in which other human processes have environmental effects and these have been known for a considerable time' (Butler 2000: 344).

Tourism environmental impacts may be categorised as resource issues and pollution issues (Aronsson 2000: 101–13; Holden 2000). Coccossis (1996: 3) defined four broad categories of tourism impacts: (a) impacts on natural ecosystems and resources; (b) impacts on the built environment, including architectural heritage; (c) impacts on local societies, including their cultures, values and attitudes; and (d) impacts on local, regional and national economies. While they may be analysed separately, these four types of impact are interrelated. Williams (1998: 104–11) proposed a five-fold classification of tourism environmental impacts that includes both positive and negative influences; those categories are defined as biodiversity impacts, erosion and physical damage, pollution, resource base impacts, and visual/structural change. A summary of this classification is provided in Table 18.1. Here the approach of Williams (1998) is adopted, although it also draws on the succinct account by Holden (2000).

Tourism impacts on biodiversity include direct and indirect influences on the flora and fauna of destinations; the balance of those impacts is strongly negative. Direct loss of habitats results from the construction of tourism infrastructure: hotels, apartments, attractions, roads and airports (Holden 2000: 85; Williams 1998: 104). Ecological degradation also results from human trampling and from damage by vehicles, which leads to the destruction of plants, changes in community composition, soil erosion, biodiversity losses and declining populations of insects, birds and small mammals. Impacts on larger animals – even within protected areas – include the disruption of their feeding, breeding and migration patterns as well as their destruction due to hunting and poaching of wildlife for food and sport, and through the collection and sale of biological specimens (Holden 2000: 86, 89; Williams 1998: 104–6).

Erosion and physical damage occurs primarily due to trampling by visitors, with significant local degradation of architectural sites and of soils near to footpaths. However, erosion and physical damage also occurs indirectly, as where the use of beach material for hotel construction leads to beach erosion. Sand and coral mining occur to supply building materials, and the removal of coastal vegetation, including mangroves and palm trees,

TABLE 18.1   Some environmental impacts of tourism

Area of Effect	Negative Impacts	Positive Impacts
Biodiversity	Disruption of animal breeding, feeding and migration patterns Killing of animals for leisure (hunting) or for souvenir trade Loss of habitats Change in species composition Destruction of vegetation	Encouragement to conserve animals as attractions Establishment of protected or conserved areas to meet tourism demands
Erosion and physical damage	Soil erosion Damage to sites through trampling Overloading of key infrastructure (e.g. water supply networks)	Tourism revenue to finance ground repair and site restoration Improvement of infrastructure prompted by tourist demand
Pollution	Water pollution (sewage, fuel spillage and littering) Air pollution (e.g. vehicle emissions) Noise from traffic and tourist attractions (e.g. bars and discos) Littering	Cleaning programmes to protect the attractiveness of locations
Resource base	Depletion of ground and surface water Diversion of water (e.g. for golf courses and swimming pools) Depletion of local fuel sources Depletion of local sources of building material	Development of new or improved sources of water supply
Visual/structural change	Land transfers to tourism (e.g. from farming) Detrimental visual impact through tourism development Introduction of new architectural styles Changes in (urban) functions Physical expansion of built-up areas	New uses for marginal or unproductive lands Landscape improvement (e.g. to clear urban dereliction) Regeneration and/or modernisation of the built environment Reuse of disused buildings

Source: Adapted from Williams (1998: 105).

leads to beach erosion and can result in reduced flood protection for coastal settlements. (Holden 2000: 79; Mieczkowski 1995). Erosion and physical damage are closely linked with biodiversity impacts – especially where wetlands are 'reclaimed' through the draining, dredging and filling of coastal marshes and saltwater lagoons (Holden 2000: 82).

Pollution is a critical tourism environmental issue – especially the pollution of water resources (since many tourism activities occur on or around water). Water pollution is acute in places where rapid tourism growth has out-paced the capacity of local services to cope, as along parts of the Spanish Mediterranean coast. The direct contamination of water with sewage, other organic and inorganic wastes and fuel oil is unsightly and promotes the spread of water-borne diseases such as gastro-enteritis, hepatitis, dysentery and typhoid (Williams 1998: 106). Indirect water pollution occurs due to the disposal of inadequately treated sewage and the run-off of fertilisers from the adjacent coast. The consequent eutrophication results in localised losses of aquatic biodiversity and in the rampant growth of some plant species, as exemplified by the occurrence of algal blooms in summer in the Adriatic Sea and by the deterioration of coral reefs in the Great Barrier Reef World Heritage Area (Furnas 2003: 5; Williams 1998: 108).

Air pollution is another significant tourism environmental issue due to the strong association between tourism and transport (Holden 2000: 93). Chemical emissions from traffic in the vicinity of airports and major roads – especially emissions of nitrogen oxides (NO_x) and particulate matter (PM) –contribute to local and regional air pollution, leading in turn to human respiratory complaints and to the acidification of water courses. In tourism destination areas, air quality may also deteriorate due to the construction of infrastructure (Holden 2000: 94). Increasingly, the impacts of air transport pollution on global climate are receiving scrutiny; those impacts include the radiative forcing of climate due to emissions of greenhouse gases such as carbon dioxide (CO_2) and aerosols, and the additional climate effects resulting from aircraft contrails and enhanced cirrus cloudiness (IPCC 1999; see also the discussion below).

Noise pollution also accompanies transport for tourism, although its impacts are generally highly localised around airports and major transport routes, and additional noise pollution occurs in and around the entertainment districts of major tourism resorts. Noise can lead to increased stress levels, especially in the vicinity of major airports, and is particularly disruptive in places renowned for their tranquillity (Holden 2000: 93–4; Hume and Watson 2003: 68–70; Thomas and Lever 2003: 99). Significant noise is also generated during the construction of tourism facilities (Briguglio and Briguglio 1996).

Resource base impacts represent another major category of tourism environmental impact. Of the various resource base issues, Holden (2000: 71–4) cited the construction and development of airports as one of the most important impacts of tourism. Airports are vital in tourism development and they generate considerable employment opportunities; however, the resulting environmental effects can be severe. Airport development involves the replacement of large areas of agricultural and recreational land with runways, taxiways, aprons and terminal buildings. The loss of agricultural land presents particular challenges for small island developing states, where airport development can lead to increased reliance on food imports (Briguglio and Briguglio 1996). Airport development also requires additional infrastructure, including roads and railways, which in turn lead to further land use change and pollution. In addition to airports, the development of other tourism facilities and infrastructure requires the transformation of land that may previously have been used for agricultural or industrial production, or for recreation (Williams and Shaw 1998: 40).

Water resources are of critical importance for tourism. Intensive tourism development, combined with the lifestyle demands of relatively affluent tourists, results in high rates of water use for tourism resorts, hotels, swimming pools and golf courses. Tourism development in areas with limited water resources may result in the over-abstraction of water, water restrictions among local people, and the modification of watercourses and aquifers. Locally, over-abstraction can mean that water must be imported and can cause conflicts between tourism developers and local communities (Holden 2000: 74–5). Similar disputes may arise over other scarce resources as, for example, when local fuel supplies are depleted or when local people are excluded from beaches or other recreational areas in favour of tourists – or even are displaced from their homes to make land available for tourism infrastructure.

Another category of impact – visual or structural change – includes the aesthetic pollution which often accompanies tourism development, especially where this takes place with inadequate planning. Where tourism development occurs with scant regard for local architectural styles, building traditions or the natural landscape, the result has been described as the 'anarchic urbanisation of the coasts' (Burac 1996: 71). Another aspect of visual/structural change includes the social and cultural transformation of places in response to the demands of tourists: the introduction of particular types of businesses (such as bars, casinos and shopping arcades), the adoption of more permissive standards of dress and behaviour, and increases in waste and littering (Holden 2000: 89). Such changes occur partly as a result of the 'demonstration effect' as local people attempt to emulate the leisured behaviour of tourists (Burns 1999: 101).

In addition to the negative environmental impacts of tourism, some positive influences can occur (Table 18.1): the long term economic success of tourism may depend upon maintaining particular standards of environmental stewardship; certain parts of the environment may be ascribed economic values; and some derelict landscapes may become valuable sites for post-industrial regeneration. However, the more positive influences of tourism generally take the form of enhanced protection of environments, habitats and species from yet more damaging economic activities (such as logging or mining) rather than being beneficial for the environment *per se* (Holden 2000: 97). Furthermore, they are probably far outweighed by the negative impacts of tourism development – at least at the local scale – and tourism environmental impacts also frequently contribute to larger environmental impacts. Overall, therefore, tourism development requires careful management and effective environmental planning if natural ecosystems and resources are not to be degraded (Holden 2000: 127).

Several factors exacerbate the environmental impacts of tourism. First, in common with many other economic activities, the external costs of tourism – including its environmental impacts – are often unaccounted for or underestimated. Second, the rapid growth of tourism (4.5 per cent in 2006; UNWTO 2007b) means that those absolute environmental costs are likely to increase significantly. In turn, rapid tourism growth will mean more intensive impacts, or impacts in more locations, or both. Third, the impacts of tourism are highly seasonal in their occurrence, with periods of intensive tourism activity each year (Coccossis 1996: 4–5). Fourth, tourism development is highly concentrated geographically, with marked differences in tourist sources and destinations at scales ranging from the global to the local (Williams and Shaw 1998: 40). Fifth, the strong link between tourism and transport – particularly air transport – and the dependence of the latter on carbon-based fuels means that tourism is inevitably a source of local air pollution, noise nuisance and global climate impacts. All of these factors suggest that the environmental impacts of tourism may increasingly constrain the growth of the industry; achieving sustainable tourism will ultimately require that the industry compensates entirely for the environmental consequences of its growth (WCED 1987: 43).

The environmental impacts of tourism transport are inherently large due to the long distances travelled by many tourists (as on flights from Europe to Australasia) and because of the high volume of traffic (such as the extensive charter operations between northern Europe and the Mediterranean). Recent studies suggest that a substantial proportion of tourism's contribution to climate change arises from air travel (Amelung and Viner 2006: 364; Becken and Patterson 2006: 338; Dubois and Ceron 2006: 400). Dubois and Ceron (2006: 405) argued that transport for tourism is responsible for about 80 per cent of the contribution of tourism to overall global warming potential in France. Amelung and Viner (2006: 364) acknowledged that 'most of the tourism-related greenhouse gas emissions are linked to transport, which is also one of the fastest growing sectors in terms of emissions:

people travel further, more frequently and for shorter periods of time than a few decades ago.' The main implications of this for sustainable development are: (a) ways of uncoupling tourism and transport growth need to be identified (Dubois and Ceron 2006: 410); and (b) in the longer term, the price of a holiday might be determined by how far tourists fly – and could be significantly higher than today.

THE ENVIRONMENTAL IMPACTS OF AIR TRANSPORT

Above, it has been argued that many of the environmental impacts of tourism are due to, or compounded by, air transport: the construction and development of airports, noise, local air pollution and influences on global climate. Conversely, significant demand for air travel is generated by tourism; hence, air transport and tourism are strongly linked and considerable overlap exists between their environmental impacts. In this section, further explanation is provided of the main environmental impacts of air transport, of which the most prominent are global climate impacts, local air pollution, and noise nuisance. The main aviation environmental impacts are listed in Table 18.2.

Global Climate Impacts

Concerns about human impacts on global climate have become prominent in international policy debates and climate change is becoming the most critical environmental issue for many governments, industries, businesses and individuals (Houghton 2004: xxiii). Climate change is a complex environmental issue for several reasons: (a) the complexity of the earth's climate system; (b) the comparative scarcity of scientific data for an adequate time period; (c) the interaction of natural and anthropogenic causes of climate change; (d) the interplay of climate change with other environmental impacts (including stratospheric ozone destruction and acidification) and the difficulty in separating these various issues; (e) the very large spatial and temporal scale of the issue; and (f) the social, cultural and political challenges involved in monitoring and addressing that issue, given the extent to which the global economy is dependent upon carbon-based fuels. Nevertheless, the scientific basis for understanding the nature and likely impacts of climate change is well established and debates now focus on the design and implementation of policies for mitigating and adapting to the effects of climate change. In particular, the emphasis is now on:

- the reduction of greenhouse gas emissions to 1990 levels – especially emissions of CO_2 (the greenhouse gas responsible for the majority of the radiative forcing of climate);

- the stabilisation of global climate, which involves limiting global average temperature rise to 2°C (associated with CO_2 concentrations of about 430 parts per million); and

- the decarbonisation of human economies so that they are less reliant on carbon-based fuels and instead are based on renewable energy sources.

TABLE 18.2   Some environmental impacts of air transport

Area of effect	Impacts	Causes
Global climate change	Emissions of greenhouse gases, particularly carbon dioxide (CO2) Emissions of aerosols, including sulphates Contrail formation Enhanced cirrus cloudiness	Aircraft main engines Auxiliary power units (APUs) Airside ground service vehicles Surface transport to and from airports
Local air pollution	Emissions of nitrogen oxides (NOx) Emissions of particulate matter (PM) Emissions of volatile organic compounds (VOCs)	Aircraft main engines Auxiliary power units (APUs) Airside ground service vehicles Surface transport to and from airports
Noise	Nuisance to residents close to airports and beneath approach/departure routes	Aircraft main engines and airframe Engine testing
Biodiversity	Conversion of land to paved areas or ecological monocultures Habitat destruction Soil and water contamination	Airport infrastructure development Aircraft de-icing
Resource and waste issues	Fossil fuel consumption Water consumption Modification of watercourses and water supplies Soil and water contamination	Airport energy consumption Airport water consumption Airport waste production and disposal

Source: Authors.

These all pose considerable challenges for aviation. Nevertheless, such actions are recommended by the Intergovernmental Panel on Climate Change (IPCC) and progress towards their implementation has commenced (Houghton 2004: 260).

Although presently a relatively small overall contributor to climate change, being responsible for 3–5 per cent of human greenhouse gas emissions, aviation is nevertheless an important polluter, for several reasons. First, the rapid growth of air transport – which is projected to continue until at least 2030 – means that the industry will contribute increasingly to climate change in the future. Second, climate models indicate that the actual climate effects due to aviation could be several times greater than the effects of aviation-derived CO_2 alone (DfT 2003b: 40). This enhanced impact occurs because aircraft create other greenhouse gases in addition to CO_2; because aircraft emissions are injected directly into a climatically-sensitive region of the atmosphere, near to the tropopause; and because other consequences of air transport (such as the formation of contrails and enhanced cirrus cloudiness) are themselves responsible for radiative impacts on climate. The effects of contrails and enhanced cirrus cloudiness caused by aircraft at cruise levels remain an important source of uncertainty in global climate modelling (Rogers *et al.* 2002).

Despite the efforts of some governments to slow or reduce greenhouse gas emissions, aviation impacts are expected to increase significantly until 2030, to the extent that DfT forecasts indicate that UK aviation could be responsible for approximately 25 per cent of UK greenhouse gas emissions by that year (DfT 2003b: 39). It is highly unlikely that this trend will be politically – let alone environmentally – sustainable. The most important implications for tourism are likely to be significant increases in airline operating costs (due to increases in the cost of jet fuel) and a potential reduction in tourism demand if the costs of air travel become too high. For airlines, climate change presents a significant business risk that may most profitably be managed by increasing the rate of fleet renewal and the introduction of advanced technologies and operational practices.

Local Air Pollution

Local air quality in the vicinity of airports is determined by several factors. The major pollution sources are ground transport, aircraft emissions and apron activities (such as the refuelling of aircraft). Aircraft emissions include pollutants emitted by main engines, auxiliary power units (APUs), brakes and tyres, all of which produce significant quantities of particulate matter (PM) that is associated with human respiratory illnesses (DfT 2006b; Rogers *et al.* 2002). Aircraft engines also generate nitrogen oxides (NO_x) which cause respiratory irritation and the acidification of ecosystems. These emissions are compounded by the pollution generated by large fleets of airside ground support vehicles and by the surface transport required to take passengers to and from airports. In terms of human exposure, the importance of airport-related emissions varies between sites depending upon the location of the airport relative to centres of human population.

   Airports are large commercial sites with considerable environmental impacts (A. Graham 2003); their operation is often the most significant source of pollution in a locality. Generally, airport emissions are not directly regulated, but local air quality legislation, nonetheless, has the potential to constrain airport growth either by restricting aircraft movements or road traffic. For example, air quality legislation at Zurich Airport – particularly in relation to NO_x and volatile organic compounds (VOCs) – prompted the introduction of aircraft emissions charges and an aggregate emissions limit for the airport which, if exceeded, requires a mitigation plan to be produced (Unique 2006: 3). Some airport operators are planning to achieve absolute reductions in emissions of local air pollutants – especially from ground vehicles and stationary plant (where reductions can most easily be achieved) – including ensuring that sufficient land is available to develop public transport infrastructure in anticipation of the need to reduce surface traffic emissions.

Aircraft Noise

At the local scale, aircraft noise nuisance usually represents the single most important issue affecting the operation and development of airports – and hence their capacity. Aircraft noise nuisance is a complex issue related to the frequency and sound output of aircraft movements, their timing and predictability, and the location of local populations relative to airports and to their arrival and departure routes. The monitoring and management of aircraft noise have received considerable attention and aircraft and engine manufacturers have made significant technological improvements (Lewis *et al.* 1999). However, these improvements have been offset by the rapid growth in air transport, with the result that most major airports are now subject to operational constraints or capacity limits based on measures of aircraft noise. In many cases, those constraints relate variously to the use of quieter aircraft, night-time curfews or operational limits based on noise budgets or noise contours (DRDNI 2003; Thomas and Lever 2003: 99, 105–6).

The recent history of Amsterdam Schiphol Airport illustrates how aircraft noise issues can severely curtail airport growth. Schiphol Airport is subject to legislative regulation that limits the level of noise exposure permitted in surrounding communities each year; the airport has been designated as a 'fully noise-coordinated airport' since 1998 (Krul 2003: 218). However, despite the development of a sophisticated aircraft noise management and mitigation programme, the airport reached its operational noise limit in November 2000 and (in principle) would have had to cease operations until the end of that year; the impasse was resolved through Dutch parliamentary action. However, it became clear that with existing infrastructure it would be impossible to sustain the growth of the airport in the longer term. Consequently, a fifth runway was constructed to allow aircraft to be routed away from residential areas, thereby releasing additional 'noise capacity' and permitting further growth to 600,000 movements in 2010 (Krul 2003: 219–20). In the UK, many airports – including Heathrow, Gatwick, Stansted, Manchester and Birmingham Airports – are subject to night-time noise constraints and most airports have noise monitoring and management programmes (DfT 2005).

The continuing, rapid growth of air traffic is likely to expose more people to aircraft noise. While the noise of individual aircraft movements has declined, air traffic frequency has increased, with the result that the primary cause of nuisance at some airports is becoming the frequency with which people are over-flown, rather than the disturbance caused by each aircraft. Noise nuisance is also a highly subjective issue related to human perception; tolerance of noise tends to decline with increasing affluence and democratisation. As a result, levels of disturbance that are now considered 'acceptable' in Western societies may not be regarded as acceptable in the future. Therefore, the issue of noise nuisance – and community opposition – around airports is not anticipated to reduce in the future; instead, it can be expected to get worse (DRDNI 2003).

One implication of aircraft noise for tourism is that the development of the industry may rely on the provision of appropriate noise respite: the adoption of policies to alleviate aircraft noise disturbance – either temporally or spatially. Noise respite may be achieved if airport operators and air traffic controllers purposefully attempt to distribute the impacts of aircraft noise more equitably through varying the selection of active runway(s) or by modifying departure and arrival procedures. The aim of noise respite is to provide local residents with some degree of predictability and relief in the scheduling and routing of aircraft movements, so that people can plan their lifestyles (to some extent) in relation to quieter periods. However, many issues remain in designing and implementing effective noise respite policies – and in ensuring that those policies are both equitable and economic.

Biodiversity, Resource and Waste Issues

By their nature, airports require large land areas and create zones that are either hostile to wildlife (paved and built) or are ecological monocultures (mown grassland). However, the areas surrounding airports may be of considerable ecological value, particularly if the airport is located close to a major urban conurbation, as is often the case. The ability of airport operators to extend the airport boundaries or even to build on parts of their land may be curtailed by the ecological value of the habitats threatened. This problem is most acute in parts of Europe, where sites protected by national or international conventions have prevented or restricted airport development. Given the commitments made by many nations at the Rio Earth Summit in 2002 – and Local Agenda 21 commitments – to protect biodiversity, such constraints are likely to become more stringent in the future (Baker 2006: 55–9; UN 2002). Other environmental concerns relate to the resources needed to deliver adequate air passenger services and to provide for the normal operation of airports. Some European airport operators have expressed concerns that they will be unable to ensure adequate and secure supplies of energy and water in the future, for instance. Similarly, forecasts of waste generated at airports suggest that significant additional infrastructure will be required for the handling, processing and transport of waste from and within airports. Waste management, therefore, is another potential constraint of airport growth.

SYNERGIES BETWEEN AVIATION AND TOURISM

The discussion in the preceding sections suggests that the relationship between air transport and tourism is one of substantial overlap: air travel constitutes a significant part of the environmental impact of tourism, while tourism generates considerable demand for air transport. Tourism represents a particular form of consumption, and air transport facilitates such consumption as part of an increasingly globalised economy. Several authors have acknowledged that a reciprocal relationship exists between these two sectors: air transport is important in supporting the growth of the tourism industry; in turn, leisure travel is stimulated by tourism development (Harrison 1995; Williams and Baláž 2000; Williams and Shaw 1998). Furthermore, Button and Nijkamp (1997: 218) argued that internationalisation and the move toward greater globalisation would be impossible without recent technical and structural changes in transport, including aviation.

Some authors have highlighted that the relationship between aviation and tourism is one of high dependency and vulnerability. Shaw and Thomas (2006: 206) reported the view of the UK Government that failure to accommodate air transport growth 'would have serious ramifications for tourism, the finance sector, and other businesses that rely on world markets'. Janelle and Beuthe (1997: 199) drew attention to the dualistic role of transport – including air transport – as a pro-active agent of globalisation and as a beneficiary of its development. Such a view implies that air transport and tourism are currently bound in a cycle that will generate ever-increasing environmental and social impacts unless fundamental changes in their operation and organisation occur. Such dependence also represents a risk to the air transport and tourism industries in an increasingly interconnected market; hence Janelle and Beuthe (1997: 205) argued that globalisation exposes transportation to severe vulnerability, with implications for the economic viability of some air routes and tourism destinations.

One particular aspect of the relationship between air transport and tourism is that it is largely supply-side driven (see B. Graham 1999). The wider availability of affordable air transport – particularly by low fare airlines – can create demand for tourism products in destinations that may be unable to cope with the scale of operations facilitated by modern air transport. Thus the introduction of new services from Auckland to Tonga and Rarotonga, in October and November 2005 respectively, by the low cost carrier, Pacific Blue, resulted in increased pressure on the capacity of local tourism infrastructure and other services at those destinations put considerable pressure on the capacity of local services. The imperative to compete in increasingly global markets may drive tourism operators and airlines to expand more rapidly than their supporting services. Conversely, sudden downturns in the economic performance of airlines – as occurred following the terrorist attacks of September 2001 – may result in route networks being reduced and abrupt contraction of the tourism products that rely on those air services, with consequences for local economies.

Due to the linked nature of aviation and tourism, and the fact that air transport may drive considerable demand for tourism products and generate intensive environmental impacts, some authors have attempted to reconcile air transport and tourism with sustainable development principles. Hence, Gudmundsson and Höjer (1996: 269) emphasised the need to incorporate development principles (increasing well-being and equity) as well as sustainability principles (preserving natural and man-made capital) in transport planning. In general, several authors have acknowledged that fundamental changes in technology, operation, design and financing are needed if air transport and tourism are to become more sustainable (Greene and Wegener 1997: 177; Paterson *et al.* 2006). Above all, the development of these two sectors – being so closely linked – needs to be strategically planned in a coordinated manner in order to ensure that benefits achieved by one sector are not simply absorbed by the other. For instance, the construction of new airport infrastructure to accommodate larger, more efficient aircraft may deliver emissions reductions, but those reductions may be offset by increased surface transport emissions as well as the destruction of pristine habitats. Strategic planning of both tourism and air transport development – based on an effective environmental impact assessment process – is therefore required if overall improvements in sustainability are to occur.

Chapman (2007: 354) has argued that, while there is a tendency to focus on long-term technological solutions to the environmental impacts of transport, short-term behavioural changes are necessary if the benefits of new technology are to be fully realised. These comments are of particular relevance to aviation, since air travel – to a greater extent than other forms of transport – may be regarded as a luxury, at least when it is undertaken for leisure. Furthermore, the options for achieving 'step-changes' in aviation technology are limited in comparison with those that may be achieved in other forms of transport; the use of biofuels, for example, is already feasible for surface vehicles but is still in its infancy for commercial aircraft. Consequently, some commentators focus on encouraging behavioural change amongst consumers in their purchasing decisions about air travel and tourism. Even the assumption that increasing mobility is desirable is itself being challenged, given that equivalent levels of consumer satisfaction might be achieved in other ways (Gudmundsson and Höjer 1996: 269).

Given practical constraints, however – including the need to deliver stable economic growth, the need to safeguard the livelihoods and welfare of those who depend on the air travel and tourism industries, and the need to achieve a return on investments already made in tourism and aviation technologies – few options remain to radically alter the projected course of air transport and tourism development. For both sectors, therefore, responding to the sustainability challenge involves maximising the eco-efficiency of their operations and attempting to use economic instruments to incentivise a basic level of environmental protection. Organisations in sectors now attempt to define, monitor and report their eco-efficiencies using performance indicators, with the result that a large increase in benchmarking and eco-labelling activity has occurred. Achieving improvements in environmental performance now depends upon firmly embedding 'polluter-pays' principles into corporate cultures – and upon providing adequate information to consumers for them to make purchasing decisions that take account of the environmental performance of air transport and tourism companies (Graham and Guyer 1999: 165; Lynes and Dredge 2006: 116).

MEASURES TO MITIGATE AVIATION ENVIRONMENTAL IMPACTS

Various measures are currently used to mitigate aviation environmental impacts; some of these measures are listed in Table 18.3. Technological measures include advances in airframe and engine design, such as the development of low NO_x combustor technology in jet turbine engines. Regulatory and legislative measures include the noise and emissions certification of engines, airport noise restrictions and local air quality standards. Operational measures involve procedures and technologies to optimise the environmental efficiency of flights, such as continuous descent approaches (which dispense with inefficient level segments during the approach to land) and air traffic flow management (which reduces the time that aircraft wait in 'stacks' prior to landing). Planning measures incorporate the management of aviation environmental impacts into land use planning processes, promoting environmental good practice in airport design, and fleet planning based on the environmental performance of aircraft. Economic instruments, including the UK Air Passenger Duty and the EU emissions trading scheme, are also used to mitigate aviation environmental impacts, although the details of their implementation are contested. Environmental management systems and corporate environmental responsibility approaches are also used by some airlines and airports to monitor, audit and report their environmental performance. Finally, community liaison, community development and partnership approaches can reduce or offset the disruption caused to local communities by aviation environmental impacts (Becken and Patterson 2006: 114–5; Moss et al. 1997).

Mitigation measures are hindered by the fact that the interrelationships between aviation environmental impacts are complex and they vary with geographical scale. At the local scale, the precise balance of those impacts depends on the particular circumstances at an airport. While climate change represents the most important environmental impact of air transport at the global scale – and the issue that presents the greatest and most immediate threat to the growth of the industry – local air pollution and noise may be more critical in the vicinity of airports. The management and mitigation of these impacts requires global and local impacts to be evaluated: in particular, climate change, local air pollution and noise need to be carefully balanced. Hence, the management of aircraft environmental impacts requires that trade-offs be made between conflicting impacts. For instance, the design of aircraft engines can be optimised either for NO_x reduction or for better fuel efficiency, but not for both. Another trade-off is made when noise reductions are achieved by routing aircraft away from noise-sensitive areas, thereby requiring longer track routes to be flown and hence greater fuel consumption and emissions. Such a trade-off is made at Belfast City Airport, where a local preference for routing aircraft over Belfast Lough (to avoid over-flying the city at low level) can add significantly to the overall track distances flown. At Cairns International Airport, aircraft departure routes are designed to minimise flight over the city, but aircraft consequently fly over the Great Barrier Reef World Heritage Area (GBRWHA) at low level, dispersing noise and emissions over an important tourism destination. Decisions about overall aviation environmental impacts therefore involve balancing different impacts that are unevenly distributed and that have consequences of varying severity according to their nature and location. This complexity illustrates one aspect of the challenge faced by aviation in addressing the demands of sustainable development and sustainable tourism.

TABLE 18.3 Measures to mitigate aviation environmental impacts

Type of Measure	Improvements	Examples
Technological measures	Airframe improvements Engine improvements Improved navigation and track-keeping performance Improved apron services	Low drag aircraft skin design Low NOx combustors Automatic Dependent Surveillance – Broadcast (ADS-B) technology Fixed electrical ground power (FEGP) provision at airport stands
Regulatory and legislative measures	Noise and emissions certification Local air quality standards Noise limits Carbon dioxide emissions reductions	International Civil Aviation Organisation (ICAO) engine certification UK Air Quality Standards (AQS) UK noise contours and night-time noise quotas Kyoto Protocol targets
Operational measures	Improvements in take-off efficiency Improvements in climb efficiency Improvements in cruise efficiency Improvements in approach efficiency Improvements in landing efficiency Improvements in ground movement efficiency	Reduced thrust take-off procedures Noise abatement departure procedures Noise preferential routes Arrival and departure management Continuous descent approaches (CDA) Low power / low drag (LP/LD) approaches Optimised use of reverse thrust and wheel braking
Planning measures	Improved land use planning Environmental good practice in airport design Fleet planning based on environmental performance	Airport relocation Energy efficient airport infrastructure Fleet upgrades
Economic measures	Environmental taxes Emissions trading Carbon offset	UK Air Passenger Duty EU Emissions Trading Scheme (ETS) Climate Care
Environmental management systems	Integrated environmental management Use of environmental performance indicators	ISO14001
Corporate responsibility approaches	Environmental reporting Environmental auditing	Aircraft eco-labelling
Community approaches	Community liaison Community development Partnership approaches	Sound insulation schemes Education projects Training and work experience opportunities

Source: Authors.

CONCLUSION

In this chapter, the environmental impacts of aviation and tourism have been reviewed and some possibilities for their mitigation have been considered. Tourism results in profound environmental impacts, many of which are attributed to air travel and its associated infrastructure. Air transport also causes considerable environmental impacts and a strong link exists between the two industries. Increasingly, consumers express preferences for more sustainable air travel and tourism; nonetheless, both industries are projected to grow significantly and, for air transport at least, the rate of growth already exceeds the rate of technological and operational improvements. The relationship between aviation and tourism is not simply one of overlap: affordable air transport drives tourism demand and the two industries are mutually-reinforcing, with the result that their environmental impacts are likely to intensify. Hence, the growing impacts of air travel and tourism – which are already unsustainable, at least in their effect on global climate – are projected to worsen unless dramatic improvements in environmental performance are achieved.

Those environmental impacts can be mitigated, at least in part, using a range of measures; but those measures need to be robust and comprehensive if they are to adequately address the challenge of sustainable development, since sustainability requires that the environmental costs of aviation and tourism are fully taken into account. Those measures will probably result in higher average airfares, with significant implications for tourism products and services and for leisure demand. Shorter routes may become preferable to longer ones, since their carbon costs will be less. Higher load factors may be further incentivised, with the result that the most economic routes will be those with the highest traffic volumes. The result may be a greater concentration of air travel on high-value routes between major hub airports, and some marginal tourism destinations may become non-viable as increasing fuel costs and higher airfares put them beyond the affordability of many tourists. Finally, the challenge of sustainable development suggests that both aviation and tourism and require strategic planning and fully integrated environmental management if they are to thrive in an increasingly carbon-constrained world (Hall 1999: 186).

PART VI

Destination Case Studies

19

Brazil

Respicio Espirito Santo Jr.

INTRODUCTION

In terms of contiguous territory Brazil is larger than the United States, with a population of over 180 million. Brazil is a country where air travel is very necessary. Like the United States, Russia, India, China, and Australia, Brazil has continental dimensions (see Map 19.1), which means that road transport is not suitable for linking the majority of State capitals, plus the most visited tourist sites to the five major cities (São Paulo, Rio de Janeiro, Brasília, Belo Horizonte, and Salvador). Moreover, international air transport is needed to bring the many tourists which it receives from the United States and Europe, especially Portugal, Germany and Italy.

This chapter looks at aviation and tourism in Brazil by initially considering the comparative domestic and international passenger flows. It then goes on in detail to discuss some major and important developments which have occurred as regards the Brazilian airline industry in recent years. This is followed by a discussion of tourism trends and an assessment of the importance of aviation to tourism.

THE BRAZILIAN AVIATION MARKETS

The necessity for domestic air transport, combined with economic growth and stability as the result of the Real Plan in 1994, has led to substantial growth rates in domestic traffic since this year. In comparison, international traffic has grown more slowly, particularly as a down-turn was experienced in the early 2000s following the global crisis in long-haul travel as a result of 9/11 (Figure 19.1).

Surveys conducted in 2003–2004 by the former Department of Civil Aviation (DAC), now the National Civil Aviation Agency (ANAC), reveal that more than 70 per cent of the domestic air travel in Brazil is done for business and/or events/congresses purposes and so domestic leisure travel is currently not that important – particularly when compared with international travel. The main buyer of domestic airline tickets is the federal government (the Executive, the Brazilian Congress, and the Judiciary), followed by the government-run organisations (such as Petrobrás, BNDES, Banco do Brasil), the large multinationals, and state/city governments.

Air travel in Brazil is highly concentrated in the Southeast, particularly over São Paulo, Rio de Janeiro, Brasília (in fact the Brazilian capital is located in the Center-West region,

MAP 19.1   Brazil – A continental country

Source: Cartography and Geo-Informatics Laboratory, Geography Department, University of the Aegean, Greece.

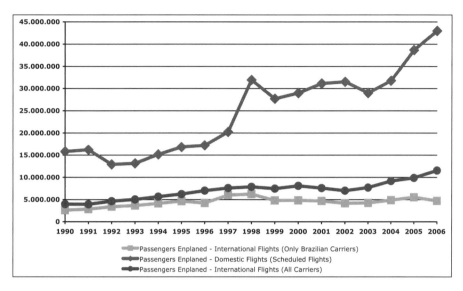

FIGURE 19.1 The Brazilian scheduled passenger market: 1990–2006

Source: Department of Civil Aviation/DAC, now Civil Aviation Agency/ANAC.

but very close to the Minas Gerais border) and Belo Horizonte. Other cities with high volumes of passengers are Salvador and Recife in the Northeast (both cities with a very large leisure tourism activity) plus Porto Alegre and Curitiba in the South (both cities with significant inbound/outbound business, events/congresses, and VFR tourism, plus a substantial outbound leisure travel market). Table 19.1 shows the predominance of the Southeast region in the Brazilian economy. Although the agriculture sector has encouraged a large amount of business travel in recent years, it is the secondary and, most importantly, the tertiary industries that are the greatest generators of the need for travel. Hence, it is the Southeast and the South regions which generate most travel in the country.

Other significant generators for air travel are Brasilia (like any country capital it is a very large generator for inbound/outbound business traffic) and the Northeast (in particular Salvador, Recife, and Fortaleza for inbound traffic). Brasilia has been used by several major carriers in the recent years as a key concentration/distribution node for flights originating in the South/Southeast and arriving in the North/Northeast, and vice-versa. Forecasts produced in late 2004 by the former Department of Civil Aviation (DAC) regarding scheduled passenger growth at the major airports in each region are presented in Table 19.2. In the short-term, domestically the traffic in the Southeast and South regions is expected to continue to grow the most whereas international traffic is forecast to grow at a higher rate in the other regions.

THE BRAZILIAN AIRLINE INDUSTRY

There has been considerable volatility within the Brazilian airline industry in recent years. After the demise of Transbrasil (in late 2001) and VASP (in 2004), there remained three key players, namely VARIG, TAM and Gol. However, with VARIG in continual financial crisis between 2002–2006 (which culminated in its near-collapse in July 2006) TAM and

TABLE 19.1   Brazilian social and political indicators by region (2004)

Region	No. of States	Area (% of Brazil)	GDP (% of Brazil)	GDP Distribution (Per Sector) [%]		
				Primary	Secondary	Tertiary
Southeast	4	10.9	55.2	32.2	60.5	56.3
South	3	6.8	18.6	33.4	18.4	15.7
Northeast	9	18.2	13.9	13.6	12.5	14.5
Center-West	4	18.9	14.3	14.3	3.4	9.2
North	7	45.2	6.5	6.5	5.2	4.3
BRAZIL	27	100	100	100	100	100

Source: Brazilian Institute of Geography and Statistics/IBGE.

TABLE 19.2   Forecasts of scheduled passenger movements by region

Region	DOMESTIC			INTERNATIONAL		
	2010	2015	2025	2010	2015	2025
Southeast	53,416,340	74,042,693	142,019,674	16,323,476	22,140,976	37,091,163
South	14,114,646	19,790,843	38,851,915	690,928	946,624	1,613,107
Northeast	17,589,749	24,990,086	50,374,783	913,864	1,237,926	2,069,257
Center-West	18,076,107	25,027,902	47,914,438	65,330	88,907	149,747
North	6,375,860	8,841,347	16,980,839	153,811	209,037	351,307
BRAZIL	109,572,702	152,692,871	296,141,649	18,147,409	24,623,470	41,274,581
Average annual growth rate (%)						
Southeast	8.93	6.75	6.73	9.28	6.29	5.29
South	8.62	6.99	6.98	9.61	6.50	5.47
Northeast	7.51	7.28	7.26	11.86	6.26	5.27
Center-West	7.46	6.72	6.71	16.53	6.36	5.35
North	8.16	6.76	6.74	11.75	6.33	5.33
BRAZIL	8.36	6.86	7.28	9.45	6.29	5.30

Source: Department of Civil Aviation/DAC, now National Civil Aviation Agency/ANAC.

Gol became the dominant airlines for both domestic and international travel, with the two being responsible for over 87 per cent of all domestic traffic in RPK terms (Figure 19.2). In their duopolistic condition, Gol's advantage over TAM is in terms of higher productivity, lower costs (both unit costs and overall costs), and higher profitability. Both have gone public via IPOs, having good acceptance in both Brazilian and US stock markets.

VARIG re-emerged as "New VARIG" after it was acquired by its former cargo subsidiary VarigLog, along with international and Brazilian investor groups (Volo), in December 2006, and the new airline was expected to regain market-share specifically over TAM and Gol, exactly the ones that drove passengers away from VARIG during its crisis. In February 2007 LAN [Chile] injected more than US$17 million in the New VARIG, while opening conversations with the Brazilian and U.S. groups that rescued the carrier from bankruptcy, so it could participate more closely in the airline's operations and management strategies. Although a more intimate link between New VARIG and LAN was expected for 2007, on March 28th Gol announced that it had officially acquired the New VARIG for approximately US$ 320 million, thus pushing aside any further actions by LAN. One day later Gol stated that the New VARIG would function as a higher service level arm of the group, mainly in terms of on-board service and cabin layout (a two-class configuration for New VARIG aircraft will most probably be exercised for domestic routes in the future).

Newcomers in the scheduled domestic market like BRA (which operated for several years as a VARIG partner for charter flights), OceanAir, and Webjet are extremely important to secure any sort of real market competition for Brazilian travelers. In May 2007 BRA and OceanAir announced a broad all-domestic network alliance, starting June 18th. One of the main points behind this alliance is not only to build market-share but, most of all, to try and guarantee the survival of both carriers in the short/medium term.

In recent years the level of air fares in Brazil has been substantially reduced. Fare wars between the major carriers are not new, but since 2001, when Gol entered the market with a low-cost/low-fare approach, the intensity of price competition significantly increased.

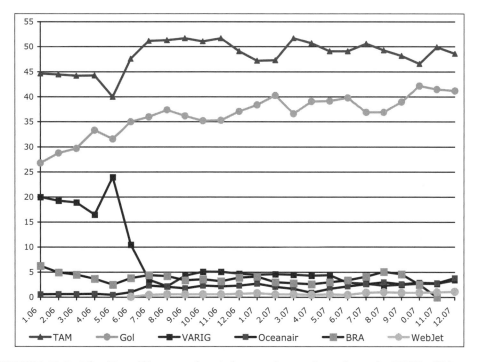

FIGURE 19.2 The Brazilian carriers' domestic market share in RPKs (%):
January 2006 to December 2007

Source: Department of Civil Aviation, now National Civil Aviation Agency.

Originally Gol had relatively low fares but nowadays travellers can often get better deals from the newcomers such as Webjet, OceanAir, and BRA. Sometimes even TAM offers a better deal in terms of price and convenience (i.e. schedule and/or direct flights) than Gol. In an investigation undertaken in July 2006, not only was Gol not the lowest-fare carrier, but on the contrary, it was close to being the highest fare player in both markets examined (Table 19.3). Indeed, if Oceanair's way to go from Rio de Janeiro to Porto Alegre through the Sao-Paulo-Congonhas busy airport is ignored, Gol had the highest fare of all in the GIG-POA flights under the conditions presented. Moreover, it had the second highest fare for the GIG-SSA route, only surpassed by BRA, another self-acclaimed low-cost/low-fare carrier (which, however, ceased operations in November 2007).

With regard to competition from the car and bus/coach, Brazil has traditionally had a very strong medium- and long-range bus network, in spite of its vast size. This is primarily because the majority of its population has low income. For example in 2003, more than 75 per cent of all Brazilian families had an average monthly income of less than 1,500 Euros per month (Brazilian Institute of Geography and Statistics (IBGE, 2007). Therefore travelling by bus, even on long distances, was the norm until the airlines entered a more vigorous competitive era in the mid-90s which produced a shift to air. This shift was further encouraged after Gol entered the market which prompted more fare wars. More recently and more importantly, the Brazilian middle-class has become more numerous and with more purchasing power, particularly as the government has lowered interest

TABLE 19.3   Lowest web-fares published by major carriers (July/2006): Rio-Porto Alegre (GIG-POA) & Rio-Salvador (GIG-SSA) one-way (July 10) and roundtrip flights (July 10–20)

Flight	Carrier	One-way lowest webfare	Roundtrip lowest webfare
GIG–POA	Gol	R$340.00	R$680.00
GIG–POA	TAM	R$199.50	R$629.00
GIG–POA	VARIG	R$199.00	R$398.00
GIG–POA	BRA	R$219.00	R$438.00
GIG–POA	Oceanair	R$1,002.00	R$1,934.00
GIG–POA	WebJet	R$215.00	R$430.00
GIG–SSA	Gol	R$247.00	R$494.00
GIG–SSA	TAM	R$159.50	R$319.00
GIG–SSA	VARIG	R$189.00	R$378.00
GIG–SSA	BRA	R$359.00	R$718.00
GIG–SSA	Oceanair	R$190.00	R$340.00
GIG–SSA	WebJet	R$153.00	R$306.00

Conditions set for the investigation: (1) Web fares as published by the airlines' websites June 1st, 2006 for planned one-way flights July 10, and roundtrip flights July 10–20, 2006; (2) Lowest web fares represent the cheapest fares published in the websites for the flights and conditions herein mentioned; (3) Search made as a leisure traveler with time to spend, but price-sensitive; (4) Oceanair flight GIG-POA via São Paulo downtown airport, then only the lowest fare for this option was picked; (5) All fares exclude passenger terminal charges (enplaning taxes, in Brazil).

rates and the banks have started to multiply the credit opportunities available to the lower middle-class and the high-end of the less rich. All this, combined with carefully targeted price promotions aimed at this segment from the airlines, and the use of easy paying options by credit cards, has produced a further shift from medium-to-long distance bus travel to air travel. Boeing (2006) reported how in the case of the Rio de Janeiro-São Paulo and São Paulo-Curitiba routes, journey time could be reduced from six hours to one hour with a shift to air, with only a slight increase in one way fares from around US$20–30 to US$30–40. For the longer routes of Belo Horizonte-Salvador and Rio de Janeiro-Salvador, savings in journey time could be greater (23–24 hours to 2 hours) and in fact the air fares at around US$ 80–90 could be marginally cheaper as well.

In terms of opportunities there is still much scope for future growth, particularly as there is some unexplored potential in the markets to/from Rio de Janeiro, as well as other specific links to/from cities now being served only by TAM and/or Gol. TAM has relatively high prices plus a far from immaculate safety record, whereas Gol's extremely fast growth has resulted in it losing its caring, charismatic and sympathetic appeal. Combining these facts with actual price searches shown in Table 19.4 suggests that there is ample room for a distinguished, customer-focused, value-proposition carrier to enter a Rio de Janeiro-based market. Up to the present moment neither BRA nor OceanAir fit in this profile, since neither is based in Rio or is focusing to being recognised as a distinguished, customer-focused, value-proposition carrier. As regards the New VARIG, even after it was acquired by Gol, and with the later stating that a higher on-board service could be expected for the acquired carrier, it is still not likely that it will fit in the role of the distinguished, customer-focused, value-proposition carrier. Moreover, since mid-2007 there appears to be a growing political will to raise the foreign ownership and control limit on Brazilian carriers from the current 20 per cent to 49 per cent, which could further encourage the setting up of a new strong and innovative Rio de Janeiro-based carrier.

INTERNATIONAL TOURISM

Brazil is geographically located far away from the main air travel axis – all three being located in the north hemisphere (Europe–North America, North America–Asia-Pacific, and Europe–Asia-Pacific) – and so incoming and outgoing tourists heavily depend on air transport. Within the states of Rio de Janeiro (where the city of Rio is located) and São Paulo (where the largest economic engine, the most important and most populated city of São Paulo is located), air transport has been responsible for an average of 98 per cent and 99 per cent of foreign tourist arrivals, respectively, in the last five years (Embratur, 2007).

International tourist arrivals have increased overall since 1996 albeit that the numbers reduced in the early 2000s because of the crisis in long-haul travel after 9/11. (Figure 19.3). Ten countries account for around three quarters of tourist arrivals. These are Argentina, the United States, Portugal, Italy, Uruguay, Germany, France, Spain, Paraguay, and Great Britain. Their share of arrivals has remained relatively constant in recent years (e.g 74.7 per cent in 2004; 73.6 per cent in 2005; 73.1 per cent in 2006) (Embratur; 2007).

As regards arrivals by air, Table 19.4 shows the importance of air transport for international tourism in Brazil. The increased dependence on air, from 50 per cent in 1999 to 73 per cent in 2006 is mostly explained by the large number of Argentineans entering Brazil via highways back in 1999 and the more recent trend towards using airlines, since is much more cheaper to fly from Buenos Aires to São Paulo, Rio or Salvador than is to go by

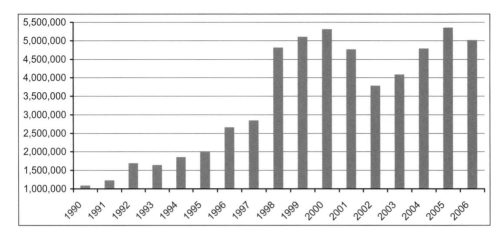

FIGURE 19.3 International tourist arrivals to Brazil: 1990–2006
Source: EMBRATUR (Brazilian Institute of Tourism), Ministry of Tourism.

TABLE 19.4   International tourists arrivals by mode of transport: 1999–2006

	Air	%	Sea	%	Road & Rail	%	River	%
1999	533,621	50	78,520	2	2,445,947	48	49,081	1
2000	2,723,029	51	121,148	2	2,429,301	46	39,985	1
2001	2,960,304	62	109,372	2	1,677,821	35	25,078	1
2002	2,634,670	70	95,781	3	1,040,459	28	12,490	≈0
2003	3,083,143	75	40,746	1	993,061	24	15,897	≈0
2004	3,568,777	74	53,593	1	1,150,610	24	20,723	≈0
2005	3,938,063	73	80,362	1	1,314,143	25	25,602	≈0
2006	3,680,095	73	88,261	2	1,215,780	24	34,855	1

Source: EMBRATUR (Brazilian Institute of Tourism), Ministry of Tourism.
Note: Data is rounded to the nearest whole numbers.

bus or car. However there are some Argentineans, who have bought summer homes in the Southern Brazilian states' beaches, and who still prefer to travel by car for their vacations in Brazil. This number tends to increase when the economic conditions in Argentina are favourable.

RIO DE JANEIRO: THE MOST VISITED CITY IN BRAZIL

In the last 20 or more years, Rio has been the mostly visited city in the country. Brazil received 5.4 million tourists in 2005; of these, nearly 1.9 million visited Rio. The main countries sending tourists to Rio are the United States (22 per cent), Argentina (12 per cent), Portugal (8 per cent), and France (6 per cent). Also, in 2005 more than 5 million domestic tourists visited Rio. These Brazilian visitors together with the 1.9 million foreigners, doubled the Rio annual population. In terms of origins of the domestic visitors, most were generated in São Paulo (26 per cent) followed by Minas Gerais (18 per cent), Rio Grande do Sul (5 per cent), Bahia (3 per cent), and Paraná (3 per cent) (Embratur, 2007).

Due to the high concentration by major Brazilian carriers in São Paulo Congonhas (the downtown airport) and Guarulhos (the international airport), this city is already very well served in terms of point-to-point air links. However, any minor event at either São Paulo airport generates a chain reaction throughout the entire network of all carriers relying directly on these facilities for quasi-hub operations. This means that all carriers (except Webjet) are significantly dependent on both Congonhas and Guarulhos for arriving, connecting, and departuring flights. As a result of this, Galeão/Tom Jobim International Airport in Rio is far from being a congested facility and also does not seem to be a target in the near future for a major carrier to establish a hub or quasi-hub operation. Moreover in June 2007, the only Rio de Janeiro-based airline operating large aircraft – WebJet – was acquired by the mega-tourism operator group CVC, based in São Paulo. Since the airline will be realigning its business plan under the new owner, at the time of writing it was unclear if it would continue to be home-based in Rio or move to São Paulo.

CONCLUSIONS

As a country with continental dimensions, domestically Brazil has to rely heavily on air transport. However, because its middle-class' average income is still low if compared to the developed nations, Brazil still has a small volume of passengers travelling by air compared to its population. Therefore, it is certain that there is much more room to grow in terms of domestic tourists being moved by air, the number of airlines, the cities served, and generally in terms of more opportunities for new entrants to capture underdeveloped markets.

With the growth that has occurred with domestic air flows in recent years, it was not really a "Gol effect" (paraphrasing the "Southwest effect" in the US during the 80s and 90s) that grew the numbers and neither was it a consistent growth of the Brazilian economy. Instead, it was more due to the huge credit given by financial institutions and the marketing done by the airlines. Internationally, the high dependence of international tourists on air transport has meant that tourism growth has increased the international air traffic, with the precise impact being very much influenced by the tourist flows from Argentina, which is Brazil's largest market.

20

India

John F. O'Connell

INTRODUCTION

India, home to one-sixth of the world's population, has recently been in the midst of an economic transformation – its GDP growth rate surged by 120 per cent over the years 2002 to 2006. India is now the fourth largest and second fastest growing economy in the world, while the Airbus Global Market Forecast (2004–2023) claimed that both China and India are set to become the world's largest consumer markets within the next 25 years with a combined purchasing power five times greater than that of the US today. Its information technology sector is the engine that is driving its economic boom. Tripathi (2006) pointed out that the revenue from the IT sector grew from US$5 billion in 1997–1998 (1.2 per cent of GDP) to over US$28 billion by 2004–2005 (4.1 per cent of GDP) and is expected to reach 7 per cent of GDP in 2008 when IT exports are expected to produce 35 per cent of India's total exports.

In addition, India is also leading the globe in call centres and outsourcing activities as cheap labour rates and well educated English speaking Indians have attracted some of the world's leading Fortune 500 companies. For example IBM, GE and HSBC Banks all set up Indian operations employing 60,000, 12,000 and 10,000 respectively by 2006 (Dossani and Kenny, 2007). Pfannenstein and Tsai (2004) have calculated that the US banking industry, for example, saved between $6 billion to $8 billion annually by outsourcing to India – this acts as a solid platform for other companies considering outsourcing their activities and will have a considerable knock-on economic impact for India. Consequently, this strong economic activity has transformed the social classes and there are now around 300 million middle class Indians, growing by 30 million each year. These middle classes have a much higher disposable income ($13,000 per year) relative to the previous generation and their per capita incomes are growing at around 5 per cent per annum. The economic boom has spread to India's tourism as Tretheway and Mak (2006) stated that tourism expenditure in India is growing at the rate of 10–12 per cent per year, while spending on tourism by Indians has now exceed $1 billion per annum.

Given this background, this chapter aims to explore aviation and tourism issues in India by first examining how these relatively stagnant sectors of a few years ago are now going through a period of rapid change. It begins by looking at aviation developments related to the domestic market and then the international market. This is followed by a discussion of the consequences for airport development. Finally, the implications of these major aviation changes on the tourism industry are assessed.

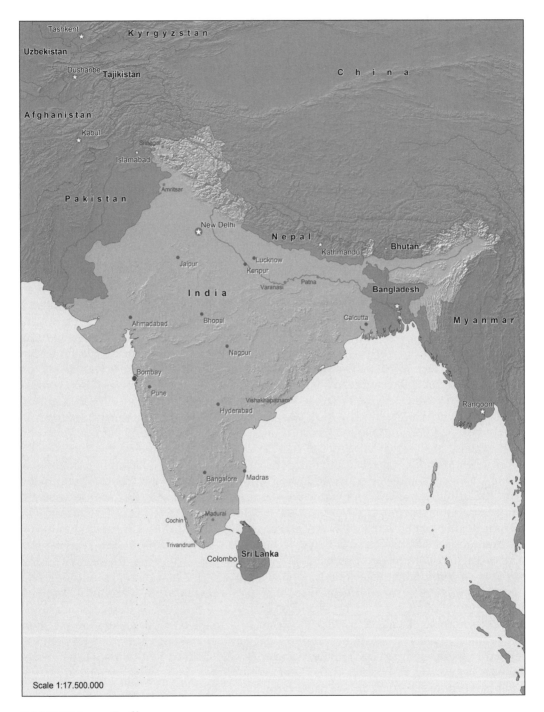

MAP 20.1   India

Source: Cartography and Geo-Informatics Laboratory, Geography Department, University of the Aegean, Greece.

INDIA'S AIR PASSENGER MARKETS

The Historical Situation

India's aviation sector had been stagnant for decades. O'Connell (2005) showed that the number of commercial aircraft operating in India had remained basically the same since 1948, with only 170 aircraft registered by 2004. Less than 1 per cent of India's population travel by air each year – while 14 million people relied daily on the cheaper, but outdated 150-year old railway system. In 2003, Indian carriers transported 14.7 million domestic passengers, roughly equal to five days demand in the US. The propensity for air travel in India is currently 0.1 trips per person per year, a fraction of the global average of 2.0. Ionides (2003) pointed out that one of the principal reasons for India's stagnant air transport industry was because domestic fares were 23–30 per cent higher than domestic fares in other countries for a comparable distance. Incoming tourism had also remained sluggish for years due to the government's inadequate aviation policy and its short-sightedness regarding the country's tourism potential.

O'Connell and Williams (2006) suggested that there were two principal reasons that constrained India's aviation market: the bureaucratic environment and its tight regulatory control. Saraswati (2001) stated that India's political and bureaucratic interference made management ineffective on critical airline decisions such as operations, finance and staffing. The lack of investment, excessive taxation, ownership restrictions and a very restrictive regulatory practice had taken a toll on India's airlines. Its airport infrastructure was equally inadequate, furthered by the fact that no new airport could be built within 150 km of an existing one. In essence, India's economic reformation was being constrained by its obsolete aviation policies which urgently needed overhauling.

India enacted a new aviation policy to allow air travel to grow and become synchronised with India's economic prosperity. O'Connell's and Williams' (2006) research found that the Ministry of Civil Aviation published a landmark document in 2003, entitled the 'Naresh Chandra', which became the road map to the reformation of India's outdated aviation policy. Around the same time, a liberal thinking Civil Aviation Minster, Praful Patel, was appointed to oversee the way forward and forever change the outdated policies that had hindered India's aviation industry. The report produced a comprehensive set of revisions to the archaic legislation and provided the foundation for deregulating India's aviation sector. Within a short time period, India, along with China, became the world's newest bright-spot in global aviation and is quickly becoming one of the world's most dynamic markets.

Table 20.1 shows India's domestic and international passenger growth over the period 1999–2007. It clearly illustrates that passenger traffic had stagnated up until 2002, but thereafter it showed exceptional growth, with the domestic market in particular expanding exponentially – it increased by 10 million passengers between 2005 and 2006, registering 28 per cent growth against a global average of just 5.9 per cent.

The Increase in India's Domestic Traffic

Up to 2003 there were four airlines operating in the Indian domestic market – namely state owned Air India and Indian Airlines together with privately owned Jet Airways and

TABLE 20.1   India's passenger growth 1999–2007

	International		Domestic		Total	
	Number of Passengers (millions)	% Increase	Number of Passengers (millions)	% Increase	Number of Passengers (millions)	% Increase
1999–00	13.3	2.9%	25.7	6.9%	39.0	5.5%
2000–01	14.0	5.4%	28.0	8.8%	42.0	7.7%
2001–02	13.6	-2.7%	26.3	-5.9%	39.9	-4.9%
2002–03	14.8	8.8%	28.9	9.6%	43.7	9.4%
2003–04	16.6	12.3%	32.0	10.9%	48.6	11.4%
2004–05	19.4	17.0%	40.1	25.0%	59.5	22.3%
2005–06	22.3	15.1%	50.9	27.9%	73.3	23.7%
2006–07E	25.5	14.4%	69.8	36.8%	95.3	30.0%

Source: Airports Authority of India.

Air Sahara. Air India is India's flag carrier and largely operates on international sectors, while Indian Airlines operates the domestic routes. Indian Airlines is one of the world's largest domestic carriers, operating to both domestic and regional destinations, and it carried 8.3 million passengers in 2006, 75 per cent of which were domestic, with 56 aging narrowbody aircraft together with 3 widebodies. However, Indian Airlines' market share has fallen dramatically from 52.3 per cent in 1997 to 23.1 per cent by 2006 (Directorate General of Civil Aviation, 2005–06). It's consistently falling market share is attributable to the surge of new carriers that entered the market when deregulation allowed the market to open. Table 20.2 shows the market share of the various carriers operating in the domestic market by 2006.

The inefficiency of Indian Airlines is apparent on analysis of their staff/aircraft ratio as the carrier employs 19,500 staff, which equates to around 414 employees per aircraft (125 or fewer is a typical Western equivalent for a full service carrier). In addition, the media within India have widely publicised that Indian Airlines ranks towards the low end of the scale in relation to customer service, reliability and on-time performance. Moreover, O'Connell and Williams (2006) pointed out that it did not meet the expectations of either leisure and business class passengers. To gain critical mass, Air India and Indian Airlines merged in 2007 under the name of 'Air India' – the joint partnership would allow a thoroughfare between a readymade international network and a vast domestic one, and this would generate extensive economies of scope. In 2006, Air India placed the largest ever order by an Indian airline for 68 Boeing aircraft with a list price of $11.6bn, while Indian Airlines has 43 aircraft on order. The merger will allow the state owned airlines to become a formidable challenger in the Indian market: Aviation Strategy (2007b) stated that the consolidated airline will control 70 per cent of the airport slots at Mumbai and New Delhi airports, which are India's largest and most important gateways, while its 'Air India' brand will allow it to retain its strong international identity.

Jet Airways and Air Sahara are two of India's oldest operating private full service airlines. Jet Airways carried 10.7 million passengers with 61 aircraft in 2006, while Air

TABLE 20.2   Indian domestic market share (2006)

	Jet Airways	Indian Airlines	Air Deccan	Air Sahara	Kingfisher	Spice Jet	Go Air	IndiGo	Paramount
Market share	31.2%	21.5%	18.2%	8.8%	8.7%	6.9%	2.7%	1.3%	0.7%

Source: Directorate General of Civil Aviation, 2006.

Sahara transported over 3 million with 21 aircraft over the same period. The majority of these passengers (around 95 per cent) were transported domestically. Jet Airways had the distinction of being repeatedly judged India's 'Best Domestic Airline' and has won several national and international awards. Despite its reputation as a quality carrier, Jet Airways market share fell from 44 per cent to 31.2 per cent between 2003–04 and 2005–06 (Directorate General of Civil Aviation, 2005–06) reflecting the level of competition that now exists within the Indian market. To ensure that Jet will maintain its market leadership within India, it has agreed to purchase Air Sahara (after a revised bid) for $327 million. Air Sahara will be rebranded as JetLite and will be used primarily to feed domestic traffic to Jet Aiways' hubs. The consolidated airline will have almost 40 per cent of India's domestic market, thereby positioning it as India's strongest carrier.

Air Deccan, India's first low cost carrier, began operations in August 2003 with four turbo-prop ATR-42 aircraft and, by mid 2007 it operated 39 aircraft (19 A320s and 20 ATRs) carrying 5.8 million passengers, up 68 per cent over 2005. This pioneering budget airline is strategically based at Bangalore, the centre of the booming IT industry. It has quickly captured market share – it had 10 per cent of the market by mid-2005 and, just two years later, it had secured over 18 per cent. O'Connell and Williams (2006) provide an explanation for its rapid growth: their research showed that Air Deccan sells around half of their fares at rates that are 50 per cent below the regular fare, while the remaining fares are priced at 25–40 per cent lower. In addition, Air Deccan sells 1000 tickets every month for one Rupee[1], with the next block of tickets sold at Rs 500 plus taxes, and this strategy drives awareness and brand image. Air Deccan aims to target passengers travelling by rail and it has been closing the gap between air and rail fares, while taking a fraction of the time to reach the destination, as shown below in Table 20.3. The potential is enormous – Indian Railways reported that it transported around 5.7 billion people in 2005–06 and, even if only 5 per cent of this traffic decides to take an aircraft, it will represent an additional 220 million air passengers (Indian Railways, 2007). By 2011, Air Deccan will receive an additional 90 aircraft as it acknowledges the growth opportunities that exist.

One of the most startling new entrants to the Indian market is Kingfisher, a full service airline which commenced operations in May 2005. It holds the status of having the strongest brand in India and is a wholly-owned subsidiary of United Breweries Holdings. Few start-up airlines have the financial capability to order 84 aircraft within 18 months of operation, as seen below in Table 20.4. It has continued to set a trailblazing pace by ordering a further 50 Airbus at the 2007 Paris air show (15 A350-800s, 10 A330-200s, 5 A340-500s and 20 A320-family jets). Kingfisher strongly differentiates itself from the other carriers via its superior inflight products: it offers a multi-channel, in-flight entertainment system installed at every seat, hot meals, model-like fashionable cabin crew and pre-assigned

---

1   One Rupee equals US$0.02 cents (Natwest bank London, July 30th 2007)

TABLE 20.3   Fare comparison of selected rail and airline routes in India (Indian Rupees)

Sector	Rail Fare (return)		Air Deccan fare (return)			
	2nd AC Sleeper[†]	Journey Time	2 Months	1 Month	3 Days	Journey Time
Delhi–Mumbai	4,100	17 hours	4,256	5452	6448	1 hr. 45 min
Delhi–Bangalore	5,700	35 hours	6,656	8,248	9,648	2 hr. 30 min
Mumbai–Bangalore	3,000	23 hours	3,656	4,952	5,448	1 hr. 35 min

[†] second class air conditioned sleeping carriage.

Source: Indian Railways and Air Deccan website.

seating. It has garnered numerous awards in the past 18 months including the "Best New Airline of the Year" award in the Asia-Pacific and Middle East region from the Center for Asia Pacific Aviation, "Service Excellence for a New Airline" award from Skytrax, and the "Best New Domestic Airline for Excellent Services and Cuisine" award from Pacific Area Travel Writers Association. The carrier gained almost 9 per cent of the domestic market in only 18 months and is also consolidating the market by purchasing 26 per cent of Air Deccan in June 2007 for $136 million with the aim of purchasing it outright at a later date – which will enable Kingfisher to become India's third dominant airline (ATI, 2007b).

Altogether, there were 12 airlines competing in the domestic market by 2007 including a new low cost carrier startup, called Indigo, which unexpectedly placed an order for 100 narrowbody aircraft at the 2005 Paris air show. Table 20.4 shows that India is set to change beyond recognition as there were 480 aircraft on order by the start of 2007, which is a record number of aircraft to be delivered to one country. Moreover, according to OAG (June 2007), there was a 25 per cent increase in the number of Indian based flights scheduled for May 2007 compared with the same month in the previous year. This represented an additional 8,631 flights or 1.7 million extra seats. Low cost carriers represented 62 per cent of the increase. Orient Aviation (2006) outlines that eight additional airlines are proposing to launch operations within the next two years, which include Magic Air, Yamuna Airlines, Visa, AirOne, InterGlobe, Paramount, Indus Air and Skylark, and the Travel Agents Association of India (TAAI) have estimated that around 20 airlines will be operating in India by the end of the decade.

The Increase in India's International Traffic

India's international operations had also stagnated and needed urgent rejuvenation. Up until 2003, Air India was the country's principal flag carrier. It operated the international sectors with just 27 widebody aircraft and its domestic flights formed part of its international services. Its fleet had an average age of more than 16 years and the bureaucracy at Government level curtailed ordering new aircraft as state owned airlines had to wait ten years after submitting applications to purchase aircraft before approval was granted. Due to a capacity shortfall, Air India could only serve 19 out of a possible 96 international destinations (Aviation Strategy, 2001). Subsequently, for the past few years Air India has

TABLE 20.4 The fleet size of India's major airlines and the fleet on order (January, 2007)

Airline		Current Fleet		Fleet on order
Indian	73	A300/A320/A319/B737 ATR42/DO228	43	A321/320/319
Jet Airways	58	B737/A340/A330/ATR72	40	B777/B737/A330
Air India	45	B747/B777/B737	68	B787/B777/B737
Air Deccan	39	A320/ATR	90	A320/ATR
Air Sahara	28	B767/B737/CRJ	10	B737
Kingfisher	22	A320/A319/ATR72	84	A380/A350/A330/A321 A320/A319/ATR
Spicejet	9	B737	20	737
Go Air	7	A320	20	A320
Indigo	5	A320	95	A321/A320
Paramount	5	ERJ	10	ERJ
Total	**292**		**480**	

Source: Centre of Asia Pacific Aviation, Air Transport Intelligence, Companies.

been steadily losing passengers to international airlines such as British Airways, KLM, Emirates, Qatar Airways, Etihad, Gulf Air and Singapore Airlines. Air India's share of outbound traffic from India had come down to just 20 per cent from 40 per cent in the 1970s due primarily to capacity shortfalls. Indian Airlines was designated as a secondary carrier on many of the international routes to South East Asia and the Middle East but was restricted from operating to Europe and the US due to capacity shortfalls. Consequently, it had only 10.1 per cent of the international market share by 2003–04, and, like Air India, was steadily losing market share (Directorate General of Civil Aviation, 2003–04).

Thus, Air India and Indian Airlines were forced to give some of their unused seat capacity (47,000 seats) to foreign carriers, which showed the first signs that India's International market was finally beginning to open (O'Connell, 2005). In 2004, India initiated a limited five month 'open skies' policy from November 2004 through to March 2005 whereby it granted an additional 275,000 seats to foreign carriers in order to boost international arrivals and make up some of the capacity shortfall that India's state carriers were unable to fill, of which 65 per cent came from the Gulf based carriers. Qatar Airways, for example, almost tripled its frequencies to India during the limited open skies policy from 19 flights per week to 51 – a 168 per cent increase (ATI, 2005).

However, regulatory constraints imposed by India restrict the traffic between India and the Gulf in order to protect its state owned airlines which were not able to compete commercially with the Arabian Gulf based carriers. Part of the master plan of the Gulf based airlines is to amass market share in nearby India by feeding passenger traffic through their respective hubs in the Gulf via fifth freedom traffic rights, taking advantage of India's growing middle class and strengthening economy. Emirates is considering configuring an all-economy class version to some of its 45 A380s, especially for the Indian market because of its enormous potential (Clark, 2007). Air India responded to the threat of the Gulf carriers by setting up a low cost carrier subsidiary, called Air India Express, in early 2005 connecting 10 Indian Cities with 8 major cities in the Arabian Gulf and offering a cheaper travel alternative to the 2.4 million Indian residents that live in the region.

India is set to permanently change the dynamics of its international regulatory framework. It signed an open skies agreement with the US in March 2005 and Air India plans to increase its services to the US from 28 to 37 per week, serving New York, Chicago and Los Angeles, and will add new destinations, such as San Francisco, Washington and Houston, when new aircraft begin arriving. US carriers have also taken advantage of the open skies policy between the US and India as Delta commenced daily services from New York to Chennai; Continental Airlines links New York to New Delhi; American Airlines connects New Delhi to Chicago, while Northwest operates to Mumbai via Amsterdam. This will significantly boost the annual 1.5 million passengers that had previously travelled between India and the US, positively impacting tourism. India has also completely overhauled its bilateral agreement with the UK by allowing 56 weekly services to foreign airlines linking London Heathrow to Mumbai and Delhi, up from 19 from just two years earlier. It also extended the bilateral to allow UK carriers to serve the Silicon Valley of India that included 14 flights a week to Bangalore and Chennai, while at the same time allowing a daily service from the UK to any other destination in India. Virgin Atlantic, British Midland and Jet Airways joined Air India and British Airways with direct connections to India, and by 2006 there were 121 non-stop frequencies between the UK and India – up from 34 just two years earlier. The landmark bilateral also removed the restrictive controls on pricing that had hindered competition: fares have plunged with return tickets from Mumbai to London costing only $300, while return fares to Singapore are $240 and the yield decline is further exacerbated by the Arab based airlines which are likewise cutting fares.

The opening up of India's skies has triggered Jet Airways to order a large number of long-range aircraft (10 777s and 10 A330s) and it is now priming itself to become a key international operator. Currently, Jet Airways operates to Colombo, Kathmandu, London Heathrow, Kuala Lumpur, Singapore and Bangkok, and it inaugurates services to New York via Brussels from August 2007, followed by services to San Francisco via Shanghai a few months later. As long-haul capacity increases, Jet will expand onto other destinations, such as the Arabian Gulf, South Africa, Kenya and Mauritius, and include more UK based cities (Jet Airways, 2007). However, the other domestic airlines that currently operate in India (i.e. Kingfisher, SpiceJet, Go Air, IndiGo, Paramount, etc) must operate for a period of five years before being allowed to fly internationally, thus confining the recent surge of domestic airlines to operations within India's borders. However, speculation is now ripe in India's aviation circles that this five year law will be amended shortly to allow all carriers access to international routes, regardless of their operating history (ATI, 2007c; Aviation Strategy 2007b). This would instantly trigger an explosion of international traffic to India, completely transforming the aviation landscape and its tourism profile.

THE RESHAPING OF INDIA'S AIRPORTS

Inadequate airport infrastructure has remained problematic for India's growing airlines as they have not been able to cope with the continuous increase in air traffic. The problems include: an inadequate number of runways and taxiways; insufficient number of aircraft parking bays making passenger handling very difficult; and shortage of ground handling equipment. Also, outdated air traffic control equipment and staff shortages reduce the number of aircraft movements to 35 per hour, while many of their western counterparts allow for 60 movements per hour. Many of India's primary airports, such as Mumbai, New Delhi, Kolkata, Bangalore, and Hyderabad, are close to saturation. New Delhi airport, for example, had a passenger throughput of almost 10 million passengers in 2003 – just three years later this figure had doubled, straining the infrastructure and way beyond its design limitations. It is typical for aircraft to circle for up to one hour at these airports before getting landing clearance because of their infrastructural constraints, which forces airlines to carry extra fuel – significantly adding to their cost structure. In addition, about one-third of all aircraft must wait at least 15 to 20 minutes after landing to proceed to the terminal due to ground congestion and insufficient gates (Airports International, 2007). In response, several of the privately owned airlines have applied a $3.40 air traffic congestion surcharge per ticket because of the worsening conditions with the aim of pressurising the government into acting quickly to resolve the issue (ATI, 2006).

The Indian government, however, is beginning to respond to the airport crisis and is planning to invest US$9 billion to upgrade and modernise some of the countries airports. The Naresh Chandra liberalisation roadmap allows the Airport Authority of India to form joint ventures with foreign multinationals, which will allow them to invest up to 74 per cent of the required equity, while Airport Authority of India (AAI) will retain a 26 per cent interest. New Delhi is constructing a third runway together with domestic and international terminals, while its existing terminals are also being expanded. It will have a throughput of around 50 million passengers a year and will be fully operational by 2010, at a cost of $2.5 billion. Plans for Mumbai airport are two-fold as the existing airport is getting new terminals and a third new runway. A new airport is also being constructed and it will be equipped with two runways accommodating 40 million passengers by 2011 – this will ease the strain on the existing airport (ATI, 2007c).

The AAI is also modernising and expanding Kolkata airport (formerly known as Calcutta) by installing a third runway, new terminals, aerobridges, cargo facilities, aircraft parking bays, etc. at a cost of $230 million. New greenfield airports are also being constructed at Bangalore and Hyderabad (known as the Silicon Valley of India), funded by overseas investors at a cost of $428 million and $390 million respectively, and will be operational by mid 2008. The AAI is also extending its investment to its smaller airports in more diverse parts of the country and plans to modernise 35 non-metro airports at an estimated cost of around $1.04 billion by 2011. These 35 airports are located in Ahmedabad, Amristar, Guwahati, Jipur, Udaipur, Trivandrum, Lucknow, Goa, Madurai, Mangalore, Agatti, Aurangabad, Khajuraho, Rajkot, Vadodara, Bhopal, Indore, Nagpur, Vishakapatnam, Trichy, Bhubaneswar, Coimbatore, Patna, Port Blair, Varansi, Agartala, Dehradun, Imphal, Ranchi, Raipur, Agra, Chandigarh, Dimapur, Jammu and Pune (Gupta, 2007).

The Air Finance Journal (2007) has indicated that India's airports will need $30 billion worth of financing, of which $9 billion has already been identified, in order to bring the countries airport infrastructure up to par with its international counterparts while at the same time accommodating the continuous growth in passenger traffic. When all the airport construction is finally completed, India's airports will be capable of handling over 400 million passengers per year by 2020. However, the future looks very promising as there have been multiple offers from joint-venture consortiums eager to invest in

India's booming aviation industry. This investment will propel India towards becoming a formidable challenger in world aviation.

THE CHANGING DYNAMICS OF THE INDIAN TOURISM MARKET

Yahya (2003) stated that prior to the 1980s, successive Indian governments paid little attention to service industries such as tourism. After liberalisation of the Indian economy in 1991, the tourism industry as well as other economic sectors began to expand rapidly and by 2001 tourism had become India's third largest export industry after garments and jewellery. By this time, tourism's contribution to GDP was double that of agriculture and manufacturing despite the fact that Indian federal government had been investing only 1 per cent of its public funds into the sector. However, the number of international tourists is alarmingly low for a country with such vast diversity. Weightman (1987) stated that India had only 860,000 international tourists in 1982 and that this had only increased to 4.4 million by 2006. This was largely due to India's inadequate aeronautical infrastructure as it had a closed regulatory aviation market, while at the same time the Government protected its flag carriers against foreign competition by not extending any international bilateral traffic rights to overseas international carriers, which caused tourism to stagnate. Most international passengers were forced into the core metro cities of Mumbai, New Delhi and Kolkata, and connections to outlying domestic cities were poorly scheduled as they lacked frequency. Gopinath (2007) stated that there are 400 airports in India, nearly half of which have no service, even including areas such as national parks, the temples of Mahabalipuram and world treasures such as the Taj Mahal.

Another problem contributing to the poor influx of tourists was India's inadequate hotel infrastructure. Yahya (2003) pointed out there were only 61,000 rooms, while there was a demand for 90,000. In particular, there was an evident lack of hotel accommodation for mid-income level tourists looking for mid-range priced hotels. However, this sector is currently being overhauled: 150 IndiOne economy hotels will be built within the next 5 years at a cost of US$328 million; a joint venture between InterGlobe Enterprises and Accor is erecting a further 25 Ibis economy hotels; and the Bird group is planning to construct 20 hotels (Deloitte, Tourism Hospitality and Leisure 2006).

Table 20.5 shows the international passengers visiting India from the top ten most popular countries. It shows that the old colonial link between India and the UK has continued to prove fruitful as the British represented the highest proportion of arriving passengers. Sharpley and Sundaram (2005) pointed out that almost 40 per cent of these are travellers visiting friends and relatives (VFR). Europe remains the biggest market, accounting for around 34 per cent of all international arrivals. The US visitor is India's second most frequent tourist and this traveller segment is set to grow exponentially as new long-range aircraft are delivered to Air India and Jet Airways, and US carriers are taking advantage of the Open Skies policy and adding Indian destinations to their schedule portfolio. The new airport developments being constructed around India will entice International airlines to serve airports other than the main metro cities. These latest aeronautical developments will exponentially increase international traffic, boosting tourism to record levels. In 2002, the Ministry of Tourism profiled a campaign, called 'Incredible India', which gives prospective tourists a snapshot of what India offers

TABLE 20.5   Tourist arrivals from top 10 countries to India (2003)

Country of Nationality	Tourist Arrivals	% of total arrivals
UK	430,917	15.8%
USA	410,803	15.1%
Sri Lanka	109,098	4.0%
Canada	107,671	3.9%
France	97,654	3.6%
Japan	77,996	2.9%
Germany	76,868	2.8%
Malaysia	70,750	2.6%
Australia	58,730	2.1%
Singapore	48,368	1.8%

Source: Bureau of Immigration

with the aim of developing the country into a sustainable tourism industry. It seems to have paid off as Conde Nast Traveller ranked India as the fourth most preferred travel destination and Lonely Planet selected the country as among the top five destinations from 167 countries for 2006.

India is also one of the fastest growing outbound travel markets in the world as 7.2 million Indians travelled abroad in 2005. According to a forecast by the World Travel and Tourism Council (WTTC), over the next 10 years India will be among the fastest growing countries in the world, with an annual growth rate of 8.6 per cent. Domestic tourism is also big business as Bandyopadhyay's and Morais's (2005) research established that there were around 230 million domestic tourists in 2003, while Trivedi (2007) revised that figure to around 290 million by 2007. According to the Ministry of Tourism (2004, p107), the major mode of transport for domestic tourist trips is by bus, representing at least 70 percent of all trips across all purposes of travel, and 20 per cent are by train. Now that air fares are becoming more closely aligned to rail fares, more people will be encouraged to travel more frequently and this has the potential of exponentially expanding the domestic tourism industry given the number of aircraft on order.

CONCLUSION

India is in the midst of an economic reformation. India always had a tourism industry but it was stagnant for decades as bureaucracy and government interference choked all growth. However, India's booming economy triggered change in the antiquated regulation of its air transport system and it began to create a roadmap by deregulating its domestic market, while at the same time opening its skies to other overseas airlines by significantly increasing its bilateral traffic rights. A domino chain of events occurred which completely changed the face of Indian aviation: the number of airlines have tripled, the number of aircraft have increased almost five-fold and around $30 billion will be set aside for airport redevelopment, which in turn has sparked the construction of hotels throughout the country. This activity has become India's blueprint for tourism and its roadmap for the future – which now looks very bright as tourism is set to become one of the countries largest and most exciting export industries.

21

China

Zheng Lei

INTRODUCTION

Situated in East Asia and on the western coast of the Pacific Ocean, China is the most populous country in the world with a population of 1.3 billion and the third largest state covering a total land area of 9.6 million square kilometres (see Map 21.1). Modern tourism in China started in 1929, when the first travel agency was set up in Shanghai. In the same year, China's first airline, China Aviation Corporation started operation (Oum and Yu 2000). However, the development of aviation and tourism was very slow over the next few decades due to wars and political unrest. In 1980, China only received less than 6 million inbound tourists (CNTA 2000) and its aviation sector just ranked 33rd in the world in terms of revenue passenger kilometres (RPK) performed (ICAO 1981). However, since then China has been developing so rapidly that in 2005, inbound tourists to China reached 47 million, making China the fourth largest destination in the world in terms of international tourist arrivals (UNWTO 2007). As for the aviation industry, China emerged as the second largest market only behind the United States measured by either RPK or revenue tonne kilometres (RTK) performed (CAAC 2007). Within such a short period, how has China gone from a situation where its aviation and tourism industries were insignificant to one today where it ranks among the top nations? This case study attempts to answer this question and the remainder of this Chapter is structured as follows. Section 2 reviews historical development and Section 3 examines current trends. Section 4 discusses major policy issues followed by Section 5 outlining the way forward.

HISTORICAL DEVELOPMENT

The development of aviation and tourism after the establishment of the People's Republic of China in October 1949 may be divided into four stages. Each stage has its distinctive characteristics and is discussed in the following sub-sections.

The First Stage: 1949–1978

Between 1949 and 1978, China was isolated from the outside world, partly due to the hostile environment between China and western countries and partly due to the rigid

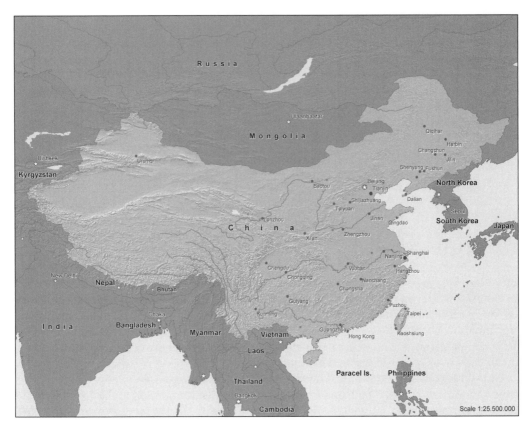

MAP 21.1   China

Source: Cartography and Geo-Informatics Laboratory, Geography Department, University of the Aegean, Greece.

communist rule imposed by its late leader, Chairman Mao. Tourism primarily served the political purpose of promoting the achievements of socialist China, to expand China's political influence through receiving invited guests and tourists (Han 1994). During this period, people from the West had to obtain a special permit to visit China, mainly for the purpose of diplomacy. People with relatives in China had to apply through the China Travel Service for a travel permit. The net result of this restriction was very few international tourists visiting China before 1978. Outbound travel was limited to few government officials and diplomats, while domestic tourism hardly existed.

During most of this period, the air transport industry was controlled by Air Force under the management of Civil Aviation Administration of China (CAAC). CAAC was structured as a four-level administration system: CAAC, six regional civil aviation bureaus, twenty-three provincial civil aviation bureaus, and seventy-eight civil aviation stations (Zhang and Chen 2003). CAAC not only acted as an industry regulator but also an owner representing the state for asset management and an operator involved in daily operation of airlines and airports. Every aspect of the industry, such as market entry, route entry, frequency, ticket price and even passenger eligibility for air travel, was heavily regulated by CAAC (Zhang and Chen 2003).

As a result of China's economic and political isolation, CAAC served very few foreign destinations. The situation was made further worse by two disastrous events – the Great Leap Forward (1958–1962) and Cultural Revolution (1966–1976) – which severely damaged China's economic base. During this period, China's air transport industry grew very slowly. In 1978, CAAC only carried 2.31 million passengers and traffic volume was just 0.3 billion RTKs.

The Second Stage: 1978–1987

After Mao's death in 1976, Deng Xiaoping emerged as the new leader of China. In 1978, the Chinese Communist Party held the Third Plenary Session of its 11th Congress. The Congress endorsed the economic reforms advocated by Deng and paved the way for introducing market mechanism into the communist economy, representing the policy shift from political struggling to economic reconstruction.

Following Cultural Revolution, China's economy was on the verge of bankruptcy. It was in deep need of foreign exchange to finance further economic development activities. The importance of tourism as a means of accumulating foreign exchange was recognised. From October 1978 to July 1979, Deng gave five talks about using tourism as an option to stimulate economic development, emphasising "Developing tourism should first develop those businesses, which could earn more money" (Cited in Xiao 2006; Zhang *et al.* 1999).

Owing to its superb natural and cultural tourism resources, when China started lifting restrictions on entry to many locations in 1978, overseas tourists flooded into China. To cope with the suddenly released huge demand, in 1984, the State Council announced that government agencies at national and local levels, state-owned companies and even private sector could invest in tourism development projects (Zhang *et al.* 1999). The decentralised policy has seen the dramatic increase in the supply of tourism facilities and the constraints were effectively eased.

In the meanwhile, administrative reform of CAAC was also implemented. In 1980, CAAC was transferred from Air Force to the State Council. In the same year, Deng pointed out that the civil aviation industry needed to be market-oriented. Beginning in 1981, the central government adopted the policy of "Self-responsible for losses and extra-profit retention" towards the airline sector. Within CAAC, six regional civil aviation bureaus became basic units for recording profits and losses in 1979. The practice was further extended to twenty-three provincial civil aviation bureaus a year later and more autonomy in marking operational decisions was delegated (Zhang and Chen 2003). But compared with the bold policy initiatives in the tourism sector, aviation reform in this stage was cautious and the pace of change was still slow.

The Third Stage: 1987–2002

Due to its well-proved record of earning much needed foreign exchange, inbound tourism development was included in the national plan for social and economic development for the first time in 1987 (Zhang 1995). Various policies were formulated to promote inbound tourism, with the focus on encouraging the construction of tourist hotels. However, as the development of aviation was lagging behind, hotel supply quickly moved ahead of the availability of airline flights and seats. The problem was particularly serious between 1985 and 1988. Tisdell and Wen (1991) note that hotel occupancy rates were low at some top tourist destinations like Shanxi and Guangxi due to inadequate air links. China's much criticised aviation industry was viewed as a major constraint to its tourism development.

To cope with the rapid development of inbound tourism and economy, structural reform of CAAC was undertaken in 1987 with the passage of the *"Report on Civil Aviation Reform Measures and Implementation"* by the State Council. The main goal of this reform programme as Zhang and Chen (2003) state was to separate the regulator from also being the operator, and to break the CAAC monopoly. Six major airlines, namely, Air China, China Eastern, China Southern, China Southwest, China Northwest and China Northern airlines were spun off from the old CAAC's six regional bureaus between 1987 and 1991. Many more regional carriers were formed following the experimental market liberalisation. Several of them were affiliated with CAAC through equity holdings by the six major airlines whereas the majority of them were established by provincial and municipal governments and state-owned business enterprises in the aim of promoting regional economic development (Le 1997).

Coincident with the structural reform in the airline industry, measures to decentralise airport management from CAAC to local authorities were piloted in selected cities aiming to encourage local governments to invest in airports and other infrastructure. Xiamen Airport was the first to be transferred to the local government in 1988 followed by Shanghai Hongqiao International Airport – the third largest airport in China – in 1993 (Zhang and Chen 2003). Following the smooth transfer of these assets, CAAC then decided that other airports would be decentralised gradually while new airports would be managed by local governments from inception (Zhang and Chen 2003). The decentralisation policy was very successful. It is observed that of the 46 airports built, upgraded, or expanded during 1986–1992, 70 per cent of the construction cost was met by local governments (Zhang and Chen 2003). In addition, in 1996, Xiamen Airport was floated on the stock exchange, followed by Shanghai Hongqiao International Airport and Shenzhen Airport in 1998 and Beijing Capital Airport in 2000. But the majority of those airports' shares were still controlled by the state.

On the airline side, the policy of encouraging market entry promoted by CAAC saw the total number of routes served in 1992 triple compared to 1980 (Zhang and Chen 2003). The aviation bottleneck for tourism development was largely eased. However, the explosive development of the airline industry put severe strains on aviation infrastructure and airline safety was at risk. Several passenger aircraft crashed in the 1990s and these fatal accidents not only damaged Chinese airlines reputation but also put off international tourists. In response to these problems, CAAC stopped issuing new airline licences since July 1994 and concentrated on improving safety record.

Another adverse consequence of the rapid expansion is that the traffic growth did not translate into profitability as most regional carriers were losing money as a result of small size and ineffective management (Zhang and Chen 2003). To compete for market share, price wars broke out among Chinese airlines. For the first time since 1978, the industry lost RMB2.1 billion (US$0.25 billion) in 1998 with the majority losses incurred by small airlines. The loss led CAAC to re-announce its price regulation. Although there were 34 airlines in China in 1999, their combined RTKs produced were around 10.6 billion, just about the same as Singapore Airlines (Thomas 2000). Under these circumstances, a plan to consolidate the industry was proposed by CAAC in 1999.

The Fourth Stage: 2002 to Present

Aviation reforms in the 1980s separated the role of CAAC as regulator and operator. However, CAAC still represented the state as the owner for some airlines and most airports. In 2002, three major policies were announced by the State Council to separate the regulator from also being the owner. First, nine CAAC-controlled airlines were ordered to consolidate into three airline groups around Air China, China Southern and China Eastern. There are two reasons for that. One is that China wanted to build strong and profitable airlines with the ability to confront competition from foreign rivals. The other is that CAAC wanted to reduce damaging price wars between its own airlines and rationalise costs. The consolidation process was formally completed in 2005. Air China acquired China Southwest and CNAC Zhejiang Airlines. China Southern took over China Northern and Xinjiang Airlines, while China Eastern gained control of China Northwest and Yunnan Airlines. Upon completion of the consolidation, the assets of the three airline groups were transferred to the newly-formulated State Assets Supervision and Administration Commission and CAAC no longer represented the state to own the airlines. All the three airlines were listed with the majority of shares being controlled by the state. In 2006, Air China, China Southern and China Eastern were all in the process of joining a major airline alliance.

During the consolidation process, other small airlines were urged to join one of the three groups. To facilitate the consolidation, in 2002, CAAC barred airlines not based at the main hubs of Beijing, Guangzhou and Shanghai from operating between those cities. This measure made the survival of many small airlines very difficult as routes between those cities accounted for the majority of revenue for them. Under the pressure, a number of small airlines chose to merge with one of the Big Three. Still, a few stronger regional airlines survived as independent entities, notably, Hainan, Shanghai and Shenzhen airlines, which formed the second tier airlines in China.

The second major policy announced by the State Council was to transfer all civil airports, except for those in Beijing and Tibet, to regional governments, giving them incentives to invest. The process was completed on July 8 2004, when the last airport, Gansu Airport was transferred to the regional authority. The airport reform saw CAAC transfer the ownership of 90 regional airports to local governments, and involved RMB40 billion (US$4.96 billion) in assets and 50,000 staff (Thomas 2005a). Most regional governments have created new airport corporations to manage and operate their airports and this represents an important step in the evolution of airport management in China.

The final major policy was to restructure those companies responsible for aviation oil supply, ticketing distribution and aircraft purchasing into three groups. Like airline reform, the asset management of these newly founded companies was transferred to the State Assets Supervision and Administration Commission from CAAC. By implementing these three major aviation reforms, CAAC's role as an owner was effectively separated from its regulatory function, representing a major step forward.

Partially due to domestic market consolidation and partially due to a bounce back in demand after the 2003 SARS epidemic, total passenger and freight traffic increased 34 per cent to 23 billion RTKs, passenger boarding jumped 38 per cent to 120 million and cargo/mail carriage climbed 24.5 per cent to 2.7 million tons (Thomas 2005b) in 2004. The civil aviation sector made a profit of RMB8.69 billion (US$1.04 billion), equal to the total profit over the previous 10 years.

CURRENT TRENDS

The Big Three – Air China, China Southern and China Eastern – are considered to be the backbone of China's airline industry. CAAC recently outlined its aviation growth plans aiming to help them rank among the world's top 10 by 2020 (In 2005, Air China, China Southern and China Eastern were ranked the 23rd, 31st, and 38th largest airlines, respectively, in terms of revenue) (Knibb 2006).

In any case, however, a new type of airlines is gradually emerging in China. In March 2005, the first new airline in China for a decade – Okay Airways – started operation. More strikingly, Okay Airways was 100 per cent owned by the private sector. Although private ownership in China dramatically increased from almost non-existence in 1978 to 60 per cent of total production in 2006 (Lindbeck 2007), this was not the case in the airline industry. For a long period, private investment was barred from entering this sector. As the aviation reform deepens, CAAC gradually lifted its restriction on domestic private investment on airlines. In June 2005, CAAC formally released its policy of *"Provisional Regulation on Domestic Investment on Civil Aviation"* to open up the domestic aviation market to more competition. In 2005 alone, 18 licences were issued by CAAC for privately-owned airlines (Thomas 2006).

The opening up of the domestic aviation market led to the emergence of the low-cost carriers when a number of start-ups modelled themselves on the US Southwest Airlines. This trend will potentially have profound impact on the airline, airport and tourism industries. The first Chinese low-cost carrier, Spring Airline, was set up by a tour company in Shanghai with its maiden flight from Shanghai to Yantai taking off on July 18 2005. The airline's cheapest airfare was RMB199 (US$25), massively undercutting the average ticket price of RMB800 (US$99) charged by majors on the same route and cheaper than a train ticket. Officially, on domestic routes, the maximum discount is 45 per cent of standard price set by the "Domestic Air Transportation Price Reform Plan", which came into effect on April 20 2004. Therefore, the cheap fare quickly became a cause for concern among major airlines. Although Spring Airlines later bowed to pressure and raised the cheapest price, the publicity generated by the dispute prompted the travelling public calling for abolishing the "minimum fare restriction". Consequently, CAAC announced its intention to end "minimum fare restriction" in the near future. Although the policy has not been officially abolished yet, since the end of 2006, low fares have become a commonplace in China. On many routes, the cheapest fare sold by Spring Airlines and other low-cost carriers was as low as RMB1 (US$0.13).

Although minimum fares virtually do not exist as a barrier in China, there are still a number of obstacles hindering the further development of China's low-cost carriers. First, it is estimated that only 3 per cent (about 40 million people) of people in China have credit cards (Jones 2005) and the development of e-commerce has been slow, resulting in selling tickets online difficult. Consequently, budget carriers in China have to mainly rely on travel agents to sell tickets. Nonetheless, travel agents usually lack incentives to act as a distribution channel for low-cost carriers as low fare means low, and sometimes, non-existence, commission. A more serious threat is from major airlines which adopted various anti-competitive practices such as not allowing their partner agents to deal with the budget airlines, in an attempt to drive those start-ups out of the market. Furthermore, China is in a severe shortage of pilots and skilled flight personnel to meet the demand from the low-cost sector. In addition, the en route charge is high and domestic fuel market is still monopolised by the state controlled Aviation Oil Supply Company and the price is usually 20 per cent higher than that in the international market (Jones 2005). Most seriously, low-cost carriers are generally prohibited from entering the most profitable trunk routes.

Despite these barriers, there are also some positive factors in favour of low-cost carriers' development. The first drive is from the need for tourism development. As one of the world's top destinations, in 2006, inbound tourists to China reached 50 million and generated US$34 billion revenue (UNWTO 2007a). But most of China's greatest attractions are located in the peripheral regions, traditionally suffering from inadequate air links. Moreover, China had the largest domestic tourism market in the world with 1.4 billion trips made in 2006 (CNTA 2007). Many of these trips were made by air due to the sheer size of China's territories. The domestic air travel market could be greatly stimulated if low fares are readily available. All these provide low-cost carriers with huge opportunities to meet the soaring demand for tourism. The second drive comes from the abundant regional airports. There are 147 airports in China and the majority of them are loss marking. Currently, airports tend to follow pricing guidelines set by CAAC. As airport commercialisation is underway in China, it is likely that these airports will provide discounts to low-cost carriers when they are seeking to increase passenger throughput to reach the critical mass of traffic.

The development of low-cost carriers is still in the very initial stage and their financial performance is mixed. On the one hand, the majority of low-cost carriers have been losing money since their first flight. On the other hand, a few led by Spring Airlines claimed that they had started to make a profit. CAAC recently indicated that it intended to provide a level playing field for the budget airlines and vowed to maintain fair competition (Ionides 2007). Given China's commitment towards a fully deregulated aviation market, it is envisaged that a strong low-cost sector could emerge in China in the foreseeable future.

In contrast to the recent relaxation of private investment in the domestic airline industry, foreign investors have been allowed to enter joint ventures, or buy stock in China's airlines since 1994, although there was a limitation of no more than 35 per cent of capital share and 25 per cent of voting stock. The motives, explained by Zhang and Chen (2003), were to attract foreign capital and enhance Chinese airlines operational efficiency. In 1994 alone, 15 joint ventures on aircraft maintenance and ground services were set up in China and Hainan Airlines became the first airline to receive foreign investment (Zhang *et al.* 1999). In the airport sector, Aéroports de Paris has had a 9.9 per cent stake in Beijing International Airport since 2000, while Copenhagen Airport acquired 25 per cent stake in Hainan Meilan Airport in 2002 (Airfinance 2006).

However, foreign direct investment into China's aviation sector was still very limited compared to the exponential increase of passenger and cargo traffic. To further stimulate foreign investors' interest in China's aviation industry, in August 2005, the limit of foreign investment in domestic airlines was raised to 49 per cent, with each individual foreign investor allowed a maximum holding of 25 per cent (Yeh 2006a). Areas that foreign capital could be invested were expanded to the areas of cargo, airport construction, jet fuel sales and storage, and computer-based air-ticketing systems.

To take advantage of the new policy initiatives, a string of international carriers announced deals to set up joint venture cargo airlines in China to capture a share of the rapidly growing market. Lufthansa was the first one that set up a joint venture, namely, Jade Cargo, with Shenzhen Airlines in 2005 flying to Amsterdam and Seoul (Yeh 2006b). The US regional carrier, Mesa Air Group, became the first foreign airline to operate regional jets on domestic routes by investing RMB245 million (US$30 million) for 49 per cent stake in a joint venture with the Shenzhen Airlines. The first joint venture airport was announced in October 2006 between Hong Kong Airport and Zhuhai Airport. The former also acquired a stake in Xiaoshan International Airport.

In the area of travel services, as an experiment, the first fully foreign-funded travel agency, Jalpak International China Co. Ltd, and the first joint venture, TUI China Travel Co. were approved in December 2003. The policy, which allows overseas controlled or wholly owned travel agencies, was formally announced in June 2004 as part of China's promises for WTO accession. Despite the apparent openness of the policy, there are still a number of restrictions imposed on foreign-controlled or wholly funded travel agencies. First, their business is restricted to inbound and domestic tours only. Moreover, the applicants must have an annual business turnover of at least RMB330.8 million (US$40 million) for a joint venture and RMB4 billion (US$500 million) for a wholly-owned travel agencies (Travel and Tourism – China 2006). Given the small margin in the travel intermediary sector, it remains to be seen the extent to which this policy could effectively stimulate foreign investment.

MAJOR POLICY ISSUES

Traditionally, China adopted very restrictive approach towards international aviation. Zhang and Chen (2003) assert that this was due to four main reasons – (1) to protect China's non-competitive airlines, (2) to restrict Chinese citizens travelling abroad, (3) constraints in its infrastructure, and (4) lack of international experience. Even under such restrictive agreements, Chinese airlines load factors on international routes were usually lower than their foreign counterparts that operated in highly competitive markets under more liberal agreements (Le 1997).

China's conservative approach to international capacity supply resulted in limited air traffic rights between China and the rest of world. For example, despite being the biggest city and the economic hub, Shanghai only had 25 international routes in 1998 (Zhang and Chen 2003). Moreover, the protective policy failed to build a strong and profitable airline industry and hampered China's national and regional economic development. Further reforming the aviation policy has become a burning issue faced by policymakers in the wake of China's accession to the World Trade Organisation in 2001 and its broader trade expansion goal (Zhang and Chen 2003). Over the past few years, China has seen major policy shifts towards a liberalised aviation regime.

Firstly, China has greatly opened up its skies to foreign airlines. By the end of 2006, China has signed 106 bilateral air service agreements (ASAs) with foreign countries and territories; there were 93 airlines from 51 countries flying into China's 31 cities with 1262 weekly scheduled passenger flights and 307 scheduled cargo flights. Among the many liberal bilateral ASAs signed between China and other countries, the one signed with the United States is most noteworthy. In April 2001, China and the US implemented the final stage of an expanded ASA, which included a fourth carrier from each side and an increase in weekly services from 27 to 54. Three years later, the air service agreement between China and the US was replaced by a sweeping liberalisation pact that quadrupled the number of flights between the two countries – from 54 to 249 (Airline Business 2004). Restrictions were lifted on US market access to any Chinese city, and code-sharing with Chinese airlines is unlimited. For all-cargo US flag carriers, 21 additional flights were allowed in 2004, while access to all mainland cities and the right to establish hubs were guaranteed (Airline Business 2004). The 2004 agreement was justified on the ground of economic development. For example, it is argued that a single daily flight by a jumbo jet from the US could generate an annual US$213 million in economic activity in China (Miller 2007).

Although China received the reciprocal traffic rights, its major airlines strongly opposed the bilateral agreement as US carriers were able to fully utilise their traffic rights, while Chinese carriers could not exhaust their full route capacity due to their weak competitiveness. Zhang and Chen (2003) observe that on most international routes served by both Chinese and foreign airlines, the former usually shared only one third of the market, albeit with lower prices and load factors. Heavy loss was a common characteristic for Chinese airlines on competitive international routes. But CAAC made it clear that it would not protect its airlines any more. In a recent interview, Mr Yang Yuanyuan, CAAC Minister, stated:

> "We believe that pure protection is not enough for the healthy growth and development of Chinese airlines ... Chinese airlines can accumulate certain experience and learn lessons from their counterparts, and they will grow in the process of liberalisation" (Ionides 2007).

In a move to further force Chinese airlines to improve their competitiveness, AirAsia, the most successful low-cost carriers in Southeast Asia, was granted rights to fly to three secondary Chinese cities (Xiamen, Chengdu and Kunming) in 2005. CAAC also abolished its policy prohibiting Chinese travelling on foreign airlines for official trips in an attempt to put pressure on Chinese airlines to improve their service level (Thomas 2001).

In the meantime, China's government substantially liberalised the previous tight restrictions on international travel by ordinary Chinese citizens. In 2002, China began to simplify application processes for passports, which were previously highly complicated and restrictive. The government also greatly eased restrictions on travel to Hong Kong and Macao, allowing people from most mainland provinces to travel to the territories under individual travel schemes. The destinations that Chinese citizens could visit in the 1990s were no more than a dozen under the so called "Approved Destination Status" (ADS) and most of them are Southeast Asian countries. By the end of 2006, 132 countries have achieved ADS, including most Western countries.

As a result of the relaxation of outbound travel, past few years have seen China quickly emerged as an importance source for outbound tourism. From Table 21.1 it can be seen since China started to allow its citizens travelling abroad for leisure purposes in 1984, it took China 17 years to reach the first 10 million outbound trips in 2000, but just 3 years to record the second 10 million in 2003 and only 2 years to achieve the third 10 million. The outbound spending by Chinese residents was over US$20 billion in 2005 (Zhang 2006). The World Tourism Organisation (1997) predicts that there will be 100 million Chinese outbound travellers by 2020. Undoubtedly, the exponential increase of Chinese outbound tourists will support Chinese airlines expansion on international routes.

Contributing to regional tourism development also facilitates CAAC's move towards an even broader liberalisation. The opening of Hainan province, the largest Special Economic Zone in China, to foreign airlines represents an interesting case of closer cooperation between aviation and tourism. With superb tropical beaches, abundant sunshine and rare fauna and flora, Hainan has had a vision to develop itself to an internationally renowned holiday destination. However, lack of adequate international air links severely prevented Hainan from reaching its goal. Strongly lobbied by the provincial government, in 2003,

TABLE 21.1   Chinese outbound trips and travel expenditure

Year	Trips abroad	Annual growth (%)	Outbound Spending (US$bn)	Annual growth (%)
1998	8,425,600	-	9.205	-
1999	9,232,400	9.60	10.864	18.02
2000	10,472,600	13.40	13.114	20.72
2001	12,000,000	11.50	13.909	6.06
2002	16,600,000	36.96	15.398	11.44
2003	20,220,000	21.80	15.187	-1.37
2004	28,850,000	42.68	19.149	26.09
2005	31,000,000	7.50	21.795	13.82

Source: Yearbook of China Tourism Statistics: Balance of payment sheet, China. Cited from Zhang (2006).

CAAC declared Hainan an "open skies" zone, giving all foreign and domestic airlines unlimited third, fourth and fifth traffic rights to operate passenger or cargo flights to and through the province's two main airports at Haikou and Sanya on a unilateral basis. Since the introduction of this policy, a number of domestic and foreign airlines have carried out market survey in Hainan and many international air links have been established. CAAC indicated that the experiment would expand to other parts of the country should it achieve desirable outcomes.

THE WAY FORWARD

This case study illustrates how aviation and tourism in China has evolved from an insignificant presence to one of the top nations in the world. Needless to say, the spectacular development of both sectors capitalised on China's dramatic economic growth. But, the proper strategies adopted by the government also played an important role. China's economic reform is unprecedented in the modern human history and it could not simply transfer experiences that had worked in other countries. Mistakes are inevitable but a unique feature in China's aviation and tourism reform is that it first started with experiments in a designated area. So, severe system-wide shocks could be avoided if the experiment goes wrong. Successful experiments are then endorsed retrospectively by the central government and become the basis for a formal policy (Le 1997).

Through a series of reforms, CAAC gave up its role as an operator and owner of airlines and airports and focused entirely on regulatory matters. Over the past few years, a clear trend has emerged and China is gradually shifting from a conservative aviation regime to a liberal competitive-driven policy. As a result, low-cost carriers have emerged while majors are encouraged to participate in global competition. China is becoming more and more open to foreign airlines typified by the liberal bilateral agreements and opening up of traffic rights in Hainan. Strategic use of aviation policy to stimulate tourism and economic development is becoming a consensus for CAAC and central government. This process is likely to be further reinforced by the recent decentralisation of airport ownership to regional governments as the latter will actively seek more air links at their airports to support regional development and raise the value of their airports. With forecasted strong economic growth over the next decade, it is likely that China will persist in the aviation and tourism policy reform and further open itself to the outside world.

ACKNOWLEDGEMENTS

The author would like to thank Mr Guoxian Cai of Civil Aviation Administration of China for his helpful comments on a previous version of this chapter.

22

The Middle East

John F. O'Connell

INTRODUCTION

The Middle East comprises Bahrain, Iraq, Jordan, Kuwait, Lebanon, Palestine, Oman, Qatar, Saudi Arabia, Syria, the United Arab Emirates, Yemen and Israel (see Map 22.1). The six main countries that are classified as the engines of the Middle East comprise Bahrain, Kuwait, Oman, Qatar, Saudi Arabia and the United Arab Emirates and are known as the GCC (Gulf Cooperation Council) countries. Amidst the doom and gloom of numerous wars, the Middle East air transport market is leading the world in growth and prosperity. The Middle East based airlines currently account for just 3 per cent of passengers transported worldwide and total traffic flown by all carriers to, from and within the region amounts to only 5.6 per cent of the world's total. The region is leading the world in aircraft orders with around $85 billion being ordered over the last number of years, with $21 billion being ordered alone at the 2007 Paris air show. Their growth has caused a tectonic shift in the marketplace as the Middle East based airlines now account for over 70 per cent of the manufacturers' long-haul aircraft backlog. To support the excessive capacity on order, the governments have also committed a further $26 billion to develop the regions airports, which will undoubtedly pivot the Middle East into becoming the new face in global aviation.

The effect of these new developments is beginning to take hold as the Middle East recorded the highest passenger growth for 2006, registering 15.4 per cent, against a world average of just 5.9 per cent (IATA 2007b). ACI also confirmed that the world's airports handled 5.7 per cent more passengers in 2006 over the previous year, led by the Middle East which was up 10.4 per cent or 4.9 per cent of global international passenger numbers. Overall, the region has posted double-digit growth in 41 of the past 43 months.

Given this growing significance which the Middle East region has within the global aviation environment, it is the aim of this chapter to explore in greater detail the market for the aviation services, the growth planned by the home carriers and the associated airport expansion which is occurring. This discussion is then related to tourism developments within the region.

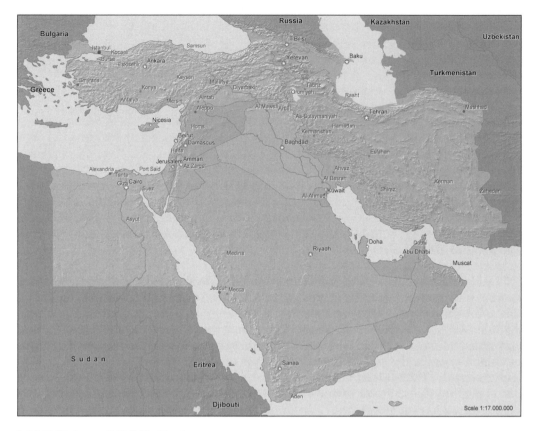

MAP 22.1   Middle East

Source: Cartography and Geo-Informatics Laboratory, Geography Department, University of the Aegean, Greece.

THE MIDDLE EAST'S ECONOMIC ENGINE, ITS RAGING CONFLICTS AND THE AIRLINE INDUSTRY

Historically, the Middle East has been synonymously associated with holding the reins of oil power across the globe while at the same time being immersed in a constant state of conflict. Feiler and Goodovitch (1994) have stated that the demand for air travel to the Middle East had always been linked to the oil industry. Hydrocarbon resources are the main economic commodities in the Middle East as they hold 64 per cent of the world's oil reserves and 40 per cent of the natural gas reserves (OPEC 2003; British Petroleum 2003). The Middle East will export US$791 billion of oil this year – up US$500 billion in four years, while the economy is steadily growing at 5 per cent each year. This revenue has allowed the Middle Eastern countries to capitalise various projects including the development of its aviation industry (Organisation of Arab Petroleum Exporting Countries 2003, 2007). The wealth of oil is not evenly distributed as Yemen and Dubai, for example have little oil, while Bahrain has 70 per cent of its exports accruing from this sector (Nakibullah and Islam 2007). However, many of the Middle Eastern countries have failed to diversify into other unrelated industries, which is short-sighted given the finite geological reserves of oil and gas.

The Middle East region has also been plagued by both regional and international conflicts which have kept it in the spotlight of international attention. Hollier (1991) outlined that many Europeans chose to avoid flying over the Gulf and especially making stopovers in the Emirates states during the first Gulf war. Feiler and Goodovitch (1994) pointed out that the first Gulf war in 1991 caused the traffic of European airlines to fall by 12 per cent (Lufthansa experienced a 30 per cent traffic decrease across its network), while the Middle East based airlines had cancelled 32 per cent of their flights as a result of a 38 per cent drop in traffic. However, today's passengers appear to coexist with the plight of terrorism and war as the number of passengers now travelling through Middle Eastern airports has soared, largely attracted by the premium service being offered by the Arabian Gulf carriers and their low fares. Alder and Hashai (2005) calculated that air traffic flows within the Middle East itself could increase by 51 per cent if there was a reduction in the violence under the assumption of regional deregulation. However, the current Iraq and Israeli–Lebanon conflicts have cast a shadow of persistent instability over the region and consequently, it is difficult to imagine that Arab based airlines are in fact changing the landscape of global aviation.

THE MIDDLE EAST'S TRANSFORMING AVIATION MARKET

The Nature of Passenger Traffic in the Middle East

There were approximately 17.2 million domestic passengers and 57.9 million international passengers transported by the 23 member airlines of the Arab Air Carriers Organisation in 2006 (Arab Air Carriers Organisation 2006). The number of international passengers carried by these carriers rose by almost 43 per cent over the period 2003–2006 largely due to extra capacity being added by Emirates, Qatar Airways and Etihad. Foreign airlines transported an additional 41 million passengers to the Middle East and North Africa in 2006 and the total air transport market stood at around 116 million passengers with a high concentration of the traffic centred in the Arabian Gulf states. Figure 22.1 shows that the passenger and cargo traffic at Middle Eastern based airports has increased by 97 per cent and 74 per cent respectively from 1997 to 2005. Boeing's forecasts indicate that the Middle East based airlines will double the number of passengers that they carry by 2014. Airbus predict that airlines in the Middle East and North Africa will need to acquire around 950 aircraft, worth $94.5 billion by 2022 (Mathews 2004).

Air transport within the Middle East is still highly regulated and is strictly ruled by bilateral agreements, although some governments have adopted liberal policies to promote air services and traffic growth. The UAE, Bahrain, Lebanon, Kuwait and Oman are the regional leaders in deregulation as they have all initiated open skies policies, which will play a key role in developing their tourism industries and have been instrumental in their home carriers' success in gaining access to numerous long-haul international markets. The dual forces of new entrant low cost carriers and intergovernmental liberalisation are combining to force rapid change. This change is evident in Saudi Arabia, which had one of the world's most closed aviation markets, but by 2007 it had allowed two low cost

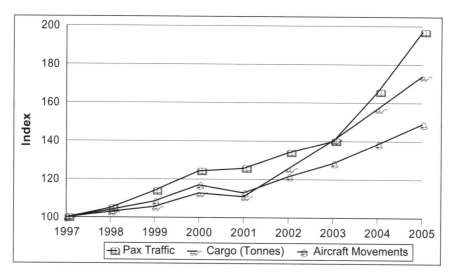

FIGURE 22.1 Passenger, cargo and aircraft movements data for Middle East airports 1997–2005

Source: AACO, ACI.

carriers (i.e. Sama and Nas Air) to enter the domestic market providing competition to the national flag carrier Saudia which had a monopoly since 1945. Table 22.1 shows the major airlines that operate in the Middle East and gives a breakdown of its traffic markets. Many of these airlines rely extensively on international traffic which emanates outside the Middle East region and this is evident in the table as Emirates and Etihad carry 82 per cent and 74 per cent of their traffic internationally outside the Middle East and consequently they have extensively developed their hubs to accommodate this volume of international traffic.

The Middle East is roughly equidistant between Europe's Northern Hemisphere and Asia's Southern Hemisphere which allows traffic to be easily routed through a central hub. An estimated 5.5 billion people reside within an 8-hour fight time of the Arabian Gulf based cities and the principle objective is to capture a chunk of this enormous market. Doganis (2006: 290) agrees that the business plans of Emirates, Qatar Airways, Etihad and Gulf Air are largely focused on transferring long-haul traffic between Europe, Asia, India and Australasia via an operating hub, while Taneja (2003: 88; 2004: 181, 2005: 28) shows that part of the success of Emirates is attributable to the hub and spoke system that it has created in Dubai. Clark (2007) stated that 50 per cent of Emirates traffic is presently transiting through its Dubai hub, down from 75 per cent a decade earlier, as more passengers are terminating at Dubai due to its developing tourism, conference and business industries. O'Connell and Williams (2006) stated that 53 per cent of the traffic between India and the UK is connecting via airports in the Arabian Gulf and these carriers are now firmly establishing themselves in order to capture a significant slice of India's exploding passenger market. Emirates is establishing a firm presence in both Europe and Asia: it has 91 flights per week to the UK (56 flights a week to London) and is also expanding its secondary markets, such as Glasgow, Venice Nice, etc., offering a one-stop service via Dubai to Africa, Asia and Australia, matching, and in many cases exceeding, the schedule offerings of European network carriers. Emirates for example, have carried

TABLE 22.1   Middle East airline majors and their traffic distribution (Summer 2006)

Airline	Est.	Hub Airport	Weekly Seats on Offer	Traffic Breakdown		
				Domestic	Within M.E.	International
Emirates	1985	Dubai	436,956	0.9%	17.3%	81.8%
Etihad	2003	Abu Dhabi	98,656	0.0%	26.0%	74.0%
Gulf Air	1950	Bahrain	214,816	0.0%	45.9%	54.1%
Kuwait Airways	1954	Kuwait	76,668	0.0%	38.7%	61.3%
Middle East Airlines	1945	Beirut	39,138	0.0%	35.6%	64.4%
Oman Air	1981	Muscat	44,146	11.7%	58.6%	29.7%
Qatar Airways	1993	Doha	191,546	0.0%	33.5%	66.5%
Royal Jordanian	1963	Amman	68,701	2.8%	42.1%	55.0%
Saudi Arabian Airlines	1945	Jeddah, Riyadh, Damman	488,192	62.8%	8.7%	28.5%
Syrian Arab Airlines	1946	Damascus	70,858	16.2%	32.3%	51.5%
Yemenia	1961	Sana'a	56,252	28.4%	32.1%	39.4%

Source: ATI, OAG-Max, Airline Websites.

350,000 passengers from Glasgow since inaugurating the route in 2004 and its traffic on the route has increased by 30 per cent each year as passengers prefer direct routing rather than transiting through London Heathrow's congested hub, necessary on British Airways network. Figure 22.2 shows the origin and destination traffic for the Arab based carriers. It shows the effectiveness of having hubs equidistant from Europe and Asia as almost 60 per cent of the traffic flows between both continents, and this is set to grow as the airlines continue to add capacity.

There are also two well established low cost carriers operating on international intra-regional routes in the Middle East notably, Air Arabia (founded in 2003, Sharjah based) and Jazerra (founded in 2005, Kuwait based). The latter has 35 aircraft on order, which is showing similar growth trends as that witnessed by Ryanair and easyJet in their early days (see Chapter 9), which will undoubtedly change the landscape of the Middle East aviation market as deregulation begins to creep through the region. In addition, there are around 130 million people that reside in the Arabian Gulf, 50 per cent of whom are under 25 years of age and it is this segment in particular that will fuel the growth of the low cost carriers. Air Arabia transported around 1.7 million in 2006 from zero just three years earlier with its nine aircraft and this exponential growth is primarily attributable to its low fare offering as a result of its low cost unit operating costs. Air Arabia's CASK (Cost per Available Seat Kilometre) was 50 per cent lower than Emirates in 2005, which

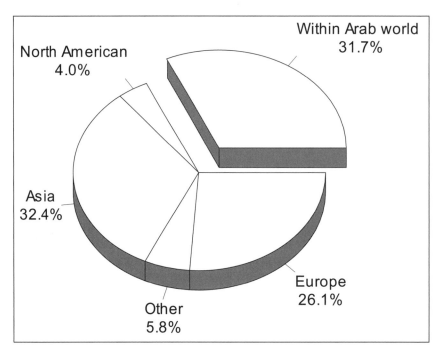

FIGURE 22.2 Geographical distribution of origin and destination markets served by Middle East based carriers (January 2007)

Source: Arab Air Carriers Organisation.

has stimulated many passengers to opt for the low cost carrier (Shuaa Capital 2007). It has taken 6 per cent of the Intra Gulf market by 2006.

The Growth Planned by the Arabian Gulf Carriers

The growth planned by Emirates, Qatar Airways and Etihad, which all reside within a 350 km radius of each other, is unprecedented. Since 1985, on average Emirates has doubled in size every three to four years, while Qatar Airways is quickly catching up. These airlines are unique as they offer a five star service while at the same time keep operating costs well below competing legacy airlines such as British Airways, KLM and Qantas etc. This allows the Arabian Gulf carriers to offer low fares which has significantly stimulated their traffic. In addition, Emirates and Qatar Airways have also set high standards and they have consistently won various product and service excellence wards by Skytrax, which is a global barometer of passenger opinions on airlines around the world.

However, what sets these airlines apart from all other carriers is the remarkable portfolio of aircraft that they have ordered from both Boeing and Airbus. It has caused a tectonic shift in the marketplace as the Middle East based airlines now account for around 70 per cent of all the long-haul aircraft orders. Emirates currently operates a fleet of 97 wide-body aircraft and has a further 134 aircraft on order including 55 A380s (around one-third of total A380s ordered) and 43 Boeing 777s – it also has options on a further 67 wide-bodies. Qatar, a small country with a total population of around 750,000 (25 per cent native and 75 per cent foreign), has also created a stir in aviation circles as it placed an order at the 2007 Paris air show for 80 A350s and 3 additional A380s, while in the previous year it ordered 20 777s at the Farnborough air show. ATI (2007a) has stated that the carrier has also placed an additional order for 30 787s in July 2007. In comparison, British Airways has only placed orders for 4 long-range aircraft while Cathay Pacific secured 23. Both Emirates and Qatar will become global challengers and will displace a lot of air traffic that currently flies on weaker Asian and European carriers, and their respective hubs at Dubai and Doha will become enormous transit points with the option for passengers to spend time at these cities and embrace a different culture in a wealthy environment. Etihad started operations in 2004 and it subsequently placed the world's largest order for a new start up airline of 24 wide-body aircraft worth approximately $7 billion. It ordered 12 more aircraft in June 2007 and it will double its current fleet within the next five years.

Other countries in the Middle East also wish to capitalise on the success of their neighbours: Husain (2007) has pointed out that Saudi Arabian Airlines is negotiating the purchase of an additional 60 aircraft valued at $12 billion, while Kuwait Airways is also planning to replace its entire fleet and acquire 34 aircraft. Meanwhile, the Omani government has dissolved its long-term partnership with Gulf Air, which had provided Oman's long-haul network – it has decided that it will develop its own long-haul route structure with 9 A330s and explore the option of obtaining newer generation wide-body aircraft while at the same time creating a hub at Muscat. Funding for new aircraft is always a major constraint, but the Middle East based carriers have a clear advantage as the long-term loans are underwritten by the countries proven oil reserves, a measure that secures favourable interest charges on borrowings. Pilling (2006) describes how Qatar Airways' loans are fully backed by the government sovereign guarantees.

The pace of growth of these Arab carriers has sent shock waves throughout the industry: they will pose a huge threat to the European and Asian Airlines as new capacity is added along with the latest technological in-flight products, while at the same time triggering lower fares which will in effect cause a paradigm shift in the dynamics of moving passenger traffic between Europe and Asia and visa versa.

The Reshaping of Middle Eastern Airports

Airports within the Middle East are also developing at lightning speed. The exponential passenger growth will be catered for by similar growth in airport capacity. This forward planning will eliminate any air traffic bottlenecks caused by the enormous volume of airline seat capacity that will be added to the region over the next few years. Over $26 billion will be invested in airports to support the growth of airline traffic over the next decade, as shown in Table 22.2. The majority of the GCC countries are expanding their existing facilities, while two states (Dubai and Doha) are building new airports. In comparison, only one airport has been built in the USA in the last 25 years. Dubai's new Jebel Ali Airport will become the world's largest airport as it will be equivalent to the combined size of London Heathrow and Chicago O'Hare when operational, handling 120 million passengers per year. It will feature six parallel runways, three passenger terminals and a cargo terminal capable of handling 12 million tons of cargo per year. It will accommodate a number of hotels, shopping malls and a dedicated executive jet centre, while an express railway network will link Jebel Ali to the existing airport.

TABLE 22.2   Airport development plans for Middle East (2005–2012)

	Airline Operating Base	Cost (US$)	Passenger Throughput (millions)	Planned Additional Capacity (millions)	Total Capacity (millions)
Dubai (Expansion)	Emirates	$4.1 billion	22	48	70
Dubai[†] (New)	Emirates	$8.2 billion	----	120	120
Doha (Expansion)	Qatar Airways	$150 million	8	12	20
Doha (New)	Qatar Airways	$5.5 billion	----	50	50
Abu Dhabi (Expansion)	Etihad	$6.8 billion	6	31	37
Jeddah (Expansion)	Saudi Arabian	$1.5 billion	10	30	40
Kuwait	Kuwait Airways	$460 million	6	14	20
Bahrain	Gulf Air	$815 million	10	8	18
Muscat	Oman Air	$300 million	3	9	12
Sharjah (UAE)	Air Arabia	$22 million	2	6	8

[†] Jebel Ali will be ten times larger than Dubai's existing airport and will be larger than Chicago O'Hare and London Heathrow combined.

Source: Airports Council International, AACO, ATI, Booz Allen and Hamilton.

Some 80 km along the coast, Abu Dhabi is investing $6.8 billion in the expansion of its existing airport in order to meet the growing demand generated by Etihad whose passenger numbers increased by 20 per cent to almost 6.5 million in 2006. In neighbouring Qatar, another major construction project is underway – a new airport is being built from land reclaimed from the sea. It is situated a mere 4 km from the existing airport which will be integrated to form one airport with multiple terminals. It will be fully operational by 2015, handling 50 million passengers a year with 80 contact gates. It is the world's first airport built specifically to accommodate the A380, which indicates that Qatar Airways may order additional units of such aircraft, similar to Emirates' strategy (Paylor 2007).

THE TOURISM MASTER PLAN OF THE ARABIAN GULF STATES

The Arabian Gulf appears to be laying down a grand tourism master plan. They are simultaneously building and expanding their airport infrastructure while at the same time ordering multiple numbers of long range aircraft. Their hubs are roughly equidistant between Europe's Northern Hemisphere and Asia's Southern Hemisphere which allows traffic to be easily routed through a central hub. In spite of the conflicts, the Middle East has been one of the most dynamic tourism regions in the past few years. It has consistently shown higher than average and often double-digit growth rates of international tourist arrivals. According to preliminary estimates, the Middle East surpassed 40 million international tourist arrivals in 2006, corresponding to a gain of 16.5 million when compared to 2000 (+70 per cent) (United Nations World Tourism Organisation 2007a). Currently, the Middle East is the fastest growing tourism market in the world, recording an annual growth rate of around 7.1 per cent, and the World Tourism Organisation (2005) has forecast that this rate of growth will continue until 2020.

This tourism growth is synchronised with the prolific expansion of the Arabian Gulf carriers. IATA (2007b) showed that the Middle East had the world's strongest Revenue Passenger Kilometres (RPKs) growth registering 19.2 per cent in 2005. Boeing's forecasts are along similar lines as it stated that the Middle East based airlines will double the number of passengers that they carry by 2014. According to the World Travel and Tourism Council (2005), travel and tourism in the Middle East in 2005 posted US$128.6 billion of economic activity (total demand) and will grow to US$220 billion by 2015. The Middle East's travel and tourism economy (direct and indirect impact) in 2005 accounted for 9.7 per cent of GDP and four million jobs (9.1 per cent of total employment). Historically, these countries had exhibited an over-reliance on oil production and had failed to diversify and source new methods of generating different revenue streams (Ayish 2005).

Table 22.3 shows the number of international tourists from 1990 to 2005. It shows that Saudi Arabia accounted for around one-third of the tourist population to the Middle East – 46 per cent of the total number of the inbound tourism trips were for religious purposes (particularly hajj pilgrimages), followed by business visits 25 per cent, with a further 13 per cent were visiting friends and relative's trips, and 5 per cent of all the inbound tourist trips represents vacation trips (Supreme Commission for Tourism 2005). However, Saudi Arabia is aggressively pushing the development of its non-religious tourism industry as Saudi's Supreme Commission for Tourism is introducing a hotel rating system,

TABLE 22.3   Middle East – International arrivals by destination

	International Tourist Arrivals (000s)				Market Share (%)	
	1990	1995	2000	2005	1995	2005
Bahrain	1,376	1,396	2,420	3,967	13.8	13.2
Iraq	748	61	78	-	0.6	-
Jordan	572	1,074	1,427	2,987	10.6	9.9
Kuwait	15	72	78	92	0.7	0.3
Lebanon	-	450	742	1,320	4.4	4.4
Oman	149	279	571	817	2.8	2.7
Palestine	-	-	330	40	-	0.1
Qatar	133	288	325	680	2.8	2.3
Saudi Arabia	2,209	3,325	6,585	9,100	32.8	34.8
Syria	562	815	1,416	3,368	8.0	11.2
UAE	973	2,315	3,907	7,600	22.8	25.2
Yemen	52	61	73	145	0.6	0.5
Total	**6,789**	**10,136**	**17,952**	**30,116**	**100%**	**100%**

Source: World Tourism Organisation, Tourism Market Trends, 2005 Edition – Annex, Abu Dhabi Tourism Authority.

encouraging archaeological and museum visitors and licensing tourist companies. These are revolutionary measures given the countries' relatively closed environment and the Secretary General of the Tourism Higher Authority (THA) boldly predicted that Saudi Arabia would have 45.3 million tourists by 2020 (Library of Congress 2006). This type of activity may trigger other Arab countries to develop similar tourism related projects.

However, the United Arab Emirates in particular is quickly becoming the world's newest tourism hub as it is developing multiple tourism projects in a setting that has year round sunshine. Table 22.3 illustrates that it had over 25 per cent of Middle East's tourism traffic by 2005. Dubai had one of the lowest oil reserves in the UAE and the government set out a blueprint that would allow it to diversify into other industries and provide it with a long-term and steady income. Tourism was top of its agenda when it was planning to diversify. The master plan to develop a mega tourism hub in Dubai is well underway as Emirates have secured a large quantity of the wide-body aircraft production capacity at Boeing and Airbus over the next few years, while at the same time the airport infrastructure is being expanded to synchronise with the continuous increase in aircraft deliveries. Concurrently, multiple tourism based projects have also been established to give the tourist variety. Dubai's 64 km of coastline now has facilities for sailing, water skiing, windsurfing, diving, fishing and golfing, while the surrounding deserts offer a unique setting for camel safaris, dune driving, sand skiing, falconry, etc. It has also erected a number of tourism development projects (See Chapter 12 by Debbage and Alkaabi). To complete the Dubai tourism master plan, hotels are also being erected: 77 additional hotels are being earmarked for construction, supplementing the existing 99 hotels and providing 126,150 rooms by 2010, an increase of 156 per cent over current levels (TRI Hospitality Consulting 2006). Hotel development has been facilitated by the relaxation of the rules on land ownership and leasing in the UAE which will attract many of the world's leading hotel brands, further developing its tourism potential.

Qatar and Abu Dhabi have taken the blueprint of Dubai's successful tourism model and are beginning to follow a similar approach, while Oman is also strongly contemplating the development of such a master plan. There is no doubt that the tourism landscape in the Arabian Gulf has reached a new dimension and its innovative and dynamic master plan will enable the region to become a tourism leader within the next decade. A recent study quoted by Global Futures and Foresight (GFF) which covers 13 Middle East countries stated that US$3.4 trillion will be invested in tourism infrastructure (hotels, airports, airlines, etc.) by 2020 (Centre for Asia Pacific Aviation 2007).

CONCLUSION

The airlines in the Middle East are currently experiencing very substantial growth rates. They are leading the world in aircraft orders and the capacity of the airports is expanding rapidly. This is creating huge tourism opportunities but the region has traditionally been an unassuming tourism destination, since it has been embroiled in constant conflict and its vast oil reserves has kept it in the spotlight of international attention for decades.

However, amidst this setting, some Middle East countries are laying down a tourism blueprint that will transform their dependence from oil, while at the same time quell the perception that the region is an unattractive holiday destination. The Middle East's geographical position between Europe and Asia allows the region's carriers to move traffic easily between the two continents – the potential is enormous as 5.5 billion people reside within an 8-hour flight time from cities such as Dubai, Doha, Abu Dhabi, etc. Concurrently, multiple tourism based projects are being erected which will attract passengers to layover while transiting through hubs, and at the same time encourage holiday makers to try out a unique new tourism product, unparalleled in the global marketplace. The vision to transform a desert into a tourism mega hub is currently being carved out and its potential is boundless – a true blueprint for other undeveloped regions of the world.

23

Africa

Pavlos Arvanitis and Petros Zenelis

INTRODUCTION

Africa is an area experiencing many controversial phenomena. It is a vast region (see Map 23.1) combining low growth in development indices and abundance of natural resources. On the other hand, the African continent has suffered from warfare and internal fighting that impeded its tourism development. This oxymoronic situation is also observed in the air transport and tourism sectors. The expansion of the airline services in the African region is rather uneven. Some African countries witness satisfactory results in the air transport operations but what is important here is the unobstructed, smooth, expeditious and unvarying spread of the air services throughout the continent so as to provide reliable services to those wishing to be transferred within its territory. Countries situated in the north, southern and eastern parts of Africa may not be sufficiently developed in the aviation field but they are in a better position compared to the French speaking, sub-Saharan countries. The main areas of the African airline industry that are problematic and inconsistent with the internationally accepted standards of aviation are safety, aged fleet, airport infrastructure and qualifications of the personnel employed. Similarly, tourism arrivals and receipts vary significantly amongst the African subcontinents and countries. This chapter examines historical developments in aviation and tourism markets in Africa followed by a discussion of current trends, major policy issues and the way forward.

HISTORICAL DEVELOPMENTS

The last fifty years were very important for the gradual development and slow but stable establishment of the air transport industry in Africa, as many countries gained their independence in the 1960s. There were, and still exist, several constraints that impeded the air linkage of the African countries not only with each other but also with the rest of the world. Apart from the transportation of people, commerce and trade are positively affected by the expansion and establishment of the aviation services. Still, today there are two dominant groups, the francophone countries (former French Colonies) and the British Commonwealth countries; these countries tend to receive more tourists to some degree, as they still have links with their former metropolis. The exception is the sub-region of North

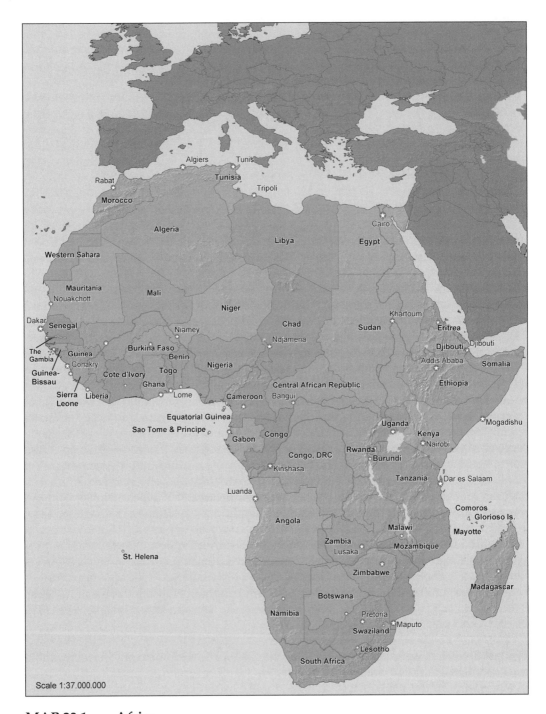

MAP 23.1   Africa

Source: Cartography and Geo-Informatics Laboratory, Geography Department, University of the Aegean, Greece.

African countries, where the close proximity to Europe has influenced their development as tourist destinations.

Africa has traditionally been attracting visitors willing to admire its natural beauties and national parks, the beaches and the game reserves. This trend is still strong, but significant progress has been achieved to attract more forms of tourism including business and conventions. Africa has improved its image as a tourist destination in the last 15 years; in 2005 it accounted for 4.7 per cent of world tourism arrivals whereas in 1990 it accounted for 3.4 per cent. During the same period, Africa recorded a 9 per cent increase in tourism receipts, which reached US$22 billion in 2005 (UNWTO, 2006). The insufficiency of air transport services between Africa and the rest of the world though is not encouraging tourism development.

In 1958, the United Nations Economic Commission for Africa (ECA) was established and, amongst others, was committed to assist responsibly in the reinforcement of the regional air transport. Since its launch the ECA has played a very important role in the development and the establishment of airlines across the continent. Its first substantial interference took place in November 1964 when it called the first African Conference on Air Transport with the support of International Civil Aviation Organisation (ICAO). One of the most important aftermaths of the Conference was the introduction of the African Civil Aviation Commission[1].

Since its establishment, ECA managed to compose, and activate several programmes and policies that contributed to the development and improvement of the airline industry in Africa. Among others, there was the United Nations Transport and Communication Decade for Africa, the Mbabane Declaration on the Freedoms of the Air, the Yamoussoukro Declaration of 1988, the Mauritius Conference[2] of 1994 and the Yamoussoukro Decision of 1999.

In particular, and thanks to the "linking" nature of the air transport services, the African airlines were experiencing the combined after-effects of the deregulation in the USA and the liberalisation process in the EU aiming to a single European airline market. The rapid transformation occurring in the rest of the world was the main reason that made African ministers in charge to meet in Yamoussoukro, Côte d'Ivoire on October 7th, 1988. They realised that they had to agree upon a new framework which had to be adopted by the airlines of the entire continent. The main points discussed in the Yamoussoukro Declaration had to do with the traffic rights among the African countries and their granting procedure, the promotion of cooperation among African airline carriers and the possibilities of further investment in the air transport industry.

This convention was the first important step towards the liberalisation of the air transport in Africa because it brought about several conferences concerning the enforcement of the Declaration's propositions such as the Banjul Accord in West Africa. The Yamoussoukro Declaration, however, did not manage to instigate radical changes on the existing status quo concerning privatisation of the national airlines and liberalisation of the air transport in the continent. After the deadline of the scheme, in 1996, no important progress was accomplished, thus further actions and official meetings had to be organised for the integration of African Airlines to update the decisions and make them realistic and feasible. Traffic rights granting was the most important issue that had to be settled. In the

---

1   The African Civil Aviation Commission (AFCAC) is an autonomous body. Its conclusions and recommendations are submitted for acceptance to the concerned governments.
2   The Yamoussoukro Declaration was reviewed at Mauritius in September, 1994 so as measures to be taken for the reactivation of the Declaration's implementation.

early 90s, the air transport policy in Africa was inadequate. There were several regulatory policies across the continent adopted by the African countries and as a result many aspects of the frameworks established were not compatible to each other. Consequently the air transport sector was strongly linked and heavily depended upon fragile occasional political instability. The latter combined with the fact that the majority, if not all, African carriers are still state owned leads to high regulatory constraints and inflexibility to take strategic decisions. The introduction of the private sector participation and supervision in the air transport sector was the most important step forward accomplished by the Yamoussoukro Declaration.

The African ministers in charge met again in 1999 to evaluate the progress of the enforcement of the Yamoussoukro Declaration. The most important field of discussion was the liberalisation of air transport between the African countries so as to facilitate the mutual access to the air transport market. The key policies defined by the African Ministers were: a) gradual liberalisation of scheduled and non-scheduled intra African air transport services, b) granting traffic rights including third, fourth and fifth freedom rights, c) multiple designation, d) elimination of limitations concerning frequencies and capacities, e) government's-approval of free tariff-setting in line with the rules of fair competition, and f) safety and security standards.

As expected, the adaptation and application of the Yamoussoukro Decision was not the same by the African countries. In time terms, the transition procedure varied. Many countries moved reasonably fast while others have not set the transition procedure yet. The hindrances that occurred and impeded the policies' transformation were the lack of political determination, the existing legal restrictions (visas' granting, work permits etc), the unskilled workforce, the infrastructure and safety incoherence with the internationally accepted standards and the protectionism of the flag carriers. Some of the impacts expected to follow the application of Yamoussoukro Decision are: a) private investments, b) network development, c) falls in tariffs, d) rise of traffic, e) upgrading of the air transport services, f) mergers and alliances, etc.

CURRENT TRENDS

The air transport is undoubtedly a crucial means of transport for the continent because Africa is an immense region where the airlines offer a necessary transport service. The importance of the airline connections is crucial because of the underdeveloped land transport networks.

As far as air transport is concerned, high traffic concentration is an incontestable phenomenon. Almost 70 per cent of the total passenger air traffic flow is operated by the 10 busiest countries. First on the list is South Africa, followed by Egypt and Morocco (ATAG, 2003). Moreover, the Europe-Africa traffic accounts for a major share exceeding 80 per cent when both percentages of intra-African international and domestic traffic flow are single digits. This trend introduces the impotence of the national government bodies in charge to advance the development of the air transport and the supportive infrastructure to offer realistic and feasible airline services within the continent. Despite the fact that the absolute number of African aircraft movements has increased, the respective market share at a global level is lower than in the past. Moreover, the ticket prices in Africa are quite high bearing in mind that similar distances covered in Europe or America are much cheaper experiencing higher flight density.

The same pattern is followed on international tourist arrivals; they are highly concentrated in a relatively small number of destinations. This led the UNWTO, as the United Nations Development Programme executing agency in tourism, to provide technical assistance in many developing countries during the past three decades including African countries. In its article 70 on Africa, the Johannesburg Summit Plan of Implementation stresses the need to "Support Africa's efforts to attain sustainable tourism that contributes to social, economic and infrastructure development (p.40)". In fact the 2002 Earth Summit in Johannesburg detailed the actions needed to fight poverty through tourism.

The following year, the ST-EP (Sustainable Tourism – Eliminate Poverty) programme was launched. A small number of countries participated as pilot destinations and more have joined since then. Sub-regions with low tourism development, especially Central and Western regions participate in the programme. In the majority of the pilot destinations the results were successful, leading more countries to join the ST-EP programme.

International Tourist Arrivals and Generating Markets

As stated above international tourist arrivals are concentrated in very few countries. There has been a substantial increase but still the gaps are great between sub-regions and countries. In a region with over fifty countries and territories, six countries receive over 1 million tourists – South Africa (6.8 million), Tunisia (6 million), Morocco (5.5 million), Zimbabwe (1.9 million), Algeria (1.2 million) and Kenya (1.1 million); almost 70 per cent of all international arrivals in the region (UNWTO, 2006). Overall, however, tourism development in Africa has been quite positive in the last twenty five years. Between 1980 and 1990, the number of international arrivals more than doubled, rising from 7.3 million in 1980 to 15 million in 1990, while in the following decade the number almost doubled again. Since 1990, Africa's share in the world total rose one percentage point, from 3.4 per cent to 4.4 per cent in 2004. It is the only region that recorded positive growth in 2001 (with the 9/11 events) and 2003 (with the SARS epidemic) and the only region to record successive tourist arrival increases since 1990.

According to the UNWTO, there are five dominant generating markets visiting the region; Europe, US and Japan, China, South Africa and domestic. The North African countries tend to receive a lot of tourists from Europe, taking advantage of their geographical location and their price advantage against the euro-zone Mediterranean countries. VFR traffic is strong from the UK to South Africa, Gambia and Kenya. Leisure traffic is also important from Europe with business tourism still improving. The US market is also strengthening its position: in 2004, 630 thousand US tourists visited Africa, 2 per cent of the total US outbound market. The Japanese market, on the other hand, was severely affected by the SARS epidemic and is recovering. Business traffic has started to emerge, following the economic expansion of Japan.

China is raising its profile as a dominant generating tourism market, especially since eight African countries negotiated 'Approved Destination Status'. The Chinese market is one of the fastest growing markets in South Africa and Zimbabwe experienced a significant rise in Chinese tourist arrivals since the launch of direct flights to Beijing.

Southern and Eastern African countries depend heavily on South Africa as it is a major source of their visitors. It is considered to be a key market with relatively high spending power. On the same grounds, domestic tourism in Africa is increasing as there are significant improvements in infrastructure, tourism opportunities and services.

African Airlines and Airports

Most of the African airlines are state owned while there are few that have several European airline companies among their major shareholders (among others British Airways holds 18 per cent of Comair's shares and KLM 26 per cent of Kenya Airways' shares). Alliances phenomena are very rare among the African airlines whereas there is co-operation between carriers outside the continent and several local ones. The two major types of alliances occurring in Africa are: a) one African airline owns equity of another airline of the continent, and b) codeshare agreements between airlines in a consortium. A typical example is the codeshare agreement between SAA (South Africa Airlines) and Ethiopian Airlines in the Johannesburg – Addis Ababa route. The reason behind the low alliance performance is the fact that most of the airlines in the region are not too profitable to attract capital investments. Without capital injections the African airlines can not easily develop and support an operating network that could attract alliance contracts. An exception to this state of affairs is SAA which on April 10th, 2006 became the 18th member of the Star Alliance. SAA was the first African carrier to join such an alliance while Kenya Airways joined, on September 4, 2007, the SkyTeam Alliance, as an official associate member.

As far as the fleet is concerned, most of the aircraft operating in the continent are old. Despite the fact that only 4.3 per cent of the aircraft operating worldwide fly in Africa, the respective percentage for the aged[3] aircraft is 12 per cent. Their low price is counterbalanced, among others, by the elevated maintenance costs and the increased fuel consumption per km. Moreover, the low credit rating of the African carriers results in low levels of aircraft' leasing contracts (5 per cent of the leased aircraft worldwide).

The African airlines' operation performance is suppressed by several external factors among which is the high fuel cost, the elevated lease fees, the high insurance charges, the lack of outsourcing potentialities and the stagnation of foreign investment resulting in capital injections through loans, increased debts, high interest obligations and insolvency phenomena. Marketing incompetence of African carriers combined with their absence from international alliances results in a domino effect of perpetual low operational performance. The only exception is SAA, which achieved exceptional performance, depicted in the relative amount of revenues.

South Africa experienced the emergence of the Low Cost Carriers phenomenon in 2001. Comair launched kulula.com, South Africa's first LCC which nowadays serves 11 destinations. There was a domestic traffic boost of more than 50 per cent with a corresponding reduction in ticket prices. Apart from kulula.com, 1time & Mango are the other two LCCs operating in South Africa.

As far as Nigeria is concerned, the Nigerian government set a deadline of April 30, 2007 for all airlines operating in the country to re-capitalise or be grounded, in an effort to ensure better services and safety. The low cost airlines that satisfied the Nigerian Civil Aviation Authority's (NCAA) criteria in terms of re-capitalisation and were re-registered

---

3   Over 15 years in service.

for operation were IRS Airlines, Chanchangi Airlines and Kabo Air while Sosoliso Airlines failed and was not allowed to fly over Nigeria's airspace[4].

Morocco's two LCCs are Jet4you and Atlas Blue (subsidiary of Royal Air Maroc). Jet4you is based in Casablanca and it operates, apart from domestic flights, between Morocco and destinations in France & Belgium. Its major shareholder is TUI Group with 40 per cent of the company's shares. Atlas Blue is based in Marrakech with flight operations to Belgium, France, Italy, Spain, Switzerland, U.K. and several domestic destinations. Furthermore, European LCCs such as easyJet and Ryanair operate to Morocco. EasyJet flies to Marrakech and Casablanca while Ryanair to Marrakech and Fez.

With respect to airports and despite the fact that noteworthy efforts are taking place to improve the relevant infrastructure across the continent, the average operational level of the African airports is still below minimum requirement standards. Longsighted exceptions do exist though, primarily related to airport privatisations. ADP[5] has invested in FHB Abidjan airport while KADCO[6] was the major player in the privatisation of the Kilimanjaro airport. Algiers and Djibouti airports are two more African airports aiming at attracting private funding to become competitive and cost-effective. ICAO has been quite dynamic and vigorous in its effort to upgrade the African aviation at a level acceptable by intercontinental aviation bodies.

The busiest airport of the continent is the South Africa's OR Tambo International Airport (ORTIA, previously known as Johannesburg International Airport – JIA) with Cairo's airport occupying the second place. The main drawback and anticompetitive element of Africa's airports operational activity is the monopolistic phenomenon of ground handling services. The existence of more than one handler in an airport is rather rare while private companies are largely absent from the market. Despite the vague framework concerning the level of liberalised handling business activity, low traffic flows and lack of skilled personnel are the main reasons for the perpetuation of the stagnant situation.

As far as South Africa airports' privatisation is concerned, Airports Company South Africa (ACSA) owns and operates South Africa's nine principal airports, including the three major international airports in Johannesburg, Cape Town and Durban together with six other domestic airports[7]. In 1998, the largest African airports authority entered in a privatisation procedure when ADR (Aeroporti di Roma) successfully acquired the 20 per cent of the ACSA's shares. In October 2005, ADR sold its shares at a price over than twice their acquisition level. Other shareholders, by that time, owned 4.2 per cent while the rest of the company's shares belonged to the state.

MAJOR POLICY ISSUES

The major policy issues regarding African air transport that IATA and the national bodies in charge aim to invigorate are safety, infrastructure, aviation liberalisation and performance simplification. In particular, safety is IATA's number one concern that African airlines have to tackle. Some progress has been admittedly accomplished but the statistics indicate that further continuation of the effort is needed for the figures to meet the global safety standards. 2004's reports showed that with less that 5 per cent of global traffic, almost 25

---

4   Nigeria Direct, The Official Information Gateway of the Federal Republic of Nigeria (www.nigeria.gov.ng).
5   Aéroports de Paris.
6   Kilimanjaro Airport Development Company.
7   Bloemfontein, Port Elizabeth, East London, George, Kimberley and Upington.

per cent of the airline accidents happened in Africa. As few African airlines have been or are expected to undertake the IOSA's[8] audit process in the near future, Africa is IATA's first priority in "Partnership for Safety"[9].

Apart from safety, infrastructure is of significant importance, although many airports across Africa have developed advanced operational systems. There are still problems with the runways, the lighting, the fencing, the meteorological data etc. Moreover, local bodies in charge have not developed reinvestment and refinancing programs that could upgrade the current infrastructure and maximise the benefits of the air transport income.

The accommodation sector varies significantly amongst the African countries. There are many efforts to attract foreign capital to invest in the sector or promote PPP (Private-Public-Partnerships). On the land transport side, there is a significant lack of road infrastructure which creates inevitably mobility issues, both regionally and intra-regionally. Sub-regions such as North Africa and countries like South Africa experience a significantly higher infrastructure profile compared to other African countries.

Liberalisation and Legislation

Liberalisation is not established across Africa yet, and that is a major problem for the intra-continental air transport market. The airlines should enjoy the freedom to design their operational strategies without being bounded by exogenous factors. It is very disappointing that 19 years after the "Yamoussoukro Declaration" the liberalisation process is still pending. The relaxation of restrictions could advance the competitiveness of the carriers and achieve economies of scale through mergers and alliances.

In the tourism sector, a number of countries are revising the regulations regarding the granting of licenses for tourism businesses and rewriting their national legal framework. Other countries are introducing measures to grade their accommodation sector. Morocco is a good example as it is in the process of liberalizing its skies and LCCs are already operating to the country.

Simplification

The simplification of the African airline industry was a project initiated in 2003 by IATA. It was divided in five major air transport categories aiming at operational cost reduction: a) overall transfer to e-ticketing, b) paperless logistics procedures, c) development of modern baggage management techniques, d) bar coded boarding passes and e) speed up of check-in procedures. The most important project is the e-ticketing introduction where much work has to be done. As discussed by Sigala in Chapter 16, the deadline for the implementation of the adaptation of the electronic ticketing method was at first December 31st, 2007. On June 4, 2007, IATA voted for the extension of the deadline to May 31st, 2008 after it became clear that several carriers would not meet the target. Africa was among those regions that were expected to miss the original deadline because of issues concerning the regulation framework and the delays in the IT systems conversion.

---

8   IOSA is IATA's Operational Safety Audit. It began in 2003 and is trying to build safety standards in collaboration with ICAO.
9   Partnership for Safety is a programme aiming s to help airlines reach the IOSA's safety standards.

Despite the major issues mentioned above there are secondary concerns that need to be waned such as the prolongation of subsidies granting, the lack of collaboration among African airlines and the discouragement of external investments.

Tourism Policy and Development

Africa is the region where the spending per tourist is the lowest in the world. The total receipts for Africa in 2005 represented just 3 per cent of the world total. It has to be stated though, that there are significant differences in spending amongst Africa's regions. The Southern Africa region accounts for 40 per cent of all tourism receipts and the spending per tourist is significantly higher compared to the region's average (US$760 in Southern Africa region compared to US$505 in the other four sub-regions) (UNWTO, 2006). On the other hand, there are countries in the continent which have introduced more taxation on the tourism sector, whereas others are using investment incentives and tax relief to facilitate tourism development. Visa requirements have been relaxed by several countries to encourage tourism. Mauritius for example allows tourists from certain countries to stay for up to 15 days without a visa, whereas other countries do not require a visa when on organised tours.

Zimbabwe has launched the 'Look East' Policy, aiming to attract the vast Asian market. South Africa has launched branding strategies. Other counties are or have introduced various policies on development, marketing even e-commerce. Each policy is tailor-made to attract either domestic or international tourists, depending on the infrastructure and resources available.

THE WAY FORWARD

The reform of the air transport industry was first introduced more than 20 years ago, in several parts of the world. Africa is still experiencing a transition period. The national airline carriers remain held back on overlooking the major benefits of the multilateral airline agreements. To improve the situation, the Yamoussoukro Decision's propositions have to be implemented. The coordination of the stakeholders, the handling services, the tourism companies, the organisations and agencies could advance the operational efficiency.

One major step forward is the collaboration between the airlines that could result in stronger negotiation potentiality on fuel and insurance charges, economies of scale in several aspects of air transport operation, more financing sources and higher load factors. Moreover, the establishment of regional airline companies could become the solution for the satisfaction of the continental air transport needs and the development of a prosperous network.

Africa seems to be in a transitional period, not just in its aviation sector, but in its tourism industry too. North African countries are expected to achieve high growth, especially since the relaxation of their aviation policies. South Africa is also implementing an aggressive marketing campaign which may generate a double digit tourism growth rate in the years to come in conjunction with the organisation of the 2012 World Football Cup and the related infrastructure development.

Many countries in Africa are investing heavily on the tourism industry. This is not just on accommodation infrastructure or National Parks. They tend to invest on infrastructure, such as roads, ports and airports in order to attract investment and tourists to their countries. They invest on business and convention bureaus; they build conference facilities to compete not just against each other but also against other regions. Countries in the sub-regions which experience lower numbers of tourist arrivals, namely Central and West Africa are the ones investing the most.

The African air transport industry has to reciprocate to the commands of the liberalised airline industry. The development process across the world indicates that the African bodies in charge should:

- Upgrade and refine the safety procedures to meet up to the international standards.

- Coordinate and promote the actions necessary for the wide implementation of the Yamoussoukro Decision's recommendations.

- Update and modify the framework across Africa for the introduction of private financing opportunities into the airline industry.

- Further relax the visa restrictions among the African countries to promote mobility across the continent.

- Encourage the cooperation between the airlines to achieve lower price levels and make the African carriers competitive in the global air transport market.

African governments and airlines should collaborate for the upgrading of the continental aviation because it constitutes a fundamental factor for tourism, economic growth and prosperity. The harmonisation of the strategies mentioned above could lead to a win-win situation for the development of the airline and tourism industry as a whole.

24

Mauritius

Neelu Seetaram

INTRODUCTION

Tourism brings enormous economic benefits to the island of Mauritius. With the decline in revenue and buoyancy of the two other main industries of the island, namely the textile and sugar industries, the tourism sector is being called upon to play an even more prominent economic role. Traditionally, since the early days of this industry, it has been a government policy to encourage 'up-market' as opposed to mass tourism. The government tried to achieve this objective by encouraging the supply of premium accommodation only and by strictly regulating the air transportation services in order to restrict air access to the island. These measures have resulted in a relatively high accommodation rate and airfare making the cost of a holiday to Mauritius affordable to only the higher income holiday makers. The tourism industry has nevertheless been booming with a steady increase of arrivals over the last 36 years. The aim of this chapter is to look at how the government of Mauritius has formulated and implemented aviation polices in order to achieve its objectives for the tourism industry and to discuss whether this is still a sound strategy given the changing economic situation that the nation is now facing.

HISTORICAL DEVELOPMENTS

The Republic of Mauritius is a volcanic island situated in the Indian Ocean, 800 km to the east of Mozambique, Africa (Map 24.1). It has a total area of 2,040 km^2, 64 km in length and 47 km in width. The capital of Mauritius is Port Louis. Mauritius has a population of approximately 1.2 million and the Mauritian society is multi-ethnic. The local currency is the Mauritian rupee[1]. In 2006 the Gross Domestic Product (GDP) per capita was €7,803. The main sources of income are the textile, tourism and sugar industries. The unique landscape, pristine beaches, diverse fauna and flora, the rich cultural mix of the island, along with the island's reputation of being very hospitable, has made Mauritius an ideal holiday destination. The national carrier, Air Mauritius, flies to 25 destinations (Map 24.1) with approximately 80 weekly flights.

According to Wing (1995), the initial stage of the development of this industry can be traced back to the eighteenth century when Mauritius (then called *Ile de France*), as a

---

1   € 1.00= Rs 41.84 as on 18/05/2008 from the Bank of Mauritius website: http://bom.intnet.mu/

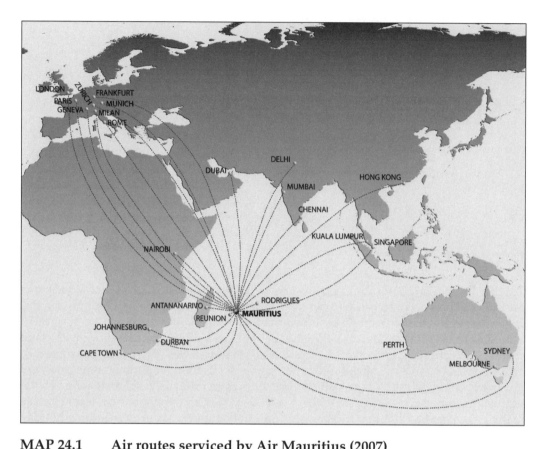

MAP 24.1   Air routes serviced by Air Mauritius (2007)

Source: Cartography and Geo-Informatics Laboratory, Geography Department, University of the Aegean, Greece.

French colony attracted visitors from mainland France for 'rest' and 'relaxation'. Since Mauritius was strategically located on the main navigation routes of the Indian Ocean, it was a popular destination for visitors in transit as well.

The main air route to Mauritius was created in 1952 and the first airline to fly to Mauritius was Qantas which used Mauritius as a transit point on its Australia–South Africa route. South African Airways joined this route five years later. Tourism to Mauritius was given a boost when European airlines added Mauritius to their routes. Air Mauritius, the local carrier, was incorporated in June 1967. In 1972, it started operations modestly with flights to the neighbouring islands. These initial years could be described as the 'exploration stage' of the tourism industry whereby the facilities offered to visitors were limited and there were no hotels of reasonable international standards.

The tourism industry in Mauritius started to expand significantly in the early 1970s when the government provided a number of fiscal and other incentives to attract both foreign and local capital for the development of local tourism businesses. The direct consequence of these was a rapid increase in the number of hotels on the island (Cleverdon 1992; Durbarry 2004). During the same time period, specific objectives for the tourism industry were established in the National Development Plan of 1971–1975. These objectives stipulated that Mauritius targets the 'up-market tourist' as a priority.

The development of the industry over the last two decades occurred taking these governmental objectives into consideration. In fact, it can be argued that the main rationale behind the aviation policy of the Mauritian government has, until very recently, been to protect the national carrier as well as to restrict access to the island in order to prevent mass tourism. This strategy was reinforced by the strict monitoring of the hotel sector. Construction of new hotels and the expansion of existing ones are subject to a number of governmental controls. The regulatory measures have been complemented with promotion campaigns by the Mauritius Tourism Promotion Authority which led Mauritius to acquire the image of an exclusive holiday destination.

CURRENT TRENDS IN AIR TRANSPORT AND TOURISM

The air access policy of Mauritius is not explicitly described in any government publication on national policies, but de facto emerges through the implemented strategies. In 2004, Mauritius had Bilateral Air Services Agreements (BASAs) with 30 countries and these were restrictive in terms of capacity and prices (NACO BV 2005). Some of the strategies adopted in this sector directly affected the level of competition on the air routes to Mauritius as they included the continuation of a ban on charter carriers and the unwillingness to grant 5th freedom rights. Furthermore, although listed at the Stock Exchange of Mauritius, Air Mauritius remains primarily a publicly owned company with the Mauritian government owning 37.46 per cent of the total shares of Air Mauritius Holdings (Air Mauritius Ltd. 2007).

Air Mauritius has a monopoly power in several of its services including its Australian, Swiss and Indian routes. Currently, the flight to India is operated on a code share basis with Air India which holds 8.8 per cent of shares in Air Mauritius Holdings and is serviced by Air Mauritius aircraft only. The two densest routes in terms of number of passengers are Mauritius–London and Mauritius–Paris. The London route is also serviced by British Airways, which flies to Heathrow and to Gatwick in London. Air France operates a code share with Air Mauritius on the Paris route. According to Oum *et al.* (1996), the code sharing effects on airfare and quality of customer services vary. Code sharing can increase flight frequency, reduce price and raise the quality of service when it leads to competitive behaviour between the code share partners. On the other hand, collusive behaviour can result in an increase of the partners' joint market shares; this may lead to greater market control and harm passenger welfare. Given that the bilateral agreements signed by Mauritius are not competition-driven (NACO BV 2005) and that British Airways Associated Companies Limited and Compagnie Nationale Air France hold 9.58 and 13.24 per cent of the shares of Air Mauritius Holdings respectively (Air Mauritius Ltd 2007), it is reasonable to expect collusive behaviour on these routes.

The limited competition faced by Air Mauritius allows the company to price discriminate based on nationality and the origin of the travel. The different sets of prices charged can also reflect cross subsidisation of certain air fare classes. It can be noted that in 2006, approximately 66 per cent of the passengers carried to Mauritius were foreigners. Examples of price discriminating practices by Air Mauritius are the followings:

1. Return airfares from Mauritius are considerably lower to return airfares to Mauritius. For example, a ticket Mauritius–Melbourne–Mauritius costs almost 40 per cent cheaper than a ticket Melbourne–Mauritius-Melbourne.

2. Special discounts are given to students under 30 with Mauritian passports en route to Mauritius. For example the full economy fare to Mauritius from Melbourne in 2006 was approximately €1010, while a Mauritian student pays only approximately €750. Parents of students travelling abroad for the graduation ceremony of their children also receive some special discounts.

3. Special discounts are available on a few of the main routes during off-peak seasons. For example, the return ticket to London can cost up to 30 per cent cheaper during off-peak season. The same type of discount is available on flights to India, South Africa and Australia. These special discount tariffs are applicable only for return flights from Mauritius and not on flights to Mauritius.

4. Air Mauritius also offers discounted airfares to civil servants and employers of semi governmental organisations in Mauritius.

5. The special fares are also extended to business travellers of selected companies registered in Mauritius.

The operating cost of the airline which was € 0.27 per km in 2002–2003, fell to € 0.25 but rose back to € 0.28 in 2005/2006. During the same time period the yield, has fallen from € 0.47 in 2002/2003 to € 0.43 in 2005/2006. Air Mauritius attributed these increases in the operating cost primarily to the rise in the price of fuel which accounted for 35 per cent of the total operating cost of the airline (Air Mauritius Ltd 2007). Given the lack of effective competition, Air Mauritius had little incentive to increase efficiency in its operations. It may be argued that this led to a dead weight loss borne by the Mauritian society and the passengers of Air Mauritius. The special fares offered to Mauritians can be seen as a compensation mechanism whereby Air Mauritius has been trying to 'export' the welfare loss to foreign passengers.

Trends in the Tourism Industry

Figure 24.1 illustrates the total number of visitors to Mauritius (by air and sea) from the year 1970 to 2005. More than 90 per cent of the arrivals are for leisure purposes. In the early 1970s the industry registered a growth of more than 30 per cent. From 1980 to 1999, this industry grew faster than the manufacturing and the agricultural sectors and prospered into a major source of foreign exchange and employment in Mauritius, second only to the manufacturing sector (Durbarry 2002). According to Durbarry (2004), the growth rate of real tourism exports was the single most important determinant of the economic growth rate of Mauritius. From 1999 to 2004, arrivals grew on average at 2.6 per cent compared to 9.1 per cent for the previous decade. This can be explained by unfavourable international conditions which affected demand. The decrease in the average growth rate of arrivals was unanticipated since according to the Tourism Development Plan (TDP) of 2002, arrivals were projected to rise steadily to 2 million by the year 2020.

Seetanah (2006) attributed the changes in arrivals from 1970 to 2004, to five main factors namely, changes in income of the home country, the relative cost of holidays to Mauritius, the level of development in Mauritius, the number of rooms supplied and air

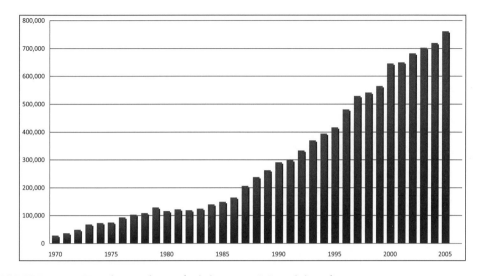

FIGURE 24.1 Total number of visitors to Mauritius from 1970–2005

Source: Data for this graph were obtained from the Central Statistics Office (2004) and the Ministry of Tourism, Leisure and External Communications (2007).

liberalisation, as measured by the number of BASAs signed by the Mauritian government. Although he finds that the effect of air liberalisation is relatively much lower than that of the other factors, this effect is statistically significant. Khadaroo and Seetanah (2007) analysed the effect of infrastructure on the number of arrivals to Mauritius. They found that the transport infrastructure of the island has been contributing positively to tourist numbers, particularly from Europe, America and Asia. Non-transport infrastructure of the island is a determining factor for arrivals from Europe and America.

The main source of arrivals to Mauritius is France (Figure 24.2). The share of tourist arrivals from this country has increased from 18 per cent in 1983 to 23 per cent in 2005. Reunion Island is legally part of France. Thus, the total number of French travellers to Mauritius accounts for 36 per cent of total arrivals and the gross earnings from these travellers accounts for approximately 37 per cent of the total gross earnings of the industry (Table 24.1). According to Archer (1985), Mauritius is popular among the French travellers because of the island's long history of French culture and the similarity of the local language to French. Tourists from Europe are the highest spenders in Mauritius, and in 2005, the average duration of their stay was higher than the overall average stay of all visitors, which was 10.1 days.

The gross earnings from tourism in 2005 increased by 9 per cent compared to 2004 and represented 16 per cent of the total gross export earnings of Mauritius. In 2004, employment in the tourism sector accounted for 21 per cent of total employment on the island and the share of real GDP attributable to this sector was 7.6 per cent.

In the TDP put forward in 2002, the government reconfirmed its policy towards targeting the 'up-market tourist' and made a commitment towards enhancing the tourism product of Mauritius. In order to increase expenditure per day and also to raise the average duration of stay which had been declining in the previous years, the government proposed the provision of more leisure opportunities to visitors. Following the publication of the TDP, substantial investments took place in the hotel sector and the total number of rooms

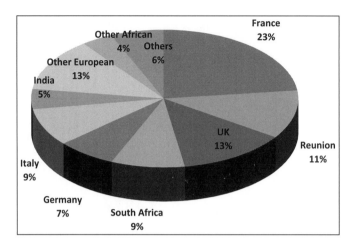

FIGURE 24.2 Distribution of international visitors to Mauritius in 2006 by main markets

Source: Data for this graph were obtained from the Minsitry of Tourism, Leisure and External Communications (2007).

TABLE 24.1   Characteristics of international visitors from the main markets

	France	Reunion Island	UK	South Africa	Germany	Italy
Duration of Stay* (nights)	10.9	7.5	11.7	8.4	12.3	9.2
Average Expenditure per Holiday† (Rs.)	32,928	16,328	45,509	25,911	39,865	33,672
% of Total Gross Tourism Receipt+	29.97	6.82	18.24	5.9	9.02	6.01

* 2006
† 2004

Source: Data for this table were obtained from Central Statistical Office (2004) the Ministry of Tourism, Leisure and External Communications (2007).

increased by 39 per cent to 10,497 in 2005. With room availability rising faster than arrivals in Mauritius, and the duration of stay continuing to fall, average hotel occupancy rate fell from 64 per cent in 1996 to 55 per cent in 2005.

In spite of the oversupply of hotel rooms, the average rate of rooms went up by almost 30 per cent (NACO BV 2005). Furthermore, it was also pointed out that there is no significant difference between hotel rooms rates charged in off-peak seasons as compared to peak seasons even if the difference in occupancy rate can be as high as 20 per cent. This is an indication of the inefficiency in price setting of this sector which could have resulted from the absence of a locally competitive accommodation market. The decline in occupancy rates can be partly attributed to a rise in the average cost of holidays to Mauritius (NACO BV 2005).

Over the last 10 years increasing demand for bed-nights in private bungalows has led to a proliferation of rooms in the informal sector as well. It is estimated that the total number of rooms offered is 7,000 and the number of room nights sold in the formal sector is three times the number of those in the informal sector (NACO BV 2005). It should be noted however, that the two markets are quite distinct since the boom in the informal sector is attributable to increasing demand from regional tourists (NACO BV 2005) whereas the majority of long haul tourists stay in hotels. The level of competition between the formal and informal sectors is negligible.

MAJOR POLICY ISSUES IN THE TOURISM AND AVIATION SECTORS

The main issues that the tourism industry is now facing are declining occupancy rates and duration of stay. These have been the main concerns for the government for the last five years. The growing pressure from a shortfall in revenue from the sugar and the textile industries which are facing increasing international competition and the fact that unemployment in the country is reaching 10 per cent, has made the economy of the country more dependent on the tourism sector. These factors have led the Mauritian Government to review its aviation policy.

Although the number of BASAs signed by Mauritius rose from 10 to 29 between 1983 and 2003 (Seetanah 2006), the first step towards actual liberalisation was taken in 2002 when Emirates Airlines started flying to Mauritius. Air Mauritius and Emirates Airlines signed a code share agreement on the Mauritius–Dubai route. Emirates Airlines did not compete directly with Air Mauritius as it did not operate any direct flights from the island. It offered, however, competitive tariffs to passengers travelling on the two main air routes of Air Mauritius, namely Paris and London by charging 6th freedom tariffs (NACO BV 2005). A number of developments occurred in the aviation sector as from 2005. More BASAs were signed by the Mauritian government and Air Mauritius signed a few additional code share agreements. As from 2006/2007 frequencies of flights to several destinations have gone up while some routes have been terminated. For example, Mauritius is no longer connected to Vienna by a direct flight ever since Austrian Airlines cancelled its weekly flight to Mauritius. The entry of Virgin Atlantic on the London route and that of Corsair on the route to France in 2007 are expected to raise competition on these routes, leading to an eventual fall in air-fares on two of the major tourism markets of Mauritius.

The annual report of Air Mauritius (Air Mauritius Ltd 2007) stated that the increasing competition on its main air routes explained to some extent the relatively poor financial performance of the company in 2006/2007 as compared to the previous year. The company registered a loss of €7,918,000 in 2006/2007, and a fall in the average prices at which its shares were traded on the Mauritius Stock Exchange (Table 24.2). During this year, capacity increased by 7 per cent and the number of passengers carried rose by 1.7 per cent, while the load factors fell by 2.3 per cent. Currently 37 per cent of the seats offered by Air Mauritius are on the European routes.

The poor performance of the airline in 2006/2007 has prompted Air Mauritius to take measures aiming at upgrading the quality of services provided, increasing efficiency and productivity in every sector of activity. These include improving sales practices and customer services and targeting markets with potential growth (Air Mauritius Ltd 2007).

TABLE 24.2   Performance indicators for Air Mauritius

	2005–20061	2006–2007[†]
Passengers Carried (No.)	1,156,820	1,176,663
Capacity (No.)	1,533,382	1,644,977
Load factor (%)	76.90	74.60
Operating Cost per Available tonnes per Kms (€)	0.28	0.27
Yield per Revenue Tonne Km (€)	0.47	0.4
Operating Revenue (€ million)	413	410
Traffic Revenue (€ million)	372	356.8
Profit / (Loss) for the year after taxation (€'000)	7,298	(7,918)
Earning/(Loss) per Share (Rs.)	2.59	(3.44)
Average Price per Share (Rs.)	20.18	18.97

[†]As at financial year ending June 30.
Source: Data for this table were obtained from Air Mauritius Ltd. (2007).

The total number of visitors to Mauritius grew by approximately 9 per cent in 2006. The main concern, however, is the long term effect of the gradual liberalisation of the air transportation industry of Mauritius. Given that more air routes to Mauritius are expected to open in the near future, and that the government is contemplating signing new BASAs, it may be expected that competition in the long term will eventually drive the airfares down, even if Mauritius maintains a no-charter policy. This measure may aid in enabling Mauritius to achieve its target of 2 million visitors by 2020. On the other hand, it conflicts with the tourism objective of encouraging only the 'up market' travellers. The high supply of cheaper accommodation in the informal sector and lower air fares may result in increased arrivals of low spending mass-tourists. This will result in Mauritius losing its image as an exclusive destination.

Major shortcomings of the TDP are the lack of information on how the target of 2 million visitors (a more than 100 per cent increase in arrivals in 20 years) will be realised, and the expected economic significance of this increase in the number of visitors to the island. Given that the tourism sector is expected to be the next engine of growth for the economy, an important matter that needs to be addressed is to find out whether the increase in arrivals to 2 million (assuming that this target is achievable) leads to sustainable economic growth on the island in the long run. The TDP does not identify the specific type of impact that is required or expected. Furthermore, the rationale behind targeting the 'up-market tourist' only has not been clearly defined.

In the past, the country has significantly benefited from the high spending tourists, in terms of income generation, employment and revenue. At this stage, however, the question raised is which tourist-type is likely to have the highest net positive economic impact on the island. Increasing the number of low expenditure mass tourists to the island can also generate economic benefits. For example, if lowering the cost per night can be compensated by a significant increase in the number of nights sold, then this may lead to increased revenue for the island. There is a need, therefore, to segment the different markets (high expenditure up-market tourism and lower expenditure mass-tourism) and assess their potential individual impacts on the economy, in terms of the contribution to GDP, employment creation, revenues, usage of the natural resources of the island as well as potential environmental impact. This can be done by carrying out economic forecasting exercises, and simulating the effect of the increase in number of visitors to Mauritius. Results of such studies can enable policy makers to take more informed decisions as to which tourism strategy is likely to be the most beneficial for the country.

CONCLUSIONS

Traditionally, the main tourism objective of the government of Mauritius has been to maintain the image of the island as an exclusive destination and to target visits by up-market tourists only. The government was able to achieve this goal by implementing restrictive aviation polices which limited access to the island. More recently, while the tourism policy of the island remained mostly unaltered, steps have been taken to gradually liberalise the air access to Mauritius. Increased competition has negatively affected the financial performance of Air Mauritius but benefited tourism to the island. It is argued that in the long term, reductions in the cost of travel to Mauritius will tend to encourage lower spending visitors to the island, which contradicts with the up-market policy reiterated in the Tourism Development Plan of 2002. Leaving environmental concerns aside, however, this need not necessarily be a cause for concern for the authorities since it may have the potential to generate sustainable economic benefits to the island in the long run.

25

South Pacific

Semisi Taumoepeau

INTRODUCTION

Aviation and tourism have become integral to modern world commerce and they are also assuming increasing importance in the economies of island nations in the South Pacific. The majority of countries and territories in the region are small island states, spread over a large area of the vast Pacific Ocean, remote from the main metropolitan centres and are characterised by small populations. Opportunities for economic growth tend to be limited, reflecting a narrow base, small size of the domestic markets and high transport costs to external markets. Tourism is the main economic sector throughout the region, highlighting the significance of regional air transportation. This chapter explores historical developments in the aviation and tourism markets of the South Pacific Region, followed by a discussion of current trends, major policy issues and the way forward.

HISTORICAL DEVELOPMENTS

For the most part in the early years, air transport links to the South Pacific islands were provided by airlines from Australia, New Zealand and Pacific Rim countries (Kissling 1984). This put these small tourist destinations in a double bind. On the one hand, their tourist industries could not survive without the tourist traffic generated by air carriers and foreign tour companies, leaving them vulnerable to the corporate and government pressures of foreign countries. On the other hand, the minor importance of island destinations meant that they were becoming increasingly marginal stop-over points given the recent changes in international aviation economics and technology (Taumoepeau 1989; Kissling 2002).

One element which contains a degree of commonality to the many South Pacific islands, is the ever close proximity of the sea, the smallness and fragmented character of the land areas comprising the various sovereign states, and the vast distances which have to be spanned to maintain contact within any one island group let alone between groups or with the rest of the world (Kissling 2002). Map 25.1 shows the great isolation of the South Pacific islands with proliferation of many small national airlines to provide essential services and to lure much needed tourist traffic from several metropolitan centres.

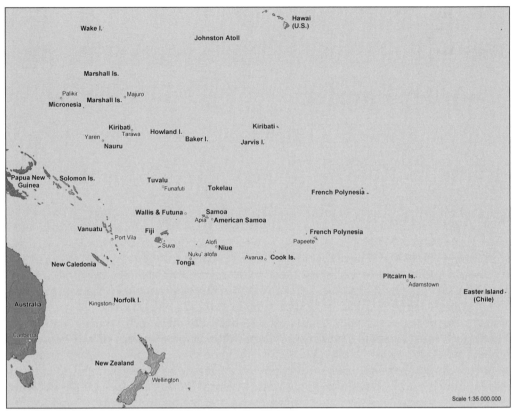

MAP 25.1   South Pacific Islands

Source: Cartography and Geo-Informatics Laboratory, Geography Department, University of the Aegean, Greece.

CURRENT TRENDS

In the South Pacific region, the degree and scope of government support both to the tourism and airline industries tends to depend on the stage of economic development in general, and the size and stage of development of the tourism industry in particular. The majority of the small airlines of the South Pacific are government owned[1]. Government ownership in the past has not been the only reason for policies designed to protect national airlines: all kinds of other reasons, including national defence, national pride and prestige have played their part in the South Pacific (Kissling 1989). Most South Pacific national carriers have repeatedly faced financial problems due to insufficient commercial planning and mistakes in the choice of right aircraft for the routes served. Generally, aircraft have been too large and the ownership and operating costs have been too high. The pattern of inbound tourism to the region reflects the existing air transportation network (Campbell 2002b; King 2002, Taumoepeau 2007).

---

1   Government-owned airline in this chapter means either wholly or partially owned. Also it is normally referred to as the national airline or flag carrier of the island or country.

Aviation

In recent years, the spectacular financial losses of some of the South Pacific airlines, such as Royal Tongan Airline, Polynesian Airline, Air Niugini, Air Kiribati, Air Tahiti Nui and Air Vanuatu, have dominated recent trends. Some governments of the South Pacific have imposed little financial discipline on their airlines, which has decreased their incentive to undertake efficiency-enhancing measures (King 2002; Taumoepeau 2007).

Regional Routes Challenges in Scheduling and Services   There is an existing challenge with the economic scheduling of flights as traffic tends to be seasonal with 'thin' uneconomical routes being very common throughout the islands. The types of aircraft used at times are not considered technically suitable for some airfields resulting in the aircraft's payload being drastically reduced (Kissling 2002). This problem is common in the South Pacific airlines with small fleets and low frequency of service. Maintenance schedules also need to be allowed for, and while market requirements should prevail in the South Pacific, there may not be a great deal of flexibility in the arrangements for maintenance and overhaul of aircraft (Campbell 2002b). To transverse the Pacific one often has to fly via New Zealand or Australia to move between two island countries separated by only a few hundred miles of ocean, e.g. Tonga to Rarotonga, via Auckland.

There are also some aviation infrastructure issues in the region. Modern jets are quite large and heavy. Many island runways are small, old and do not have a "depth" of concrete on thresholds. Runways "break up" with modern jet landing impacts. Many terminals struggle with a full aircraft load and security is poor. Some airports have night curfew or are closed on Sundays (Kissling 2002; Taumoepeau 2007). Table 25.1 shows the varying degree of government support depending on the stages of economic development in the region. There is a tendency for the least developed economies to receive more government support and subsidies than the more developed ones. The aviation policy is still regulated through out the islands.

Pricing and Yield Management   The level of fares for travel within the South Pacific region is high. The tourist, however, is used to travelling on group or other discount fares. These are available between the majority of the islands, at between 30 and 40 percent of the full fare (King 2002; Taumoepeau 2007). The opening up of a deregulated environment in Australia and New Zealand also manifests itself in giving rise to low cost airlines such as Virgin Blue, Pacific Blue, Jetstar and Freedom Air (later grounded by its parent company Air New Zealand in 2007). These have been instrumental in the development of increased tourism in the two countries, but with slow implication or influence on air travel in the islands as yet, except to Fiji at this stage.

Lack of Capital and Financial Resources   For local airlines, mostly government-owned, the responsibility for the provision of capital lies with governments, which in most cases are unable to continue to inject further capital into national airlines that are consistently losing money. Without sound long-term finance, airlines are thus forced to enter into more expensive short-term arrangements. As the business expands, so should the equity capital base of the airline, but this is not so in the islands. As such, the airlines are engaged

**TABLE 25.1   South Pacific governments support to tourism and air
transportation**

Stage of development in the Pacific States	Funding of Air Transport Infrastructure	Tourism Investments	Aviation Policy Regulations or Deregulations	Destination Marketing	Direct Subsidisation of Air Transportation
Developed economy with mature tourism destination e.g. Fiji	Partly by the government, partly by the private sector	Decreasing government involvement, mostly private sector	Regulated	Partly government, partly private sector	Not normally except in crisis situation
Developing economy with mature tourism destination e.g. Tahiti, New Caledonia	Fully by the government	Funded partly by government, partly by the private sector	Regulated	Partly government, partly private sector	Partly subsidised
Developing economy with developing tourism destination e.g. Tonga, Samoa, Vanuatu, Solomon Islands	Fully by the government	Funded partly by the government, partly by the private sector	Regulated	Mostly government	Fully subsidised
Developing economy with small tourism destination e.g. Kiribati, Tuvalu	Fully by the government	Core investment undertaken by government	Regulated	Mostly government	Fully subsidised

Source: SPTO 2005; Taumoepeau 2007.

in a small domestic and sub-regional network with limited returns and insufficient capital for expansion (King 2002; Taumoepeau 2007).

High Maintenance Costs and Regulatory Constraints   Airlines in the region require high seat factors to breakeven, typically around 75 per cent year round. There are no small costs in airlines. A representative breakdown of a South Pacific airline operational costs is as follows: Typical lease costs for a new B737 over a 60 month lease are a fixed US$270,000 per month, plus overhaul reserve of US$260/hr for a typical 4000 hours per annum giving a total cost of US$ 4.24 million per annum; In addition, there are direct operating costs of fuel; catering and ground handling; en route and air navigation fees; landing and airport terminal charges; freight handling, insurance, crew salaries and other expenses. Direct operating costs are at least double the lease and maintenance costs (Campbell 2002b). High cost of imported fuels at island airports is a significant factor, which increased from about 15 per cent of the total airline operational cost in 2001 to about 30% in 2006 (Drysdale 2002; Taumoepeau 2007). Maintenance, spare parts, expatriate engineering and pilots are also main features of the airlines' costs in the islands. Since the 9/11 tragedies, additional costs in security, insurance and operations are making it especially hard to run an airline profitably, both globally and regionally (ASPA 2001; Drysdale 2002).

Small aircraft giving higher frequency are costly to operate, lack comfort, lack range and payload and most airlines do not operate turbo prop aircraft, except domestically. Regional jets (70–90 seat size) are not operated by any South Pacific airline as they are costly to obtain and operate, and are not suitable for major market operations, often not suited for domestic operations on rugged and remote airways and are not supported with spares, training and maintenance by any major airline on most networks (King 2002; Taumoepeau 2007).

The airlines of the region operate under civil aviation authorities based on regulatory systems of several different countries like Australia, France, USA, United Kingdom and New Zealand (ASPA 2001). This reduces opportunities for the sale or leases of aircraft to other regional operators, and occasionally results in the non-recognition of other countries' airworthiness licenses for particular aircraft types (Taumoepeau 2007).

Tourism

In global terms, tourism in the South Pacific is small with the region receiving less than 1.0 per cent of world tourist arrivals. Although there are approximately 1,700 tourism related businesses in the region, the majority of these are small and medium sized businesses (SPTO 2005). The modest size of this industry, leads to limited business opportunities for new entrants (SPTO 2005).

The established tourist destinations of the South Pacific, such as Fiji and Tahiti, started to develop during the 1960s as they were originally refueling points for piston aircraft on the trans-oceanic routes and consequently possessed fully equipped international airports (Kissling 1984). Other smaller destinations in the region developed gradually, reflecting parallel development in regional air services during the 1970s (Taumoepeau 1989).

Air transport and international tourism are inter-dependent, and need each other for growth in the South Pacific islands. However, the level of tourism activity, the size of the industry, the degree of foreign participation, and the rate of tourism development all differ markedly from country to country and in most cases are influenced by the airline network and air transportation pattern in the region. Tourism is being ranked as the main foreign exchange earner for the region. The level of contribution from the tourism sector to the GDP varies depending on the size of the industry and the degree of development of other sectors of the economy such as the agriculture and the fisheries sector. There is large variation in the number of hotel rooms in the region with the lack of hotel investment in the smaller islands being a major constraint. Table 25.2 shows some key tourism and economic figures for the countries of the South Pacific region.

South Pacific countries with developed infrastructure and adequate hotel room stock such as Fiji and Tahiti, with more than 200,000 air visitors annually will be able to sustain their national carriers. Those national airlines serving other smaller destinations will continue to struggle, as the tourism industry is not yet large enough to sustain a viable air service. Benefits from the ever growing tourism industry still need to be optimised, distributed out regionally and continually developed further (SPTO 2003).

Nature of the Tourist Traffic to the region   Tourists are drawn to the islands from a range of northern and southern hemisphere markets, depending on available airline networks and extent of destination awareness and marketing activities carried out. The major source markets are (SPTO 2005):

- Australia and New Zealand especially for destinations in the western Pacific

- North America in the eastern Pacific

- France in French speaking countries such as French Polynesia and New Caledonia

- Other European markets for destinations across the region.

Much of the traffic moving to and from the region consists of passengers travelling primarily for leisure purposes and for VFR (visiting friends and relatives). While this is the market sector, which undoubtedly has the greatest long-term potential for growth, it tends to exhibit low revenue yields and volatility as it responds to changes in levels of economic activity in tourism-generating countries like Australia, New Zealand and USA (Milne 2005; Taumoepeau 2007).

The air traffic volume and geographic characteristics of the region impose additional problems and unique requirements not experienced perhaps by airlines of developing countries in other parts of the world. The traffic densities tend to be low, thus affecting frequencies; distances are long and over water with market dependence on the nearest countries of Australia and New Zealand. Even longer distances are involved for those travelling from tourists' home countries, particularly for Europeans and North Americans. Here, it is important to minimise travel times, reduce the number of interchange points and offer attractive through fares to the final South Pacific destination. The lack of region-wide interlining of air routes, schedules and fares, including through fares from origins

TABLE 25.2   Tourism data in the South Pacific during 2004/2005

Country	Est. No. of Hotel Rooms 2005	Est. of Tourism Contribution to GDP % 2005	Tourism Rank as Foreign Exchange Earner	Major Tourist Market Source	No. Int. Air Visitors 2004
Cook Islands	1320	47%	1	Australia, NZ, USA	83,333
Fiji	6500	35%	1	Australia, NZ, USA	507,000
French Polynesia (Tahiti)	3900	45%	1	France, USA	211,893
Kiribati	179	14.5%	3	Australia, NZ	2,882
New Caledonia	2062	20%	2	Australia, France	99,515
Niue	123	15%	2	New Zealand	2,558
Papua New Guinea	1300	6.5%	3	Australia	59,022
Samoa	845	12%	2	Australia, NZ	98,024
Solomon Islands	811	3%	3	Australia	6,000 (est)
Tonga	740	9.5%	2	Australia, NZ	41,208
Tuvalu	75	3.0%	3	Australia, NZ	1,214
Vanuatu	946	17%	1	Australia, NZ	60,611

Source: Milne 2005, SPTO 2005, Taumoepeau 2007.

outside the region to destinations beyond the major gateways of the region, unavoidably constrain the accessibility of the region and the effort to spread the tourist traffic within the region (King 2002; Taumoepeau 2007).

MAJOR POLICY ISSUES

From a Regulated to a Liberalised Air Transport Environment

Currently in the South Pacific region there is extensive proliferation of air services agreements, with up to 77 bilateral air service agreements (ASAs), 25 bilateral agreements with island members, 16 bilateral agreements with other forum members and 36 bilateral agreements with the rest of the world (Guild 2002). The South Pacific Forum (regional forum of heads of governments in the South Pacific) is investigating various ways in which the aviation sector could further promote economic reform in the region, encourage private sector development, and enhance competitiveness of national economies and further development of tourism (SPTO 2005; Taumoepeau 2007). The ultimate aim is to pursue open, liberal and transparent investment policies and to work towards a common goal of free and open trade and investment. The expected benefits from such regional multilateral air services could increase tourism, improve access to regional air routes and efficiency improvements for airlines and expand inter-island tourism. Airlines in many small island states are infant industries and therefore may still need protection, as against mature airlines in most developed nations (ASPA 2001). Several small South Pacific countries feel it is crucial to have their own airlines, to ensure that adequate and continuous air links domestically and with the outside world are maintained.

Cooperative Strategy for Aviation and Tourism

In the early 1970s, the concept of a single regional airline to operate the air rights entitlements of the various island states was mooted and considered by most to make much economic sense. Several governments decided to work towards a regional airline, earmarking Air Pacific for the role (King 2002). However, some governments argued that Fiji was getting all the benefits such as jobs, destinations and service priorities and tourism promotion. Other governments wanted prestige as well as having a national airline with a focus on meeting national priorities. The question of forming a regional airline has been discussed again at several fora but politically the islands have not been willing to create a regional airline (Taumoepeau 2007).

The way forward is sharing of training equipment and risk sharing arrangements where these are feasible. These strategies can at least reduce costs and for airlines flying in the most difficult circumstances contribute towards a break-even result, and even a small profit (Campbell 2002b). A cooperative strategy would avoid wasteful duplication of effort, ensure the highest levels of productivity for both equipment and personnel, guarantee commonality of equipment and minimise spare part inventories. Such a strategy would be able to provide air services to island airports of little or no interest to global airlines and be more effective at the bargaining for air traffic bilateral exchanges with developed Pacific Rim countries (Taumoepeau 2007).

Creation of Alliances and Code Sharing

Another strategy is where South Pacific airlines cooperate with each other using various commercial agreements such as formation of alliances and code sharing arrangements. Isolation from the main gateways and the small size of the intra-Pacific market would warrant a cooperative strategy between the intra-Pacific and the trans-Pacific airlines (Taumoepeau 2007). As the latter typically have long range jets designed to operate non-stop between Pacific Rim countries, intra Pacific flights would be loss making for them; hence, they could consider "partner" arrangements with South Pacific airlines to provide network feed for them. South Pacific airlines could thus link up and deliver tourists to meet the tourism infrastructure and national earnings needs. Another challenge is to consider appropriate links with the highly seasonal VFR (visit friends and relatives) market and overseas local workers, the source of substantial repatriated income (King 2002).

Code sharing offers Pacific islands airlines a way to co-operate with each other, something that has proved difficult in the past. Air Pacific of Fiji has code share arrangements on routes to and from Nadi with several airlines in the region (Campbell 2002a; Taumoepeau 2007). Most South Pacific airlines have, as the primary mission, flights between their home country and major tourism/business/VFR source markets, such as from Asia, North America, Australia and New Zealand, implying potentially economically sustainable code share routes on a north-south rather than an east-west axis (Kissling 2002).

Creation of a Managed Integrated Independent South Pacific Airlines (MIISPA) System

In order for the small airlines of the South Pacific to ensure economic sustainability a MIISPA system for airlines of the region is proposed (Taumoepeau 2007). This is to establish in a cooperative manner, a well managed integration of the airlines in the region to enable economies of scale and scope, pooling of managed resources, code shares, spare-parts inventory, joint training programmes, cooperative marketing, common reservation systems and deliberate cutting down of costs of operation in all areas. Yet maintaining identities and flight codes amongst the participating airlines is a challenge (Taumoepeau 2007). Airlines that could participate in such a new regional system include the new national Tongan airline, Polynesian airline (PH), Solomon airline (IE), Air Vanuatu (NF), Air Kiribati (VK), Air Fiji (PC), Aircalin (SB), Air Tahiti (VT), Air Tahiti Nui (TN), Air Niugini (PX), Air Nauru (ON) and Air Pacific (FJ). The MIISPA system would allow various South Pacific governments and their airlines first to identify appropriate points of entry for a feasible operation and second to adopt relevant strategies appropriate to the system. This regional system is considered to be politically acceptable; it could dovetail to national aspirations; enable regional cooperation amongst stakeholders; and sustain commercial operations and resource pooling between the regional carriers (Taumoepeau 2007).

CONCLUSIONS

The future growth of tourism in the South Pacific Islands is dependent almost wholly on the provision of frequent, continuous and reasonably priced air transportation to and within the region. Similarly, the growth of aviation in the region depends almost entirely on the growth of the tourism market and traffic from outside the region, as the state of the island economies and the size of population in the islands are unable to sustain improved air services. In order for tourism to continue to grow and play a more significant role in the economic development of the South Pacific, closer coordination amongst regional stakeholders and improved services amongst the airlines of the region are needed.

PART VII

Conclusions

26

Conclusions: Themes and Future Issues

Peter Forsyth
Andreas Papatheodorou
Anne Graham

The studies in this book have covered a wide range of aspects of aviation, leisure tourism, and the linkages between them. By way of conclusion, we draw together some of these themes which have been discussed- these cut across the different chapters. Some key themes which emerge are:

- The changing aviation industry

- Aviation policy and its implications for leisure tourism

- The tyranny of density

- The emergence of airports as tourism stakeholders

- Constraints on growth

- Innovation and its impacts

Both aviation and leisure tourism are industries which are undergoing changes – we have highlighted some of the more significant of these. Naturally, uncertainties exist, and the outcomes of several issues and processes, and their implications for these industries, have yet to be resolved. Thus, some of the unresolved issues are:

- Future developments of airline business models

- Climate change and its implications

- Resolving the development versus environment trade-off

- The emerging giants: India and China

We discuss these themes and unresolved issues in turn.

THEMES

The Changing Aviation Industry

Perhaps the most significant and obvious development in aviation and leisure tourism has been the transformation of the aviation sector in the past two decades or so. This has had major impacts on the growth and patterns of leisure tourism. Liberalisation has enabled the development of more competitive airline markets, and lower fares, but it has also led to a change in the nature of the airline industry. The rise of the low cost carriers (LCCs) is the most important aspect of this (Barrett, Ch. 9). However, this has led to other changes, such as the decline of the share of the market enjoyed by charter airlines (Williams, Ch. 8), especially in Europe, and it has forced the full service carriers (FSCs) to change the products they are offering, for example, emphasising long haul travel through major hubs (Debbage and Alkaabi, Ch. 12; B Graham, Ch. 17). From being an industry oriented towards serving mainly business travel markets, the airline industry is now more oriented towards meeting the needs of leisure travellers. In addition, new and very effective airline competitors, such as the airlines from the Middle East, have emerged and are now impacting on travel patterns (O'Connell, Ch. 22). The LCCs themselves have been developing new leisure tourism markets, such as short break holidays and travel to regions previously not well served by air. This is partly in response to limitations in airport capacity in traditional destinations. Airlines are also changing in response to external factors. One of the more important of these is changing demographics, such as the "greying" of the major industrial countries (A. Graham, Ch. 3). As with other services, demand patterns are affected by changes in real incomes over the longer term, as well as factors which can change sharply in the short term, such as exchange rates and relative prices (Li, Ch. 3).

The airlines themselves are reassessing what products they wish to provide, and developments in the leisure market are influencing this (Shaw, Ch. 4). Thus the LCCs have emphasised providing a cheap, simple product, but they have been reviewing what the market wants. Do leisure travellers simply want the cheapest product, or are they prepared to pay for some comfort and convenience? The FSCs are reviewing what networks they wish to operate, and thus which services they wish to offer to their customers. Some are lessening their involvement in short haul markets, and emphasising long haul travel, perhaps through their major hub (Debbage and Alkaabi, Ch. 12). They are also assessing the roles of airline alliances, which can offer the passenger a set of connected flights to a distant destination, but which impose coordination costs on participating airlines (Iatrou and Tsitsiragou, Ch. 11). Charter airlines have been under pressure- leisure travellers are less prepared to buy the more constrained products the charter airlines offer, especially since LCCs are offering low fares to the destinations they wish to visit. Thus, some charter airlines are turning themselves into LCCs (Williams, Ch. 8). Aviation and tourism enterprises have long experimented with vertical integration, but apart from the integrated tour companies with charter airlines, now under threat (Williams, Ch. 8), no sustainable models have developed.

Aviation Policy and its Implications for Leisure Tourism

Changes in aviation policy have had a profound impact on leisure tourism growth and the patterns it has taken. In most markets around the world, aviation policy was more directed towards protecting home airlines than to stimulating tourism development (Barrett, Ch. 9). Not surprisingly, airlines tailored their services to appeal to business and other high yield travellers, and paid only limited attention to leisure markets. Over time, countries have relaxed or removed their regulation of aviation, thus removing a key impediment to the development of leisure travel. US domestic airline deregulation was a watershed, and since this happened, many countries and regions have liberalised their domestic markets and international routes (Papatheodorou, Ch. 5; Forsyth, Ch. 7). European liberalisation is an excellent example of how liberalisation can lead to the development of a new sector of the airline industry which specifically targets leisure travel, such as the LCC sector. There is a similar story in other regions and countries. Most developed countries have opened up their airline markets, and some large developing countries, such as Brazil, have deregulated domestic aviation, leading to a boom in new airlines and airline traffic (Espirito Santo, Ch. 19). Probably the biggest impacts in the near future will come in two countries, India and China. Aviation liberalisation in India is now well under way, with many new airlines, many of them LCCs, and international services are rapidly opening up, with a boom in inbound tourism (O'Connell, Ch. 20). As in India, aviation was tightly regulated in China, though there has been a gradual process of liberalisation (Lei, Ch. 21). China air travel is booming, though regulation still remains a constraint on growth.

Some countries have been slower to liberalise, partly because they have been less interested in increasing tourism numbers. Thus, Mauritius prefers to keep air fares relatively high, and to emphasise having a smaller number of high yield tourists (Seetaram, Ch. 24). Malta, another island nation with limited tourism capacity, had a similar approach, though since joining the European Union (EU) it has had to conform to EU aviation policy, and open up its markets (Zammit, Ch. 10). This is imposing an adjustment problem on its airline, Air Malta.

It is important to realise that aviation liberalisation does not lead to the resolution of all aviation policy problems. In most airline route markets, there are only a few competitors, and the threat of market power is quite real (Papatheodorou, Ch. 5; Debbage and Alkaabi, Ch. 12). Fares are not always as low as they could be because the airlines serving a route do not compete very strongly with each other. Even in the largest domestic market, that of the US, other sources of market power can develop, such as market power which emerges from the domination by one or two airlines of the services to and from major hubs. Mergers also become an issue, since they can lessen the number of competitors on route markets, and increase the scope for airlines to use market power. Some of these problems can be addressed by national competition policies, which are increasingly being applied to airlines.

The Tyranny of Density

Economies of density are an important aspect of airline economics, and they have important implications for tourism patterns and flows. On a per seat or per passenger basis, costs are lower for large than for small aircraft. Thus, the costs per seat kilometre are low on large long haul aircraft such as the Boeing 747 or Airbus A380, but they are high for small aircraft, such as the regional jets. This means that dense or busy routes, which can support large aircraft, will have lower fares than low density or thin routes. In addition, denser routes will have more services and will be more convenient for travellers.

Lack of economies of density makes it difficult for tourism development in many countries or regions. This is particularly the case for the island nations of the South Pacific, where populations are very low, and air routes are long and thin (Taumoepeau, Ch. 25). As a consequence, flights to South Pacific destinations are expensive and inconvenient, and this severely curtails the ability of these nations to make effective use of their potential for leisure tourism. Low density is a problem for the remote regions of Europe, such as the Northern regions (Halpern and Niskala, Ch. 15). While Africa does not lack population, only a small proportion of its population have high enough incomes to afford air travel, and as a result, routes both within Africa, and to Africa, are expensive (Arvanitis and Zenelis, Ch. 23). Only a few African destinations, especially those along the Mediterranean, have been able to achieve traffic flows high and air fares low enough to make their tourism industries competitive. Some small island destinations such as Mauritius have not been too concerned about visitor numbers, and have been able to develop higher yield tourism (Seetaram, Ch. 24).

There are, of course, positive aspects to economies of airline density. When markets grow, per passenger airline costs fall, and this enables lower fares which further stimulate the market. India is experiencing this, with markets opening up, traffic volumes increasing and fares falling. If a country or region is small, with limited scope for high traffic volumes, there is not much it can do. If they are part of a larger, well off community, such as the EC, then low density routes can be subsidised centrally- this happens with low density EC routes. However, for countries like the South Pacific nations, which are neither large nor wealthy, there is little scope to do this. Hence it is particularly important to minimise the disadvantages of low density through means such as cooperation between airlines.

The Emergence of Airports as Tourism Stakeholders

Recent years have seen the emergence of airports as distinct players in the aviation and tourism industry. In earlier years, airports were simply seen as public utilities which provided places for aircraft to land and passengers to board them. There were some problems associated with them – lack of capacity could be a constraint on tourism development, and there were environmental problems, such as noise associated with them. These days, airports take on much more pro active roles.

Retail and related functions have taken on a much more important role than they did before, especially since the privatisation of the London airports. Airports seek to increase their non aeronautical revenues, partly to keep their aeronautical charges down, and partly to enhance their own profits (Brilha, Ch. 13; Echevarne, Ch. 14). Passengers see airports as attractive places to go shopping in, especially since they may spend a considerable amount of time waiting at them. Leisure passengers are willing shoppers at airports, and the passengers of LCCs are neither poor nor unwilling to spend, though the types of retail outlets they patronise may be different from those which appeal to business travellers.

Airports also realise that different types of airlines require different types of facilities. The LCCs in particular want simpler facilities at a lower price. They also wish to achieve fast turnarounds for their aircraft, so they are keen to avoid congested airports. As a consequence of this, airports are developing specialised LCC terminals, with less lavish facilities, and lower usage charges, to cater for the LCCs (Echevarne, Ch. 14).

Many of the LCCs are willing to use secondary airports, possibly at some distance from the Central Business District (CBD) of the cities they are serving. Until 15 years ago, there was little competition between airports, and the major airports of a city served most or all of its traffic. Where there are several airports within range of a city, competition will develop between them to attract LCCs (Echevarne, Ch. 14). Even regions which do not have major cities close by, but which have some prospects for tourism development, are possible destinations or bases for LCCs. Regional authorities see attracting LCCs to their airports as an effective means of stimulating tourism and more general development. Hence they are sometimes willing to subsidise them to keep charges low (or even negative). This has posed policy problems, such as those arising from discrimination between airlines, which authorities have had to resolve. Airports, and especially secondary airports in regions adjacent to large cities, are now seen as an arm of tourism development policy in ways not imagined only fifteen years ago.

Constraints on Growth

Any expanding sector, such as leisure tourism, will encounter constraints on growth, and several of these have been discussed in this book. There can be constraints at the level of the tourism industry itself- for example, the lack of supply of hotel accommodation. For most countries, these are not particularly limiting, though they are or have been for some countries- China being an example. Several of the constraints are at the aviation level. Policy constraints which limit entry and development through regulation, have been significant, and have been discussed above.

One form of constraint which has been important, especially in Europe, but also in the US, and increasingly, Asia, are physical infrastructure constraints. Demand to use major airports is pressing up against inadequate capacity. This is resulting in congestion and delays (especially in the US) and in unmet demand (especially in Europe). Substantial additions to capacity are unlikely in the near future except in a few places. The problem can be lessened, though not resolved, by more efficient utilisation of capacity already in place. The more extensive use of secondary airports, which is common in Europe but now taking place elsewhere, is helping to relieve the pressure on airport capacity. Air Traffic Control is another form of infrastructure which is limiting aviation and tourism development. In Europe and elsewhere, flight routings are longer, and delays are more extensive, than they need to be (Vasiliadou, Ch. 6). Movement towards better coordination of ATC under a single European Sky should help, but integrating individual countries' ATC systems is a slow process.

Constraints which come about because of environmental concerns are also important. Aviation and tourism generally have significant environmental impacts (Daley, Dimitriou and Thomas, Ch. 18). Often, expansion of airports is held up or stopped because of environmental reasons. Larger airports generate more noise and emissions, and nearby residents oppose such developments. Environmental controls, such as noise curfews or restrictions on flight paths can also lessen the effective capacity of airports. Environmental aspects have to be addressed and environmental costs factored into decisions. It is important that this is done in a cost effective manner, so that aviation and leisure tourism can continue to grow without imposing unacceptable environmental costs.

Innovation and its Impacts

The past twenty or so years have seen a strong pace of innovation in aviation and leisure tourism, especially in the aviation aspects. We have mentioned several of the product innovations. These include the simpler, no frills services offered by the LCCs, the more convenient multi stage services offered by the FSCs through their alliances, and services to new destinations (especially those outside the main cities and tourism resorts). In addition to these product innovations, there has been extensive process innovation, which has helped reduce real air fares and stimulate tourism.

The most frequently discussed of these is the use of the internet by airlines. Internet booking has significantly reduced the cost to the airlines of accepting bookings – it was pioneered by the LCCs, and it is now being adopted by all airlines. The internet has also changed the way airlines services are marketed- airlines now market their services direct to the traveller, bypassing the travel agent. Less obvious, but still significant, has been the use of airline booking systems to make more effective use of airline capacity. Load factors are significantly higher for most FSCs than they were 20 years ago, and this has led to falls in real costs and air fares.

Airports are also the setting for extensive innovation, and several of the more apparent innovations are taking place with airport processes (Sigala, Ch. 16). Airports host many processes, such as check in, baggage handling, security screening, passport control and customs control. Most of these processes are being changed. Thus, over the past five years, airlines have moved to check in kiosks and away from manual check in, and further developments, such as online check in are being introduced. Biometric identification is now being used, and electronically readable passports are impacting on passport control and security checking. Further developments are likely with baggage tracking. The results of all these changes should be lower cost processing of passengers, more productive use of space in terminals, and less time being spent by passengers undergoing the necessary processes (leaving them more time to shop in the terminal).

UNRESOLVED ISSUES

Future Developments of Airline Business Models

The last couple of decades have seen a revolution in business models of the airline industry, with the emergence of LCCs, with consequent implications for leisure tourism. Will the future bring comparable changes?

The growth of the LCCs has transformed short haul leisure markets. Nonetheless, the jury is still out on whether the LCC model can be applied successfully to long haul travel. There are important differences in markets and long haul airlines will need to provide better in flight facilities to their passengers, and will not be able to save as much, in proportional terms, through operational advantages such as short turnarounds. However, long haul LCCs will still be able to achieve considerable cost advantages relative to their FSC competitors through greater productive efficiency and lower input costs, and they should be able to offer reductions in fares sufficient for them to win market share. Already, several long haul LCCs are flying, and more routes are planned. Significantly, several of the long-haul LCCs (e.g. Jetstar International and Tiger) are subsidiaries of successful FSCs.

Another growing trend on long haul markets has been competition from sixth freedom carriers. Originally, it was Asian carriers, such as Singapore Airlines which thrived on sixth freedom traffic but more recently, the Middle Eastern carriers have been making their mark. These carriers have aggressive growth plans. In addition, some more of the Asian carriers may emulate the Singapore Airlines strategy, and could develop into effective low cost competitors in long haul markets.

This all suggests that it could be in long haul markets that we see the most change over the next decade. Many FSCs have shifted their emphasis to long haul in the face of strong competition in short haul markets from LCCs- now their long haul markets will be coming under pressure. They will be forced to adapt to survive. Some may be able to reduce costs by improving their productive efficiency. Another option, which some are already employing, is to outsource more of their operations and staffing. They need not do all their maintenance at home if doing so is expensive, and they can employ staff on an international basis, rather than employing most staff from the home country, which can be very costly. Finally, as noted before, they can fight fire with fire by setting up their own LCCs. The extent to which LCCs and sixth freedom carriers make inroads in long haul markets will depend on the extent to which they can gain access to those international routes which are still regulated. While the general trend has been one of moving towards liberalisation, some of the long haul "flag" carriers may see opposing liberalisation of Air Services Agreements as a means of holding up the development of their competitors.

Climate Change and its Implications

Climate change is an issue which has rapidly gained prominence recently. It has the potential to influence aviation and leisure tourism in several ways. In particular, it will directly impact on tourism attractions, and measures to mitigate climate change will impose costs on aviation and tourism.

Global warming, resulting from climate change, will directly impact on tourism attractions, especially those which are nature based. Ski fields may become too warm to be viable, beach resorts may become inundated, and attractions such as the Great Barrier Reef in Australia may be damaged or even destroyed. While most of the effects will be negative, there are some which will be positive – for example, some areas which are now not suitable for skiing will become suitable, and extended seasons for summer sport based attractions will become possible. To an extent the damage done by global warming can be lessened through adaptation – but adaptation is costly. Overall, climate change will result in different patterns of tourism, and tourism to some countries is likely to fall in absolute terms. Clearly, however, there are major uncertainties associated with these effects.

Tourism will also be affected by policies introduced to mitigate the extent of climate change. Related mitigation policies will make activities which generate greenhouse gas emissions more expensive, either through the imposition of carbon taxes, or as a result of the workings of emissions trading schemes. In addition, specific restrictions could be put on particular activities, such as short haul flying.

Both the aviation and the ground content of tourism generate greenhouse gas emissions. Transport is the most important source of tourism's emissions, and aviation is a major contributor. While aviation is not responsible for a high proportion of total emissions at present (its contribution is variously estimated at around 2 per cent), it is a rapidly growing source. Tourism demand is growing, and aviation is winning market share. In addition, demand for air services is growing rapidly in the Asia Pacific, and especially in India and China. There is little scope for significant reductions in aviation's contribution to emissions on a per passenger basis. Aircraft are becoming more fuel efficient, and generate lower emissions, but this in only a gradual process and it takes a long time to replace airline fleets. Major technological break-throughs are not likely in the short to medium term. As a consequence, aviation is very likely to account for growing aggregate emissions, and an increasing proportion of the total.

At the very least, climate change mitigation policies will make aviation more expensive, though not prohibitively so. These higher fares will affect tourism demand. However, the growing contribution of aviation to emissions is leading to calls for special measures to limit aviation – if implemented, these would further restrict growth. How countries and communities of nations such as the EC tackle the emissions problem has yet to be determined, but this creates a major area of uncertainty for aviation and leisure travel.

Resolving Development Versus Environmental Trade-offs

Environmental considerations are often behind many of the physical limits to the growth of aviation and tourism, such as through airport expansion or provision of ground infrastructure. It may be difficult to expand an airport because of the noise, emissions and traffic congestion it will generate. Resort developments may be constrained so as to not impact adversely on local ecosystems. Environmental factors are taken very seriously in Europe, North America, and increasingly, Asia.

How effectively the development versus environment trade-off is resolved will be a key determinant of how aviation and tourism evolve over the coming decades. Environmental values are important to local residents, and increasingly, visitors, so it is critical how they will be incorporated into decision-making. For some countries or regions, it may be feasible to put an overall cap on tourism flows and development, thereby controlling their environmental impacts. However, most regions and countries will try to strike a balance, and permit tourism growth but seek to limit its adverse impacts. There are many ways in which they can do this. They can build airports further from the CBD, in less populated areas; they can permit resort development in less sensitive areas, while preventing such development in the more vulnerable ones; or they can lessen congestion around transport hubs such as airports by improving rail access and shifting surface traffic to rail. Investments in technology can also alter the trade-off – new aircraft are quieter and produce lower emissions, reducing the adverse impacts of air traffic. The less environmentally damaging solutions will often be more costly, and this will add to the cost of travel, to some extent reducing demand. The issue is not so much one of whether environmental problems will give rise to constraints on the growth of aviation and tourism as one of designing ways of ensuring that environmental values can be preserved at least cost to communities through the impacts on mitigation measures on aviation and tourism growth.

The Emerging Giants: India and China

As discussed, India and China are the emerging giants of aviation and tourism – will the expectations be fulfilled? Starting from a small base around the year 2000, they are projected to grow very rapidly, and be medium-sized tourism countries very soon and very large tourism countries in a few decades. Their very large populations, who are now enjoying higher living standards, will become big generators of demand for aviation and tourism, both domestic and international. In addition, they are countries with many tourist attractions, which hitherto have been less accessible, and better and more convenient air services will facilitate considerable inbound tourism growth.

The most likely scenario is for continued rapid growth. This is conditional and it could falter. If growth in real GDP slackens off, this will impact on tourism growth. In addition, policies need to be in place to enable the growth to take place. India's aviation markets are opening up, though China's remain relatively restricted. If regulation remains in place, it will be necessary for additional airline capacity to be approved so that it is adequate for demand. In some cases, infrastructure, for both tourism and aviation, could be a problem, as it has sometimes in the past, but over the longer term is should be feasible to address infrastructure problems.

This greater mobility within India and China, along with growth in outbound and inbound travel, will impact heavily on tourism industries. The home industries will need to expand rapidly to cater for domestic and inbound growth. Growth in outbound travel will make a noticeable impact on tourism flows in the Asia Pacific region. In particular, the impacts on some smaller destinations and countries could be very large. Direct flights to some smaller destinations, such as Fiji, could stimulate tourism strongly, lessening those countries' problems of lack of scale and remoteness.

With this last note on the emerging superpowers of the 21st century, we would like to close the discussion of this edited book. We hope that all twenty-six chapters enabled the reader to acquire a solid understanding of the structurally intertwined relationship between aviation and tourism and we anticipate that as a result of this publication, further research will be inspired on this fascinating area!

Bibliography

Abeyratne, R. (2001), *Aviation Trends in the New Millennium* (Aldershot: Ashgate).

Abrahams, M. (1983), 'A Service Quality Model of Air Travel Demand: An Empirical Study', *Transportation Research* 17A:5, 385–93.

Abu Dhabi International Airport, (2007), *Statistics Section* (Personal correspondence).

ACARE (Advisory Council for Aeronautics Research in Europe) (2004), *Strategic Research Agenda*, Vol. 1 (Brussels: ACARE).

Adams, J. (1999), *The Social Implications of Hypermobility* (Paris: OECD).

Adams, P.D. and Parmenter, B. (1995), 'An Applied General Equilibrium Analysis of Tourism in a Quite Small, Quite Open Economy', *Applied Economics* 27:10, 985–94.

Adams, W.M. (2001), *Green Development: Environment and Sustainability in the Third World*, 2nd Edition (London: Routledge).

Adler, N. and Hashai, N. (2005), 'Effect of open skies in the Middle East region', *Transportation Research Part A: Policy and Practice* 39:10, 878–94.

African Union (2005), *Overview of the State of Air Transport in Africa*, Meeting of African Ministers Responsible for Air Transport, 1st Ordinary Session, May, 16–19, Sun City, South Africa.

African Union (2006), *African Air Transport Development Strategy – Plan of Action*, High-Level Meeting of African Airlines, May, 29–30, Tunis, Tunisia.

Agarwal, V. and Talley, W.K. (1985), 'The Demand for International Air Passenger Service Provided by U.S. Air Carriers', *International Journal of Transport Economics* 12:1, 63–70.

Air Malta (1999), *Annual Report and Consolidated Financial Statements year ended 31 March 1999*.

Air Mauritius Ltd (2007), *Annual Report 2006/2007*, <http://www.airmauritius.com>, accessed 26 October 2007.

Air Transport Action Group (2003), *The Contribution of Air Transport to Sustainable Development in Africa* (Geneva: ATAG).

Air Transport Action Group (ATAG) (2005), *The Economic and Social Benefits of Air Transport* (Geneva: ATAG).

Air Transport World (2005), *First Choice Airways Goes After the Upper End of the Leisure Market*, May, 48.

--- (2006a), *Success Squared*, January, 44–8.

--- (2006b), *World Airline Report: Location, Location, Location*, July, 26–37.

Airfinance Journal (2005), *Charting the Future*, March, 31–33.

--- (2006), *Spotlight falls on airports*, November, 10.

--- (2007), *Indian Aviation Market Sobers Up*, April, 12–5.

Airbus (2005), *Market Survey 2005* (Toulouse: Airbus).

Airbus Global Market Forecast (2004–2023), <http://www.airbus.com>, accessed 23 November 2007.

Airline Business (2001), *Special Report: Alliance Survey* July, 39–70.

--- (2003), *IT Trends Survey 2003* (CD-ROM).

--- (2004), *USA and China Free Markets*, July, 8.

--- (2005), *Concern Mounts Over Airport Aid Rules*, February, 19.

--- (2007), *Package Deals*, September, 74–76.

Airports Company South Africa (ACSA), <http://www.airports.co.za>, accessed 14 June 2007.

Airports Council International (2003), *Policy Handbook* (Geneva: ACI).

Airports International (2007), *Indian Ups and Downs* 40:4, 14.

Amelung, B. and Viner, D. (2006), 'Mediterranean tourism: exploring the future with the tourism climatic index', *Journal of Sustainable Tourism* 14:4, 349–66.

Anonymous (2006a), *Future traveller tribes 2020*, Report for the Air Travel Industry developed by Henley Centre in partnership with Amadeus.

--- (2006b), *Las Vegas Airport bets on RFID*, <http://www.rfidjournal.com/article/view/643>, accessed 18 August 2007.

--- (2007), 'Registered travel – just another document?', *Biometric Technology Today*, October, 8–10.

Arab Air Carriers Organization (2006), *Arab Air Carriers Organization Annual Report*, 39th Annual General Meeting (Kuwait City: AACO).

Archer, B. (1985), 'Tourism in Mauritius: An Economic Impact Study with Marketing Implications', *Tourism Management* 6, 50–4.

Aronsson, L. (2000), *The Development of Sustainable Tourism* (London: Thomson).

Artus, J.R. (1970), The Effect of Revaluation on the Foreign Travel Balance of Germany, *International Monetary Fund Staff Papers* 27, 602–17.

Ashford, N., Stanton, H., Moore, C. (1997), *Airport Operations* (New York: McGraw-Hill).

Ashford, N., Stanton, H., Moore, C. (2006), *Airport Operations*, 2nd Edition (New York: McGraw-Hill).

Ashworth, G.J. (1998), 'The Conserved European City as Cultural Symbol: The Meaning of the Text', in B. Graham (ed.), *Modern Europe: Place, Culture, Identity* (London: Arnold), 261–86.

Ashworth, G.J., Graham, B. and Tunbridge, J.E. (2007), *Pluralising Pasts: Heritage, Identity and Place in Multicultural Societies* (London: Pluto Press).

Ashworth, G.J. and Tunbridge, J.E. (2000), *The Tourist-historic City: Retrospect and Prospect of Managing the Heritage City* (London: Pergamon/Elsevier).

Association of European Airlines (2006), *Yearbook 2005*, (Brussels: AEA).

Association of South Pacific Airlines (2001), *Report on Forum Aviation Proposal on Pacific Islands Air Services Agreements (PIASA)* (Nadi: ASPA).

ATI (2005). *Qatar pushing for more Destinations in India*, 21st February.

--- (2006), *Govt Upset Over Indian Carriers' Congestion Surcharge*, 6th December.

--- (2007a), *Qatar 787 Order Revealed by Logo on Aircraft at Roll-Out*, 9th July.

--- (2007b), *PARIS 2007: India Likely to Clear Kingfisher for Int'l Flights*, 21st June.

--- (2007c), *India's Govt Approves New Airport for Mumbai*, 1st June.

Aviation Strategy (2001), *Will India Finally Fulfil its Potential?*, January, 3–5.

--- (2004), *Charter Airline Legacy: The Case of MyTravel*, January, 2–6.

--- (2005), *European Charter Airlines: Adapting to a Declining Market*, June, 2–9.

--- (2006*), Air Berlin's IPO: Just Bad Timing?*, May, 7–13.

--- (2007a), *Germany: Restructuring or Just Juggling?*, Jan/Feb, 2–9.

--- (2007b), *Jet/Sahara vs Air India/Indian in the Battle for International Markets*, June, 10.

Aviation Week and Space Technology (2003), *Sixth Freedom Blues* 159:22, 44

--- (2006), *Alliance Expected to Grow Even Larger*, May 8:44.

--- (2007), *First Steps: The Newly Ratified U.S. –Europe Aviation Deal Sets a Demanding Agenda for the Second Phase*, April 2:60–1.

Ayish, M. (2005), 'Virtual Public Relations in the United Arab Emirates: A Case Study of 20 UAE Organizations' Use of the Internet', *Public Relations Review* 31:3, 381–8.

Bacchetta, F. (2007), What's wrong with PSO routes. In 4th *Forum on Air Transport in Remoter Regions*, 17–19 April, Lisbon.

Bailey, E.E. and Baumol, W.J. (1984), 'Deregulation and the Theory of Contestable Markets', *Yale Journal of Regulation* 2, 111–37.

Baker, C. and Field D. (2001), 'Jumping the Tracks', *Airline Business*, June 2001.

Baker, C. (2005), 'Leisure Travel: New Horizons', *Airline Business*, August, 19.

Baker, S. (2006), *Sustainable Development*, Routledge Introductions to Environment Series (London: Routledge).

Bandyopadhyay, R. and Morais, D. (2003), 'Representative Dissonance: India's Self and Western Image', *Annals of Tourism Research* 32:4, 1006–21.

Barbot, C. (2006), 'Low-cost airlines, Secondary Airports and State Aid: An Economic Assessment of the Ryanair-Charleroi Airport Agreement', *Journal of Air Transport Management* 12, 197–203.

Barrett, S. (1987), *Flying High – Airline Price and European Deregulation* (London: Gower).

--- (2004a), Airports and Communities in a Deregulated Market, in *Hamburg Aviation Conference*, 20 February, Hamburg.

--- (2004b), 'How do Demands for Airport Services differ between Full-Service Carriers and low-cost carriers?', *Journal of Air Transport Management* 10, 33–9.

--- (2004c), 'The Sustainability of the Ryanair Model', *International Journal of Transport Management* 2, 89–98.

Bauman, Z. (1998), *Globalization: The Human Consequences* (New York: Columbia University Press).

Baumol, W.J. (1982), 'Contestable Markets: An Uprising in the Theory of Industry Structure', *American Economic Review* 72, 1–15.

Baumol, W.J., Panzar, J.C., and Willig, R.D. (1982), *Contestable Markets and the Theory of Industrial Structure* (New York: Harcourt Brace Jovanovich).

Baumol, W.J. and Willig, R.D. (1986), 'Contestability: Developments since the Book', *Oxford Economic Papers* 38:9–36.

BBC News online (2004), *Ryanair Slates Charleroi Ruling*, 3 February.

Becken, S. and Patterson, M. (2006), 'Measuring National Carbon Dioxide Emissions from Tourism as a Key Step towards achieving Sustainable Tourism', *Journal of Sustainable Tourism* 14:4, 323–38.

Bieger, T and Wittmer, A. (2006), 'Air Transport and Tourism – Perspectives and Challenges for Destinations, Airlines and Governments', *Journal of Air Transport Management* 12:1, 40–6.

Black W.R. (1996), 'Sustainable Transportation: A US Perspective', *Journal of Transport Geography* 4, 151–9.

Blake, A. and Sinclair and M.T.; Sugiyarto, G. (2003), *The Economic Impact of Tourism in Malta* (Nottingham: Christel DeHaan Tourism and Travel Research Institute).

Blum, A. (2005), 'JetBlue's Terminal takes wing', *BusinessWeek*, 21 July.

Bodine, K. (2005), *Best and Worst of Kiosk Software* (Cambridge, Mass.: Forrester Research).

Boeing (2006), *Current Market Outlook* (Seattle: Boeing).

Borenstein, S. (1989), 'Hubs and High Fares: Dominance and Market Power in the U.S. Airline Industry', *Rand Journal of Economics* 20, 344–65.

Borenstein, S. (1990), 'Airline Mergers, Airport Dominance, and Market Power', *American Economic Review* 80:2, 400–4.

--- (1992), 'The Evolution of U.S. Airline Competition', *Journal of Economic Perspectives* 6:2, 45–73.

Boston Consulting Group (2006), 'Decline of the Mega-hub', *Airline Business* 22:10, 72–6.

Bovagnet, F. (2006), 'How Europeans go on Holiday', *Eurostat: Statistics in Focus*, 18 (Luxembourg).

Bows, A. and Anderson, K.L. (2007), 'Policy Clash: Can Projected Aviation Growth be Reconciled with the UK Government's 60% Carbon-reduction Target?', *Transport Policy* 14, 103–10.

Bows, A., Upham, P. and Anderson, K. (2005), *Growth Scenarios for EU and UK Aviation: Contradictions with Climate Policy*, Summary of research by the Tyndall Centre for Climate Change Research for Friends of the Earth Trust Ltd, 16 April 2005, Manchester, Tyndall Centre for Climate Change Research (North).

Brassington, F.B. and Pettit, S. (2007), *Essentials of Marketing*, 2nd Edition (Harlow: Prentice Hall).

Briguglio, L. and Briguglio, M. (1996), 'Sustainable Tourism in the Maltese Isles', in L. Briguglio, R. Butler, D. Harrison and W. L. Filho (ed.) *Sustainable Tourism in Islands and Small States* (London: Pinter), 161–79.

British Airways (2007), 'Carbon Offset', <http://britishairways.com/travel/envoffset/public/en_gb>, accessed 5 July 2007.

British Petroleum (2003), *BP Statistical Review of World Energy* (London: BP).

Britton, S. (1991), 'Towards a Critical Geography of Tourism', *Environment and Planning D Society and Space* 9, 451–78.

Brueckner, J.K., Pels, E. (2005), 'European Airline Mergers, Alliance Consolidation, and Consumer Welfare', *Journal of Air Transport Management* 11, 27–41.

BSCA (2007), <http://www.charleroi-airport.com>, accessed 04 November 2007.

Bull, A. (1995), *The Economics of Travel and Tourism*, 2nd Edition (Sydney: Longman).

Burac, M. (1996), 'Tourism and Environment in Guadeloupe and Martinique', in L. Briguglio, R. Butler, D. Harrison and W.L. Filho (ed.) *Sustainable Tourism in Islands and Small States* (London: Pinter), 63–74.

Burkart A.J. (1975), 'The Regulation of Non-Scheduled Air Services in the United Kingdom 1960 to 1972', *The Journal of Industrial Economics* 23, 51–64.

Burns, P. (1999), *An Introduction to Tourism and Anthropology* (London: Routledge).

Butler, R.W. (2000), 'Tourism and the Environment: a Geographical Perspective', *Tourism Geographies* 2:3, 337–58.

Button, K.J. (2001), 'Are Current Air Transport Policies Consistent With a Sustainable Environment?', in E. Feitelson and E.T. Verhoef (eds), *Transport and Environment: In Search of Sustainable Solutions* (Cheltenham: Edward Elgar), 54–72.

Button, K. and Nijkamp, P. (1997), 'Social Change and Sustainable Transport', *Journal of Transport Geography* 5:3, 215–8.

CAAC (2007), Civil Aviation Development in China: 2006–2007 (in Chinese), <http://www.caac.gov.cn>, accessed 20 August 2007.

Cabrini, L. (2005), International and European Tourism: Recent Trends and Outlook, *Public-Private Partnerships in Tourism Seminar*, Moscow, Russian Federation, 22 March.

--- (2006), 'Overview of International and European Tourism: 2005 Results and Short Term Outlook', *45th Meeting of the UNWTO Commission for Europe*, Almaty, Kazakhstan, 26 April.

Cairns, S. and Newson, C. (2006), *Predict and Decide (II): The Potential of Economic Policy to Address Aviation-Related Climate Change* (Oxford: UK Energy Research Centre, University of Oxford).

Cambodia Airports (2007), 'Data News 2007: Siem Reap International Airport', <http://www.cambodia-airports.com/statistics/DATANEWS2007Rep.pdf>, accessed 1 October 2007.

Campbell, J. (2002a), 'Status of South Pacific Airlines', *ASPA Annual Meeting*, Nuku'alofa, Tonga, June.

--- (2002b), 'Connecting the Pacific Islands to Enhance Growth and Development', *Air Transport Pacific Roundtable Pacific Economic Cooperation Council*, Noumea, New Caledonia.

Caplan, H. (2001), 'Passenger Health – Who's in Charge? The Passenger, of course', *Air & Space Law* 26:4–5, 203–17.

Castree, N. (2004), 'Economy and Culture are Dead! Long Live Economy and Culture', *Progress in Human Geography* 28, 204–26.

Cater, E. and Goodall, B. (1992), 'Must Tourism destroy its Resource Base?' in S. R. Bowlby and A. M. Mannion (eds), *Environmental Issues in the 1990s*, (Chichester: Wiley), 317–21.

Central Intelligence Agency (2007), *The World Factbook*, (Washington: CIA).

Central Statistics Office (2004), *Digest of International Travel and Tourism Statistics - Historical Series*, <http://www.gov.mu/portal/sites/ncb/cso/hs/tourism/hs.htm>, accessed 12 April 2007.

Centre for Asia Pacific Aviation (2007), *Global Airport Privatisation Report*, 2nd Edition, (Sydney: CAPA).

--- (2007), *Middle East Aviation Outlook: The Next Generation Aviation Market* (Sydney: CAPA).

Chapman, L. (2007), 'Transport and Climate Change: a Review', *Journal of Transport Geography* 15 (5): 354–367.

Chatzinikolaou, R. (2005), *Air Transport of Passengers* (Athens: Sakkoulas) (in Greek).

Cheng, B. (1962), *The Law of International Air Transport* (London: Stevens & Sons Limited).

Chesshyre, T. (2007), *How Low Can You Go?* (London: Hodder and Stoughton).

Civil Aviation Authority (CAA) (1990–2006), *UK Airports* (London: CAA).

--- (2000, 2003, 2006), *UK Airlines* (London: CAA).

--- (2005a), *Demand for Outbound Leisure Air Travel and its Key Drivers* (London: CAA).

--- (2005b), *Financial Protection for Air Travellers and Package Holidaymakers in the Future*, CAA Advice to the Government, CAP 759 (London: CAA).

--- (2005c), *Passenger Survey Report* (London: CAA).

--- (2005d), *UK Regional Air Services*, CAP754 (London: CAA).

--- (2006a), *International Air Passenger Traffic to and from UK Reporting Airports* (London: CAA).

--- (2006b), *No-Frills Carriers: Revolution or Evolution*. CAP770 (London: CAA).

--- (2006c), *UK Airline Financial Tables* (London: CAA).

--- (2007), *Connecting the Continents: Long-haul Passenger Operations from the UK*, CAP 771 (London: CAA).

Clark, L. and Fulena, U. (2001), 'Deep Vein Thrombosis – A New Risk Exposure Area?', *Air & Space Law* 26:4–5, 218–24.

Clark, P. (2007), *Buying the Big Jets*, 2nd Edition (Aldershot: Ashgate).

Clark, T. (2007), '21st Century Civil Aviation; Raising the Game', *Lindbergh Lecture*, 13th March, Royal Aeronautical Society, London.

Cleverdon S. (1992), *Tourism Development Impact: Assessment and Policy Formulation*, (Port Louis: Ministry of Economic Planning and Development, Mauritius).

Climate Care (2007), *Flights Calculator*, <http://www.climatecare.org>, accessed 5 July 2007.

CNTA (2000), *Yearbook of China's Tourism Statistics* (Beijing: China Tourism Publishing House) (in Chinese).

--- (2007), *Major Statistics of Domestic Tourism 2006* (in Chinese), <http://www.cnta.gov.cn>, accessed 20 August 2007.

Coccossis, H. (1996), 'Tourism and Sustainability: Perspectives and Implications', in G. K. Priestly, J. A. Edwards and H. Coccossis (eds) *Sustainable Tourism? European Experiences* (Wallingford: CAB International), 1–21.

Compton, P. (2005), 'Timetable for success', *Airport World* 10:2, April-May, 56–7.

Corrodi, B. (2007), 'Driving Tourism Growth through Consumer-Centric Marketing', in World Economic Forum, *The Travel & Tourism Competitiveness Report 2007*, <http://www.weforum.org/en/initiatives/gcp/TravelandTourismReport/index.htm>, accessed 25 March 2007.

Cresswell, T. (2006), *On the Move: Mobility in the Modern Western World* (London and New York: Routledge).

Crouch, G. (1995), 'A Meta-Analysis of Tourism Demand', *Annals of Tourism Research* 22, 103–18.

Cruise Lines International Association (2006), *Cruise Industry Overview* (Fort Lauderdale: CLIA).

Crump, E. (2004), 'Rovaniemi Santa Claus Airport', *Airliner World*, February, 48–51.

Dagtoglou, P. (1994), *Air Transport and the European Union*, 2nd Edition (Athens: Sakkoulas/ Kluwer) (in Greek).

Davy Stockbrokers (2006), *Ryanair as a Consumer Growth Company* (Dublin: Davy).

Dearden, S.J.H. (1994), 'Air Transport Regulation in the European Union', *European Business Review* 94:5, 15–9.

Debbage, K.G. (1990), 'Oligopoly and the Resort Cycle in the Bahamas', *Annals of Tourism Research* 17:4, 513–27.

--- (1993), 'U.S. Airport Market Concentration and Deconcentration', *Transportation Quarterly* 47:1, 115–36.

--- (1994), 'The International Airline Industry: Globalization, Regulation and Strategic Alliances', *Journal of Transport Geography* 2:3, 190–203.

--- (2004), 'Airlines, Airports and International Aviation' in L. Pender & R. Sharpley (ed.) *The Management of Tourism* (London: Sage Publications Ltd), 28–46.

Deloitte & Touche (2002), *Tourism Development Plan for Mauritius* (Port Louis: Ministry of Economic Planning and Development, Mauritius).

--- (2003), *Evaluation des Retombées Economiques générées par les Activités de l'Aéroport de Charleroi*, Study commissioned by SOWAER, December.

--- (2006), *Hospitality 2010, a Five-Year Wake up Call* (London: Deloitte & Touche).

Department of Information Malta (2006), *Call for Proposal from Low-Cost Airlines to Operate New Routes To and From Malta* (Valetta: Department of Information).

Department for Transport (DfT) (2003a), *Night Flying Restrictions at Heathrow, Gatwick and Stansted* (London: The Stationery Office).

--- (2003b), *The Future of Air Transport* (London: The Stationery Office).

--- (2005), *Night Flying Restrictions at Heathrow, Gatwick and Stansted Airports* (London: The Stationery Office).

--- (2006a), *Public Experiences of and Attitudes to Air Travel*, <http://www.dft.gov.uk/pgr/statistics/datatablespublications/att/publicexperiencesofandattitu1824?page=6>, accessed 30 January 2007.

--- (2006b), *Project for the Sustainable Development of Heathrow: Air Quality Technical Report*, <http://www.dft.gov.uk/pgr/aviation/environmentalissues/heathrowsustain>, accessed 2 August 2006.

Department of Transport (2007), *Essential Air Services Program*, <http://ostpxweb.dot.gov/aviation/X-50%20Role_files/essentialairservice.htm> accessed 23 August 2007.

Diederiks-Verschoor, I. (2001), 'The Liability for Delay in Air Transport', *Air & Space Law* 26:6, 300–14.

Dieke, P. (1991), 'Policies for Tourism Development in Kenya', *Annals of Tourism Research* 18, 269–94.

Directorate General of Civil Aviation (2003–2004), *India Air Transport Statistics*, <http://dgca.nic.in/reports/stat-ind.htm> accessed 05 October 2007.

--- (2005–2006), *India Air Transport Statistics*, <http://dgca.nic.in/reports/stat-ind.htm> accessed 05 October 2007.

Dixon, P. and Parmenter, B. (1996), 'Computable General Equilibrium Modelling for Policy Analysis and Forecasting' in H. Aman, D. Kendrick & J. Rust (ed), *Handbook of Computational Economics* (Oxford: Elsevier), 1, 4–85.

Dobruszkes, F. (2006), 'An Analysis of European Low-Cost Airlines and Their Networks', *Journal of Transport Geography* 14, 273–86.

Doganis, R. (1991), *Flying off Course – The Economics of International Airlines*. 2nd Edition (London: HarperCollins).

--- (1992), *The Airport Business* (London: Routledge).

--- (2001), *The Airline Business in the 21st Century* (London: Routledge).

--- (2002), *Flying Off Course: The Economics of International Airlines.* 3rd Edition (London: Routledge).

--- (2006), *The Airline Business,* 2nd Edition (London: Routledge).

Donaghy, K., Rudinger, G. and Poppelreuter, S. (2004), 'Societal Trends, Mobility Behaviour and Sustainable Transport in Europe and North America', *Transport Reviews* 24, 679–90.

Doran, N. (2006), *The Customer-Enabled Airline and the Contribution to Competitiveness,* Presentation given at the 5th eTourism Futures Forum at the University of Surrey, 27th March.

Dossani, R. and Kenny, M. (2007), 'The Next Wave of Globalization: Relocating Service Provision to India', *World Development* 35: 5, 772–91.

DRDNI (Department for Regional Development Northern Ireland) (2003), *A Good Practice Guide to the Assessment and Management of Aircraft Noise Disturbance around Northern Ireland Airports* (Belfast: DRDNI).

Dresner, M. (2006), 'Leisure versus Business Passengers: Similarities, Differences, and Implications', *Journal of Air Transport Management* 12:1, 28–32.

Drysdale, A. (2002), 'Update on Global and Regional Aviation Scene'. *Air Transportation Round Table Pacific Economic Cooperation Council,* Noumea, November.

Dubai International Airport, (2007), 'Facts and Figures', <http://dubaiairport.com/DIA/English/TopMenu/About+DIA/Facts+and+Figures/>, accessed 21 April 2007.

Dubois, G. and Ceron, J.-P. (2006), 'Tourism and Climate Change: Proposals or a Research Agenda', *Journal of Sustainable Tourism* 14:4, 399–415.

Durbarry, R. (2002), 'The Economic Contribution of Tourism in Mauritius' *Annals of Tourism Research* 29: 3, 862–5.

--- (2004), 'Tourism and Economic Growth: the Case of Mauritius', *Tourism Economics* 10:4, 389–401.

Durbarry, R. and Sinclair, M.T. (2003), 'Market Shares Analysis: The Case of French Tourism Demand', *Annals of Tourism Research* 30, 927–41.

eBusiness Watch (2006), 'ICT and e-business in the Tourism Industry'. *ICT Adoption and e-business Activity in 2006* (Brussels: European Commission).

Egan, M. (2001), *Creating a Transatlantic Marketplace: Government Policies and Business Strategies* (Washington, D.C.: The Johns Hopkins University).

Elliott, J.A. (2006), *An Introduction to Sustainable Development,* 3rd Edition, Routledge Perspectives on Development Series (London: Routledge).

Embratur (2007), *Embratur Statistics Yearbooks,* <http://embratur.gov.br>, accessed 15 December 2007.

Emirates Group (2007), *Annual Report 2006–2007,* <http://www.ekgroup.com/Annualreports/2006–2007>, accessed 9 April 2007.

Euromonitor International (2006), *Travel and Tourism – China: Country Market Insight* (London: Euromonitor International).

European Commission (2001), *European Transport Policy for 2010: Time to Decide* (Luxembourg: Office for Official Publications of the European Communities).

--- (2004), 'The Commission's Decision on Charleroi Airport promotes the Activities of Low-Cost Airlines and Regional Development', Press Release, 3 February, (Brussels: European Commission).

--- (2005), *Community Guidelines on financing of Airports and Start-up Aid to Airlines departing from Regional Airports,* 2005/C 312/01, (Brussels: European Commission).

--- (2007a), *Consultation Paper on the Possible Revision of Regulation 2299/89 on a Code of Conduct for Computerised Reservation Systems* (Brussels: European Commission).

--- (2007b), *EU-US First Stage Air Transport Agreement,* Presentation made by the Directorate-General Energy and Transport / Air Transport Directorate (Brussels: European Commission).

--- (2007c), *Proposal for a Directive of the European Parliament and of the Council on Airport Charges* (Brussels: European Commission).

--- (2007d), *Proposal for a Regulation of the European Parliament and of the Council on a Code of Conduct for Computerised Reservation Systems* (Brussels: European Commission).

--- (2007e), *Public Service Obligations: List of Routes Concerned* (Brussels: European Commission).

European Communities (2006), *Panorama on Tourism* (Luxembourg: Office for Official Publications of the European Communities).

European Community (1981), *Report on Scheduled Passenger Air Fares in the EC* (Brussels: EC).

European Low Fares Airlines Association (2004), *Liberalisation of European Air Transport: the Benefits of Low Fares Airlines to Consumers, Airports, Regions and the Environment* (Brussels: ELFAA).

Fan, T. (2006), 'Improvements in Intra-European Inter-city Flight Connectivity, 1996–2004', *Journal of Transport Geography* 14, 249–64.

Favotto, I. (1998), 'Not all Airports are Equal', *Airport World*, December, 17–18.

Feiler, G. and Goodovitch T. (1994), 'Decline and Growth, Privatization and Protectionism in the Middle East Airline Industry', *Journal of Transport Geography* 2:1, 55–64.

Finavia. (2007), *Air Traffic Statistics 2006* (Vantaa: Finavia).

Findlay, C. (1985), *The Flying Kangaroo: an Endangered Species? An Economic Perspective of Australian International Civil Aviation Policy* (Sydney: Allen and Unwin).

Flamm, M. and Kaufman, V. (2006), 'Operationalising the Concept of Motility: A Qualitative Study', *Mobilities* 1, 167–89.

Flight International (2002), *Rebel Skies – The Future*, April.

--- (2007a), *TUI to Unify Airline Brands*, January.

--- (2007b) *Environmental Special: How EU Plan Affects Europe's Airlines*, September.

Florida, R. (2002), *The Rise of the Creative Class* (New York: Basic Books).

--- (2005a), *Cities and the Creative Class* (Abingdon: Routledge).

--- (2005b), *The Flight of the Creative Class: The New Global Competition for Talent* (New York: HarperBusiness).

Flybe (2007), *Eco-Labelling Scheme*, <http://www.flybe.com/environment/eco-labels.htm>, accessed 5 July 2007.

Forrester Research (2007), *Humanizing the Digital Travel Experience*, August 2007.

Forschungsgemeinschaft Urlaub und Reisen e.V (2007), *Reiseanalyse 2007*, <http://www.fur.de/downloads/Reiseanalyse_2007_engl.pdf>, accessed 30 April 2007.

Forsyth, P. (2006), 'Tourism Benefits and Aviation Policy', *Journal of Air Transport Management* 12:1, 3–13.

--- (2007), 'The Impacts of Emerging Aviation Trends on Airport Infrastructure', *Journal of Air Transport Management* 13:1, 45–51.

Forsyth, P., King, J. and Rodolfo L. (2006), 'Open Skies in ASEAN', *Journal of Air Transport Management* 12:2, 143–52.

Francis, G., Dennis, N., Ison, S. and Humphreys, I. (2007), 'The Transferability of the Low-Cost Model to Long-Haul Airline Operations', *Tourism Management* 28:2, 390–8.

Francis, G., Humphreys, I. and Ison, S. (2004), 'Airports' Perspectives on the Growth of Low-Cost Airlines and the Remodelling of the Airport – Airline Relationship', *Tourism Management* 25, 507–14.

Francis, G., Humphreys, I., Ison, S. and Aicken, M. (2006), 'Where Next for Low Cost Airlines? A Spatial and Temporal Comparative Study', *Journal of Transport Geography* 14, 83–94.

Frechtling, D.C. (2001), *Forecasting Tourism Demand: Methods and Strategies* (Oxford: Butterworth-Heinemann).

Freiberg, K. and Freiberg, J (1996), *Nuts, Southwest Airline's Crazy Recipe for Business and Personal Success* (New York: Bard Press).

Frühling, P. and Eyskens, W. (2004), 'Current and Future Issues Relating to Slot Management and Mobility in the European Union', *Air & Space Law* 29:2, 79–113.

Furnas, M. (2003), *Catchments and Corals: Terrestrial Runoff to the Great Barrier Reef* (Townsville: Australian Institute of Marine Science).

Gillen, D., Harris, R. and Oum, T. (1996), *Assessing the Benefits and Costs of International Air Transport Liberalisation* (Ottawa: Transport Canada).

Gillen, D.W., Morrison, W.G., Stewart, C. (2003), *Air Travel Demand Elasticities: Concepts, Issues and Measurement* (Ottawa: Department of Finance).

Gimeno, J., Cool, K. and Buccela, A. (2003), *A Note on the European Airline Industry* (Fontainebleau: INSEAD).

Goetz, A.R. and Graham, B. (2004), 'Air Transport Globalization, Liberalization and Sustainability: Post-2001 Policy Dynamics in the United States and Europe', *Journal of Transport Geography* 12, 265–76.

Goetz, A.R. and Sutton, C.J. (1997), 'The Geography of Deregulation in the US Airline Industry', *Annals of the Association of American Geographers* 87:2, 238–63.

Gopinath, G. (2007), Against the Trend, *Aircraft Economics*, January/February, 79, 18–19.

Graham, A. (2003), *Managing Airports: An International Perspective*. 2nd Edition (Oxford: Elsevier).

--- (2006), 'Have the Major Forces Driving Airline Traffic Changed?', *Journal of Air Transport Management* 12:1, 14–20.

Graham, B. (1999), 'Airport-specific traffic forecasts: a critical perspective', *Journal of Transport Geography* 7, 285–9.

--- (2002), 'Heritage as Knowledge: Capital or Culture?', *Urban Studies* 39, 1003–17.

--- (2003), 'Air Transport Policy: Reconciling Growth and Sustainability?', in I. Docherty and J. Shaw (eds), *A New Deal for Transport? The UK's Struggle with the Sustainable Transport Agenda* (Oxford: Blackwell), 198–225.

--- (forthcoming), 'UK Air Travel: Taking Off for Growth', in I. Docherty and J. Shaw (eds), *Traffic Jam: Ten Years of 'Sustainable' Transport in the UK* (Oxford: The Policy Press).

Graham, B., Ashworth, G.J. and Tunbridge, J.E. (2000), *A Geography of Heritage: Place, Culture, Identity* (London: Arnold).

Graham, B. and Goetz, A.R. (2008), 'Global Air Transport', in R.D. Knowles, I. Docherty and J. Shaw (eds), *Transport Geographies* (Oxford: Blackwell), 137–55.

Graham, B. and Guyer, C. (1999), 'Environmental Sustainability, Airport Capacity and European Air Transport Liberalization: Irreconcilable Goals?' *Journal of Transport Geography*, 7 (3), 65–180.

Graham, B. and Shaw, J. (forthcoming), 'Low-cost Airlines in Europe: Reconciling Liberalization and Sustainability', *Geoforum* 37.

Graham, B. and Vowles, T.M. (2006), 'Carriers Within Carriers: A Strategic Response to Low-cost Airline Competition', *Transport Reviews* 26, 105–26.

Gray, H. P. (1966), 'The Demand for International Travel by United States and Canada', *International Economic Review* 7, 83–92.

Greene, D.L. and Wegener, M. (1997), 'Sustainable Transport', *Journal of Transport Geography* 5:3, 177–90.

Groth L. (1999), *Future Organisational Design; the Scope for the IT-based Enterprise* (New York: John Wiley and Sons).

Gudmundsson, H. and Höjer, M. (1996), 'Sustainable development principles and their implications for transport', *Ecological Economics* 19, 269–82.

Guild, R., (2001), *Proposal for Multilateral Air Services Agreements (2001)*, South Pacific Forum, Suva, Fiji.

--- (2002), 'A Single Aviation Market for the Pacific', *Air Transport Round Table Pacific Economic Cooperation Council*, Noumea, New Caledonia.

Gunn, C.A. (1988), *Tourism Planning*, 2nd Edition (New York: Taylor and Francis).

Gupta, R. (2007), 'Common Ground', *Air Finance Journal*, April, 40–2.

Hacan ClearSkies (2003), 'It's the Economy, Stupid', <http://www.hacan.org.uk>, accessed 18 January 2005.

Haitovsky, Y., Salomon I. and Silman, L.A. (1987), 'The Economic Impact of Charter Flights on Tourism to Israel', *Journal of Transport Economics and Policy* 21, 111–34.

Hall, C.M. and Lew, A.A. (1998), 'The Geography of Sustainable Tourism Development: an Introduction', in C. M. Hall and A. A. Lew (eds) *Sustainable Tourism* (Harlow: Prentice Hall), 1–12.

Hall, C.M. and Page, S. J. (2006), *The Geography of Tourism and Recreation: Environment, Place and Space* (London: Routledge).

Hall, D.R. (1999), 'Conceptualising Tourism Transport: Inequality and Externality Issues', *Journal of Transport Geography* 7, 181–8.

Halpern, N. (2005), 'Airport Marketing and the Development of Tourism in Remoter Regions', in *3rd Forum on Air Transport in Remoter Regions*, 24–26 May, Stockholm.

--- (2006), *Market Orientation and the Performance of Airports in Europe's Peripheral Areas* (Unpublished PhD Thesis, Cranfield University, United Kingdom).

Han, K.H. (1994), *China: Tourism Industry* (Beijing: Modern China Press).

Hanlon, P. (1999), *Global Airlines – Competition in a Transnational Industry*, 2nd Edition (Oxford: Butterworth-Heinemann).

Harrell Associates (2002), *The Internet Travel Industry: What Consumers Should Expect and Need to Know, and Options for a Better Marketplace* (New York: Harrell Associates).

Harrison, D. (1995), 'International Tourism and the Less Developed Countries: the Background', in D. Harrison (ed.) *Tourism and the Less Developed Countries* (Chichester: John Wiley and Sons), 1–18.

Harrison, D. and Hitchcock, M. (eds) (2005), *The Politics of World Heritage: Negotiating Tourism and Conservation* (Clevedon: Channel View Publications).

Harrop, P. (1999), *New Earning Streams for Airports* (Hampshire: Footnote).

Harteveldt, H.H. & Epps, S.R. (2007), *Self-service Check-in Clicks with Travellers. Mobile Check-in and Better Merchandising will increase Self-Service Appeal* (Cambridge, Mass.: Forrester Research).

Heracleous, L. & Wirtz, J. (2006), 'Biometrics: the Next Frontier in Service Excellence, Productivity and Security in the Service Sector', *Managing Service Quality* 16:1,12–22.

Hermida, J. (2001), 'The New Montreal Convention: The International Passenger's Perpective', *Air & Space Law* 26:3, 150–5.

Hickman, L. (2007), The *Final Call: In Search of the True Costs of Our Holidays* (London: Transworld/ Guardian Books).

Highlands and Islands Airports Limited (2005), *HIAL Targets Tour Operators at VisitScotland Expo 2004*, (Inverness: HIAL Press).

HM Government (2005), *Securing the Future: Delivering the UK Sustainable Development Strategy* (London: HMSO).

Holden, A. (2000), *Environment and Tourism* (London: Routledge).

Holden, E. (2007), *Achieving Sustainable Mobility: Everyday and Leisure-Time Travel in the EU* (Aldershot: Ashgate).

Hollier, R. (1991), 'Conflict in the Gulf: Response of the Tourism Industry', *Tourism Management* 12:1, 2–4.

Holmér, J. (2007), 'Rethinking PSOs in Sweden: Reflections and Actions', In *4th Forum on Air Transport in Remoter Regions*, 17–19 April, Lisbon.

Hotels (2006), *Corporate 300 Rankings* 40(7):40–52.

Houghton, J. (2004), *Global Warming: The Complete Briefing*, 3rd Edition (Cambridge: Cambridge University Press).

Howrey Europe (2004), 'Ryanair/Charleroi Decision – when are Incentives granted to Airlines by Regional Airports Lawful', *Howrey Client Alert*, February.

Hume, K. and Watson, A. (2003), 'The Human Health Impacts of Aviation', in P. Upham, J. Maughan, D. Raper and C. Thomas (eds) *Towards Sustainable Aviation* (London: Earthscan Publications), 48–76.

Hunter, C. and Shaw, J. (2006), 'Applying the Ecological Footprint to Ecotourism Scenarios', *Environmental Conservation* 32, 294–304.

Husain, S.R. (2007), 'Saudi airline to buy 60 planes worth $12bn', <http://www.dawn.com/2007/01/05/ebr10.htm>, accessed 5 January 2008.

Iatrou, K. (2004), *The Impact of Airline Alliances on Partners' Traffic* (Bedford: Cranfield University).

Iatrou, K. and Oretti, M. (2007), *Airline Choices for the Future: From Alliances to Mergers* (Aldershot: Ashgate).

Indian Railways (2007), *Annual Statistical Statements 2005–06*, <http://www.indianrailways.gov.in/deptts/stat-eco/YB-05-06/key-statistics.pdf> accessed 10 November 2007.

Instituto Brasileiro de Geografia e Estatística (2007), 'Monthly Survey of Industrial Employment and Wages', <http://www.ibge.gov.br>, accessed 15 December 2007.

Instituto de Estudios Turísticos (2004), 'Compañías Aéreas de Bajo Coste', <http://www.iet.tourspain.es>, accessed 10 November 2007.

Intergovernmental Panel on Climate Change (1999), *Aviation and the Global Atmosphere*, A Special Report of IPCC Working Groups I and III in collaboration with the Scientific Assessment Panel to the Montreal Protocol on Substances that Deplete the Ozone Layer, (ed.) J. E. Penner, D. H. Lister, D.J. Griggs, D.J. Dokken and M. McFarland (Cambridge: Cambridge University Press).

International Air Carrier Association (2006), *Statistical Overview* (Brussels: IACA).

International Air Transport Association (2005), *Industry Statistics: Revenues, Expenses, Operating Profit & Net Profit* (Geneva: IATA).

---(2007a), *European Leisure Air Travel Survey*, <http://www.iata.org/NR/rdonlyres/FA3E6ED3-2342-4D48-BD20-DA157DD72356/0/LATS2007ProductInformationPackfinal.pdf>, accessed 20 December 2007.

--- (2007b), *Industry Times, Steady, More Profitable Growth in 2006*, News Release February (Montreal: IATA).

--- (2007c), 'RFID Business Case for Baggage Tagging', *IATA Simplifying the Business Project* (Montreal: IATA).

---(2007d), *Simplifying the Business*, <http://www.iata.org/stbsupportportal/index>, accessed 15 February, 2007.

International Air Transport Association/United Nations World Tourism Organisation (2002), *General Guidelines for using Data on International Air Passenger Traffic for Tourism Analysis* (Madrid: UNWTO).

International Biometrics Group (2005), *About IBG*, <http://www.biometricgroup.com>, accessed 12 July 2005.

International Civil Aviation Organization (1981), *Annual Report: The State of International Civil Aviation* (Montreal: ICAO).

--- (2007), *Profits and Traffic up for World's Airlines in 2006*, News Release, <http://www.icao.int/icao/en/nr/2007/pio200703_e.pdf>, accessed 5 July 2007.

International Reports (2006), *Dubai's GDP registered around 16 Percent Growth in 2005*, <http://www.internationalreports.net/middleeast/dubai/2006/gdp.html>, accessed 7 June 2007.

Ioannides, D. and Debbage, K. (1997), 'Post-Fordism and Flexibility: the Travel Industry Polyglot', *Tourism Management* 18:4, 229–41.

Ioannides, D. and Petridou-Daugthrey, E. (2006), Competition in the Travel Distribution System: the US Travel Retail Sector, in Papatheodorou, A. (ed.) *Corporate Rivalry and Market Power: Competition Issues in the Tourism Industry* (London: IB Tauris), 124–42.

Ionides, N. (2003), Indian Promise, *Airline Business*, May, 37–41.

--- (2007), Piloting change, *Airline Business*, September, 38–43.

InsiderVLV.com, (2007), *20 Largest Hotels in the World*, <http://www.insidervlv.com/hotelslargestworld. html>, accessed 4 June 2007.

Janelle, D.G. and Beuthe, M. (1997), 'Globalization and Research Issues in Transportation', *Journal of Transport Geography* 5:3, 199–206.

Jarach, D. (2005), *Airport Marketing: Strategies to Cope with the New Millennium Environment* (Aldershot: Ashgate).

Jet Airways (2007), *Jet Airways Reports Profit for Q2 FY 2007–08*, Press Release, <http://www.jetairways. com/Cultures/en-US/United+Kingdom/About+Us/Press+Room/Press+Releases/Profit_for_Q2_ FY08.htm>, accessed 10 November 2007.

Jones, D. (2005), 'China's Low-Cost Revolution', *Airfinance Journal*, April, 279, 28–30.

Jones, L. (2006), *easyJet: The Story of Britain's Biggest Low-Cost Airline* (London: Aurum).

Keeling, D.J. (2007), 'Transportation Geography: New Directions on Well-worn Trails', *Progress in Human Geography* 31, 217–25.

Kester, J. (2005), 'Leisure Traffic and Tourism: New Strategies for Airlines, Airports and the Travel Trade', *8th Hamburg Aviation Conference*, February.

Khadaroo, J. and Seetanah, B. (2007), 'Transport Infrastructure and Tourism Development', *Annals of Tourism Research* 34:4, 1021–32.

King, J. M. C. (2002), 'Issues for Tourism in Aviation Management', *ATRI Outlook Conference: Plotting the Future*, 16–17 October, Sydney, Australia.

Kirby, T. (2006), *Britons with Second Home Abroad Up 45% in Two Years*. The Independent, 22 November, <http://news.independent.co.uk/uk/this_britain/article2004223.ece>, accessed 10 August 2007.

Kissling, C. (ed.) (1984), *Transport and Communications for Pacific Microstates: Issues in Organisation and Management* (Suva: Institute of Pacific Studies).

--- (1989), 'International Tourism and Civil Aviation in the South Pacific: Issues and Innovations', *GeoJournal* 19:3, 309–15.

--- (2002), 'Pacific Air Travel Connectivity 1975–2002', *Air Transport Round Table Pacific Economic Cooperation Council*, Noumea.

Knibb, D. (2006), 'China unveils Aviation Leap forward', *Airline Business*, April, 26.

Krugman, P. (1986), Introduction: New Thinking about Trade Policy in P. Krugman (ed.) *Strategic Trade Policy and the New International Economics* (Cambridge, Mass.: MIT Press), 1–22.

Krul, J. (2003), 'Environmental and Economic Factors in Airport Capacity', in P. Upham, J. Maughan, D. Raper and C. Thomas (ed.) *Towards Sustainable Aviation* (London: Earthscan Publications), 218–220.

Kulendran, N. and Witt, S.F. (2003), 'Forecasting the Demand for International Business Tourism', *Journal of Travel Research* 41, 265–71.

Lafferty, G. and Fossen, A.V. (2001), 'Integrating the Tourism Industry: Problems and Strategies', *Tourism Management* 22, 11–9.

Langedahl, T.B. (1999), 'Attracting Business to Remote Airports in Norway', In: *1st Forum on Air Transport in Remoter Regions*, 2–4 April, Nairn.

Larsen, I. (2002), *Regime of Liability in Private International Air Law - with Focus on the Warsaw System and the Montreal Convention of 28 May 1999*, <http://www.rettid.dk/artikler/speciale-20020002. pdf>, accessed 03 March 2007.

Lawton, T.C. (2002), *Structure and Strategy in the Low Fare Airline Business* (Aldershot: Ashgate).

Le, T. T. (1997), 'Reforming China's Airline Industry: From State-Owned Monopoly to Market Dynamism', *Transportation Journal* 36, 45–62.

Le Figaro (2006), *Ryanair prend racine dans le nouvel aéroport de Marseille*, 13 November.

Lennon, J. and Foley, M. (2000), *Dark Tourism: The Attraction of Death and Disaster* (London: Continuum).

Lewis, J.S., Niedzwiecki, R.W., Bahr, D.W., Bullock, S., Cumpsty, N., Dodds, W., DuBois, D., Epstein, A., Ferguson, W.W., Fiorentino, A., Gorbatko, A.A., Hagen, D.E., Hart, P.J., Hayashi, S., Jamieson, J.B., Kerrebrock, J., Lecht, M., Lowrie, B., Miake-Lye, R.C., Mortlock, A.K., Moses, C., Renger, K., Sanpath, S., Sanborn, J., Simon, B., Sorokin, A., Taylor, W., Waitz, I., Wey, C.C., Whitefield, P., Wilson, C.W. and Wu, S. (1999), 'Aircraft Technology and its Relation to Emissions', in J.E. Penner, D.H. Lister, D.J. Griggs, D.J. Dokken and M. McFarland (ed.) *Aviation and the Global Atmosphere* (Cambridge: Cambridge University Press), 291–70.

Li, G., Song, H. and Witt, S.F. (2005), 'Recent Developments in Econometric Modeling and Forecasting', *Journal of Travel Research* 44, 82–99.

Library of Congress (2006), *Federal Research Division Country Profile: Saudi Arabia*, September, <http://lcweb2.loc.gov/frd/cs/profiles/Saudi_Arabia.pdf>, accessed 8 July 2007.

Lindbeck, A. (2007), 'Change for Better', *South China Morning Post*, May 2.

Low Fare and Regional Airlines (2007), *New-Style Sustainable Expansion*, May 24:4, 16–7.

Lynes, J.K. and Dredge, D. (2006), 'Going Green: Motivations for Environmental Commitment in the Airline Industry. A Case Study of Scandinavian Airlines', *Journal of Sustainable Tourism* 14:2, 116–38.

Makridakis, S., Wheelwright, S.C. and McGee, V. E. (1983), *Forecasting: Methods and Applications*, 2nd Edition (New York: John Wiley).

Malta International Airport (2007a), *Annual Statistical Summary 2006* (Luqa: Malta International Airport).

--- (2007b), *2006 Business Report and Financial Statements* (Luqa: Malta International Airport).

Mangion, M. (2001), *Carrying Capacity Assessment for Tourism in the Maltese Islands* (Valetta: Ministry for Tourism).

Manuhatu, F. (2000), 'Aviation Safety Regulation in Europe – Towards a European Safety Authority', *Air & Space Law* 25:6, 264 – 72.

Marcussen, C.H. (2007), *Trends in European Internet Distribution of Travel and Tourism Services*, Centre for Regional and Tourism Research – Denmark, <http://www.crt.dk/uk/staff/chm/trends.htm>, accessed 25 November 2007.

Marseilles Airport (2006), *'Un nouveau terminal pour le développement des Bouches-du-Rhône et de la Provence'*, (Marseille: Marseille Airport).

Marseilles Airport (2007), *Voyagez Low-Cost avec l'Aéroport Marseille – Provence*, <www.mp2.aeroport.fr>, accessed 3 November 2007.

Mathews, N. (2004), 'All Hail Oil', *Aviation Week and Space Technology*, 13 December, 53.

McGrath, G. (2007), 'Ryanair to go Long-Haul', *Times Online*, 12 April.

Mendes, P. (2006), 'The Fight Against Terrorism Through Aviation: Data Protection Versus Data Production', *Air & Space Law* 31:4–5, 320–30.

Meyer, M. (2001), 'Deep Vein Thrombosis – Blood Flow v. Profit Flow', *Air & Space Law* 26:4–5, 225–30.

Middleton, V.T.C. and Clark, J. (2001), *Marketing in Travel and Tourism*, 3rd Edition (Oxford: Butterworth-Heinemann).

Mieczkowski, Z. (1995), *Environmental Issues of Tourism and Recreation* (Lanham: University Press of America).

Miller, T. (2007), 'China and US close to an Agreement on 'Open Skies' Deal', *South China Morning Post*, 14 April.

Milmo, D. (2007), 'British Hotels attack Budget Airlines', *The Guardian Unlimited*, 22 January, <http://travel.guardian.co.uk/article/2007/jan/22/travelnews.theairlineindustry.hotels> accessed 10 August 2007.

Milne, S. (2005), *The Economic Impact of Tourism in SPTO Member Countries*, August (Suva: SPTO Publications).

Ministry of Tourism (2004), *India Tourism Statistics 2003*, <http://tourism.gov.in/rtia/..%5Cstatistics%5CFTAIS2003.pdf>, accessed 3 October 2007.

Ministry for Tourism and Culture (2006), *Tourism Policy for the Maltese Islands 2007–2011: Draft for External Consultation* (Valletta: Ministry for Tourism and Culture).

Ministry of Tourism, Leisure & External Communications (2007), *Handbook of Statistical Data 2006*, <http://www.gov.mu/portal/site/tourist/menuitem.79cbb79e172f03797d97dde8a0208a0c/>, accessed 12 August 2007.

Mintel (2005), *Activity Holidays – UK*, September (London: Mintel).

--- (2007), *Health and Wellness Holidays – UK*, February (London: Mintel).

Morrison, S. and Winston, C. (1986), *The Economic Effects of Airline Deregulation* (Washington DC: Brookings Institution).

Mosedale, J. (2006), 'Tourism Commodity Chains: Market Entry and its Effects on St. Lucia', *Current Issues in Tourism* 9:4–5, 436–58.

--- (2008), The Internationalisation of Tourism Commodity Chains. In C.M. Hall, and T. Coles (eds), *International Business and Tourism: Global Issues, Contemporary Interactions* (London: Routledge), forthcoming.

Moss, D., Warnaby, G., Sykes, S. and Thomas, C.S. (1997), 'Manchester Airport's Second Runway Campaign: The Boundary Spanning Role of Public Relations in managing Environmental Organisational Interaction', *Journal of Communication Management* 2:4, 320–34.

Mowforth, M. and Munt, I. (1998), *Tourism and Sustainability: New Tourism in the Third World* (London: Routledge).

NACO BV (2005), *Master Plan on Air Transportation in Mauritius*, <http://www.gov.mu/portal/goc/externalcomm/file/rhfinal.pdf>, accessed 27 October 2007.

Nakibullah, A., Islam, F. (2007), 'Effect of Government Spending on Non-Oil GDP of Bahrain', *Journal of Asian Economics* 23:6, 34–42.

National Statistics Office (2007), *Various Releases*, <http://www.nso.gov.mt>, accessed 27 March 2007.

Neufville, R., Odoni, A. (2003), *Airport Systems – Planning, Design and Management* (New York: McGraw-Hill).

Newsweek (2006), *The Wings of Dubai Inc.*, 17 April, <http://www.msnbc.msn.com/id/12225864/site/newsweek/>, accessed 19 September 2007.

Njegovan, N. (2006), 'Elasticities of Demand for Leisure Air Travel: A System Modelling Approach', *Journal of Air Transport Management* 12, 33–9.

Nolan, P. (2007), *Ryanland: A No-frills Odyssey Across the New Europe* (Dublin: Hodder Headline Ireland).

O'Connell, J.F. (2005), 'The Scramble for India', *Aircraft Economics* 79, January/February, 30–1.

O'Connell, J.F. and Williams, G. (2006), 'Transformation of India's Domestic Airlines: A case study of Indian Airlines, Jet Airways, Air Sahara and Air Deccan', *Journal of Air Transport Management* 12:6, 358–74.

OAG (2006), *European Low Cost Carriers White Paper*, <http://www.oag.com/graphics/lowcostcarriers.pdf>, accessed 03 September 2007.

OAG (2007), *India's Aviation Growth Phenomenon*, <http://www.oag.com/oag/website/com/en/Press+Room/Press+Releases+2007/Indias+aviation+growth+phenomenon+05060701>, accessed 21 November 2007.

Office of Fair Trading (2007), *British Airways to pay Record £121.5m Penalty in Price Fixing Investigation*. Press Release August 1st, (London: Office of Fair Trading).

Office of Travel and Tourism Industries (2005), *Various News Releases* (Washington DC: Department of Commerce).

Organization of Arab Petroleum Exporting Countries (2003), *The Annual Statistical Report*, <http://www.oapecorg.org/Publications.htm>, accessed 23 November 2007.

---(2007), *Secretary General Annual Report*, <http://www.oapecorg.org/Publications.htm>, accessed 07 November 2007.

Organization of Petroleum Exporting Countries (2003), *The Annual Statistical Bulletin*, (Vienna: OPEC).

Orient Aviation (2006), *India: The pressure is on*, April, 10–4.

Oum, T. H., Park, J.-H., and Zhang, A. (1996), 'The effects of Airline Codesharing Agreements on Firm Conduct and International Airfares', *Journal of Transport Economics and Policy* 30, 187–202.

Oum, T. H. and Yu, C. (2000), *Shaping Air Transport in Asia Pacific* (Aldershot: Ashgate).

Oxford Economic Forecasting (1999), *The Contribution of Aviation to the UK Economy* (Oxford: OEF).

Oxford Economic Forecasting (2006), *The Economic Contribution of the Aviation Industry in the UK* (Oxford: OEF).

Pacific Asia Travel Association (2007), *Annual Reports 2000–2006*, <http://www.pata.org>, accessed 22 November 2007.

Palaskas, T., Papatheodorou, A. and Tsampra, M. (2006), *Cultural Heritage as a Growth Factor in the Greek Economy* (Athens: Academy of Athens) (in Greek).

Papatheodorou, A. (2002), 'Civil Aviation Regimes and Leisure Tourism in Europe', *Journal of Air Transport Management* 8:6, 381–8.

Papatheodorou, A. and Busuttil, L. (2003), 'EU Accession and Civil Aviation Regimes: Malta and Cyprus as a Case Study', *2003 World Conference of the Air Transport Research Society*, Toulouse, France.

Papatheodorou, A. and Iatrou, K. (2007), 'Leisure Travel: Implications for Airline Alliances, *2007 World Conference of the Air Transport Research Society*, Berkeley, United States.

Papatheodorou, A. and Lei, Z. (2006), 'Leisure Travel in Europe and Airline Business Models: A study of Regional Airports in Great Britain', *Journal of Air Transport Management* 12:1, 47–52.

Parkin, M., Powell, M. and Matthews, K. (1997), *Economics*, 3rd Edition (Harlow: Addison-Wesley).

Patterson, T., Bastianoni, S. and Simpson, M. (2006), 'Tourism and Climate Change: Two-Way Street, or Vicious/Virtuous Circle?', *Journal of Sustainable Tourism* 14:4, 339–48.

Paylor, A., (2006), 'Thomsonfly finds a Niche, The UK leisure Carrier combines Traditional Holiday Charters with Low-Fare Seat only Sales', *Air Transport World*, August, 36.

--- (2007), 'Peninsula of Promise', *Jane's Airport Review* 19:4, 8–11.

Pearce, B. (2007), 'Investing in Air Transport Connectivity to Boost National Productivity and Economic Growth', in World Economic Forum, *The Travel & Tourism Competitiveness Report 2007*, <http://www.weforum.org/en/initiatives/gcp/TravelandTourismReport/index.htm>, accessed 25 March 2007.

Perry, A. (2006), 'Will predicted Climate Change compromise the Sustainability of Mediterranean Tourism?', *Journal of Sustainable Tourism* 14:4, 367–75.

Pfannenstein, L. and Tsai, R. (2004), 'Offshore Outsourcing: Current and Future Effects on American IT industry', *Information Systems Management* 21:4, 72–80.

Pilling, M. (2005), 'Concern Mounts Over Airport Aid Rules', *Airline Business*, February, 19.

Pilling, M. (2006), 'Total Control', *Airline Business*, March, 4.

--- (2007), 'Opportunity knocks for Air Berlin', *Airline Business*, August, 4.

Pitt, M., Wai, F.K. & Teck, P.C. (2002), 'Technology Selection in Airport Passenger and Baggage Systems', *Facilities* 20:10, 314–26.

Poon, A. (1993), *Tourism, Technology and Competitive Strategies* (Oxford: CAB International).

Pragma Consulting/ARC Retail Consultants (2006), *Study of the Commercial Potential Development for a New European Airport* (Twickenham: Pragma Consulting).

Priestly, G.K., Edwards, J.A. and Coccossis, H. (eds) (1996), *Sustainable Tourism? European Experiences* (Wallingford: CAB International).

Pustay, M.W. (1993), 'Towards a Global Airline Industry: Prospects and Impediments', *Logistics and Transportation Review* 23:1, 103–28.

Quinn, J.B. (1992), *Intelligent Enterprise; a Knowledge and Service-Based Paradigm for Industry* (New York: Free Press).

Raguraman, K. (1997), 'Airlines as Instruments for Nation Building and National Identity: Case Study of Malaysia and Singapore', *Journal of Transport Geography* 5:4, 239–56. *Statistics* (Personal correspondence)

Reynolds-Feighan, A.J. (1995), 'European and American Approaches to Air Transport Liberalisation: some Implications for Small Communities', *Transportation Research Part A: Policy and Practice* 29:6, 467–83.

Rogers, H.L., Lee, D.S., Raper, D.W., Forster, P.M. de F., Wilson, C.W. and Newton, P. (2002), 'The Impacts of Aviation on the Global Atmosphere', *The Aeronautical Journal*, October, 521–46.

Rovaniemi Tourism and Marketing (2007), *Press Release: Rovaniemi and Santa Claus* (Rovaniemi: Rovaniemi Tourism and Marketing).

Ryanair (2005), *Annual Report 2005*, <http://www.ryanair.com/site/EN/about.php?page=Invest&sec=download&ref=2005>, accessed 10 June 2007.

--- (2006), Half-Year Results, *Roadshow Presentation Dublin*, September.

Sager, T. (2006), 'Freedom as Mobility: Implications of the Distinction between Actual and Potential Travelling', *Mobilities* 1, 465–88.

Sambracos, E. and Rigas K. (2007), 'Passenger Reactions to Market Deregulation: First Results from the Experience of the Greek Islands Market', *Journal of Air Transport Management* 13, 61–6.

Sambrinvest (2007), *Missions of Sambrinvest*, <http://www.sambrinvest.be>, accessed 10 November 2007.

Saraswati, S. (2001), 'Operating Environment for a Civil Aviation Industry in India', *Journal of Air Transport Management* 7:2, 127–35.

Scobie, B. (2007), 'Business flair - All Premium Operations', *Airline Business*, August, 90–4.

Seetanah, B. (2006), 'Air Access Liberalization and Tourism Development', *Journal of Travel and Tourism Research* 6:1, 1–11.

Sewill, B. (2005), *Fly Now, Grieve Later: How to Reduce the Impact of Air Travel on Climate Change* (London: Aviation Environment Federation).

Shannon Airport (2006), *Shannon Airport Traffic Development Schemes 2006* (Shannon: Shannon Airport).

Sharjah International Airport, (2007), *Passenger Movements 1999–2006*, <http://www.shj-airport.gov.ae/statistics.htm>, accessed 21 April 2007.

Sharpley, R. and Sundaram, P. (2005), 'Tourism: a Sacred Journey? The Case of Ashram Tourism, India', *International Journal of Tourism Research* 7:3, 161–71.

Shaw, S. (1982), 'Airline Deregulation and the Tourist Industry', *Tourism Management* 3:1, 40–51.

--- (2007), *Airline Marketing and Management*, 6th Edition (Aldershot: Ashgate).

Shaw, S. and Thomas, C. (2006), 'Social and Cultural Dimensions of Air Travel Demand: Hyper-mobility in the UK?', *Journal of Sustainable Tourism* 14, 209–15.

Sheldon, P. (1997), *Tourism Information Technology* (Wallingford: CAB International).

Shuaa Capital (2007), *Air Arabia: Equity Research*, Pre IPO Coverage, 12 March.

Sigala, M. (2002), 'The Impact of Multimedia on Employment Patterns in Small and Medium Hospitality and Tourism Enterprises (SMTHEs) in UK.', *Information Technology and Tourism* 4:3–4, 175–89.

--- (2003), 'The Information and Communication Technologies Productivity Impact on the UK Hotel Sector', *International Journal of Operations and Production Management* 23:10, 1224–45.

--- (2004), 'Collaborative Supply Chain Management in the Airline Sector: the Role of Global Distribution Systems (GDS)', *Advances in Hospitality and Leisure*, 1, 103–21.

Sinclair, M.T. and Stabler, M. (1997), *The Economics of Tourism* (London: Routledge)

Smith, L.J. (2006), *The Uses of Heritage* (London: Routledge).

Smith, M. (2003), *Issues in Cultural Tourism Studies* (London: Routledge).

South Pacific Tourism Organisation Annual Reports (2003), *Regional Tourism Strategy for the South Pacific Central Pacific – Strategy for Growth*, <http://www.spto.org>, accessed 20 January 2007.

--- (2005), *Annual Reports 1998–2005*, <http://www.spto.org>, accessed 25 April 2007.

Stern, N. (2006), *The Economics of Climate Change: The Stern Report* (Cambridge: Cambridge University Press).

Sobie, B. (2007), 'SkyTeam completes Slot Shuffle', *Airline Business*, 19 December, <http://www.flightglobal.com/articles/2007/12/19/220407/skyteam-completes-slot-shuffle.html>, accessed 28 December 2007.

Song, H. and Witt, S.F. (2000), *Tourism Demand Modelling and Forecasting: Modern Econometric Approaches* (Oxford: Pergamon).

Song, H., Witt, S. F. and Li, G. (2003), 'Modelling and Forecasting the Demand for Thai Tourism', *Tourism Economics* 9, 363–87.

SQW & NFO (2003), *Impact of Ryanair on the Ayrshire Tourism Economy 2002–2003* (Edinburgh: SQW).

Standard and Poor (2007), *Industry Surveys – Airlines* (New York: McGraw-Hill).

STRAIR (2005), *Air Service Development for Regional Development Agencies, North East South West INTERREG IIIC.* (Stockholm: Office of Regional Planning and Urban Transportation).

Supreme Commission for Tourism (2005), Tourism Statistics. (Riyadh: SCT).

Sustainable Aviation (2005), *A Strategy Towards Sustainable Development of UK Aviation* (London: Sustainable Aviation).

Taneja, N. (2003), *Airline Survival Kit: Breaking Out of the Zero Profit Game* (Aldershot: Ashgate).

--- (2004), *Simpli-Flying: Optimizing the Airline Business Model* (Aldershot: Ashgate).

--- (2005), *Fasten Your Seat Belt: The Passenger is Flying the Plane* (Aldershot: Ashgate).

Taumoepeau, S.P. (1989), *Air Transportation and Development of Tourism in Tonga*. Unpublished MSc thesis, University of Surrey, UK.

--- (2007), *A Blueprint for the Economic Sustainability of the Small National Airlines of the South Pacific.* Unpublished PhD thesis, University of the Sunshine Coast, Australia.

Teufel, S., Merten, P. S., & Steinert, M. (2007), A mobile Computing and Commerce Framework. In D. Taniar (Ed.), *Encyclopaedia of mobile computing and commerce* (Hershey: Idea Group Publishing).

Teye, V. (1986), 'Liberalisation Wars and Tourism Development in Africa. The Case of Zambia', *Annals of Tourism Research* 13, 589–608.

--- (1988), 'Prospects for Regional Tourism Cooperation in Africa', *Tourism Management*, 221–34.

The Guardian (2006), '70 per cent of Leisure Passengers deterred by Rail Prices', 13 July, <http://www.guardian.co.uk/travel/2006/jul/13/travelnews.uknews.transportintheuk>, accessed 13 July 2007.

Thomas, C. and Lever, M. (2003), 'Aircraft Noise, Community Relations and Stakeholder Involvement', in P. Upham, J. Maughan, D. Raper and C. Thomas (ed.) *Towards Sustainable Aviation* (London: Earthscan Publications), 97–112.

Thomas, G. (2000), 'China's Long-Haul', *Air Transport World*, October, 49.

--- (2001), 'Unscrambling the Egg', *Air Transport World*, August, 29–33.

--- (2005a), 'China's Runway Challenge', *Air Transport World* February, 32–5.

--- (2005b), 'Will China go Low-Cost?' *Air Transport World*, May, 36–39.

--- (2006), 'Yin Yang', *Air Transport World*, February, 25–30.

Thomas, R. (1997), *Quantitative Methods for Business Studies* (London: Prentice Hall).

Timothy, D. and Boyd, S.W. (2003), *Heritage Tourism* (Harlow: Prentice Hall).

Tisdell, C. and Wen, J. (1991), 'Foreign tourism as an element in P.R. China's Economic Development Strategy', *Tourism Management* 12:1, 55–67.

Tompkins, G. (2001), 'Deep Vein Thrombosis (DVT) and Air Carrier Legal Liability – The Myth and the Law', *Air & Space Law* 26:4–5, 231–35.

Tretheway, M. and Mak, D. (2006), 'Emerging Tourism Markets: Ageing and Developing Economies', *Journal of Air Transport Management* 12:1, 21–7.

TRI Hospitality Consulting (2006), *Ready for 30 Million Room Nights?*, <http://www.thehotelshow. com/hotel/downloads/TRIreport-Feb06.pdf>, accessed 30 July 2007.

Tribe, J. (1995), *The Economics of Leisure and Tourism*, 2nd Edition (Oxford: Butterworth-Heinemann).

Tripathi, M. (2006), 'Transforming India into a Knowledge Economy through Information Communication Technologies — Current Developments', *The International Information & Library Review* 38:3, 139–46.

Trivedi, V. (2007), *Airlines 2007: Opportunities & Challenges*, <http://www.ficci.com/media-room/ speeches-presentations/2007/feb/air-con/session3/vishwapti.ppt>, accessed 18 November 2007.

Tunbridge, J.E. and Ashworth, G.J. (1996), *Dissonant Heritage* (Chichester: Wiley).

Tunnacliffe, I. (2003), *Self-Service Solutions for Airport Check-In Increase as Technology improves* (Cambridge, Mass.: Forrester Research).

Tyndall Centre (2005), *Decarbonising the UK: Energy for a Climate Conscious Future* (Norwich: Tyndall Centre).

UAE Interact (2007), *UAE Yearbook 2007*, <http://www.uaeinteract.com/uaeint_misc/pdf_2007/index. asp>, accessed 24 April 2007.

Unique Flughaven Zürich AG (2006), *2005 Environmental Report* (Zürich: Unique).

United Nations (2002), *World Summit on Sustainable Development: Johannesburg, 2002* (New York: United Nations).

United Nations World Tourism Organisation (1994), *National and Regional Tourism Planning: Methodologies and Case Studies* (London: Routledge).

--- (1997), *Tourism: 2020 Vision* (Madrid: UNWTO).

--- (2000), *WTO Seminar on Tourism and Air Transport* (Funchal, Madeira, Portugal 25–26 May) (Madrid: UNWTO).

--- (2005), *Tourism Highlights: 2005 Edition* (Madrid: UNWTO).

--- (2006), *Tourism Market Trends: Africa 2005 Edition* (Madrid: UNWTO).

--- (2007a), *Tourism Highlights: 2007 Edition* (Madrid: UNWTO).

--- (2007b), *International Tourists 1995 - 2006*, <http://www.world-tourism.org>, accessed 14 April 2007.

--- (2007c), *Tourism Market Trends:* Africa 2006 Edition (Madrid: UNWTO).

--- (2007d) *World Tourism Barometer* 5:1, January (Madrid: UNWTO).

--- (2007e), *World Tourism Barometer* 5:2, June (Madrid: UNWTO).

United States General Accounting Office (1990), *Airline Competition: Higher Fares and Reduced Competition at Concentrated Airports* (GAO: Washington DC).

--- (1996), *Airline Deregulation: Changes in Airfares, Service, and Safety at Small, Medium-Sized, and Large Communities* (GAO: Washington DC).

--- (1999), *Airline Deregulation: Changes in Airfares, Service Quality, and Barriers to Entry* (GAO: Washington DC).

Upham, P. (2001), 'Environmental Capacity of Aviation: Theoretical Issues and Basic Research Directions', *Journal of Environmental Planning and Management* 44:5, 721–34.

Upham, P., Maughan, J., Raper, D. and Thomas, C. (2003), *Towards Sustainable Aviation* (London: Earthscan).

Upham, P., Thomas, C., Gillingwater, D. and Raper, D. (2003), 'Environmental capacity and airport operations: current issues and future prospects', *Journal of Air Transport Management* 9, 145–51.

Urry, J. (2000), *Sociology Beyond Societies: Mobilities for the Twenty-first Century* (London: Routledge).

--- (2002), *Small Worlds and Large Distances* (London: Freedom to Fly).

Uysal, M. (1998), 'The Determinants of Tourism Demand: A Theoretical Perspective', in D. Ioannides and K.G. Debbage, (eds), *The Economic Geography of Tourism* (London: Routledge), 79–95.

Uysal, M. and Crompton, J. L. (1985), 'An Overview of Approaches Used to Forecast Tourism Demand', *Journal of Travel Research* 24, 7–15.

Vanhove, N. (2005), *The Economics of Tourist Destinations* (Amsterdam: Elsevier).

Vasiliadou, A. (2006), *Consumer and Passenger Protection in a Liberal Aviation Market.* Unpublished MSc Thesis, (Patras: Hellenic Open University) (in Greek).

Victorian Auditor General's Office (2007), *State Investment in Major Events* (Melbourne: Victorian Government Printer).

Virgin Atlantic (2007), *Virgin Atlantic's Plans to Cut Carbon Emissions gain Ground as Airports Prepare for December Trials*, <http://www.virginatlantic.com/en/gb/allaboutus/pressoffice/pressreleases/news/pr041206c.jsp>, accessed 5 July 2007.

Virgin Blue (2007), *Carbon Offset: A Virgin Blue Initiative*, <https://secure.virginblue.com.au/public/system/carbon> accessed 23 August 2007.

VisitBritain (2006), 'Inbound Tourism – the Global Context', *Foresight,* 34, August.

Wall, G. (1994), 'Tourism Alternatives in an Era of Global Climatic Change', in V. L. Smith and W. R. Eadington (eds) *Tourism Alternatives* (Chichester: John Wiley and Sons), 194–215.

Walton, C., (2005), 'easyJet', *UBS Transport Conference*, 20 September, London.

Wassenbergh, H. (2000), 'Common Market, Open Skies and Politics', *Air & Space Law* 25:4–5, 174–83.

Wegter, J. (2006), 'The ECJ Decision of 10 January 2006 on the Validity of Regulation 261/2004: Ignoring the Exclusivity of the Montreal Convention', *Air & Space Law* 31:2, 133–48.

Weightman, B. (1987), 'Third World Tour Landscapes', *Annals of Tourism Research* 14:2, 227–39.

Wells, A. and Young, S. (2004), *Airport Planning and Management* (New York: McGraw-Hill).

Wessels, D. (2006), *Customer Loyalty in the Airline Industry* (Philadelphia: The Wharton School of Business).

Whalen, T. (2000), 'The New Warsaw Convention: The Montreal Convention', *Air & Space Law* 25:1, 12–26.

Wheatcroft, S. (1994), *Aviation and Tourism Policies – Balancing the Benefits* (London: Routledge).

Whitelegg, J. and Cambridge, H. (2004), *Aviation and Sustainability* (Stockholm: Stockholm Environment Institute).

Williams, A.M. and Baláž, V. (2000), *Tourism in Transition: Economic Change in Central Europe* (London: IB. Tauris).

Williams, A.M. and Shaw, G. (1998), 'Introduction: Tourism and Uneven Economic Development', in A.M. Williams and G. Shaw (eds) *Tourism and Economic Development: European Experiences* (Chichester: John Wiley and Sons), 1–16.

Williams, G. (2001), 'Will Europe's Charter Airlines be replaced by "No-Frills" Scheduled Airlines?', *Journal of Air Transport Management* 7, 277–86.

--- (2002), Airline Competition - Deregulation's Mixed Legacy (Aldershot: Ashgate).

Williams, G., Mason, K. and Turner, S. (2003), *Market Analysis of Europe's Low Cost Airlines*, Report 9 - Air Transport Group (Cranfield: Cranfield University).

Williams, G. and Pagliari, R. (2004), 'A Comparative Analysis of the Application and Use of Public Service Obligations in Air Transport within the EU', *Transport Policy* 11:1, 55–66.

Williams, S. (1998), *Tourism Geography* (London: Routledge).

Wing, P. (1995), 'Tourism Development in the South Indian Ocean: the Case of Mauritius' in M. V. Colin and T. Baum (eds) *Island Tourism Management Principles and Practices* (England: J. Wiley and Sons Ltd), 229–35.

Winter, T. (2005), 'Landscape, Memory and Heritage: New Year Celebrations at Angkor, Cambodia', in D. Harrison and M. Hitchcock (eds) *Politics of World Heritage,* 50–65.

--- (2007a), Landscapes in the Living Memory: New Year Celebrations at Angkor, Cambodia', in N. Moore and Y. Whelan (eds), *Heritage, Memory and the Politics of Identity: New Perspectives on the Cultural Landscape* (Aldershot: Ashgate), 133–47.

--- (2007b), *Post-conflict Heritage, Postcolonial Tourism: Culture, Politics and Development at Angkor* (Routledge: London).

Witt, S.F. and Witt, C.A. (1991), 'Tourism Forecasting: Error Magnitude, Direction of Change Error and Trend Change Error', *Journal of Travel Research* 30, 26–33.

Woodworth, P. (2007), *The Basque Country: A Cultural History* (Oxford: Signal Books).

World Commission on Environment and Development (1987), *Our Common Future* (Oxford: Oxford University Press).

World Economic Forum (2007), *The Travel & Tourism Competitiveness Report 2007*, <http://www.weforum.org/en/initiatives/gcp/TravelandTourismReport/index.htm>, accessed 25 March 2007.

World Travel and Tourism Council (2005). *2005 Annual Report*, <http://www.wttc.travel/eng/Home/index.php>, accessed 27 September 2007.

Wyld, D. (2006), 'RFID 101: The next Big Thing in Management', *Management Research News* 29:4, 154–73.

Wyld, D., Jones, M. and Totten, J. (2005), 'Where is my Suitcase? RFID and Airline Customer Service', *Marketing Intelligence & Planning* 23:4, 382–94.

Xiao, H. (2006), 'The Discourse of Power: Deng Xiaoping and Tourism Development in China', *Tourism Management* 27, 803–814.

Yahya, F. (2003), 'Tourism Flows between India and Singapore', *International Journal of Tourism Research* 5, 347–67.

Yeh, A. (2006a), 'Investing in China: Aviation is Slow to take-off', *The Financial Times*, 15 February.

--- (2006b), 'Mesa teams up with Shenzhen Airlines', *The Financial Times*, December 23.

York Aviation (2004), *The Social and Economic Impact of Airports in Europe*, <http://www.aci-europe.org>, accessed 18 December 2007.

Zammit, J. (2003), *Guiding Main Carrier and Airport Business Development – Case study: Air Malta plc and Malta International Airport plc* Unpublished MBA Thesis, Danube University Krems, Austria.

Zhang, A. and Chen, H. (2003), 'Evolution of China's Air Transport Development and Policy towards International Liberalization', *Transportation Journal,* Spring, 32–49.

Zhang, G. (1995), 'China's Tourism Development since 1978: Policies, Experiences, and Lessons Learned', in A. A. Lew, and L. Yu, (eds) *Tourism in China: Geographic, Political and Economic Perspectives* (Boulder: Westview Press), 3–18.

--- (2006), 'China's Outbound Tourism: An Overview', Presentation at *Tourism Business Frontiers: Looking into the Future of Tourism*, 8 November (London: World Travel Market).

Zhang, H.Q., Chong, K. and Ap, J. (1999), 'An Analysis of Tourism Policy Development in Modern China', *Tourism Management* 20, 471–85.

Zuboff, S. (1988), *In the Age of the Smart Machine: the Future of Work and Power* (New York: Basic Books).

LEGAL DOCUMENTS

COM/88/447 Final, Proposal for a Council Regulation (EEC) on a Code of Conduct for Computerised Reservation Systems (Brussels: European Commision).

COM/95/724 Final, Proposal for a Council Regulation (EC) on Air Carrier Liability in Case of Accidents (Brussels: European Commision).

COM/99/640 Final, Air Transport and the Environment. Towards meeting the Challenges of Sustainable Development. Communication from the Commission to the Council, the European Parliament, the Economic and Social Committee and the Committee of the Regions (Brussels: European Commision).

COM/2000/595 Final, Proposal for a Regulation of the European Parliament and of the Council on establishing Common Rules in the Field of Civil Aviation and creating a European Aviation Safety Agency (Brussels: European Commission).

COM/2001/123 Final/2, Action Programme on the Creation of the Single European Sky and Proposal for a Regulation of the European Parliament and of the Council laying down the Framework for the Creation of the Single European Sky (Brussels: European Commission).

COM/2005/46 Final, Strengthening passenger rights within the European Union (Brussels: European Commission).

COM/2005/48 Final, Proposal for a regulation of the European Parliament and of the Council on the information of air transport passengers on the identity of the operating carrier and on communication of safety information by Member States (Brussels: European Commission).

COM/2005/459 Final, Reducing the Climate Change Impact of Aviation (Brussels: European Commission).

Convention for the Protection of Human Rights and Fundamental Freedoms (Council of Europe) on September 2003.

Convention for the Unification of Certain Rules for International Carriage by Air, Signed at Montreal on 28 May 1999.

Convention for the Unification of Certain Rules Relating to International Carriage by Air, Signed at Warsaw on 12 October 1929.

Council Decision 2001/539/EC of 5 April 2001 on the Conclusion by the European Community of the Convention for the Unification of Certain Rules for International Carriage by Air (the Montreal Convention) , *Official Journal of the European Union* L 194 (18.07.2001).

Directive 94/56/EC of the European Parliament and of the Council of 21 November 1994 establishing the Fundamental Principles governing the Investigation of Civil Aviation Accidents and Incidents, *Official Journal of the European Union* L 319 (12.12.1994).

Directive 95/46/EC of the European Parliament and of the Council of 24 October 1995 on the Protection of Individuals with Regard to the Processing of Personal Data and on the Free Movement of Such Data, *Official Journal of the European Union* L 281 (23.11.1995).

Directive 96/67/EC of the European Parliament and of the Council of 15 October 1996 on Access to the Ground Handling Market at Community Airports Aviation, *Official Journal of the European Union* L 272 (25.10.1996).

Directive 2003/42/EC of the European Parliament and of the Council of 13 June 2003 on Occurrence Reporting in Civil Aviation , *Official Journal of the European Union* L 167/23 (04.07.2003).

Directive 2004/36/EC of the European Parliament and of the Council of 21 April 2004 on the Safety of Third-Country aircraft using Community airports, *Official Journal of the European Union* L 143/76 (30.04.2004).

European Union Charter of Fundamental Rights, *Official Journal of the European Communities*, C 364/1 (18.12.2000).

Regulation (EEC) No 2299/89 of the European Parliament and of the Council of 24 July 1989 on a Code of Conduct for Computerized Reservation Systems, *Official Journal of the European Union* L 220 (29.07.1989).

Regulation (EEC) No 295/91 of the European Parliament and of the Council of 4 February 1991 establishing Common Rules for a Denied-Boarding Compensation System in Scheduled Air Transport, *Official Journal of the European Union* L 036 (08.02.1991).

Regulation (EEC) No 2407/92 of the European Parliament and of the Council of 23 July 1992 on Licensing of Air Carriers, *Official Journal of the European Union* L 240 (24.08.1992).

Regulation (EEC) No 2408/92 of the European Parliament and of the Council of 23 July 1992 on Access for Community Air Carriers to Intra-Community Air Routes, *Official Journal of the European Union* L 240 (24.08.1992).

Regulation (EEC) No 2409/92 of the European Parliament and of the Council of 23 July 1992 on Fares and Rates for Air Services, *Official Journal of the European Union* L 240 (24.08.1992).

Regulation (EEC) No 95/93 of the European Parliament and of the Council of 18 January 1993 on Common Rules for the Allocation of Slots at Community Airports, *Official Journal of the European Union* L 014 (21.02.1993).

Regulation (EC) No 2027/97 of the European Parliament and of the Council of 9 October 1997 on Air Carrier Liability in the Event of Accidents, *Official Journal of the European Union* L 285 (17.10.1997).

Regulation (EC) No 323/1999 of the European Parliament and of the Council of 8 February 1999 amending Regulation (EEC) No 2299/89 on a Code of Conduct for Computer Reservation Systems (CRSs) , *Official Journal of the European Union* L 040 (13.02.2009).

Regulation (EC) No 889/2002 of the European Parliament and of the Counci of 13 May 2002 amending Council Regulation (EC) No 2027/97 on Air Carrier Liability in the Event of Accidents, *Official Journal of the European Union* L 140/2 (30.05.2002).

Regulation (EC) No 1592/2002 of the European Parliament and of the Council of 15 July 2002 on Common Rules in the Field of Civil Aviation and establishing a European Aviation Safety Agency, *Official Journal of the European Union* L 240 (07.09.2002).

Regulation (EC) No 2320/2002 of the European Parliament and of the Council of 16 December 2002 establishing Common Rules in the Field of Civil Aviation Security, *Official Journal of the European Union* L 355/1 (30.12.2002).

Regulation (EC) No 622/2003 of the European Parliament and of the Council of 4 April 2003 laying down Measures for the Implementation of the Common Basic Standards on Aviation Security, *Official Journal of the European Union* L 089 (05.04.2003).

Regulation (EC) No 1643/2003 of the European Parliament and of the Council of 22 July 2003 amending Regulation (EC) No 1592/2002 on Common Rules in the Field of Civil Aviation and Establishing a European Aviation Safety Agency, *Official Journal of the European Union* L 245/7 (22.7.2003).

Regulation (EC) No 1882/2003 of the European Parliament and of the Council of 29 September 2003 adapting to Council Decision 1999/468/EC the Provisions relating to Committees which assist the Commission in the Exercise of its Implementing Powers laid down in Instruments Subject to the Procedure Referred to in Article 251 of the EC Treaty, *Official Journal of the European Union* L 284/1 (31.10.2003).

Regulation (EC) No 68/2004 of the European Parliament and of the Council of 15 January 2004 amending Commission Regulation (EC) No 622/2003 laying down Measures for the Implementation of the Common Basic Standards on Aviation Security, *Official Journal of the European Union* L 10 (16.01.2004).

Regulation (EC) No 261/2004 of the European Parliament and of the Council of 11 February 2004 establishing Common Rules on Compensation and Assistance to Passengers in the Event of Denied Boarding and of Cancellation or Long Delay of Flights, and Repealing Regulation (EEC) No 295/91, *Official Journal of the European Union* L 46 (17.02.2004).

Regulation (EC) No 549/2004 of the European Parliament and of the Council of 10 March 2004 laying down the Framework for the Creation of the Single European Sky, *Official Journal of the European Union* L 96/1 (31.03.2004).

Regulation (EC) No 550/2004 of the European Parliament and of the Council of 10 March 2004 on the Provision of Air Navigation Services in the Single European Sky, *Official Journal of the European Union* L 96/20 (31.03.2004).

Regulation (EC) No 551/2004 of the European Parliament and of the Council of 10 March 2004 on the Organisation and Use of the Airspace in the Single European Sky, *Official Journal of the European Union* L 96/20 (31.03.2004).

Regulation (EC) No 552/2004 of the European Parliament and of the Council of 10 March 2004 on the Interoperability of the European Air Traffic Management Network (the interoperability Regulation) , *Official Journal of the European Union* L 96/1 (31.03.2004).

Regulation (EC) No 785/2004 of the European Parliament and of the Council of 21 April 2004 on Insurance Requirements for Air Carriers and Aircraft Operators, *Official Journal of the European Union* L 138/1 (30.04.2004).

Regulation (EC) No 793/2004 of the European Parliament and of the Council of 21 April 2004 amending Council Regulation (EEC) No 95/93 on Common Rules for the Allocation of Slots at Community Airports, *Official Journal of the European Union* L 138/50 (30.04.2004).

Regulation (EC) No 847/2004 of the European Parliament and of the Council of 29 April 2004 on the negotiation and implementation of air service agreements between Member States and third countries, *Official Journal of the European Union* L 157/7 (30.04.2004).

Regulation (EC) No 849/2004 of the European Parliament and of the Council of 29 April 2004 amending Regulation (EC) No 2320/2002 establishing Common Rules in the Field of Civil Aviation Security, *Official Journal of the European Union* L 158/1 (30.04.2004).

Regulation (EC) No 2111/2005 of the European Parliament and of the Council of 14 December 2005 on the establishment of a Community list of air carriers subject to an operating ban within the Community and on informing air transport passengers of the identity of the operating air carrier, and repealing Article 9 of Directive 2004/36/EC, *Official Journal of the European Union* L 344/15 (27.12.2005).

Regulation (EC) No 474/2006 of the European Parliament and of the Council of 22 March 2006 establishing the Community List of Air Carriers which are Subject to an Operating Ban Within the Community Referred to in Chapter II of Regulation (EC) No 2111/2005 of the European Parliament and of the Council, *Official Journal of the European Union* L 84/14 (23.3.2006).

Regulation (EC) No 1107/2006 of the European Parliament and of the Council of 5 July 2006 Concerning the Rights of Disabled Persons and Persons with Reduced Mobility when Travelling by Air, *Official Journal of the European Union* L 204/1 (26.7.2006).

Regulation (EC) No 1546/2006 of 4 October 2006 amending Regulation (EC) No 622/2003 laying down Measures for the Implementation of the Common Basic Standards on Aviation Security, *Official Journal of the European Union* L 286/6 (17.10.2006).

Glossary

- **(Bilateral) Air Service Agreements** (BASAs) (also known as **Bilateral Air Transport Agreements**) are agreements between governments which establish the rules for international scheduled air services. There are an increasing number of **Open Skies BASAs** which are much more liberal agreements.

- The **Chicago Convention** was a meeting of government officials in 1944 which set up the **International Civil Aviation Organization (ICAO)** and established many rules and standards for air travel.

- **Code Sharing** is when the flight codes of two or more airlines are used on a flight which is operated by one of the airlines. Code sharing is usually (but not exclusively) implemented in the context of **Strategic Alliances** among airlines.

- The **Demand Elasticity** is the proportional change in quantity demanded relative to the proportional change in another variable. There are a number of different elasticities such as:

    - **Income Elasticity (IED)** which is the proportional change in quantity demanded relative to the proportional change in income. The aviation and tourism products are usually regarded as income elastic, i.e. with an IED exceeding 1.
    - **(Own-) Price Elasticity (PED)** which is the proportional change in quantity demanded relative to the proportional change in the price of a product. The aviation and tourism products are usually regarded as price elastic, i.e. with an PED exceeding 1 (in absolute value).
    - **Cross Price Elasticity (CPED)** which is the proportional change in quantity demanded of a good A relative to the proportional change in the price of another product B. A positive CPED is associated with substitutes and a negative with complement goods. The aviation and tourism products are clear examples of the latter when jointly considered. Alternative destinations or routes on the other hand may be understood as substitutes.

- **Freedoms of the Air** are operating rights of airlines which are negotiated in BASAs. There are five basic rights:

1. The right to fly over another country without landing.

2. The right to land in another country for technical reasons such as refuelling.

3. The right to carry commercial traffic from an airline's home country to another country.

4. The right to carry commercial traffic back from the other country to the airline's home country.

5. The right to carry commercial traffic between two other countries on a flight which originates or terminates in the airline's home country.

There are also three supplementary rights:

6. The right to combine two sets of third and fourth freedom rights to carry commercial traffic between two other countries by using the airline's home country as a transit base.

7. The right to carry commercial traffic between two other countries without the flight originating or terminating in the airline's home country.

8. (or **Cabotage**) The right to carry commercial traffic between two domestic points in another country.

- **Regulation** refers to the erection of institutional impediments in the way a market functions. The aviation industry is characterised by strict regulations in the areas of safety and security; in the past, there was also heavy economic regulation at both domestic and international levels. Gradually, however, this has been relaxed or entirely lifted in the context of market **deregulation** and **liberalization**. In spite of the existence of a few differences (e.g. deregulation may take place within a country whereas liberalization across countries), these last two terms are often used interchangeably. Regulation in tourism is in many cases associated with planning restrictions in terms of infrastructure standards (e.g. safety and hygiene), construction and architectural styles. In the past, there was also economic regulation in certain tourism sectors but this has been globally reduced in the last two decades.

Name Index

Subject Index